S0-BNK-029

AFRICAN HISTORICAL DICTIONARIES
Edited by Jon Woronoff

1. *Cameroon,* by Victor T. LeVine and Roger P. Nye. 1974. Out of print. See No. 48.
2. *The Congo,* 2nd ed., by Virginia Thompson and Richard Adloff. 1984
3. *Swaziland,* by John J. Grotpeter. 1975
4. *The Gambia,* 2nd ed., by Harry A. Gailey. 1987
5. *Botswana,* by Richard P. Stevens. 1975. Out of print. See No. 44.
6. *Somalia,* by Margaret F. Castagno. 1975
7. *Benin [Dahomey],* 2nd ed., by Samuel Decalo. 1987. Out of print. See No. 61.
8. *Burundi,* by Warren Weinstein. 1976
9. *Togo,* 2nd ed., by Samuel Decalo. 1987
10. *Lesotho,* by Gordon Haliburton. 1977
11. *Mali,* 2nd ed., by Pascal James Imperato. 1986
12. *Sierra Leone,* by Cyril Patrick Foray. 1977
13. *Chad,* 2nd ed., by Samuel Decalo. 1987
14. *Upper Volta,* by Daniel Miles McFarland. 1978
15. *Tanzania,* by Laura S. Kurtz. 1978
16. *Guinea,* 2nd ed., by Thomas O'Toole. 1987
17. *Sudan,* by John Voll. 1978. Out of print. See No. 53.
18. *Rhodesia / Zimbabwe,* by R. Kent Rasmussen. 1979. Out of print. See No. 46.
19. *Zambia,* by John J. Grotpeter. 1979
20. *Niger,* 2nd ed., by Samuel Decalo. 1989
21. *Equatorial Guinea,* 2nd ed., by Max Liniger-Goumaz. 1988
22. *Guinea-Bissau,* 2nd ed., by Richard Lobban and Joshua Forrest. 1988
23. *Senegal,* by Lucie G. Colvin. 1981. Out of print. See No. 65.
24. *Morocco,* by William Spencer. 1980
25. *Malawi,* by Cynthia A. Crosby. 1980. Out of print. See No. 54.
26. *Angola,* by Phyllis Martin. 1980. Out of print. See No. 52.
27. *The Central African Republic,* by Pierre Kalck. 1980. Out of print. See No. 51.
28. *Algeria,* by Alf Andrew Heggoy. 1981. Out of print. See No. 66.
29. *Kenya,* by Bethwell A. Ogot. 1981
30. *Gabon,* by David E. Gardinier. 1981. Out of print. See No. 58.
31. *Mauritania,* by Alfred G. Gerteiny. 1981
32. *Ethiopia,* by Chris Prouty and Eugene Rosenfeld. 1981. Out of print. See No. 56.
33. *Libya,* 2nd ed., by Ronald Bruce St John. 1991
34. *Mauritius,* by Lindsay Rivière. 1982. Out of print. See No. 49.
35. *Western Sahara,* by Tony Hodges. 1982. Out of print. See No. 55.

36. *Egypt,* by Joan Wucher King. 1984. Out of print. See No. 67.
37. *South Africa,* by Christopher Saunders. 1983
38. *Liberia,* by D. Elwood Dunn and Svend E. Holsoe. 1985
39. *Ghana,* by Daniel Miles McFarland. 1985. Out of print. See No. 63.
40. *Nigeria,* by Anthony Oyewole. 1987
41. *Ivory Coast,* by Robert J. Mundt. 1987
42. *Cape Verde,* 2nd ed., by Richard Lobban and Marilyn Halter. 1988. Out of print. See No. 62.
43. *Zaire,* by F. Scott Bobb. 1988
44. *Botswana,* by Fred Morton, Andrew Murray, and Jeff Ramsay. 1989
45. *Tunisia,* by Kenneth J. Perkins. 1989
46. *Zimbabwe,* 2nd ed., by R. Kent Rasmussen and Steven L. Rubert. 1990
47. *Mozambique,* by Mario Azevedo. 1991
48. *Cameroon,* 2nd ed., by Mark W. DeLancey and H. Mbella Mokeba. 1990
49. *Mauritius,* 2nd ed., by Sydney Selvon. 1991
50. *Madagascar,* by Maureen Covell. 1995
51. *The Central African Republic,* 2nd ed., by Pierre Kalck; translated by Thomas O'Toole. 1992
52. *Angola,* 2nd ed., by Susan H. Broadhead. 1992
53. *Sudan,* 2nd ed., by Carolyn Fluehr-Lobban, Richard A. Lobban, Jr., and John Obert Voll. 1992
54. *Malawi,* 2nd ed., by Cynthia A. Crosby. 1993
55. *Western Sahara,* 2nd ed., by Anthony Pazzanita and Tony Hodges. 1994
56. *Ethiopia and Eritrea,* 2nd ed., by Chris Prouty and Eugene Rosenfeld. 1994
57. *Namibia,* by John J. Grotpeter. 1994
58. *Gabon,* 2nd ed., by David Gardinier. 1994
59. *Comoro Islands,* by Martin Ottenheimer and Harriet Ottenheimer. 1994
60. *Rwanda,* by Learthen Dorsey. 1994
61. *Benin,* 3rd ed., by Samuel Decalo. 1995
62. *Republic of Cape Verde,* 3rd ed., by Richard Lobban and Marlene Lopes. 1995
63. *Ghana,* 2nd ed., by David Owusu-Ansah and Daniel Miles McFarland. 1995
64. *Uganda,* by M. Louise Pirouet. 1995
65. *Senegal,* 2nd ed., by Andrew F. Clark and Lucie Colvin Phillips. 1994
66. *Algeria,* 2nd ed., by Phillip Chiviges Naylor and Alf Andrew Heggoy. 1994
67. *Egypt,* by Arthur Goldschmidt, Jr. 1994

HISTORICAL DICTIONARY OF THE REPUBLIC OF CAPE VERDE
third edition

by

RICHARD LOBBAN
and
MARLENE LOPES

African Historical Dictionaries, No. 62

The Scarecrow Press, Inc.
Lanham, Md., & London

British Library Cataloguing-in-Publication data available

Library of Congress Cataloging-in-Publication Data

Lobban, Richard.
Historical dictionary of the Republic of Cape Verde / by Richard Lobban and Marlene Lopes. — 3rd ed.
p. cm. — (African historical dictionaries ; no. 62)
Includes bibliographical references.
ISBN 0-8108-2918-5 (acid-free paper)
1. Cape Verde—History—Dictionaries. 2. Cape Verde—Bibliography. I. Lopes, Marlene, 1948– II. Title. III. Series.
DT671.C25L63 1995
966.58′003—dc20 94-17116

Manufactured in the United States of America

Printed on acid-free paper

In Deep Appreciation
to our Parents
for all they have given us.

TABLE OF CONTENTS

ACKNOWLEDGMENTS

It is something of an embarrassment to put our names as the authors of a work on history to which so many individuals have contributed by their acts: the generations of Africans, the Portuguese explorers and settlers, thousands of slaves, and the forces of nationalism and anti-nationalism in recent years, Of course, it is this collective process of history-making that gives us the material for history writing.

Richard Lobban and Marlene Lopes

In more specific terms Richard would like to thank the leadership of the PAIGC for permitting travels to Guinea-Bissau in 1973, 1975, and 1993, and to Cape Verde in 1975 and 1992.

The first edition of this book was assisted by a grant from the Rhode Island College Research Fund which helped meet some of the costs of typing and duplication. The first edition was also assisted by substantial research efforts of Linda Zangari. Similarly the first edition of this book was helped by Raymond Almeida, then of the American Committe for Cape Verde who gave critical review of many entries. Jose Aica assisted with translation and other details relating to the Portuguese language.

In the second edition the central recognition must go first and foremost to Marilyn Halter who joined me as co-author. As equal partners we took all credit or blame for that work. Special areas on women, emigration, and migration, and Cape Verdean culture benefitted especially from her participation. I want to express my appreciation and gratitude for her collaboration which is not continuing here only because of her many writing and teaching commitments.

The second edition received significant input from Peter Manuel and his specifically signed entries on various aspects of Cape Verdean ethnomusicology and musical traditions. Since his work has turned elsewhere, these topics are covered by Susan Hurley-Glowa, who is fresh from doctoral fieldwork in Cape Verde.

However, the input of Manuel continues and we are all grateful to him for his earlier and continuing role for specific entries.

The third edition has drawn encouragement from leading members of the Cape Verdean-American community. Their numbers are too many to be noted in full but several deserve special recognition for their parts. We are especially grateful to Ron Barboza, Francisco Fernandes, Virginia Gonçalves, and Oling Jackson. Although not of Cape Verdean origin, Waltraud Coli and Eva Nelson have likewise made tireless efforts in their important work in the Cape Verdean community, especially in the celebration of Cape Verdean independence and in bringing the schooner *Ernestina* to Providence. The format of this work can not reveal the degree to which the several, and very important, works of George Brooks have added to my understanding of the Senegambian region. I am most grateful to benefit from his published works, correspondence, and broad knowledge, especially on the American connections to Cape Verde and the neighboring coast. The newly made maps of Cape Verde drawn by the cartographer Richard Grant specifically for this work also enhance the book.

The third edition also received substantial financial backing from the West Africa Research Association which generously supported research and travel in Cape Verde, Senegal, and Gambia in 1992, by the Rhode Island College Faculty Research Fund. The New Bedford Public Library and the American Antiquarian Society have been helpful in providing information about the early American Consuls to Cape Verde. In Cape Verde I am especially appreciative of the support and assistance of José Maria Almeida at the Arquivo Historico Nacional and the access I was given to the 19th century slave registries. Adams Library and its Cape Verdean Studies Special Collection have also been vital in this ongoing research. My gratitude to all of these institutions and their staffs is indeed great.

Thanks also go to Carolyn and Josina Fluehr-Lobban for putting up with me during the many months that passed while working on this project. My other daughter, Nichola, deserves special mention because she accompanied me to Cape Verde in 1992. There is no question that the charm of this 11-year old opened many doors and allowed me to understand new dimensions of the warmth and richness of Cape Verdean culture.

EDITOR'S FOREWORD

Cape Verde is one of Africa's smallest and poorest countries. It is also one of the most interesting with respect to its history, population and politics. Once tenaciously held by Portugal because of its strategic location, it could again become more important than its size or wealth would ordinarily warrant. For Americans, it has an additional significance due to the large numbers of Cape Verdeans living in this country.

Partly because it was so closely controlled by Portugal during the colonial period, and not terribly open even after independence, Cape Verde's realities are hardly known abroad. In fact, the very image raised by its name of a verdant cape is exceptionally misleading. This book therefore has the arduous task of providing solid information and clearing up some misconceptions. It achieves that purpose admirably.

Like the first edition, this updated volume was undertaken by Richard Lobban, Professor of Anthropology and the Director of the Program of African and Afro-American Studies at Rhode Island College. One of our leading authorities on Cape Verde and Guinea-Bissau, he visited the islands on independence and has followed the situation closely since. That has included a 1992 research trip to Cape Verde. This time, he was assisted by Marlene Lopes who, as Curator of the Cape Verdean Collection at the Adams Library, Rhode Island College, was in an excellent position to contribute an exceptionally complete bibliography. This makes the new edition of the *Historical Dictionary of the Republic of Cape Verde* an even more useful guide.

Jon Woronoff,
Series Editor

AUTHOR'S FOREWORD

This reference book on the history of Cape Verde is unusual in that it does not start with the Portuguese sightings in the mid-fifteenth century as the beginning of Cape Verdean society and history. Rather it reaches much further back to look at the regional history of the neighboring Upper Guinea coast in West Africa from where the largest portion Cape Verdean ancestry is substantially derived. It also examines the knowledge and events which presented the Portuguese with marine technology, cartography, and information about oceanic navigation as well as the great savanna empires. This background is essential to see Cape Verde in the context of a continuing process of human and cultural expansion, creation, and development.

Although this book is now in its third edition, the limited availability of historical sources on Cape Verde in any language, and especially in English, is a difficulty to be overcome. Consequently, some less important events and individuals may have better documentation than other more significant figures and circumstances. This gives an inevitable unevenness or arbitrariness to the historiography and periodization of Cape Verdean studies. However, as this book has evolved over the last twenty years that I have been writing about Cape Verde, I believe that fewer pages of this history are left blank or incomplete. This book is also a function of many years of teaching one of the few semester-long courses on Cape Verde and Guinea. This classroom setting has included a notable portion of students of Cape Verdean origin or descent.

In any case, this book first presents the reader with a very detailed chronology which will help to anchor their research. This introduction locates the islands and sketches the overall history, and current events, while the main body of the dictionary is given both alphabetical order by topics, but also with numerous cross-listings, to make the contents accessible from differing points of interest. Finally, the bibliography is intended to be as current and complete as is reasonable within the framework of the books in this series. The references provide the sources from which the entries are derived and suggest sources for further research. In short, this book is designed to be a handy reference tool which will open the way to further Cape Verdean studies.

Richard Lobban

ABBREVIATIONS AND ACRONYMNS

ADB	African Development Bank
AID	Agency for International Development
ANP	Assembléia Nacional Popular (People's National Assembly)
BCV	Banco de Cabo Verde (Bank of Cape Verde)
BNU	Banco Nacional Ultramarino
CEAO	Communauté Economique de l'Afrique Occidentale (West African Economic Community)
CEI	Casa dos Estudantes do Império
CEL	Comité Executivo da Luta
CEN	Comissão Eleitoral Nacional
CIA	Central Intelligence Agency (USA)
CIPM	Centro de Instrução Politico Militar
COM	Comissão das Organizaçãos das Mulheres
CONCP	Conferência das Organizações Nacionalistas das Colónias Portuguesas

COSC	Comissão Organizadora dos Sindicatos Caboverdeanos
CSL	Conselho Superior da Luta
CUF	Companhia União Fabril
DGS	Direção Geral de Segurança
DiNaS	Direção Nacional de Segurança
ECA	(UN) Economic Commission for Africa
ECOWAS	Economic Community of West African States
EMPA	Empresa Pública de Abastecimento
FACCP	Frente Africana Contra O Colonialismo Português
FAL	Forças Armadas Locais
FAO	(UN) Food and Agriculture Organization
FARP	Forças Armadas Revolucionárias do Povo
FLGC	Frente de Libertação da Guiné Portuguesa e Cabo Verde
FLING	Frente de Luta Pela Independência Nacional da Guiné-Bissau
FRAIN	Frente Revolucionária Africana para a Independência Nacional das Colónias Portuguesas
FRELIMO	Frente de Libertação de Moçambique
FUL	Front Uni de Libération (de Guinée et du Cap Vert)

GADCVG	Grupo de Acção Democrática de Cabo Verde e da Guiné
ICS	Instituto Caboverdeano de Solidaridade (Cape Verdean Institute of Solidarity)
IDA	International Development Association
IFAD	International Fund for Agricultural Development
INIA	Instituto Nacional para Investigação Agricola (National Institute for Agricultural Research)
ITCZ	Intertropical Convergence Zone
JAAC	Juventude Africana Amilcar Cabral
MAC	Movimento Anti-Colonialista
MFA	Movimento das Forças Armadas
MING	Movimento para Independência Nacional da Guiné Portuguesa
MLG	Movimento de Libertação da Guiné
MLGCV	Mouvement de Libération de la Guinée Portugaise et des Îles du Cap Vert
MLICV	Mouvement de Libération des Îles du Cap Vert
MpD	Movimento para Democracia
MPLA	Movimento Popular de Libertação de Angola
NATO	North Atlantic Treaty Organization
OAU	Organization of African Unity

OMCV	Organizição de Mulheres de Cabo Verde
PAICV	Partido Africano da Independência de Cabo Verde
PAIGC	Partido Africano da Independência da Guiné e Cabo Verde
PIDE	Polícia Internacional e de Defesa do Estado
POP	Polícia de Ordem Público
PP	Pioneiros do Partido
PSD	Partido Social Democratica
PSP	Polícia de Segurança Público
PVDE	Polícia de Vigilancia e Defesa do Estado
RDAG	Rassemblement Demócratique Africaine de Guinée
SACOR	Sociedade Anônima de Refinação de Petróleos
TACV	Transportes Aereos de Cabo Verde
UCID	União Caboverdeana Independênte e Democrática
UDCV	União Democrática de Cabo Verde
UDEMU	União Democrática das Mulheres
UDG	União Democrática da Guiné
UGEAN	União Geral dos Estudiantes da Africa Negra
UGTGB	União Geral dos Trabalhadores da Guiné-Bissau

UN	United Nations
UNCTAD	United Nations Conference on Trade and Development
UNDP	United Nations Development Program
UNGP	União dos Naturais da Guiné Portuguesa
UNTG	União Nacional dos Trabalhadores da Guiné
UPA	União das Populações de Angola
UPG	União Popular da Guiné
UPICV	União das Populações das Ilhas do Cabo Verde
UPLG	União Popular para Libertação da Guiné
URGP	União des Ressortissants de la Guinée Portugaise
WADB	West African Development Bank
WHO	World Health Organization

HISTORICAL CHRONOLOGY OF THE CAPE VERDE ISLANDS

1350	Arabs visit Azores and Cape Verde Islands according to *Libro del conoscimiento,* a book of contemporary knowledge by an unknown Franciscan monk. Cape Verde Islands are reportedly shown with Arabic names.
1394	Birth of Prince Henry ''The Navigator'' who establishes a research center for navigators at Sagres, Portugal.
1433–38	Reign of Portuguese King Edward.
1434	Sailing for Prince Henry, Captains Gil Eannes and Afonso Gonçalves Baldaia reach Cape Bojador, Morocco.
1441	First slaves reported as captured by the Portuguese captains Nuño Tristão and Antão Gonçalves at Rio do Ouro in Morocco.
1443	Prince Henry monopolizes all trade south of Cape Bojador.
1444–5	Portuguese Captains Lançarote and Diniz Dias reach Cap Vert at Senegal and return to Portugal with 235 slaves.
1446	Portuguese sailors reach coast of Guinea-Bissau.

1447	Nuño Tristão killed along the Upper Guinea coast.
1455	Portuguese establish slave trading "factory" at Arguim. Some claim that in July 1455, the Genoese, António De Noli, first sights Sal, Boa Vista, Maio, São Tiago, and Fogo.
1456	Cadamosto reaches Cape Verde Islands in May.
1460	Portuguese explorers, Diogo Gomes, Diogo Afonso, and the de Noli brothers, António and Bartólomeu, initiate early settlement in some of the Sotavento group of islands in Cape Verde archipelago. Death of Prince Henry.
1461	6 December, Diogo Afonso lands on São Nicolau. A week later he is the first Portuguese on Santa Luzia.
1462	17 January, Diogo Afonso is the first Portuguese on Santo Antão, where he celebrates the first mass at the Parish of Nossa Senhora do Conceição. On 22 January, Diogo Afonso lands at São Vicente. The De Noli brothers and their nephew Rafael de Noli intensify their efforts to settle on São Tiago. 19 September, Crown grants captaincy to Diogo Afonso
1466	12 June, Royal charter grants early settlers in Cape Verde the right to trade in African slaves and other goods on the coast, except at Argium. Many settlers leave before the end of the decade. The first Franciscans arrive in the islands.
1468	First contract for export of urzella from Cape Verde.
1468–1474	Crown grants five-year trade monopoly to Fernão Gomes.
1469	30 September, Crown grants rights to the urzella trade to Castillian brothers Johan and Pero De Lugo.

1470	Fernâo Gomes reaches São Tomé.
1471	Portuguese sailors cross the equator for the first time.
1472	Free trade on coast for settlers of Cape Verde is now limited. The coastal trade monopoly is awarded to Fernão Gomes.
1473	9 April, Rodrigo Afonso appointed as *capitão* of São Tiago.
1475–79	Luso-Spanish war.
1475–1600	Period of major Portuguese slave trade on Upper Guinea coast.
1476	Spanish Admiral Carlos de Valera attacks São Tiago with 25 ships and takes António De Noli captive; as a result De Noli changes his allegiance to Spain.
1479	4 September, Papal Treaty of Alçacovas between Spain and Portugal.
1480	Start of Spanish Inquisition and expulsion of Jews.
1481–95	Death of Afonso V, Rise of Portuguese King João II.
1482–83	Columbus serves as pilot on Azambuja mission and probably returns via Cape Verde Islands.
1483	French sailors reach Cape Verde Islands.
1489	30 May, King grants land in Cape Verde to Duke of Beja. 30 November, Lopo Afonso granted *capitão* of Brava.
1490	First settlement of Maio.

1492	Rise of Spanish Inquisition. Portuguese King João II sends hundreds of Jews to São Tomé, Guinea, and Cape Verde. So many are sent that the term "Portuguese" in Africa at this time often implies "Jews."
1493	4 May, Pope Alexander VI issues Papal Bull "Inter Caetera" which demarcates Portuguese and Spanish territory in New World as east or west of a line 100 leagues west of Cape Verde.
1494	7 June, Treaty of Tordesillas adjusts the above treaty to a line 370 leagues west of Cape Verde.
1495–1521	Reign of King Manuel and "Golden Age" of Portugal.
1496	December, Portugal issues order for major expulsion of Jews.
1497	Vasco da Gama stops at Cape Verde Islands at start of his epic voyage. He reaches Sal Island on 22 July and São Tiago on 27 July. His fleet departs on 3 August on its way to India. António De Noli dies in Cape Verde Islands; his son, Dom Branca de Aguiar, inherits the royal grant.
1498	Christopher Columbus arrives in Cape Verde Islands on 27 June on his third Trans-Atlantic voyage. He visits Boa Vista, Fogo, and São Tiago before departing on 4 July.
1499–1500	Amerigo Vespucci, sailing as a Spanish pilot, stops in Cape Verde Islands at Fogo. Da Gama stops in Cape Verde in May 1499 on his return from India.
1500	9 March, Pedro Alvares Cabral sails from Lisbon with a 16-ship fleet; two ships are left in Cape Verde Islands.

1501–02 Vespucci sails by Cape Verde Islands for second time.

1502–03 Da Gama probably stops again in Cape Verde on his way to and from India.

1503–04 Vespucci stops in Cape Verde Islands for third time.

1504 Slaves from São Tomé reach Cape Verde for export.

1505 Cattle grazing land on Boa Vista leased to Pero Corea.

1506–1510 Valentine Fernandes writes of the peoples along the Guinea coast and in Cape Verde Islands.

1510 First effective and permanent captaincy system established in Cape Verde Islands, especially in São Tiago and Fogo.

1513–15 Sale of 2,966 slaves recorded in São Tiago.

1514 Gonçalo Lopez leases urzella producing lands in São Nicolau and Santa Luzia.

1515 Eighty households reported for Ribeira Grande. Maize introduced to Cape Verde Islands from Brazil.

1517 Sugar cane plantations expanded in São Tiago.

1530 Royal Charter issued for *vila* of Ribeira Grande.

1533 *Vila* of Ribeira Grande is elevated to status of *cidade* with its own Diocese and Bishop over the islands and coast. First sugar cane planted in Cape Verde Islands by a Genoese.

1537 French loot six ships in Cape Verdean waters.

1542	French raid Cape Verde Islands.
1545	Expanded settlement of Fogo and Brava by João da Fonseca.
1548	Early settlement of Santo Antão under *capela* and *morgado* systems of land ownership.
1549	Hans Stade stops in Cape Verde and notes that the islands were "rich in Black Moorish slaves."
1550	Bishop actually arrives at Ribeira Grande. Census in Cape Verde shows 13,700 slaves.
1555	Father Fernando Oliveira criticizes slave trade in Guinea.
1556	Approximate start of construction of cathedral of Ribeira Grande, in São Tiago.
1564	Volcano on Fogo erupts (and 28 times since).
1564	Hereditary captain of São Tiago dies; captaincy reverts to Portuguese Crown.
1566	English Captain John Lovell loots 5 ships in Cape Verde waters.
1572	Population of Santa Catarina at 2,400; Ribeira Grande at 1,500 including merchants, adventurers, *lançados,* and slaves.
1574	Cape Verdeans supply aid for famine relief in Senegal.
1576	Cape Verde is changed from *capitanias* to *provincias.*
1577	English Captains Hawkins and Drake seize Portuguese cargo ships, but most passengers released on Brava island.

1578 Francis Drake raids Cape Verde Islands.

1580–83 Drought and famine in Cape Verde.

1580–1640 Cape Verde becomes major slave entrepôt under Portuguese and *lançado* control regularly threatened by Dutch and English.

1581 Short-lived revolt against Spanish King Philip I on Fogo.

1582 English raids in Cape Verde Islands. Population of Fogo and São Tiago includes 13,700 slaves and 600 whites.

1585 Francis Drake stages second attack on Cape Verde when he loots São Tiago towns of Praia, Santa Catarina, and Cidade Velha with force of 600 men on 16–17 November. This causes Portuguese decision to improve island defenses and build Fort of São Filipe to protect Ribeira Grande.

1587 Portuguese improve the island defenses. Duarte Lobo da Gama becomes first Portuguese Governor of Cape Verde directly representing the royal administration.

1588 *Capitania* system of royal governors also established on coast at Cacheu, but subordinated to governor of Cape Verde.

1591 Foreigners forbidden to trade in Cape Verde Islands.

1592 Famine in Cape Verde.

1593 Approximate completion of Royal Fort of São Filipe.

1595 First church constructed at Ribeira Grande, Santo Antão.

1598	English and Dutch raid Cape Verde, especially at Maio. Flemish pirates attack São Tiago
1600s	Intensification of slave trade on West African coast. Population of São Tiago and Fogo about 1,500 free people and 14,000 slaves. Slaves are "seasoned" in Cape Verde Islands and then exported to New World.
1601	Crown gives Jews the right to settle and trade on the coast, but under Crown authority in Cape Verde Islands.
1604	First Jesuit mission established in Cape Verde.
1610	Drought and famine in Cape Verde.
1612	Governors and bishops rotate between Ribeira Grande and Praia.
1613	Eruption of Fogo.
1619	Slave traders allowed to pay Crown tax directly at Cacheu and bypass slave tax paid in Cape Verde Islands.
1620	Royal order seeks to exile Portuguese women convicts to Cape Verde to "extinguish the mulattoe race."
1621	Dutch replace Portuguese at Rufisque, Portudal, and Joal.
1625	Publication of André Donelha's *Account of Sierra Leone and the Rivers of Guinea of Cape Verde.*
1627	Catholic Church opposes presence of a Jesuit mission in the Islands.
1642	Jesuit mission in Cape Verde Islands is closed.

1643	Cape Verdean *lançados* establish trade center at Ziguinchor, Casamance.
1647	Capuchin mission opens in Cape Verde. Ribeira Grande loses its monopoly of slave trade.
1640s	Expansion of cattle export from Cape Verde Islands.
1650–70s	About 7,500 slaves exported to Brazil each year or about 150,000 for this period.
1650–1879	Guinea-Bissau administered from Cape Verde, especially to produce slaves for Brazil and South American mines and plantations.
1652	Fortified city of Praia becomes full capital; Ribeira Grande enters long process of decline. Bishop is rotated between Praia and Ribeira Grande.
1653–1665	Revolt of *capitão* Domingos Rodrigues Viegas and his brother Belchior Monteiro de Queiros against authority of São Tiago.
1655	Dutch attack São Filipe in Fogo.
1664	1,280, mostly *mestiço,* soldiers defend Ribeira Grande.
1676	Formation of Companhia Cacheu e Rios da Guiné to provide slaves and taxes on slaves for Portuguese Crown. It fails in 1682.
1677	First priest stationed in Boa Vista.
1679	*Regulos* near Cacheu revolt fearing a loss in control of trade to *lançados* and other Portuguese representatives.
1680	Eruption and lava flow in Fogo cause refugees to settle in Brava. Formation of Companhia Africano do Cabo Verde e Cacheu.

1682	Formation of Companhia Pará e Maranhão to import 10,000 slaves annually through Guinea and Cape Verde.
1686	Brava attacked by pirates and the *feitor real* is killed. Spanish Capuchins initiate anti-slavery effort in Bissau.
1687	23 January, (Jewish) Cape Verdeans are forbidden to sell *panos* to foreigners, who used them in slave trade.
1690	Formation of Companhia do Cacheu e Cabo Verde to control regional trade in slaves and ivory. This company fails in 1706 and economic stagnation returns to the region. Perhaps first Cape Verdean whalers in New Bedford. Bishop Portuense of Ribeira Grande raids priests who are sleeping with African slave concubines.
1696	Bishop Vitoriano Portuense of Cape Verde travels along Farim and Rio Grande Rivers and establishes small convent in Bissau. Revolt of Bibiana Vaz, a *grumetta* who opposed Portuguese trade monopoly.
1697	Decree requires that all Cape Verdean slaves must be baptized. Mandingos of Farim revolt against Cape Verdean *lançados.*
1700	Approximate completion of Cathedral at Ribeira Grande which adds to reluctance to transfer capital.
1701	Commercial quantities of indigo discovered in Cape Verde.
1701–08	Cape Verdean presence on coast weakened by neglect of Fort at Bissau.
1705	Creation of processing factory for indigo in the islands.

1705–21 Prolonged drought in Cape Verde Islands, especially in northern and low-lying islands.

1706 Companhia do Cacheu e Cabo Verde fails.

1712 May, French under Jacques Cassard attack Praia and Ribeira Grande on São Tiago. This is last major pirate attack, but it is decided to abandon Ribeira Grande for better defended Praia plateau.

1719 Famine noted in São Tiago.

1724 Process of abandoning Ribeira Grande, São Tiago, is underway.

1730 Population of Cape Verde reaches 38,000

1738 Cape Verdean Governor petitions King to liberalize trade in *panos* and allow their sale to foreigners.

1741–42 Francisco de Lima e Melo is head of *donatário* of Santo Antão.

1743 18 November, São Vicente administered from São Nicolau, no longer from Santo Antão. Ribeira Grande reported in ruins. Only 20 Whites in the archipelago. Many slaves (*badius*) have fled into the mountains.

1746 Revolt in Cape Verde in dispute over representation to King. Drought in Cape Verde.

1748–50 Drought in Cape Verde.

1750 Reign of King José I and Prime Minister Marquis de Pombal, who brings liberal reforms, weakens Portuguese feudalism and curbs long-lasting Inquisition. Maranhão in Brazil increases slave imports from Cape Verde and Guinea.

1754	Drought in Cape Verde.
1757	Companhia Geral do Grao Pará e Maranhão monopolizes economy and assumes effective administration of Cape Verde. Slaves are tallied and sold at Alfandega at Ribeira Grande.
1764	Cape Verde Governor notes deplorable state of island defenses. Drought in Boa Vista and Sal. Fort in Bissau is completed.
1770	Official capital of Cape Verde is transferred from Ribeira Grande to Praia; the former city enters permanent decline.
1773–76	Famine reported especially in Fogo, Brava, and São Nicolau.
1775	Some 180 people die monthly in Praia from famine, reaching a total of 12,778 dead in Praia alone, and 22,666 dead in the archipelago. All cattle of Maio and Brava are dead or eaten.
1777	End of administration by Marquis de Pombal.
1778	Companhia do Grao Pará e Maranhão is replaced by Comércio Exclusivo. Coffee is introduced to São Nicolau by António Leite. Population of Ribeira Grande is 787, including 495 free and 292 slaves.
1785	Eruption of Fogo.
1790	São Nicolau coffee crop begins to appear in the market.
1795	Plan to populate São Nicolau with people from Fogo.
1798	French attack Brava, a port for New England whaling ships.

1799	Eruption of Fogo.
1800s	European nations begin to abolish slavery. Trade in Upper Guinea coast starts slow decline, but slave trade at Bissau and Cacheu continues until mid-century.
1802–82	At least 2,433 *degredados* shipped to Cape Verde by Lisbon.
1807	Census of Cape Verde notes 1,752 "Whites." England abolishes slavery; USA formally abolishes slave imports, but this is poorly enforced.
1810	Anglo-Portuguese treaty has secret provision for British control of Bissau and Cacheu for 50 years. Cape Verde population at 51,480.
1812	British export slaves from West Africa to Cape Verde for secret sales to American slave shippers.
1814	Famine in Cape Verde causing migration from Boa Vista to Fogo and São Nicolau. English try to take Bolama from Portugal.
1815	Treaty of Vienna between England and Portugal compels Portugal to curb slave trade north of the equator.
1816	Eruption and lava flows on Fogo
1817	First elementary public school established in Praia.
1818	Samuel Hodges of Massachusetts is appointed first official American Consul to Cape Verde. On 3 December, Hodges arrives in Cape Verde. On 4 December, pirates attack Cape Verde.
1819	Anglo-American Treaty and American Slave Trade Act are further legal steps to end slave imports to United States.

	21 July, pirates attack Cape Verde.
	28 August, small slave revolt reported.
	November, American pirates from Baltimore loot citizens and sailors in Maio.
1820s	Portuguese Jewish community virtually gone following the "Liberal Wars." Jewish Miguelistas flee to Santo Antão.
1820	25 February, Portuguese say they will fire on American vessels suspected of piracy. Americans slavers fly the Portuguese flag.
1821	Cape Verde and Guinea-Bissau send one representative to King.
1822	Brazil becomes independent of Portugal.
1824	First known Cape Verdean to gain naturalized American citizenship from residence in Nantucket, Massachusetts.
	12 August, *Old Ironsides* visits Cape Verde.
1825	Famine in the islands. Governor Chepuzet sells Crown-owned urzella for famine relief; he is dismissed for violating Crown monopoly.
1826	19 May, Gardner serving as US Consul to Cape Verde.
1827	Maio and Boa Vista plundered by pirates from Buenas Aires.
	22 October, Hodges dies of malaria in Praia.
1828	Chiefs of Canhabaque called to Bissau to assert loyalty to Portuguese Governor under authority of Cape Verde.

1831–33 Severe famine in Cape Verde Islands; 30,000 die. Population of Fogo is cut by 6,000.

1832 Charles Darwin arrives in Cape Verde on HMS *Beagle;* from 15 January to 8 February he makes extensive study of flora, fauna, and geology which helps in writing his *Origin of Species.*

12 March, William G. Merrill serving as US Consul.

1834 Abolition of slavery in British colonies and Britain pressures others to follow. Population of Cape Verde put at 51,854 free and 3,974 slaves.

1836 Portuguese officially abolish slave trade, but in Cape Verde slave system and slave imports continue. Honório Pereira Barreto, a Cape Verdean, is appointed Governor of Guiné.

1837–59 Governor H. Barreto claims Bolama and Canhabaque as under Portuguese authority. Guinean economy declines with formal abolition of slave trade and increasing resistance to Portuguese from inhabitants of the area.

1837 F. Gardner is serving as American Consul.

1838 The English begin their first coal dump in Mindelo.

1840s "Pacification" of coastal peoples in Guinea-Bissau by Portuguese results in slave imports to islands.

1841 Many American whalers load salt at Sal and Maio.

1842 Anglo-Portuguese Treaty abolishes slave trade in all overseas possessions, and allows armed anti-slavery sailing cruisers.

24 August, first printing press operating in Cape Verde, the Typographia Nacional which publishes the first *Boletim Oficial do Governo Geral de Cabo Verde.*

1843	United States establishes Africa Squadron based in Cape Verde Islands for symbolic suppression of American slavers. Dock built at Furna on Brava.
	4 June, Anglo-Portuguese *Comissão Mixta* signs accord in Boa Vista to abolish slavery.
1845–46	Poor harvests in islands, especially São Nicolau and São Tiago.
1846	October, Yellow fever epidemic in Boa Vista.
1850	Mindelo elevated to status of *vila.* British Royal Mail Steam packet service begins stops in Mindelo.
	Harvests fail due to heavy rains in Barlavento islands.
1850s	Moroccan Jews arrive in Boa Vista for hide trade.
1852	American military cemetery established in Cape Verde for sailors of Africa Squadron.
1853–54	Poor harvests in the islands, especially Sal and Boa Vista.
1854	State-owned Portuguese slaves emancipated. Peanuts introduced to Santo Antão as result of a shipwreck.
1854–55	Poor harvests in all islands, especially Fogo, which has cholera epidemic killing 800.
1856	Church-owned Portuguese slaves emancipated, as well as those born of a slave mother. Census in Cape Verde notes 17 ''racial'' distinctions.
	Cholera epidemic in Mindelo kills 532.
1857	Cholera spreads in islands; 20,000 perish. Fogo erupts.

1858 Praia and Mindelo are given status of *cidade*. Portuguese decree calls for end of slavery in 20 years. Poor harvests in Maio, São Tiago, and Brava. British steam warship liberates Portuguese slaves in Bolama, which is under Cape Verdean authority.

1860 Cape Verde population at 90,000.

1861 US Africa Squadron recalled from Cape Verde for naval blockade against American secessionists after shots at Fort Sumter.

1863 19 May, Portuguese pass law reforming *latifundia* system which further undermines slavery in Cape Verde.

1863–67 Widespread famine and drought in Cape Verde which kills 30,000. General crisis causes large-scale emigration.

1864 Legislation introduced to punish coffee theft.

1866 *Liceu* established at São Nicolau. Tax introduced on production of *grogga* in Santo Antão. Drought in the islands.

1867 250 steamers call at São Vicente.

1868 BNU establishes branch in Cape Verde Islands.

1869 Slavery completely abolished in all forms and parts of Portuguese Empire. Cape Verdean sea traffic diverted to newly opened Suez Canal.

The Cape Verde Census notes 919 "Whites."

28 December, Clarimundo Martins is first Cape Verdean, naturalized as a US citizen, to serve as US Consul.

1870 US President Grant arbitrates conflict of Bolama,

	still under Cape Verdean authority, in favor of Portugal. Cape Verde population put at 80,000.
1871	Coffee introduced to Santo Antão.
1875	Decree calls for ex-slaves in Cape Verde to work for two more years for their ex-masters after 1878.
1878	Official end of slavery in Cape Verde.
1879	After 500 years, Guinea-Bissau gains a colonial administration which is independent from Cape Verde.
1881	Drought in Cape Verde. Population put at 103,000.
1883–86	Poor rains in Cape Verde. Famine, drought, and death are widespread causing general crisis and emigration.
1884–85	Partition of (''scramble for'') Africa by European powers meeting at Berlin Congress.
1886	Construction of famed Janela lighthouse in Santo Antão.
	17 April, Republican revolt in Santo Antão at Ribeira Grande.
1889–90	Brussels Anti-Slavery Conference forbids import of arms and spirituous liquors to a zone in Africa including Cape Verde.
1890	2,264 ships stop in Mindelo for coal. Famine and Locust plague in Cape Verde. Population in islands reaches 130,000
1892	Cape Verde becomes ''autonomous district'' of Portugal.

1894	Revolt in Santo Antão over election of deputy to Lisbon.
1898	2 June, Accidental fire at US Consulate in São Vicente. Considerable damage and loss of archives.
1899	Portuguese regulations provide for use of contract labor, especially in São Tomé and Príncipe. Failed harvests and famine in Fogo.
1900	Cape Verde population put at 147,000.
1900–03	Drought in Cape Verde kills 16,000 or about 17 percent of population.
1902–22	At least 24,000 Cape Verdean contract laborers sent "to the south" (i.e., to São Tomé and Príncipe); another 1,968 migrate to Brazil. At least 18,620 migrate to New England.
1910	Portuguese monarchy overthrown. Parliamentary Republican rule until 1926.
1911	Drought in Cape Verde.
1912	First publication of *A Voz de Cabo Verde.*
1914	Some Cape Verdeans gain rights to Portuguese citizenship.
1920	*Liga Africana* established in Lisbon, thus beginning a sense of unity of Africans in Portuguese colonies.
1921–22	Severe drought in Cape Verde; 17,000 die. Aid is sought from United States as was the case in 1832 famine. About 5,000 *contratados* "go south" to São Tomé and Príncipe.
1924	17 August, Journal *Pro-Guiné* starts publication to

	represent interests of the Republican Democratic Party. It is closed after 10 issues.
	12 September, Birth of Amilcar Cabral, Cape Verdean leader.
1926	28 May, Rise of Portuguese fascism under General Gomes da Costa. Republicans overthrown.
1928–30	Consolidation of fascist power by António Salazar.
1930–32	*Mocidade Africana* (African Youth) published in Cape Verde by E. Tavares and B. L. Da Silva.
1930–33	Salazar formulates *Estado Novo* as blue-print for Portuguese fascism until 1974. Famine in Cape Verde; at least 870 Cape Verdeans go to United States.
1934	4 June, Food revolt led by Carpenter Ambrosio in Mindelo. Customs House attacked and food distributed.
1936	First of four issues of *Claridade* published in Cape Verde thus starting new Cape Verdean literary tradition. The first editor is Manuel Lopes. Island population put at 162,055.
1940	Cape Verdean Catholic diocese separated from that in Guinea Bissau. British plan "Operation Sackbut" to take over Cape Verde Islands to block German attempt to control the region. Plan not put into effect. Cape Verde population at 181,286.
1940–42	Severe drought kills 20,000 in islands. From 1940–73 at least 120,000 Cape Verdeans "go south."
1941	Some 5,000 Portuguese troops arrive in the islands.

1941–42 About 20,000 Cape Verdeans die, and from 1941 to 1949 about 20,000 Cape Verdeans "go south" to São Tomé and Príncipe.

1942 January, 100 deaths reported daily in Praia from hunger.

May, Portuguese troop strength reaches 6,150.

November, Serious riots in the islands; clashes between soldiers and civilian population.

1943 The ship *Matilde* departs from Brava to America, but is never seen again, adding a new subject for Cape Verdean *mornas.*

1944 Journal *Certeza* starts publication in São Vicente.

1945 Formation of PIDE from PVDE. Anti-fascist revolt by Henrique Galvão.

1946 First publication of the *Boletim Cultural da Guiné-Portuguesa.*

1946–48 Famine in islands kills 30,000.

1947 Last issue of *Claridade* published. Henrique Galvão reports to secret session of Portuguese National Assembly on abhorrent labor conditions in Africa.

1949 Opening of Tarafal prison in Cape Verde Islands for political opponents of fascist regime in Lisbon.

1950 Third Pan-African Congress held in London with delegates of the *Liga Africana.* Cape Verde population falls to 147,096.

1950–70 Some 34,000 Cape Verdean *contratados* "sent south."

1951	Last eruption of Fogo. Status of Cape Verde changes from "colony" to "overseas province."
1956	19 September, Formation of PAIGC in Bissau.
1959	Amilcar Cabral is supported by members of British Communist Party. MLGCV is formed to launch propaganda campaign.
	January, Anti-colonial Congress in Tunis; FRAIN is formed to link PAIGC with MPLA. Formation of UPICV.
	3 August, Pijiguiti massacre in Bissau, PAIGC changes tactics toward armed struggle.
1960	*Antologia da ficção cabo-verdiana contemporânea* organized by Baltazar Lopes. Cape Verde population reaches 201,000.
1961	Formation of CONCP, which replaces FRAIN.
	13–17 July, MLGCV and PAIGC merge.
	Portuguese Captain Henrique Galvão seizes ocean liner to protest Portuguese colonial policy in Africa.
1962	First publication of *O Arquipelago.* Amilcar Cabral says that PAIGC is a party of "soldiers for the United Nations."
1963–1974	Period of nationalist war in Guinea-Bissau.
1963	21 July, Secret PAIGC meeting in Dakar discussed strategy for expanding war to the Cape Verde Islands.
1964	13–17 February, First National Congress of PAIGC inside Guinea at Cassaca. Divisions within PAIGC are eliminated or repressed.

1964–65 FLING holds some armed actions in Guinea to rival PAIGC.

1965 Américo Tomas reelected as Portuguese President.

PAIGC is selected for OAU support over FLING.

1966 The war in Guinea expands with mortars, bazookas, small cannons, and 75mm recoilless rifles.

1968 19 February, PAIGC forces attack Bissalanca Airport at Bissau and begin to gain initiative in the war.

1969 Assassination of FRELIMO President Eduardo Mondlane.

1970 1 July, Amilcar Cabral and associates meet the Pope in Rome.

1971 Amidst a revolutionary atmosphere in Europe and North America, PAIGC launches nationalist wall slogans in Cape Verde.

1972 21 September, Big anti-colonial demonstration in Praia.

DGS/PIDE broadens powers to counter anti-colonial forces.

Cape Verde population reaches 272,000.

1973 20 January, Assassination of Amilcar Cabral in Conakry.

March, PAIGC intensifies use of SAM-7's against Portugal's air force in Guinea-Bissau. Portugal loses some 20 aircraft.

25 May, Portuguese fort at Guiledge falls.

18–22 July, Second Congress of PAIGC in Boe.

September, First meeting of *Assembléia Nacional Popular* of PAIGC.

Gen. António Spinola relieved of his command of the war.

2 November, United Nations General Assembly calls on Portugal to cease all military activity in Guinea-Bissau.

19 November, Guinea-Bissau becomes 42nd member of OAU.

1974 25 April, Fall of fascist/colonial Portugal following revolt of *Movimento das Forças Armadas* led by Gen. Vasco Gonçalves. MFA restores democracy to Portugal and promises decolonization. Discussions about Luso-Guinean cooperation begin; teachers promised for next school year.

1 May, huge crowd at Tarrafal prison camp to see release of political prisoners. United Front policy adopted by PAIGC for mass mobilization.

19 May, Portuguese troops fire on demonstrators in Praia.

Big demonstrations in Mindelo.

6 June, Referendum recognizes PAIGC as leading force of United Front for decolonization.

July, Ideological struggle in Lisbon between neo-colonialist position of Spinola and decolonization position of Vasco Gonçalves.

August, PAIGC and MFA have meetings in Algiers and London to arrange for troop withdrawal.

14 September, Portugal recognizes independence of Guinea-Bissau. Spinola meets with Mobutu in Sal to discuss MPLA and Angola. Spinola blocks effort by Pedro Pires to fly from Bissau to Sal. Spinola prevented from landing in Bissau.

September, 150 Portuguese marines transferred from Guinea-Bissau in early withdrawal provoke incidents in São Vicente over decolonization.

Pedro Pires arrives in Cape Verde Islands. PAIGC influence spreads quickly and widely, but António Spinola is not yet willing to discuss independence for Cape Verde.

12 September, JAAC formed.

24 September, Guinea-Bissau becomes independent.

29 September, General strike in Cape Verde. Spinola sacks Governor of Cape Verde, Silva Horta, for being too liberal and accommodating. Horta was replaced by Serge Fonseca, an ardent colonialist, who was told to arrest PAIGC members and block arrival of any more.

Silvino da Luz, already in Cape Verde, went into hiding.

Spinola was inclined to call on Portuguese troops in Cape Verde to fire on demonstrators.

30 September, In this crisis atmosphere, Spinola was toppled by leftist members of MFA. This paved way for return of Pedro Pires and Aristides Pereira.

13 October, Pedro Pires returns to Cape Verde

15 October, Last of 30,000 Portuguese troops leave Guinea-Bissau.

19 October, Luis Cabral and Aristides Pereira enter Bissau.

Pedro Pires turns his attention to process of decolonization of Cape Verde Islands.

October, Cape Verdean lawyer, Dr. Aguinaldo Veiga calls for an independent and democratic Cape Verde. UDCV and UPICV mount opposition to political dominance of PAIGC.

1 November, Spinola denounced by MFA and PAIGC endorsed as sole party of decolonization. UPICV and UDCV are isolated by the MFA and

PAIGC for being opposed to decolonization and unity of Cape Verde and Guinea-Bissau.

7 November, Major period of negotiations between PAIGC and reconstituted leadership of MFA. This results in plan for independence in six months and jointly supervised electoral referendum in which UDCV and UPICV are excluded.

9 December, PAIGC militants led by Silvino da Luz and Luis Fonseca take over Radio Barlavento owned by pro-Portuguese Gremio Club of São Vicente.

19 December, Final agreement reached between MFA and PAIGC's Cape Verdean National Committee.

In 1974, Cape Verde Islands have 465 primary schools, 70,000 students, 1,200 primary teachers, and 247 secondary teachers. Thirteen doctors in archipelago. Cases of cholera reported. No cash reserves left.

1975 23 February, Cape Verdean Juridical Congress declares independence for Cape Verde from Boston Sheraton Hotel.

15 April, Portugal passes law for election of deputies of Cape Verdean National Assembly as a result of meetings between delegations of PAIGC and MFA.

20–26 June, PAIGC delegation of Fidelis Cabral de Almeida and José Araujo goes to Cascais, Portugal.

24–25 June, at Bissau meeting of PAIGC's CSL plans are made for a Council of Unity of the two states of Guinea-Bissau and Cape Verde. PAIGC gives "total respect to the principle of free choice, democracy, and sovereignty of the people." Cape Verde National Assembly elections will be democratic. CSL notes the blood and glorious sacrifices of our glorious people, the eternal glory of Amilcar Cabral, and the patriotism of Cape Verde.

11 May 1975, Coup by Spinola fails in Lisbon.

30 June, Elections for Cape Verdean ANP. Eighty-five percent of adult population participated, with 92 percent of votes cast for PAIGC. Parties other than PAIGC are excluded.

Elections supervised by UN Mission headed by Syrian Ambassador Hassam Kelani.

5 July, Cape Verde becomes independent by declaration of ANP. A constitution is promised in 90 days. PAIGC is identified as the Force and Guiding Light of the People of Cape Verde and Guinea-Bissau.

6 July, Independence of Cape Verde accepted by MFA led by Vasco Gonçalves.

Drought conditions continue from 1975–1977.

1976 1 May, Formation of Commission of Cape Verdean Trade Unionists on International Workers' Day.

Flora Gomes releases film *Le retour de Cabral.*

1 July, Cape Verde nationalizes bank, airport and airline, shipping, harbors and ports.

30 October, Law enacted in Cape Verde which gives DiNaS power to detain anyone in prison for 90 days without charge.

December, Cape Verde signs friendship accords with Angola.

1977 PAIGC offers transit point for Cuban troops going to Angola. PAIGC passes law allowing military to try political crimes and repressive measures taken against dissidents.

15–20 November, Third Party Congress of PAIGC.

	Carlos Veiga serves as Cape Verdean Attorney General.
1978	Prime Minister Pedro Pires visits Boston.
	Flora Gomes releases film *Anos no Ocaluta.*
	"Reshuffle" within PAIGC, and some small-scale repressive measures against younger dissidents seeking liberalization and more open access to party positions. UCID attracts some PAIGC dissidents.
1979	February, Manuel Faustino and José Veiga leave PAIGC with complaints about lack of internal democracy.
	April, PAIGC purges "Trotskyists" followed by further defections of independent and youthful members of PAIGC.
	May, Joint Guinea-Cape Verde military exercise is cancelled.
1980	5 September, Cape Verdean Constitution passed.
	7 October, Constitution put into effect granting leading role to PAIGC as sole party of the state.
	November, Guinea-Bissau President Luis Cabral overthrown by João Vieira in Bissau. Cabral imprisoned in Guinea.
	PAIGC constitution suspended and replaced with PAICV constitution. PAICV has 4,000 members in islands.
	Renato Cardoso, Carlos Veiga and others leave PAICV.
	Cape Verde census shows a population of about 320,000.
	31 December, Pedro Pires notes that unity with Guinea Bissau is a matter of internal security for PAIGC in Cape Verde with implications that FARP

troops from Guinea could not be counted on for support in Cape Verde.

1981 19 January, PAICV is officially recognized as ruling party.

12 February, PAIGC is officially disbanded in Cape Verde. Unity between Guinea and Cape Verde is suspended. OMCV is formed.

31 August, UCID leaders arrested and held without charge.

1982 January, Luis Cabral freed in Bissau and takes exile in Cuba.

26 March, Agrarian Reform Legislation is passed.

26 April, Cape Verde introduces First Development Plan.

June, Diplomatic relations restored with Guinea-Bissau.

''Group of Five'' Lusophone African nations meets in Praia.

Cape Verde signs cultural accord with Libya.

1983 1 January, Agrarian Reform Law goes into effect.

Abortive military coup is attempted in Guinea-Bissau.

''Group of Five'' Lusophone African nations meets in Bissau.

1984 Elections in Guinea-Bissau; new Constitution adopted.

''Group of Five'' meets in Maputo.

PAICV membership reaches 6,447.

1985 20 January, Amilcar Cabral Institute and School is opened.

June, Cape Verdean police sent for training in Cuba.

Abortive military coup in Guinea-Bissau is attempted by Col. Paulo Correia. ''Group of Five'' meets in São Tomé.

28 October, New ANP is opened in Praia.

1986 P. Correia and five other PAIGC opponents are executed in Bissau.

May, Conference on Social Research in Cape Verde.

PAICV-German project to construct airport in Brava.

''Group of Five'' meets in Luanda.

Membership of PAICV reaches 9,000.

1987 Airline of Cape Verde initiates flights to Boston.

1988 25–30 November, Third Congress of PAICV.

1989 Democratic elections in Gabon.

29 September, mysterious death of Renato Cardoso.

1990 March, First reference to MpD in declaration by Carlos Veiga and António Monteiro calling for greater democracy.

April, PAICV agrees to elections within ANP.

PAIGC dissidents form MpD in rejection of PAICV.

25 July, Fourth PAICV Congress.

Flora Gomes releases film, *Mortunega.*

2 September, PAIGC adopts policy of transition to pluralism.

13–21 September, PAICV and MpD meet at ANP to plan for transition to democratic pluralism.

15 September, PAICV meets with UPICV(R) to

discuss constitutional revisions leading to electoral rights.

28 September Constitutional revisions accepted. This change means that PAICV is no longer sole party in the state and ANP; it also allowed for expanded electoral rights.

6 October, New law defines rights of opposition parties.

13 October, Electoral laws passed to determine procedures, campaign regulations, and eligibility for elections to ANP, and for Presidential elections.

27 October, Law passed to regulate access to telecommunications media and right of reply.

November, MpD publishes its Political Program.

21 November, PAICV and MpD sign Code of Ethical Conduct.

First Congress of OMCV.

1991 13 January, In internationally supervised elections, PAICV is defeated by MpD which wins 56 seats, and makes Carlos Veiga the new Prime Minister, against 23 seats won by PAICV. UCID did not compete.

14 January, Pedro Pires resigns as Prime Minister.

17 January, Election for Presidency won by António Monteiro.

May, PAIGC in Bissau also abolishes provisions in Constitution making the party "the leading political force in the state and society."

May, MpD seeks to isolate the independents in its party.

September, Multi-party Constitution is approved.

15 December, Municipal elections in Cape Verde.

17 December, Election results show MpD winning ten of 14 municipal councils.

Independent candidate wins in São Vicente.

1992 January, Cape Verde assumes seat in UN Security Council. Cabinet reshuffles in Cape Verde.

31 January, Cape Verde Prime Minister Veiga at Security Council to support UN peace-keeping role in Yugoslavia and Haiti.

4–8 May, UNESCO conference in Cape Verde on "The Role of Africa and its Consequences in the Encounter Between Two Worlds."

22 June, Esparadinha airport opens in Brava.

25 June, MpD allows Cape Verdean emigrants to vote in Presidential elections and to participate in ANP.

5 July, PAICV calls a rally to support existing flag.

20 July, PAICV withdraws from Special Session of ANP which is rewriting the Constitution and designing a new flag.

Opposition poll claims that 46 percent of population are opposed to change in the flag. PAIGC complains that MpD has limited or denied access to press and TV.

21 July, Privatization policy enunciated by MpD.

24 July, New flag is officially adopted.

September, Privatization process in Cape Verde is underway.

September–October, Prime Minister Veiga visits New England.

1993 January, Luís Cabral seeks return to Guinea-Bissau.

Creation of Conferência Cabo-verdiana dos Sindicatos Livres.

Second MpD Congress, reelects C. Veiga as Party President.

April, MpD publishes list of companies to be privatized, liquidated, or partly privatized.

June, Schooner *Ernestina* is dry-docked in Massachusetts.

World Bank restructures Cape Verdean commercial sector.

5 July, 18th anniversary of Cape Verdean independence.

August, UCID elects Celso Celestino Party President.

August–September, American Congressional visit to Cape Verde.

September, PAICV Congress elects Aristides Lima the new Secretary General; Pedro Pires becomes PAICV President.

29 September, strike of air traffic controllers on Sal.

October, Cape Verdean President Mascarenhas Monteiro addresses UN General Assembly and meets Cape Verdean-Americans.

Major flu epidemic strikes Mindelo.

24 November, former President Aristides Pereira says that Cape Verdeans ''did not want independence.'' Remark stirs controversy.

November, Prime Minister of São Tomé visits Cape Verde.

Cape Verde government gives aid to Cape Verdeans living in Mozambique.

New PAICV Secretary General Aristides Lima visits Lisbon.

December, Mindelo Mayor Onesimo Silveira visits New Bedford.

Worker protests in Praia over labor laws.

Worker protests in Santo Antão over no back pay.

USAID mission in Cape Verde slated to close in FY 1994.

Creation of Cape Verdean Coast Guard.

Last year of Cape Verdean seat on UN Security Council.

Stone Inscription at Janela, Santo Antão
Photo: Richard Lobban, copyright

Slave Trading Post, Ribeira Grande, São Tiago
Photo: Waltraud Berger Coli, copyright

19th Century Schooners in Furna Bay, Brava
Source: Waltraud Berger Coli Collection

The Custom House in Praia, 1881
Source: Arquivo Historico Nacional

New England Schooner, *Maria Sony* in Mindelo, São Vicente, 1975
Photo: Richard Lobban, copyright

Trans-Oceanic Ships at Mindelo, São Vicente
Photo: Richard Lobban, copyright

Faces of the Future, São Tiago
Photo: Richard Lobban, copyright

Santo Antão, 1975
Photo: United Nations/Y. Nagota

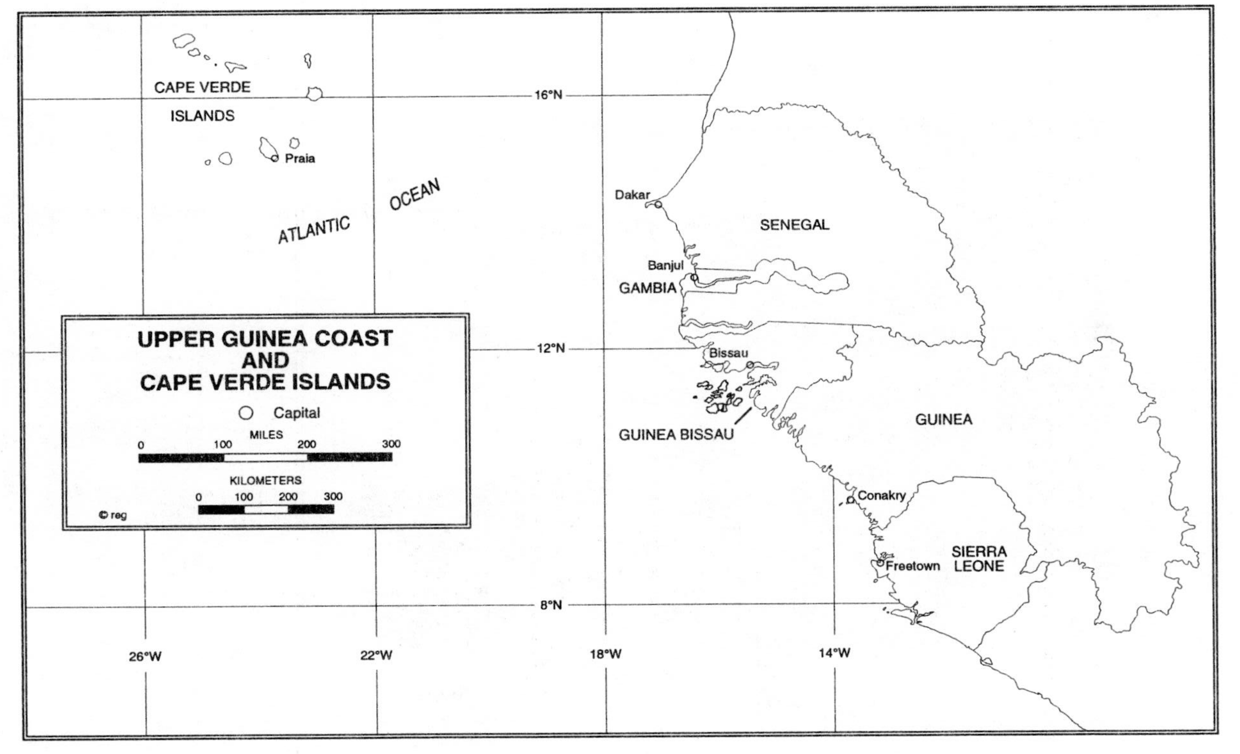
UPPER GUINEA COAST
AND
CAPE VERDE ISLANDS
Capital
MILES
0
100
200
300
KILOMETERS
0
100
200
300
© reg
CAPE VERDE
ISLANDS
Praia
ATLANTIC
OCEAN
16°N
12°N
8°N
26°W
22°W
18°W
14°W
Dakar
SENEGAL
Banjul
GAMBIA
Bissau
GUINEA BISSAU
GUINEA
Conakry
Freetown
SIERRA
LEONE

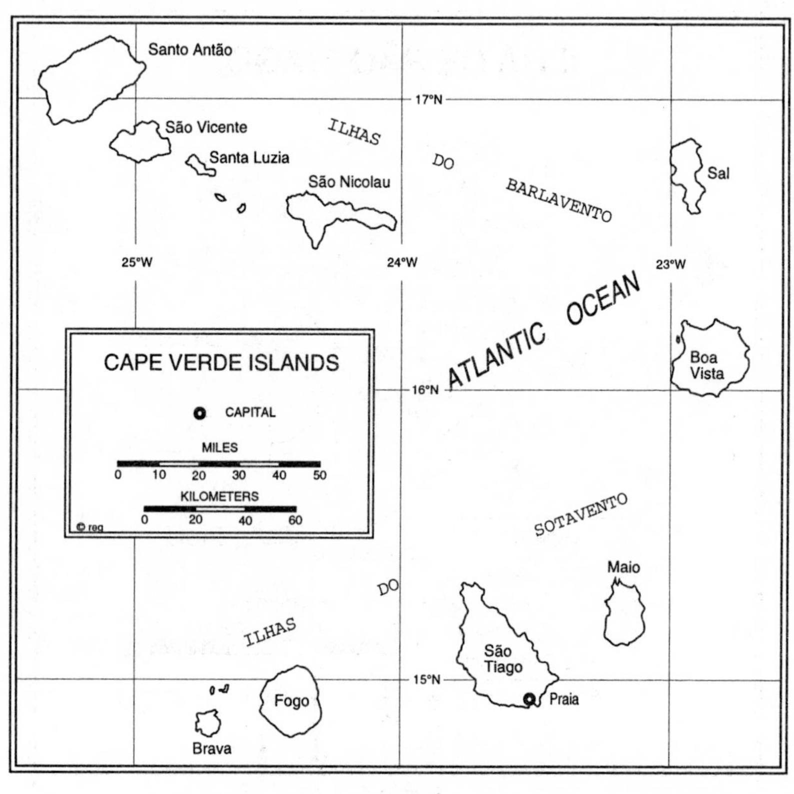
Santo Antão
São Vicente
Santa Luzia
São Nicolau
ILHAS
DO
BARLAVENTO
Sal
17°N
25°W
24°W
23°W
ATLANTIC OCEAN
Boa Vista
16°N
CAPE VERDE ISLANDS
CAPITAL
MILES
0 10 20 30 40 50
KILOMETERS
0 20 40 60
© reg
SOTAVENTO
DO
ILHAS
Maio
São Tiago
Praia
15°N
Fogo
Brava

ILHA DE SÃO TIAGO
Tarrafal
Chão Bom
ATLANTIC OCEAN
23° 30´ N
Pedra Badejo
Assomada +
1394 m
15° 00´ W
Praia
Cidade Velha
Legend
Capital
Cities
Major Roads
Other Roads
© reg
Kilometers
0
10
20
30

INTRODUCTION

Cape Verde's history has three distinct phases. From time immemorial until the mid-15th century it had no permanent human habitation although conceivably there were a few human visitors before the Portuguese. Its second phase was its very longest known history; from about 1455 to 1975 it served the strategic and commercial interests of Portuguese colonialism. Since 1975, the Republic of Cape Verde has entered its third phase as an independent nation. This experience began under the rule of a nationalist one-party state, but since 1991 this has been transformed into plural democracy.

Its people are from diverse origins, but especially they are from the adjacent African coast, and from Portugal and its various Atlantic possesssions, as well as those having Muslim and Jewish roots. Not only are Cape Verdeans immigrants from other lands, they are also a migrating people who are found more in diaspora and maritime communities around the world than in the islands themselves. A fascinating feature of Cape Verdean society is its unique Crioulo culture complete with its own language, music, literature, foods, and dress. Despite the few natural resources of Cape Verde, the character of its hard-working citizens has placed them as leaders in the movements to defeat Portuguese colonialism, to liberate their island country, and now to turn the Cape Verdean people to their next noble experiment of building plural democracy.

Physical Features

The Cape Verde Islands stretch between 475 and 720 kilometers off the coast of Senegal between the latitudes of 14° 48′N and 17° 12′N, and the longitudes 22° 41′W and 25° 22′W. The archipelago consists of 21 islands and islets, of which nine are inhabited. The name of the Republic of Cape Verde may be confused with the Cap Vert peninsula on which Dakar, Senegal is located. Cape Verde is so named because of its position opposite Cap Vert, not because it is especially green as some have proposed. In fact, for all of their known history, the islands have been deeply affected by drought conditions. Less than 25 centimeters of rain falls annually at São Tiago. Strong prevailing dry winds from the north in the winter and sometimes moist winds from the south in the summer cause some slight two-season climatic variation. These two wind systems create the broadly clashing front known as the Intertropical Convergence Zone (ITCZ). If the ITCZ does not move far enough northward in a given year it can result in the utter absence of rainfall. These circumstances in the area of Cape Verde are also responsible for creating hurricanes, which often travel westward to the Caribbean and on to American shores.

The maritime location does add some moisture to the air, but still Cape Verde is quite dry and has an annual temperature fluctuation of only 22–27° C (68–80° F). The land represents only 4,033.3 square kilometers, that is, only a bit larger than the area of Rhode Island. Some islands are particularly rocky and mountainous, while others are flat and sandy. The islands are all of volcanic origin, and the island of Fogo has had many eruptions and tremors in historical times. Only a mere 1.65 percent or 52,688 hectares of the land area may be cultivated and much of this is fallow for long periods. Abusive farming and grazing practices added to soil degradation along with feudal and colonial land ownership patterns which cared little about long-term effęcts. Aside from mountain tops which draw moisture from passing clouds, the terrain is exceptionally bleak and moon-like with sharp crags, volcanic cones, deep valleys, and pronounced erosion on many islands, while some like Sal and Boa Vista are remarkably flat and desert-like. The low-lying islands may only be a hundred meters above sea level, while the volcanic cone of Fogo rises to a majestic 2,831 meters only a few kilometers from the ocean side.

History

There is reason to believe that the Portuguese may not have been the first humans to visit Cape Verde. A case can be made for

Phoenicians to have reached the islands in the 5th or 4th centuries BC. Also there is a possibility of Moorish sailors stopping at the islands for salt in the 10th or 11th centuries. As well, coastal African fisherfolk such as the Lebou of Senegal may have known of Cape Verde. Given periodic eruptions of the island of Fogo, it is reasonable that a high altitude smoke plume may have attracted the attention of these early sailors. Irrespective of these claims, there can be no doubt that it was the Portuguese who were the first to settle there and begin a centuries-long pattern of colonialism, slavery, and trade.

The Portuguese first crossed the Straits of Gibraltar in 1415 to conquer Ceuta under the initiative and leadership of Prince Henry. Each subsequent decade saw Portuguese sailors move further and further down the Atlantic coast of Africa. In 1434, they reached Cape Bojador in Morocco, but two years later they failed to take Tangiers. By 1441, Portuguese sailors and captains such as Gil Eannes and Nuño Tristão took their first slaves from the African coast and, by 1446, they reached the portion of the Upper Guinea coast in the area of modern Senegambia and Guinea-Bissau. By the early 1450s, the Portuguese were regularly taking about 1,000 African slaves back to Portugal and to their Atlantic islands for domestic and agricultural labor. It was on a wide sweep off the coast, returning from a mission of exploration and slaving, that the southeastern islands in the archipelago were first noted by sailors of Prince Henry.

In 1455 or 1456, António de Noli, from Genoa, and Diogo Afonso, from Portugal, probably became the first Europeans to reach some of the Cape Verde Islands. The rest of the islands were discovered in the late 1450s and very early 1460s. In 1462, plans were made for their colonization and settlement under a policy of *capitanias* held by António and Bartólomeu de Noli. At the very beginning, the islands offered a healthier and strategically secure base for trade along the coast, especially by the merchant Fernão Gomes who steadily explored further down the West African coast. As the decades went by, the islands became stopover points for such famous navigators as Da Gama, Dias, and Columbus. Thus, almost from the start, the Cape Verde islands were important to those who were on the way to someplace else, whether as seafarers, merchants, or slaves exported to the New World. In a parallel fashion, the history of Cape Verde is very much a history of connections to other places. Especially, this includes ties to the human and natural resources of the African coast, to the political and economic power base in Portugal, to New World markets in Brazil and the Caribbean, and as whalers and mariners on New England ships.

But this is not the whole story, because the Cape Verde Islands represent a land and people of a unique and rich blend. Equally early in their history the population moved from being simply Portuguese and Africans to a population of Crioulos, or *Caboverdeanos.* The small population of the islands was internally diversified by variations in class, race, and ethnicity. They could range from the Portuguese *capitãos,* clerical officials, and military officers, to roving *lançados* (outcastes), and *degredados* (convicts) from Portugal. Often it was some members of these groups who were active in coastal trade for slaves, hides, dyewoods, ivory, and wax. The links to the coast were so essential that Cape Verde quickly became, and long was, the control center for the Portuguese on the entire Upper Guinea coast.

Almost from the beginning of settlement, West African slaves of Senegambian, Mande, and Fula origins were also being brought to the islands. The Portuguese used them to labor on plantations producing cotton, sugar and susbsistence crops as well as in domestic service as cooks, washers, stoneworkers, and herders. After the slave needs of the islands were met, the largest numbers of slaves in Cape Verde were exported either to Portugal and the Canaries in early decades, or to Brazil and the New World in later centuries. Cape Verde was thereby a nation founded by both slavers, slaves, and their progeny.

The discovery and settlement of the New World triggered a great intensification of the slave trade in the 16th century in which European competition grew and Portugal was no longer able to meet the demand. The Portuguese Crown issued formal slave trade monopolies on the coast, but other European "freebooting" independent merchants, African Dyula long-distance slave traders, and various Luso-African middlemen sought their own private gains by bypassing the official traders. The penetration and knowledge of the interior by Europeans was extremely superficial at this time. Europeans were content to have Africans war upon other Africans as long as coastal traders had a supply of slaves, who could be bartered for guns, rum, cloth, and trinkets.

Slaves were brought to the coast on foot or in light river craft and were then transported to regional *baracoon* slave warehouses, to await purchase and shipment to Cape Verde and the New World. Facing attacks by Spanish, English, and Dutch slave traders throughout the 16th century, the Portuguese sought to strengthen their authority by abolishing the *capitania* system in 1587 and replacing it with a Governor-General who was directly responsible to the Crown under whose authority he jointly controlled the islands and the Guinea coast.

The 17th century saw an even greater expansion of the slave trade, but the portion of slaves transported on Portuguese ships steadily declined and Portugal's concerns in Cape Verde and Guinea often turned toward military defense against its rivals. Frequent attacks, and only modest success at administrative reform, created an unpredictable and undisciplined presence of Portuguese *lançados* and *grumettas* on the coast, who relied on good ties with African peoples and states, as much as with Lisbon. Overall, the colonial economy of Cape Verde was stable, but stagnant, potentially lucrative, but precarious.

The themes from these earlier centuries carried over into the 18th century even though African slave traders had steadily drifted further down the coast toward such regions as the Slave Coast (Nigeria) and Lower Guinea (Angola). By this time Cape Verdeans would sometimes escape the conditions of drought and poverty with work on whaling or sealing ships from New England. The mid-18th century saw a substantial effort by the Marquis de Pombal, Portuguese Prime Minister, to develop Brazil. His plans included a central role for Cape Verde as a regional supply center for thousands of slaves from the African coast. Meanwhile, French attacks continued in the islands and they also pressed southward from Senegal on the coast, while the British repeatedly sought to take Bolama from Cape Verdean administration saying that it belonged to their regional domain in Sierra Leone.

In the early 19th century, the same ruling classes of the European nations which had gained great wealth through slaving, began to turn toward its abolition for moral and economic reasons. Legitimate trade in oils, hides, woods, ivory, gold, and other African products became more significant than slaves. Unfortunately, the Portuguese were especially slow to follow this course.

American, and particularly New England, merchant ships continued to acquire slaves on the coast and in the islands, where they also obtained salt and supplies. The arrival of an American Consul in Cape Verde in 1818 suggests the early significance of this tie. Indeed, sometimes the commerce with Americans even exceeded that with Portugal. In the 1840s, the American government established an Africa Squadron in Cape Verde with the ostensible task of cruising the coast to look for Americans engaged in slave shipping. For a variety of reasons, this mission was largely a failure and was curtailed completely when American ships were recalled for naval picket duty against the southern secessionists in the American Civil War.

Meanwhile, the limiting ecological conditions in the islands always meant restrictions on the development of the slave plantation systems there. Some specialty exports of the islands such as salt, urzella, coffee, horses, and *panos* also used slave labor. Among the few advantages of Cape Verde, certainly its strategic location is one of the most important, not only as a secure supply area for "seasoned" slaves, but for worldwide exploration, merchant fleets, and regular traffic to the New World which was carried down the Canary Current and across to the Caribbean. Other famed visitors who stopped in Cape Verde also include Drake, Darwin, and much later, even the Lindberghs.

The Portuguese presence on the coast diminished through the 19th century. In 1879, the Portuguese offically separated the administration of the islands from their colony on the Guinea coast, and by the time of the 1884–85 Berlin Congress they were left with mainly the estuaries of the Cacheu and Geba which constitute the largest part of Guinea-Bissau today. As the 19th century came to a close, the age of sail had been replaced by the age of steam and São Vicente became one of the great ports of call for refueling. Trans-oceanic telegraph cables also tied Cape Verde to the wider world at a rather early date.

As these exchanges were taking place over the centuries, the always sparse Portuguese population intermingled with the greater numbers of slaves to produce the distinctive majority culture of the Cape Verdean people. The interweaving of European and African cultural features is so complete that one must correctly speak of a synthesis of a uniquely Crioulo society with its own distinctive customs, folklore, cuisine, music, literature, and language.

The overthrow of the Portuguese monarchy in 1910 was followed by democratic Republicanism until the establishment of fascist rule in Portugal in 1926. These events brought little substantive change to Cape Verde which was kept as a more-or-less self-sustaining but impoverished colony, especially at times of drought. Seeing these difficult conditions, a program of peaceful appeals to the Portuguese government and international bodies, was launched by the Partido Africano da Independência da Guiné e Cabo Verde (PAIGC). This was founded in 1956 in Bissau by Amilcar Cabral and other leaders of Cape Verdean origin or descent. An answer to the PAIGC demands was given by the Portuguese in Bissau at the Pijiguiti dockyards in August 1959, when they massacred striking nationalist workers. As a result, the PAIGC determined that a program of anti-colonial armed struggle would be the only path to independence.

In January 1963 the nationalist war began. This was followed, on 22 November 1963, by Portugal declaring that Cape Verde was an "overseas province" and not a colony. This move allowed Portugal to assert that Cape Verde was an organic part of Portugal and thus not subject to the rapidly expanding movement for African decolonization. The war in Guinea-Bissau was concurrent with wars of national liberation in Angola and Mozambique, which were projected as comradely struggles and part of a general anti-colonial offensive which was designed to liberate Cape Verde, São Tomé, and Príncipe as well. The tactics of guerrilla warfare finally burdened the economy and political agenda of Portugal to the extent that the entire fascist and colonial structure was toppled by Portuguese officers on 25 April 1975. In a rapid turn of events, negotiations soon led to the independence of Guinea-Bissau on 24 September 1974 and of Cape Verde on 5 July 1975.

Initially both nations were ruled by the common political party, the PAIGC, which had long fought in the African forests for the independence of the islands. However, in January 1973, Amilcar Cabral was assassinated in a Portuguese-backed conspiracy so independence began without his crucial leadership. In Cape Verde, the PAIGC was able to defeat its political rivals, and it became the sole ruling party led by the old PAIGC militants Pedro

Pires, as Prime Minister, and Aristides Pereira, as President and PAIGC Secretary General. In Guinea-Bissau, Luís Cabral, the half-brother of Amilcar Cabral, was the President.

In 1980, Luís Cabral was overthrown in a military coup by João Vieira. This violation of party unity was viewed with great hostility by the PAIGC branch in Cape Verde which ceased diplomatic relations with its coastal counterpart and changed the name of the ruling party in the islands to the Partido Africano da Independência de Cabo Verde (PAICV). Although relations were restored in 1982, they have since been cool. Significantly, these events had made the PAICV leadership become more suspicious of its domestic rivals. In addition, they pursued their plan of reform in land ownership and the goal of expanding a socialist-oriented policy of state-owned companies. These circumstances in turn caused the PAICV to adopt restrictive, and occasionally repressive, measures against opposition groups such as the UPICV, UCID, and also dissidents within the party. While it was common in Africa to have a one-party state, the PAICV and its Assembléia Nacional Popular (ANP) allowed a forum for diverse or opposing views. As the last edition of this book was written this policy of a one-party state was still being pursued. However, since then, a new democratic movement has appeared in Africa. This movement has targeted one-party and military regimes on the continent. Its general goal is the protection of human rights and replacement of one-party states with multi-party, democratically elected governments.

Addressing this challenge, but feeling confident it would win, the PAICV leadership made constitutional and legislative changes which allowed for multi-party, internationally supervised elections in the islands. A group of PAIGC/PAICV dissidents began to coalesce around a new formation called the Movimento para Democracia (MpD) which put forward its own candidates and allowed other independents to run. In peaceful and fair elections held in January 1991, the MpD candidate for Prime Minister, Carlos Veiga, gave a stunning defeat to Pedro Pires, and the independent candidate for President, António Mascarenhas, overwhelmingly outdistanced his competitor Aristides Pereira. A new government was quickly formed in the following month.

Since 1991, the ruling MpD has maintained a good record in supporting democratic pluralism and even more parties are expected to compete in the 1996 elections. The collapse of the world communist movement has also brought an end to American-Soviet rivalries, and that has permitted a broader range of diplomatic choices for the MpD than was formerly available. On the domestic front, the MpD continues the earlier policies of improvement of educational, health, and social services, but its economic policy is aimed at reversing many of the PAICV's state-owned agencies and institutions by turning them over to private sector interests. This program of economic liberalism is designed to attract foreign investors, but is opposed by the old-line PAICV. In addition to such major economic policy shifts, the new MpD government has created a new national flag and other national icons saying that the former flag was only that of the PAIGC party, rather than of the nation of Cape Verde. Some observers have pointed out that the former flag had a style and colors similar to many African nations, while the new flag has similarities with those of European nations. As this is written it is too early to tell of the longer-term effects of these changes in form and content. The voters who were tired of the PAICV and were attracted to the theme of change with the MpD will be expectant.

To the credit of the PAIGC/PAICV administration, no mass starvation took place even during drought conditions due to huge efforts in water conservation and reforestation. This program is continued by the MpD. The PAICV foreign policy of non-alignment with a progressive slant was favored and Cape Verde maintained excellent relations with both sides in a world much divided by superpower rivalries. The MpD is also active on the world stage at important bodies such as the Organization of African Unity and the United Nations. While some human rights abuses have been noted, the PAICV again should be credited with supporting the bloodless transfer of power to its rivals.

Economic Development

Of the five former Portuguese colonies in Africa, Cape Verde has made notable strides in economic and social development, a feat made more significant given the poor base in natural resources which was inherited at the time of independence. At times, the ravages of the drought even challenged the very survival of the population.

At independence in 1975, the new Republic of Cape Verde was a remarkably poor and undeveloped nation by Western standards, although, compared with other West African countries on the continent, the levels of health and literacy were, and are, much higher. Under colonial rule, the human and few natural resources of Cape Verde were broadly neglected or abused. The main source of subsistence or wealth was generated in agriculture which has included sugar cane, cotton, bananas, fruits, peanuts, urzella, indigo, and coffee. Cotton was often exported as *pano* cloths, while sugar was refined to make *grogga;* both had been important in the slave trade. Livestock production includes fowl, pigs, goats, cattle and horses. Cape Verdean goat and cow hides have long been an export; horses from the islands were especially valued in the slave trade.

Mineral resources are equally modest, and have included salt, puzzolane (a plaster additive), stone and sand quarries. Solar and wind power are other natural resources of some merit with high technology transfer.

Subsistence production in Cape Verde is, at best, a marginal activitity and the islands long ago failed to meet their domestic food needs. Corn, a popular staple food, is almost 90 percent imported and a large part of the national budget is devoted to food imports. In the past and present, the wealthier members of Cape Verdean society have prospered with export and import monopolies and large-scale plantation production. Although slavery is long gone from Cape Verde, the conditions of rural poverty experienced by the *badiu* population have made them susceptible to work gangs or contract labor in the islands or as exported contract labor to such places as São Tomé and Príncipe. While the numbers were not great, some Cape Verdeans became modest merchants or strategic colonial middlemen in the islands and in Portugal's African colonies.

Tormented by recurrent droughts, limited arable land, and widespread erosion, only a small minority could make a comfortable living. These degraded conditions have led to a low labor cost which itself has retarded capital-intensive innovations and has kept the economy at a small scale. One hope for future economic growth and import substitution rests in certain types of intensive, specialized agriculture, but this will also require more measures for water and soil conservation. While fish represent a major natural resource for Cape Verde, the state-owned fishing fleet has not properly developed the potential with implications in earning hard currency, stimulating local canning manufacture, and nutritional improvement. Perhaps foreign technology and fishing fleets may be attracted to the abundant and diverse fish species in Cape Verdean waters.

Proposals to utilize Cape Verdean labor in light manufacture such as textiles, ceramics, or in ship services such as repair and bunkering, are advanced, but as yet they have had little widespread result in broadening the Cape Verdean economy. International and domestic air services have played a stable role in the economy of Cape Verde. International communication services using trans-oceanic cables and satellites have long found a strategic advantage in Cape Verde. Some role in international warehousing for bulk items distributed to the African coast has been discussed with Brazilian firms, such as automobile and clothing manufacturers.

The usually warm and sunny weather, and extraordinary beaches of some islands such as Sal and Boa Vista, have accounted for a steady rise in the number of hotel beds and expanding employment opportunities in the hotel and tourist industries. This might prompt an expansion of poultry, egg, and dairy farms as well a vineyards and other tourist services. Still, to an important degree, one of the chief Cape Verdean exports remains its citizens who are found throughout the world. This diaspora population, reckoned as larger than the islands', is an important source of remittances and hard currency for the nation.

Over the centuries, Cape Verdean society has evolved its own distinctive culture. This is centered around the Crioulo language and literature, which include novels, short stories, poetry and the *Claridade* literary movement. Crioulo emerged as a lingua franca in commercial relations with the coast, but it also has spawned musical and dance forms as well as a wide variety of folkways such as unique foods, games, arts and crafts, and dress. While Crioulo culture and language have gone far to unify the people of Cape Verde there are still notable differences by class, subculture, and education. These subjects are all addressed in the entry-style format of this dictionary.

THE DICTIONARY

-A-

AFONSO, DIOGO. Afonso, of Portuguese origin, is credited with discovering some of the westward islands in the Barlavento group in the late 1450s. Afonso was a nephew and heir of Prince Henry (q.v.) the Navigator and was titled as the Squire of Prince Fernando. Because of his discoveries and relationship to the royal household, Afonso was appointed as *capitão* (q.v.) of one of the two first captaincies on São Tiago island (q.v.) in 1462. Perhaps preferring his appointment as *contador* (royal accountant) of Madeira, he never initiated the colonization of his appointed captaincy in Cape Verde, unlike De Noli (q.v.). *See* INSCRIPTIONS.

AFRICA SQUADRON. From 1843 to 1861 the United States Navy officially sought to curtail the trade in African slaves. This was to be achieved by establishing the Africa Squadron, a fleet of sailing "cruisers" used to further the anti-slavery mission by boarding suspected ships and seizing their human cargoes. This effort had its roots in the 1807 Slave Importation Prohibition Act, signed by President Jefferson, but was very clearly not supported by southern slave-owners.

The Squadron was supposed to function jointly with British ships sailing under similar orders. Nevertheless, the British and Americans had not fully restored the trust broken by the American Revolution and the War of 1812, so they were still unable to fully agree to mutual inspection of each other's ships. The 1819 Anglo-American treaty and the related American Slave Trade Act were early, but small steps toward curbing the slave trade. This Act allowed for the use of armed cruisers to suppress the slave trade, but it was barely put into practice. As with America, Britain had officially abolished the trade in its colonies in 1833, but British slavers were still active.

The British Squadron was based in Sierra Leone to carry out the anti-slavery policy with a greater degree of enforcement than the American vessels. The American plan included the creation of the country of Liberia to provide a place for the disembarkation of any slaves (q.v.) captured on the high seas.

Limitations on the mission of the Squadron were proposed by U.S. Senator James DeWolfe of Bristol, Rhode Island. The DeWolfe family, especially James's brother George, was actively interested in weakening the mission since this prominent Rhode Island family had gained great wealth from the slave trade during the preceding years. According to the historian George Brooks, James DeWolfe was also the father-in-law of William Perry, a brother of Matthew Perry who was the first Commander of the U.S. Africa Squadron based in Cape Verde.

Officially, the Treaty of Washington was ratified in August 1842 and articles 8 and 9 provided for the presence of armed anti-slavery cruisers. However, as it began in 1843, the Secretary of the Navy was Abel B. Upshur who was from the slave-owning southern states as were six out of nine of his successors. As a result, Upshur assigned rather few, poorly equipped ships carrying only 80 guns for this assignment. Upshur insisted on the conservative policy which gave the highest priority to the protection of American lives, commerce, and ships. This approach added to the limitations of the possible actions of the Squadron captains. Thus, with a structural bias toward southern, and slave-trading influences, it is not surprising to learn that the Africa Squadron was largely ineffective.

Moreover, by this time, much of the slaving had moved from the Upper Guinea coast to the Lower Guinea coast at the Slave Coast (Nigeria) or further south to Angola which were far from Cape Verde. Systemic problems of supply meant that the range of the cruisers was also limited. Cape Verde, as a Portuguese colony, had itself not abolished slavery (q.v.) at this time and slaves were still being imported by the Portuguese to the very ports where the Squadron was based. The health conditions in Cape Verde were also poor and an American graveyard in Cape Verde was soon in use for American sailors dying of malaria, yellow fever, and other tropical diseases.

The coastal slavers who intended to load slaves could either wait until the Squadron cruisers had departed the area, or they could fly the Portuguese flag to circumvent the 1842 protocol which allowed American cruisers to board only American flag ships. The strict control imposed on the right to search suspected ships was a severe limit to the Squadron's effectiveness, although there were some instances of Africa Squadron cruisers seizing American slave ships which sailed under the Portuguese flag. Other limiting factors were relatively slow and under-gunned ships often in poor condition.

Some of these cruisers were based in São Vicente, others were at São Tiago (qq.v.). These sailing vessels (q.v.) included the famed *Constitution* (''Old Ironsides''), the *Constellation,* the *Consort,* the sloops *Decatur* and *Marion,* the ships *Germantown, Yorktown, Jamestown, Perry, Mohican, Mystic, Sumpter,* and *San Jacinto,* the frigate *Macedonian,* the brigs *Bainbridge, Boxer, Dolphin, Porpoise,* and *Truxton,* and the *Preble.* However, it was usual to have only four or five cruisers operating in the Squadron at any time. Its annual operating budget was about $250,000, but this was less than a third of what was budgeted for the English Squadron. The largest cost was probably in lives of officers and crew who quickly required American cemeteries to be built in São Vicente and São Tiago. Later the neglect and abuse of these cemeteries became an issue between American diplomats and Portuguese authorities.

During the 1843–45 command of the Squadron by Captain Matthew Perry in his frigate *Saratoga,* only one slaver was reported captured and this was later freed by a New Orleans court. In Sepember 1844, Perry sailed the *Preble* to Bissau as a show of force to protect American goods and merchants during a local uprising. Among Perry's successors were Commodores Read (1846) and Skinner (1846); they accomplished little more than showing the flag and protecting American commercial interests.

For the next decade, the Africa Squadron was under the command of Commodores Bell and J.H. Gregory (1851), G. C. Read (1852), LaVallete (1852–53), Mayo (1853–55), Foote (1855), Crabbe (1856), Conover (1857), and others. It was usual to seize no more than one slaver each year, and remarkably, Captain Isaac Mayo, was himself an owner of slaves. During its 16 years of operation only 19 slavers were actually brought to trial; of these, four were released and the others resulted in small fines or light jail terms for the captains. One exception to this was under the command of Inman who, in 1859, managed to seize 11 slavers, freeing almost 2,800 slaves. In the previous 18 years only 24 ships had been seized and 4,945 slaves liberated. By contrast, during this same period the British Anti-Slavery squadron had captured 595 slave ships, and freed 45,600 slaves. When the Squadron officially ended in 1862, there were ships carrying 113-guns, but the inflated prices for slaves (given their relative scarcity) still made smuggling irresistibly profitable to American, Portuguese, and Spanish slave smugglers. Brooks points out that between 1859–62 New York had still outfitted 170 slaveships, even while the north was engaged in the Civil War with the American south over this issue. This number of ships was far more than those from Europe or Cuba.

The long-lasting toleration of slavery was finally reversed only in 1859 when relations with Britain were improved and the slave system was more aggressively opposed by Lincoln to undermine the slave system in the south. As the American Civil War wore on, the Africa Squadron was transferred to naval picket duty to blockade southern U.S. ports. The Emancipation Proclamation, and the subsequent defeat of the Confederacy, brought the formal practice of the slave trade to its extinction by the mid-1860s. *See:* SLAVERY; UNITED STATES RELATIONS.

AFRICANUS, LEO (Al-Hassan ibn Muhammad Al-Wazzan Az-Zayyati b. ca. 1489–ca. 1550). Leo Africanus is the name by which the famed Moorish geographer is better known. He is noted in this book because his reports contributed to the Portuguese and Spanish interest in exploring the Guinea coast and penetrating the interior of West Africa. In addition, he gave an alternative Moorish account of the great events in 15th century Iberia. He was probably born in Fez, Morocco, to a family of Spanish Arabs exiled after the Spanish Inquisition began in 1492. He traveled as far as Turkey and Songhai (during the reign of Askia Muhammad) and to Bornu, Wadai, and Egypt. Captured by Sicilians in 1518, he was given protection by Pope Leo X in Rome who valued his traveler's reports. It was in this connection that he gained the name Leo of Africa (Africanus). His work *Description of Africa* was written in Italian and was completed in 1526 but probably not published until 1550. By 1556 translations appeared in Latin and French. These works became the classic detailed source on medieval Sudanic Africa for many years because of their primary data and incorporation of earlier scholarship.

AGRICULTURE. Although the Cape Verdean population is overwhelmingly rural, the role of agriculture in the islands is very tenuous given the inadequate supply of ground water and rainfall. The colonial economy and a fragmented system of land ownership were also detrimental to the development of productive agriculture. Arable land in Cape Verde is very limited with only 0.12 hectares available per person. The prolonged drought (q.v.) and degradation of the soils adds more severe limitations to agriculture. In combination, these factors result in a very low, irregular, and uncertain level of agricultural production. Under these circumstances agricultural production yields as little as 10 percent of the national food needs and very seldom does production reach even 50 percent of the food consumed.

The significant exports have been cane sugar and bananas, but other cash crops have included coffee, citrus fruits, castor beans, indigo (q.v.), and urzella. Valuable land was taken up by these cash crops at a time when the production of basic subsistence crops was declining. In recent years maize production, for example, only equaled 4 percent of the total demand; the balance was imported.

While banana cultivation has fluctuated quite markedly in recent years, overall production has remained very high relative to other crops. For example, bananas were produced at 3.92 tons per hectare while the next highest productivity was recorded for peanuts at 0.76 tons per hectare. Moreover, some of the land used for bananas is among the best-watered land in the archipelago including rather large privately owned plantations. The 30-hectare banana plantation of Fazenda Santa Cruz on São Tiago (q.v.) once employed 1,000 workers. This plantation was taken over by its workers after April 1974, but may be slated for re-privatization.

Agricultural Production in Metric Tons

Crop	*1968*	*1970*	*1983*	*1987*	*1989*
Sugar Cane	11,223	8,072	9,000	15,700	18,150
Bananas	6,889	8,323	3,000	4,500	5,400
Cassava	2,934	2,085	950	3,000	3,000
Sweet Potatoes	3,172	2,306	1,600	2,800	1,600
Maize	678	3,354	2,700	21,200	7,300
Potatoes			800	2,600	1,920

(Source: Cape Verdean Ministry of Rural Development)

Traditionally Cape Verdean agricultural production had some diversity in exports in such commodities as rum, *grogga* (q.v.), produced from sugar cane, salted meat, livestock (especially horses [q.v.]), and cotton. Many of these traditional exports (from as early as the 15th century) figured importantly in the trade on the African coast for slaves, ivory, plant dyes, hides, and beeswax.

Recent statistics on livestock production show notable fluctuation in the population of cattle as a result of drought conditions. The foraging potential of sheep and goats allows for stable or increasing numbers, but with risk to the environment. Pigs are especially important for Cape Verde as they can be penned and recycle wastes, or they can forage around towns and villages. Pigs are well known as high energy converters and they reproduce quickly with large litters so they provide an important source of meat to Cape Verde. Commercial poultry production has become important in recent years as a source of income and for improved nutrition.

Number of Head of Major Livestock

Type	*1970*	*1975*	*1980*	*1985*	*1986*	*1988*
Cattle	25,000	15,000	11,000	10,000	11,500	17,996
Goats	60,000	50,000	66,000	75,000	78,000	95,338
Sheep	1,800	1,600	1,600	1,700	2,300	4,193
Pigs	30,000	24,000	35,000	58,000	67,000	57,977

(Source: General Office of Livestock; Agricultural Census of 1988)

The plant dye, urzella (*Litmus roccella,*) has frequently been an export of Cape Verde. Urzella and indigo (*Indigofera sp.*) were cultivated to revive the stagnant economy but the commerce in these plant dyes was controlled by the British. While urzella and indigo were used to dye Cape Verdean textiles, especially the *panos* (q.v.) used in the slave trade, they were never of great significance as a cash crop and they were essentially replaced by the more valuable production of coffee in more recent years.

Representatives of the complex of West African crops may be found in Cape Verde. This complex underlies the establishment of the major Sahelian states of West Africa. Grains include fonio, sorghum or millet, some Guinea yam, and okra. Calabash gourds and watermelons are important. Very many of the important West African and Cape Verdean crops today are, in fact, native to the Americas and were only introduced in the 16th century. Chief among these is maize or American corn which is well suited to rainfed areas or to places cultivated by irrigation. Lima and haricot beans are common American legumes now found in common Cape Verdean foods. The diet also includes American crops such as pineapples, pumpkins, squash, tomatoes, and papaya.

Peanuts or groundnuts (*Arachis hypogaea*), *mancarra* in Portuguese, are grown in Cape Verde, especially on Fogo (q.v.), but this crop has far less significance in the islands than on the neighboring mainland. Production fluctuates very widely by rainfall. Even the high figure for 1964 was a small 164 tons, but the production of peanuts in 1970, a year of major drought, was put at just 14 tons.

About 80 percent of the Cape Verdean working population (some 77,000 workers) lives by agricultural production (mostly subsistence farming), thus when production falls drastically one may understand just how devastating and extensive the impact can be. In figures for the early 1960s it was calculated that only 1.65 percent (52,688 hectares) of the total land area of Cape Verde was being cultivated. The limitations on agriculture are even more obvious when it is considered that about 30 percent of the farmland in Cape Verde is being fallowed and only 50 percent is for permanent regular crops. This harsh picture was worsened by the exploitative systems of colonial land tenure under which 69.4 percent of the 36,309 farms were operated by sharecropping or tenant farming. For those minority farmers who owned their own land the holdings were usually small. Aside from private capitalists, the Catholic Church was a large land owner. Some narrow coastal areas and high moisture-bearing altitudes on Fogo are particularly good for peanut and coffee cultivation, but most agriculture is concentrated on São Tiago, Santo Antão, and São Nicolau (qq.v.), all of which have somewhat more regular sources of water.

During the colonial era up to independence, agricultural labor was also generated through *frentes de trabalho* (labor pools) which were compensated at the following levels: men, 30 escudos per day, women, 22.5 per day, and children, 18 per day. These rates were similar to those paid to the *brigadas da estrada* (road building crews) which have built, largely by hand, endless cobblestone roadways throughout the islands. *See* DROUGHT; ECONOMY; FISHING.

AIDS. The Acquired Immune Deficiency Syndrome (AIDS, or SIDA in Portuguese) has arrived in Cape Verde as well as most other parts of the world. At the 28th Summit of the OAU (q.v.) in Dakar in 1992, notable concern was expressed about this disease without a cure. Officially the first case of AIDS in Cape Verde was reported in 1986; by 1992 there were 56 confirmed cases and 28 known deaths. Given a dispersed and mobile population, unofficial estimates place the numbers even higher, perhaps at 0.5 percent of the population aged 15–55. Perhaps other cases were dismissed as pneumonia.

Special attention was drawn to Cape Verde when an

apparently new strain (HIV2) was identified for an individual with Cape Verdean origins who was living in New Jersey. A program of AIDS education for Cape Verdean-Americans is underway in Boston led by Dr. João Soares. In Cape Verde, Dr. Carlos Brito is coordinating the Cape Verdean League for the Struggle against AIDS in conjunction with a WHO program and other West African initiatives. The Cape Verdean Ministry of Health has initiated a study of AIDS prevalence in a sample population of 1,500, but the results are not yet known. *See* HEALTH, LIFE EXPECTANCY.

AMARILIS, ORLANDA. Amarilis is a native of São Tiago (q.v.) and was married to the distinguished Portuguese writer Manuel Ferreira in 1946. Ferreira has focused on Luso-African, and especially Cape Verdean, literature; his very important three-volume anthology, *No Reino de Caliban,* featured a number of Cape Verdean writers. This prominent literary couple went on to found the literary magazine *Certeza,* which is considered to carry on the literary traditions of the earlier *Claridade* (q.v.). Amarilis traveled and lived in India and Angola which added material and depth to her own work. Her two collections of introspective short stories examine gender aspects of Cape Verdean women as well as the complex issue of Cape Verdean ethno-racial identity. *See* CLARIDADE; LITERATURE.

ARAUJO, JOSÉ EDUARDO F. (15 March 1933–20 January 1992). After his secondary education, Araujo entered the Faculty of Law in the University of Lisbon while in his twenties. He returned to Praia in 1958, but only to travel on to Dakar and Conakry to join his comrades in the PAIGC (q.v.). He was a long-time PAIGC militant who served in many high-ranking capacities including political commissar of the permanent commission of the southern national committee in Guinea-Bissau (q.v.) during the armed struggle. Araujo was the head of the PAIGC information section in Conakry and was a member of the Executive Committee for the Struggle (CEL [q.v.]) in charge of production. After the reorganization of the CEL, Araujo became Minister of the

General Secretariat. Araujo was a member of the team that negotiated for Cape Verdean independence in 1975.

Following independence he became the organizational secretary for the PAIGC (a trouble-shooting minister without portfolio), and he served as the Minister of Education and Culture. When he discovered that the 1992 annual celebration of National Heroes' Day had a diminished role for Amilcar Cabral (q.v.) he became so upset that he was stricken with a heart attack and died that same day. Araujo is buried in Varzea cemetery in Praia.

ARMED FORCES. SEE: FORÇAS ARMADAS.

ARRENDAMENTO. SEE: MORGADOS.

ASSEMBLÉIA NACIONAL POPULAR (ANP). The People's National Assembly is the legislative branch of the government of Cape Verde elected by universal adult suffrage. This consisted of 56 deputies elected in December 1980. The ANP was formerly joined with the ANP of Guinea-Bissau until the 1980 coup of João Vieira (q.v.). The PAICV (q.v.), the former ruling party, was technically subordinate to the ANP which is the supreme legislative body of the state. While there has been overlap in membership, the functions and meetings of the bodies were quite distinct. At least a quarter of the members of the ANP were not members of the PAICV. The ANP empowered the Council of State Commissioners, passed laws, ratified decrees, and could adopt or revise the Constitution (q.v.). In turn the Council of State Commissioners acted as the executive organ of the ANP when it was not in session. The ANP meets annually for several weeks at a time.

At the first meeting of the ANP in the liberated zones of Guinea-Bissau (q.v.) during the war it adopted the Constitution and elected officers and ministers for the Council of State which had 15 members in 1973. The first meeting had 125 delegates representing various party organs and various regional councils. In April 1975 it held its first meeting after liberation. Since that time, the membership was expanded to

150 delegates and the structure has become more formalized. Since 1980 the two republics have altered the numerical composition of their now separate Assemblies, but the general form remains similar.

As a result of the democratic reforms and national elections in 1991 the ANP composition has changed markedly. Indeed, it was within the ANP that the Constitution was changed to allow for multi-party elections and from the exclusive domain of the PAIGC/PAICV in the one-party state to the PAICV being the minority party in the MpD (q.v.) government. On 25 January 1991 the new Government was formed from the ANP under a new Constitution of April 1991. This allowed the formation of a new National Program in May 1991 which enlarged the democratic process, removed party membership as a requirement for public service, reduced the instruments of state control and granted free association to trade unions and the public. On foreign policy matters the ANP endorsed relations with bodies of the UN, OAU (qq.v.) and ECOWAS. *See* APPENDIX: OFFICIALS OF CAPE VERDE; ELECTIONS; PAIGC.

ASSIMILADOS. With the Colonial Act of 1930, just prior to the onset of Salazar's (q.v.) rule and while he was Minister of the Colonies, the status of *assimilado* was assigned to those *indigenas* in the Portuguese African colonies whose cultural standards of literacy, education, financial position or other criteria would entitle them to fuller rights as Portuguese citizens. This designation was to elevate a very select few from the classification of *indigena,* also described in the Act of 1930, which applied to the vast majority of the African colonial populations, making them wards of the state who were denied their civil rights including the right to vote. This Act relegated them to the lowest paying jobs and inferior schools, and subjected them to a head tax, restricted movement, and more severe and arbitrary punishment within the criminal justice system.

Most Cape Verdeans, because of some cultural similarity to the Portuguese, were considered to be *assimilados* and therefore were citizens of Portugal and entitled access to Portuguese state schooling. Consequently, they tended to be somewhat better educated than other peoples of Lusophone Africa and many participated in Portuguese colonialism as public administrators and civil servants throughout the other colonies. However, a close examination of the reality of the *assimilados*' political and economic position, especially under the Portuguese "New State" policy, revealed a situation of discriminatory policies, limited civil rights, and notable inequality of opportunity.

The status of *assimilado* was offered to those Africans in the colonies who wanted recognition, empowerment, and social mobility. On the other hand, for anyone of European ancestry, no matter how high or low their social station, there was no need to aspire to assimilation; this was their birthright. Africans or Cape Verdeans, on the other hand, needed education, property, and unquestioned obedience to a state which negated much of their cultural and linguistic being and history. There were many who were willing to pay even this price, but as the struggle for a greater legitimacy advanced, some of those who resisted found a new resolve to go their own way. Foremost among these was Amilcar Cabral (q.v.) who suggested that the price might include "class suicide" and that national liberation was, above all, "an act of cultural liberation." Overall, the relatively small number of *assimilados* shows that this policy was never seriously meant to transform the entire population. *See* BADIUS; CLASS STRUCTURE; RACE AND RACISM.

AZAMBUJA, DIEGO DA. Portuguese knight under the reign of Dom João II (q.v.) (1477, 1481–95) who was charged with West African coastal exploration, trading for gold, and the rapid construction of the São Jorge Al-Mina fortress on the Gold Coast. Azambuja was appointed as the Captain-General of this mission. Prefabricated building materials, some 500 soldiers and sailors, and 100 construction specialists left Portugal on 12 December 1481 in ten caravels and transport ships. Captains Bartólomeu Dias, Pacheco Pereira, and perhaps Christopher Columbus (qq.v.) were members of this mission.

They reached Al-Mina on 19 January 1482 and immediately began construction at that site, where a Portuguese,

João Fernando, was already trading. The project was completed by the end of 1482 to guard the Portuguese trade in slaves and gold until they were replaced by the Dutch in the 1630s. The gold from Al-Mina and elsewhere on the Guinea coast was vital in the financing of the Portuguese economy, and for their other explorations of the period.

AZURARA, GOMES EANES DE. A well-known 15th century chronicler for Prince Henry (q.v.). Although Azurara's works were written in support of the great age of Portuguese exploration and expansion, they are considered a basic source in the documentation and chronology of this period. He wrote of the 1415 Ceuta campaign in the *Key to the Mediterranean.* In 1453 he wrote *Crônica de Guiné* which described some of the earliest seizing of Africans, and of African resistance to the predations of the early slavers.

-B-

BADIUS. Having been socialized and instructed to accept that Africa and Africans had no history, some Cape Verdeans went about seeking its recovery. With the African roots of Cape Verde so deep and yet denied, these new intellectuals rediscovered and romanticized the virtues of the life of *badius* who, in their lifeways, preserved their Africanity and their relative freedom in their remote and hard lives in the São Tiago (q.v.) interior. Oppressed by the political structure, ecology, and economy, but free to be themselves, the *badius* and their music (q.v.) came to represent a symbol of Cape Verdean legitimacy and authenticity.

The "proof" of this was the Portuguese disgust for the life of the *badius.* Thus, the new nationalists determined that if this were so bad for colonialism, then the *badius* must represent something positive for themselves. These nationalists began to see themselves in a new light, by recognizing the powerful tool of racism (q.v.) used by Portuguese colonialists to divide Cape Verdeans. In the islands it meant that the elite and middle classes should view the *badius* as mountain dwelling ruffians and renegades, and the *indigenas* (q.v.) in the forests of Guinea were projected as even worse. As the etymology of their name suggests, the *badius* of Cape Verde are wanderers and runaways. Formed at times of national weakness by pirate attack, famine, and drought, these descendants of slaves were economically marooned in their hideaways which provided a measure of freedom of social oppression while suffering the ravages of ecological degradation and cultural humiliation. Essentially the *badius* are the core of the peasant population of the interior of São Tiago who have retained a certain degree of African-based cultural distinctiveness in their customs, folklore, religious practices and dialect of Crioulo (q.v.).

Living in remote regions and maintaining a social distance from the rest of the population during the years of colonial rule, the *badius* were less assimilated to Portuguese culture than the rest of the Cape Verdean population. They were viewed as the primary representatives of an African heritage and, as such, have historically been denigrated by the colonial authorities and looked down upon by other Cape Verdeans. However, the few known instances of slave and peasant rebellions in Cape Verde were among the *badiu* populations, giving them a certain notoriety in popular mythology that has engendered a mixture of disdain and admiration toward this so-called "primitive" social group. Perhaps because of the threat that they once posed to the colonial authorities in resisting assimilation, the *badius* were more likely to be recruited for contract labor and they provided the backbone of forced emigration to the cocoa plantations in the islands of São Tomé (q.v.) and Príncipe.

For those granted privilege by external powers, the *badius* were all that could be low and negative, rough and crude. Unlettered of mind, but free of spirit and expression, the *badius* were a group of runaway ruffians who challenged authority by showing the persistence of African ways, and even African architecture in the round *funcas* of Cape Verdean basalt and thatch roofs rather than "proper" Portuguese style tile. Ask the owners of the *donatarios* (q.v.) and large proprietors about the sexuality and primal nature of the *badius*. This image says they love to dance and play, but only as marginal human beings might. Portuguese authorities went so far as to ban their dancing *batuko* (q.v.) style which was "too African, too primitive." Some *badius* in the 20th century went so far as to "outrageously" reinterpret the meaning of Catholicism with the *rebelado* (q.v.) movement. This merged a fundamental and personal spiritualism that the bishops and priests found repugnant.

One important measure of *badiu* folk culture must be found within the framework of their spiritual nostalgia, or *saudade,* which surrounds them. In turn, the soulful essence of *saudade* is especially carried forward in the *badius*' popular musical traditions since this was the main area in which survival of their Africanity was just tolerated during the centuries of slavery (q.v.) and colonialism. The primary musical genres of the *badius* are *batuko, finaçon, funana,* and *tabanka* (qq.v.). Elsewhere in this work Susan Hurley-Glowa and Peter Manuel have investigated the integration of the form and function of *badiu* music and culture. *See* CRIOULO ENTRIES.

BALILA. SEE: BATUKO.

BAM-BAM. SEE: BATUKO.

BANA. SEE: EVORA, C.; GONÇALVES, A.; MUSIC.

BANCO DE CABO VERDE (BCV). The BCV was formed in 1976 from a merger of the local branches of the Banco Nacional Ultramarino (BNU) and the Banco de Fomento. The BNU was a part of the Portuguese colonial banking monopoly, established in Lisbon in 1864 and in Cape Verde in 1868. The BNU Board of Directors was in intimate association with the colonial administration, having two former colonial secretaries as well as major shareholders associated with the Companhia União Fabril (q.v.) and its overseas linkages. In addition, the BNU had significant association with finance capital in Paris, Madrid, and London. Net profit during a typical late colonial year (e.g. 1963) was some $3 million with dividends commonly at 9 percent from colonial investments. The BNU was also associated with the major insurance firm, Companhia de Seguros A Mundial. With such extensive connections the BNU had an important influence in financing agriculture (q.v.), transport, petrochemicals, and other aspects of development in Cape Verde.

The BCV functions as a central bank issuing currency and serving as the government banker. Since the BCV was established its monetary policy has stressed the maintenance of a strong foreign reserve position. The BCV has its central office in Praia with branches in other islands.

BANCO NACIONAL ULTRAMARINO (BNU). SEE: BANCO DE CABO VERDE.

BARACOON. During the period of slavery (q.v.) on the Senegambian (q.v.) coast, slaves were warehoused in fortified or sometimes palisaded *baracoons* by *lançado* and Dyula (qq.v.) traders.

BARBOSA, JORGE (1902–1971). Noted poet and one of the founders, with Baltasar Lopes and Manuel Lopes (qq.v.), of the literary review, *Claridade,* in 1936. Barbosa's first collection of poetry, *Arquipélago,* articulated many of the themes of the new social and cultural awareness associated with the *Claridade* movement (q.v.). Actually this collection was published a year before the appearance of the first issue of *Claridade.* A native of Praia, São Tiago (q.v.), Barbosa received little formal schooling. It is ironic that much of his life was spent in Mindelo where a prominent secondary school has been renamed in his honor.

Barbosa holds a special place in the history of Cape Verdean literature as the first poet to make a definitive break with the classical tradition, by passionately stressing the hard realities of Cape Verdean life. This departure marked the beginning of modern Cape Verdean poetry, and one could say that this laid the cultural groundwork for the nationalism to come in later decades. Barbosa is widely published and translated in anthologies; he is well known for his poems, "Lost Islands" and "Poem of the Sea." Barbosa died in Lisbon but his remains were brought back to Cape Verde after independence. His impressive tomb in Varzea cemetery in Praia bears the inscription: ''Homenagen de Povo Cabo-Verdiano, Ao Poeta do Arquipleago.'' *See* LITERATURE.

BARBOSA, RAFAEL (1924–). Barbosa was born in the Safim section of Bissau (q.v.) of a Guinean mother and Cape Verdean father. He was employed in Bissau as a public works foreman when he and Amilcar Cabral (q.v.) and several others joined to form the PAIGC (q.v.) in 1956. Barbosa operated under the *nom de guerre* of Zain Lopes as the President of the Central Committee of the PAIGC until his arrest on 13 March 1962 by the Portuguese secret police in Bissau where he was carrying out his revolutionary activities. Barbosa was initially tortured and then released by the Portuguese on 3 August 1969 after seven years of imprisonment. His confinement led him to compromising and finally, from the viewpoint of the PAIGC, to betrayal, which resulted in his expulsion from the party in April 1970. He had still been considered the President of the PAIGC until February 1964.

After independence, Barbosa was charged with high crimes against the state and party for having been implicated in the assassination of Amilcar Cabral. At the conclusion of his trial on 8 October 1976, he was sentenced to death for his allegedly anti-PAIGC and pro-Spinola (q.v.) statements and activities. On 4 March 1977 his death sentence was commuted to 15 years at hard labor. Since the acceptance of democracy in Guinea-Bissau, Barbosa has been active in his own small political party.

BARLAVENTO, ILHAS DE. Northern, windward islands of Cape Verde including Santo Antão, São Vicente, Santa Luzia, São Nicolau, Sal, and Boa Vista (qq.v.). *See* Individual entries on the major islands.

BARRETO, COL. HONÓRIO PEREIRA. Barreto is believed to be the first Cape Verdean Governor of Guinea-Bissau (q.v.). This ambitious servant of colonialism was appointed Superintendent of the Portuguese fortress at Cacheu in 1834 and he became the Governor of Cacheu and Bissau in 1837. Barreto's importance also lies in his defense of Portuguese colonial interests against the intrusions of the French and British.

BATUKO, BATUCO, BATUQUE. Batuko is a music (q.v.) and dance genre performed by women (q.v.) of rural *badiu* (q.v.) communities of São Tiago (q.v.). Of all the musics of Cape Verde, *batuko* has the strongest resemblance to traditions from mainland Africa in its dance style, rhythmic organization, and call-and-response structure. *Batuko* is generally performed by a group of women who sit in a semi-circle with rolled-up *panos* (q.v.) held between their thighs. They beat contrasting rhythmic patterns on these *panos,* creating a polyrhythmic texture through the juxtaposition of twos against threes with beats called *bam-bam* and *rapica.* One person acts as the leader, beginning and ending songs in a call-and-response style common in African music.

Batuko song lyrics cover a wide range of topics but are usually limited to only a few phrases that are repeated at length by the leader and chorus. Songs can be either improvised on the spot by the group leader or have a fixed melody and text. Group members sing choruses, beat rhythms on their *panos* (q.v.), and take turns as a solo dancer. The dancer stands in the middle of the semi-circle and begins by moving slowly to the music, gradually picking up energy and speed leading to a climax of activity called *chabéta,* signified by the dancer's rapid hip movements and the strong singing and energetic pounding on the *pano* by the rest of the group. During the dance, attention is focused on the hips, which are accentuated by a low-slung *pano* tied around them. The hips gyrate in rapid, staccato movements that are sexually suggestive. At the end of each song, the dancer selects the next dancer by giving her the *pano* or placing it around her.

Although most *batuko* performers are women, *batuko* is not performed in a context without men. Men often watch the women dance and sing and onlookers of both sexes reward particularly good performers with money to show their approval. In addition, males sometimes actively participate in *batuko* performances as dancers and chorus members. One of the oldest and best known *batuko* groups in São Tiago is led by a man, Antoni Dente D'oro, who organized an ensemble in São Domingos. Dente D'oro and his ensemble are featured in the 1986 film, *Songs of the Badius* by Gei Zantzinger. Other *batuko* leaders who are famous throughout São Tiago include Bibinha Kabral (now deceased but featured in Zantzinger's film as well as in a biography by T.V. Da Silva), Nasia Gomi from Santa Cruz (also the subject of a book by T.V. Da Silva) and the lesser known Tchin Tabari and Balila, a blind *batuko* and *finaçon* (q.v.) leader from Praia. These group leaders are often hired by families or communities to perform at celebrations, and their presence can help to ensure that the *festa* (a Cape Verdean party) will be a success.

Many of the most famous *batuko* ensemble leaders also perform *finaçon* (a genre closely related to *batuko*) interspersing occasional *finaçon* performances with *batuko*. Both genres have a group leader and an ensemble of women who beat *panos*. The primary differences between *finaçon* and *batuko* are: *finaçon* features one person who relates an extended solo narrative in a rhythmic, sermon-like fashion while the group provides a rhythmic accompaniment, and *finaçon* has no dancing. The group beats time softly so as not to miss a word that the soloist says. Good *finaçon* performers often use parables to make a statement about issues of topical interest. They also function as informal oral historians, keeping the memory of events, people, and families alive through their stories. Traditionally *batuko* and *finaçon* ensembles perform for religious events such as saint's days, christenings, or the night before a wedding. Today, ensembles also perform for secular regional folk festivals, tourist events and municipal celebrations.

There are several folk theories about the origins of *batuko*. One suggests that *batuko* came about when colonial lords offered guests their pick of female slaves for sexual pleasure during a visit. The *batuko* dance was thought to be a way of displaying the charms of the various women to aid the guests in making a selection. A second theory maintains that *batuko* evolved as a means for women (q.v.) to cope with the loss of their men, either through death, departure to work abroad, or simple desertion for other women. Some say that *badiu* women dance to purge themselves of their grief and that a night of singing and dancing until dawn brings inner peace and happiness.

In communities with active ensembles, girls learn to perform *batuko* at an early age and are taught that it is something to be taken seriously. Some of the best dancers are very young girls, although women of all ages, even women in their seventies and eighties, are valued ensemble members. As life styles are changing in Cape Verde, fewer younger women from the villages in the interior are learning *batuko* and the tradition may become extinct in coming years.

SUSAN HURLEY-GLOWA

BENROS, GARDENIA (1962–). Benros was born and grew up in the Cape Verde Islands until departing at age 13. Her professional singing career was launched in 1983 when she recorded her first album. She is also a model, and former Miss Cape Verde, USA. In 1984 she won the Talent of America competition in New York as the Best Vocalist and Most Photogenic. She has sung in Europe and North America with her recordings distributed by Polygram Records. Her formal musical and drama education continued at Rhode Island College in 1991. Capturing the spirit of Cape Verdean *saudade,* she sings in her native Crioulo (q.v.) and has recorded many of the popular favorite *mornas* (q.v.) of Eugenio Tavares (q.v.), such as "Pescador," "Bidjica," and "Mal D'Amor." Benros is equally at home in Portuguese, Spanish, Italian, French, and English. Having some Jewish (q.v.) roots she also sings in *ladino* (q.v.), the 16th and 17th century language of Sephardic Jews.

BERLIN CONGRESS. Between 1884–85 the major European powers of the time met in Berlin to organize the colonial partition of Africa. The Congress was dominated by France and England, but claims to African territory were made by Portugal, Germany, Italy, Spain, and Belgium. This meeting launched the "Scramble for Africa" which triggered an era of military conquest and subjugation by European powers in order to support their claims of "effective occupation" and control.

The basic configuration of Africa's modern national boundaries has very largely descended from the Berlin Congress with various local adjustments made throughout the colonial era. Before the Congress, the European ruling classes had, in general, neglected Africa as too expensive for permanent settlement and there was remarkably little knowledge of the people and resources of the interior at that time. The age of European exploration of Africa was taking place mainly in the period just prior to and after the Berlin Congress. Many of the present African conflicts have roots in the arbitrary borders drawn a century ago.

BIKER, JUDICE. Early 20th century governor of Guinea-Bissau, best known for his 1903 documentation of the virtual slave labor conditions in São Tomé (q.v.). Biker's articles unleashed a major political scandal showing that 2–4,000 "contract laborers" went to São Tomé each year but few ever returned to Cape Verde and Angola where they originated.

BISSAGOS, BIJAGOS (ISLANDS). The Bissagos archipelago lying off the coast of Guinea Bissau (q.v.) is sometimes confused with the Cape Verde Islands since they were all under Portuguese colonial administration. These islands draw their name from the Bissagos people who have certain ethnic affinities to the coastal people in Guinea-Bissau and some were no doubt captured as slaves and taken to the Cape Verde Islands. The islands were not "pacified" until 1936 and were distinguished among the peoples of Guinea-Bissau for their persistent resistance (q.v.) to foreign penetration. The earliest case may date to the very first Portuguese explorer, Nuño Tristão (q.v.), who may have reached these islands in 1447 and was killed shortly thereafter somewhere along the coast. Large, fast-moving ocean canoes also permitted the Bissagos people to engage in the slave trade and to defend themselves effectively for many centuries.

BISSAU. Capital city of the Republic of Guinea-Bissau (q.v.) at the broad estuary of the Geba River on the north shore (11° 51′N; 15° 35′W). The first European to reach the area was the

Portuguese explorer Nuño Tristão (q.v.) in 1446, who was killed in the following year along the coast. In the 16th century Bissau became a modest coastal base for slave-trading *lançados* (q.v.) and other Luso-Africans who continued in this capacity through the late 19th century. Following attacks by European powers and virtual anarchy in the slave trade, Bissau was made a captaincy-general in 1692 in order to strengthen the Portuguese monopoly coordinated from the Cape Verde Islands. This was designed to establish a more meaningful coastal presence between Cacheu to the north and Bolama (qq.v.) to the south.

By 1696 Bissau town had a fort, church and hospital and controlled trade on the Geba and Corubal Rivers. The trade remained largely in the hands of sometimes independent *lançados.* About a dozen settlers were assigned there each year in the early 18th century; later this number was raised to 40 per year. A high death rate from tropical diseases and frequent attacks by neighboring Africans on ports and forts strongly discouraged expanded colonization. In 1869 Bissau became one of four administrative *comunas* in order to create a more effective local administration, although the Governor's residence was still at Geba, a small town much further east in the interior. When the administration of Guinea-Bissau was fully separated from Cape Verde in 1879, the capital was transferred to Bolama. The first three decades of the 20th century saw almost continuous resistance by the Papeis in the Bissau area, but in 1941 the colonial capital was moved to Bissau from Bolama. After independence in 1974 there was some discussion about moving the capital to a central place in the interior but it remains at Bissau. The population of Bissau in 1979 was put at 109,214.

On 3 August 1959 the Pijiguiti dockyards in Bissau were the scene of bloody repression against the rising nationalist movement. The Pijiguiti massacre, as it became known, caused the leadership of the nascent PAIGC (q.v.) to determine that a path of armed struggle rather than negotiation would be necessary to achieve independence.

BOA VISTA. (16° 10′N; 23° 50′W). This island was first known as São Cristovão and is the third largest (620 sq. km.) island in the Cape Verde archipelago, and the easternmost member of the Barlavento (windward, northern) group. Boa Vista was among the islands discovered by António De Noli and Diogo Gomes (qq.v.) in 1460. No serious settlement took place there until the 16th century when it was used for animal grazing when there was adequate rainfall. The animals were used in the islands and in the slave trade (q.v.). The periodic droughts (q.v.) in the islands have sometimes decimated the livestock (q.v.) population. Fishing (q.v.) and some salt production are the other main aspects of the local economy. In the 17th century the administration of Boa Vista was granted to António Correa, Lord of Bellas.

Unlike other Cape Verde islands, Boa Vista is relatively low (maximum altitude 390 meters) and sandy. During the last years of Portuguese colonialism, a West German company, AIP, had planned to develop three hotels having a 6,000 bed capacity for tourists, but this plan has not been fully realized. Since independence, the government has built a number of catchment dams and has created public works jobs for the population. The main town of the island is Sal-Rei, other villages are Gata, Fundo de Figueiras, and Curral Velho.

Population of Boa Vista

1580	50
1650	150
1720	1,000
1800	2,200
1890	3,934
1900	2,600
1927	2,495
1930	2,454
1940	2,653
1950	2,903
1960	3,309
1970	3,463
1980	3,397
1990	3,452

(Source: Duncan 1972 and Cape Verde Censuses)

BOLAMA. From the very earliest times in the Portuguese colonial administration the area of Guinea-Bissau was ruled from Cape Verde. Bolama or Bulama was thereby a strategic Guinean coastal island town under the direct administration of Cape Verde. This island town (11° 35′N; 15° 28′W) faces the tidal estuary of the Fulacunda flood basin. The Portuguese navigator Nuño Tristão (q.v.) reached Bolama in 1446 when he explored the Geba River. Throughout the period of the Cape Verdean slave trade (q.v.), but especially in the 18th and 19th centuries, Bolama offered an ideal defensive position with easy access to the riverine interior. In 1753 Portugal claimed official ownership of the island, but their authority was weak and control fell back to local African leaders, who in turn, sold a portion of Bolama to the British trader Philip Beaver and others. By the end of the 18th century all of these ventures had failed.

In 1828 the Portuguese returned to fortify the town and to restore their control. The British protested and in 1837 sent the naval brigantine, *The Brisk,* to cut down the Portuguese flag and hoist the Union Jack. For more than 30 years the conflict continued with various acts of violence and ownership shifting back and forth with the British occupying Bolama again in 1858 and claiming the Bissagos (q.v.) islands as well. In 1860 the British declared that both territories were considered incorporated within the administration of Sierra Leone. The Portuguese rejected this claim and the entire matter was sent to President Grant of the United States for final arbitration. Grant ruled in favor of Portugal and the British withdrew in January 1869. In order to improve their restored administration, the Cape Verdean authorities gave Bolama the status of a *comuna* (one of four in Guinea-Bissau) so they could intensify the effort to pacify and colonize the local population. Finally in 1879 the administration of Cape Verde was separated from Guinea-Bissau which began to be ruled as a distinct colony. Bolama was the first capital of this colony.

BRANCO AND RASO ISLETS. The two uninhabited (16° 40′N; 24° 40′W) islets of the Barlavento portion of the Cape Verde archipelago. Branco (2.8 sq. km.) and Raso (7 sq. km.) are located between Santa Luzia and São Nicolau (qq.v.) islands.

BRAVA. (14° 50′N; 24° 43′W). The second smallest island (64 sq. km.) of the ten major Cape Verdean islands, and the smallest of the Sotavento group. It is the westernmost point in the archipelago. Despite its small size, Brava is quite varied with mountainous and terraced land forms. Its highest elevation of 977 meters at Fontainhas is often shrouded in mist which can support a diversity of flowers and cool temperatures. The main port is on the north coast at Porto da Furna lying some three kilometers from the main town of Nova Sintra situated in the interior hills. With some permanent water sources its confined but fertile valleys generate export crops and livestock (q.v.) if there is no drought (q.v.).

Brava was first reached by the Portuguese on 24 June 1462 and was first called São João Baptista, in honor of the saint's day on that date. Brava attracted Europeans from Minho, Algarve, and Madeira and it is still considered the most "European" of the islands today. Settlers governed under the captaincy of Martinho Pereira arrived as early as 1573, and in more regular numbers in the late 17th century, especially from neighboring Fogo (q.v.) in 1680 following an eruption in that year. The administration of Brava in the 17th century was joined to that of Santa Luzia (q.v.) under the ownership of Luís de Castro Pereira.

In 1730 the English Captain George Roberts began the exploitation of urzella (q.v.) lichen in Brava for plant dye. In 1798 the French attacked Brava in their unsuccessful effort to dislodge the Portuguese influence there and on the coast. In 1826 Brava saw the creation of the parish of Our Lady of the Mountain which was chosen in 1836 as the residence of the Bishop of Cape Verde. During these decades Brava experienced relative prosperity through service on American and English whaleships. A public dock was first built in Furna in 1843 which is presently served by a transport ship of the same name. In the 1850s Brava began an early secondary school which attracted students from throughout the archipelago and from Guinea-Bissau. The noted Cape Verdean poet, Eugenio Tavares (q.v.), was a native of Brava.

Throughout the late 19th century Brava was considered one of the most pleasant islands in which to live. The town of Nova Sintra, at 520 meters elevation, is often breezy and cool.

The small size of the island, its tiny and secluded harbors, especially Furna, its ethnic composition, and limited agricultural land have resulted in a historic pattern of emigration from Brava, even greater than from other islands. A very large proportion of these migrants moved to the northeastern United States, especially to New Bedford, Massachusetts, where Cape Verdeans had at one time been known simply as "Bravas." Migrants from Brava also had a very significant role in the American whaling and cranberry (qq.v.) industries of Cape Cod. Because of the close links to the United States (q.v.), an American vice-consul was officially established there in 1816.

Population of Brava

1580	100
1650	400
1720	1,200
1774	3,190
1800	3,000
1890	9,784
1900	9,200
1927	6,819
1930	6,383
1940	8,510
1950	7,902
1960	8,646
1970	7,888
1980	6,984
1990	6,975

(Source: Duncan 1972 and Cape Verde Censuses)

Presently the government has emphasized irrigation and water conservation programs for Brava as well as efforts to develop agriculture (q.v.), animal husbandry and reforestation to create new jobs. In 1986 a joint German and Cape Verdean project began to construct an airport in Brava. This project was completed in June 1992 at the coastal town of Esparadinha. The airport was opened on the festival of Saint João and was named in the honor of Francisco Feijo Barbosa. The airport is only nine kilometers from Nova Sinta and it should improve communication, and emergency evacuation. The runway is 640 meters long and 30 meters wide, with an additional 360 meter extension planned for the future. Tiny Brava and its limited resources, elderly population, and few jobs have long accounted for a pattern of out-migration.

BULIMUNDO. SEE: FUNANA; MARTINS, C.

-C-

CABRAL, AMILCAR LOPES "ABEL DJASSI" (12 September 1924–20 January 1973). Cabral was born in Bafatá in Guinea-Bissau (q.v.) of Cape Verdean parents, Juvenal Cabral (q.v.) and Iva Pinhel Evora. Since his father was educated, Amilcar was sent to the Liceu Gil Eanes in São Vicente (q.v.) for his secondary education. At the age of 21 he entered the University of Lisbon's Institute of Agronomy, from which he graduated with honors in 1950. In the early 1950s he was associated with the Casa dos Estudantes do Império (CEI) (q.v.) in Lisbon where he met and discussed with revolutionary intellectuals from other African colonies. While in Lisbon he met and married his Portuguese wife, Maria Helena Rodriques, who was herself a dedicated revolutionary. With his training complete, Cabral entered the colonial agricultural service in 1950 where he applied soil science, demography and hydraulics engineering. During the period 1952–54 Cabral traveled very extensively in Guinea to conduct its first agricultural census and to gain an intimate and detailed knowledge of the land and people which would become a great asset in organizing the PAIGC (q.v.), the nationalist revolutionary party.

Cabral's first attempt at launching a nationalist movement in Guinea was in 1954 with the Recreation Association which was parallel to the MING (q.v.) movement also founded by Cabral in the same year. In the mid-1950s Cabral met with his revolutionary friends from the CEI and they formed the Movimento Anti-Colonialista (MAC) (q.v.). Finally, on 19 September 1956, Cabral, his half-brother Luís, Aristides Pereira, Rafael Barbosa (qq.v.) and two others met secretly in Bissau to form the PAIGC. Cabral could not remain in Bissau at the time as he had to return to Angola where he was at work with a private sugar company. In December 1956 Cabral, Agostinho Neto and other Angolans met secretly to form the Movimento Popular de Libertação da Angola. The clandestine organizing continued and sought to mobilize the workers of Bissau. On 3 August 1959, a nationalist oriented dockworkers' strike was met with harsh colonial repression while Cabral was at work in Angola.

Following this event Cabral returned to Bissau to discuss a change in tactics and to prepare for a protracted armed struggle to win independence for Guinea-Bissau and the Cape Verde Islands. In 1960 Cabral secretly left Bissau to continue party building and to form the FRAIN (q.v.) in Tunis; this was soon replaced by the CONCP (q.v.) in April 1961. These organizations sought to unify the struggles in the various Portuguese colonies in Africa. After 1963 the PAIGC launched its war which gained control of two-thirds of the countryside over the next ten years. In 1973 the PAIGC was able to declare itself the government of an independent Guinea-Bissau. Such actions severely demoralized a Lisbon regime which was already financially and politically exhausted from the endless wars in Africa. The April 1974 overthrow of the Caetano (q.v.) regime in Lisbon brought an end to decades of fascism in Portugal and to the Portuguese colonial presence in Africa and elsewhere. In an abortive anti-PAIGC plot Cabral was assassinated in Conakry on 20 January 1973 so that he did not personally live to see all of his objectives fulfilled only a few months later.

Achievements of such a scale for a man of such modest beginnings earned Cabral many international awards and honors. He received the Nasser Award, the Joliot-Curie Medal, and honorary doctorates from Lincoln University (USA) and from the Soviet Academy of Science. Today Cabral is widely recognized as a major African revolutionary theoretician in both analysis and practice. He is survived by his half-brother, Luís (q.v.), who became the first President of Guinea-Bissau until his overthrow, his three children and his second, Cape Verdean wife, Anna Maria Cabral, who has worked in the Ministry of Health and Social Welfare, and now resides in Praia. Until 1991, September 12th, Cabral's birthday, was celebrated as a national holiday. His image appears on coins and paper currency, but since the 1991 elections in Cape Verde and the rise of the MpD (q.v.) the position of Cabral in the political history of Cape Verde is being actively reduced as the nation moves from a single party nation guided by socialism to one with plural democracy and privatization.

CABRAL, BIBINHA. SEE: BATUKO; DA SILVA, T.V.

CABRAL, JUVENAL. (1889–?) Father of Amilcar and Luís Cabral (qq.v.) and perhaps 62 other children according to biographical notes on J. Cabral by Basil Davidson. It is reported that Cabral offered praise to the leader of Portuguese "pacification" in Guinea, so one may conclude that he was not inclined to recognize the African roots of Crioulo (q.v.) culture. He wrote for *A Voz de Cabo Verde* (1915) and he called for rural development and land reform in the islands in 1940. He was the author of *Memorias e Reflexões* (1947). Cabral studied at the Seminary of Viseu in Portugal and had a deep sensitivity to the cultural aspects of Portuguese colonial rule which caused him great personal frustration. This background was significant in the ideological development of Luís and Amilcar Cabral, but they expanded it to form their model of a program of revolutionary nationalism which sought to link Cape Verde with the struggles in Africa in general and Guinea-Bissau (q.v.) in particular.

CABRAL, LUÍS DE ALMEIDA. (1931–). One of the six original founders of the PAIGC (q.v.) in 1956 in Bissau (q.v.) where he was born. Cabral's early education led him to a position as an accountant for the CUF (q.v.) in Bissau. He left for Guinea-Conakry soon after the PAIGC was formed since the Portuguese secret police were seeking his arrest. In 1961

Cabral became the founding Secretary General of the pro-PAIGC trade union group, the UNTG (q.v.). By 1963 Cabral was in charge of the strategic Quitafine frontier zone which was militarily active at that time. In 1965 he became a member of the PAIGC Conselho de Guerra (q.v.). Following the reorganization of the PAIGC in 1970 he became a member of the Permanent Commission of the CEL (q.v.) with the responsibility for national reconstruction in the liberated zones. When the independence of Guinea-Bissau followed his brother's assassination, Luís Cabral became the first President of that new nation as well as the Deputy Secretary of the PAIGC.

By some estimates, Luís Cabral was less a leader than his internationally known half-brother. However his quiet and hard-working style made him effective as an administrator. During the period after the armed struggle some rivalries emerged between Cape Verdeans who were sometimes perceived as an outside minority and those of a wholly African origin. This tension, and increasingly autocratic rule, formed the context in which Luís Cabral was overthrown in November 1980 by João "Nino" Vieira (q.v.) who had become Prime Minister in 1978 after a strong military career. Vieira held Cabral in Guinea until his negotiated release from a death sentence and initial exile in Cuba, then in the Cape Verde Islands, and in Lisbon. Recent efforts by Guinea-Bissau and Cape Verde have restored diplomatic relations, but Cabral's overthrow fractured unity between the Republics and the original goals of the PAIGC. The strong electoral victory of the MpD in the islands may deepen this cleavage, since Vieira is thought to be of the same PAIGC "old guard" that has been voted out of office. On the other hand, with a promise to have plural democracy in Guinea-Bissau, Luís Cabral was reported in 1993 to be exploring the possibility of returning to a political life in Bissau.

CABRAL, PEDRO ALVARES. Portuguese sea captain whose fleet reached the Cape Verde Islands on 22 March 1500. Rather than travel along the West African coast he went back into the Atlantic heading far to the southwest and "accidentally" discovered Brazil in April 1500.

CABRAL, VASCO (1924?–). Cabral was born in Guinea-Bissau but was one of the very few Africans to study in Lisbon University in 1950. In 1954 he was arrested for his political views and was held in prison for almost six years including two years in solitary confinement. Upon his release in 1959 he completed his degree in economics and met with Amilcar Cabral (q.v.) who was also in Lisbon at that time. Vasco Cabral fled from Portugal in July 1962 with Agostinho Neto of the MPLA and soon joined the PAIGC (q.v.) to serve on its central committee and on the Conselho de Guerra (q.v.). Cabral also served on the Comité Executivo da Luta (q.v.) with his specialty in party ideology. Most recently he was the Minister for Economic Development and Planning in Guinea-Bissau (q.v.).

CACÃO ISLANDS. SEE: SÃO TOMÉ.

CACHASS. SEE: MARTINS, C.

CACHEN RIOS E COMÉRCIO DA GUINÉ. SEE: CACHEU.

CACHEU. Town in Guinea-Bissau (q.v.) (12° 10′N; 16° 10′W), located on the south bank of the Cacheu River in an area populated by the Manjaco and Cobiana ethnic groups. The Cacheu River was first reached by the Portuguese explorer Nuño Tristão (q.v.) in 1446. In the early 16th century, slaving (q.v.) became the notable activity at Cacheu where there was trade in salt and horses (q.v.) from Cape Verde for slaves captured and sold by *lançados* (q.v.) along the coast and from the interior tributary kingdoms of Mali (q.v.). In 1588 Cacheu became an official Portuguese captaincy under the regional authority of Cape Verde. As a captaincy it was to regulate the slave trade and establish a post for regular trade and supplies. With this prosperity beginning in the late 16th century a special Crown agreement with Jewish (q.v.) merchants, *lançados,* in 1601 gave permission to settle and trade in the Cachen Rios area and to establish a *capitão e ouvidor* (captain and overseer) who was subordinate to the Governor of Cape Verde. In the 17th century the slave trade was intensified and in 1624 the Dutch temporarily seized the Cacheu captaincy. In 1630 Cacheu partly returned to Portuguese control as it began to be developed as the economic nucleus for the province of Guinea. Security remained a problem and Cacheu was fortified in 1641 against attacks by Luso-African *lançados* and various European powers.

The 1660s brought the creation of the Cape Verdean-based slaving company Cachen Rios e Comércio da Guiné which had a slave trade monopoly from Senegal to Sierra Leone including the rivers of Guinea. In 1676 this company was reorganized as the Companhia do Cachen Rios e Cabo Verde, but its main slaving activities were still based at Cacheu which continued to dominate the slave trade in Senegambia (q.v.). The Companhia do Cachen Rios e Cabo Verde had relative prosperity but only until the close of the 17th century when it ceased its trade monopoly of the slave trade to Spanish America. With locust plagues and some reduction in slaving itself, the importance of Cacheu declined into the early 18th century with Bissau's (q.v.) importance increasing, not to mention the expansion of slavery much further along the West African coast.

In the 19th century European rivalries for African territory were intensified and the District Officer at Cacheu in the 1830s, Honório Barreto (q.v.), gained some prominence for his stalwart defense of Portuguese interests. Following administrative reorganization in 1869, Cacheu had the status of one of the four colonial *comunas,* but when the government of Guinea-Bissau was separated from that of Cape Verde in 1879, the first capital became Bolama (q.v.) rather than Cacheu. Portuguese efforts at settlement and "pacification" of the Cacheu area were sharply resisted by the Papeis people in 1891–94 and in 1904. Today Cacheu is a Guinean town of modest importance.

CACHUPA, MANCHUPA. A national dish of Cape Verde, it is a hearty mixture made of cracked whole corn, beans, onions, garlic, olive oil, bay leaves, and meat or fish, depending on what is available. "Rich" *cachupa* has lots of meat and "poor" *cachupa* consists mostly of corn and beans. The corn for *cachupa* is traditionally cracked or ground with a large wooden mortar and pestle, or *pilão,* and soaked in water a day or so before it is to be eaten. When the *cachupa* ingredients are put together in a big pot, they must simmer together under a slow flame for many hours until the beans and corn are done. SUSAN HURLEY-GLOWA

CADAMOSTA (CA DA MOSTA), ALVISE. Venetian navigator in Portuguese service who sailed twice in the Senegambian area between 1454 and 1456 in a 90-ton vessel. In 1455 Cadamosta and Usodimare, a Genoan, separately reached the estuary of the River Gambia. In 1456 the two navigators sailed on a joint two-ship mission three kilometers up the Gambia River where the ships were strongly attacked by the local population and their ship crews mutinied. Still in 1456 Cadamosta and Usodimare reached the Rio Geba (Grande) and the Bissagos Islands (q.v.) in Guinea-Bissau.

On the same voyage they reported active trade of gold in Taghaza, and merchandise and slaves (q.v.) at Arguim Island in Mauretania. Cadamosta noted that already Arguim was supplying about 1,000 slaves per year. Probably under his command, three or four armed caravels attacked coastal fishing villages in the Gulf of Arguim to capture slaves for the return voyage.

CAETANO, MARCELLO JOSÉ DAS NEVES ALVES (1906–1980). Caetano was a noted writer and professor of public law and the main author of the 1933 Constitution which institutionalized Portuguese fascism. He was the Minister of Colonies from 1944 to 1947 and was also instrumental in the 1951 revisions of the Portuguese Constitution which maintained Portugal's (q.v.) colonies in Africa. He served in the Premier's office from 1955–58 but returned to his professorial post except for brief interim ministerial appointments, but being slightly liberal he did not always agree with Prime Minister Salazar (q.v.). Caetano was appointed Prime Minister of Portugal in September 1968, following the stroke of Prime Minister Salazar. His administration was challenged in Portugal and overseas by the wars in the African colonies. His reforms were not sufficient and on 25 April 1974 he was overthrown by the Armed Forces Movement (MFA). He died in exile in Brazil in 1980. *See* PORTUGAL.

CAITENINHO. SEE: FUNANA.

CANARY CURRENT. South flowing ocean current off the Atlantic coast of Morocco, and with a natural movement toward Cape Verde. This current enabled early Portuguese sailors to pass easily down the coast in the epoch of great maritime exploration. However, without tacking vessels sailing close to the wind, the Canary Current could make the return voyage slow and difficult.

CANTA-REIS. Popular *festa* celebrated to welcome the New Year. Small groups of musicians roam through the neighborhood serenading from house to house with traditional Crioulo music (qq.v.). A special song is sung first to ask that the door be opened for *canta-reis*. The carolers are then invited inside for more singing and to partake of the customary foods, usually *canja* (chicken rice soup) or *gufongo* (cornmeal crullers) and *grogga* (q.v.) (rum) before moving on to the next awaiting household. *See* CRIOULO CULTURE; MUSIC.

CÃO, DIOGO. Born in the mid-15th century, Cão was a Portuguese navigator who in 1480 seized three Castilian vessels off the Al-Mina coast. These vessels and their Spanish prisoners were brought back to Portugal where Cão was received as a great hero. In 1482 Cão was the first to explore the west coast of Central Africa just south of the equator. He reached the Kongo kingdom in 1483.

Both Cão and Christopher Columbus (q.v.) sought to go around the Muslim world in the Middle East and secure an alternative route to India. Since Christopher Colombus sailed along the Guinea Coast between 1482 and 1484, he possibly met Cão at this time. The explorations of Cão were the forerunners to the voyages of Barthólomeu Dias and Vasco Da Gama (qq.v.).

CAPELAS. Lands owned by the church in Cape Verde, usually in feudal-like tenancies. The tenant farmers on *capela* (chapel) lands could occupy the land with an annual payment to the church, nominally for its upkeep. *Capelas* and other systems of feudal land grants were part of the colonial inheritance which was cancelled by the Agrarian Reform introduced by the PAICV (q.v.). This step and others led to some hostilities between the Catholic Church and the PAICV. *See* MORGADOS.

CAPE VERDEAN-AMERICAN EMIGRATION. Permanent, circular, and temporary emigration has long been a significant feature of the population of Cape Verde. This history of emigration spans several centuries and has resulted in enclaves of Cape Verdeans and their descendants in many parts of the world. By far the largest of these overseas Crioulo (q.v.) communities is found in the United States. It is often estimated that the number of Americans having Cape Verdean ancestry is as great as 250,000. In fact, there is no consistent or accurate measure of the Crioulo population in the United States by formal census or by self-identification. Much depends upon who consider themselves Cape Verdean and what precise definitions or generational criteria might be applied.

The 1990 population figure for the Cape Verde Islands was 337,000 and is probably greater than the maximum number claimed to represent the Cape Verdean-American population. On the other hand, it is very likely not an exaggeration to claim that more people of Cape Verdean descent live in various nations outside of the archipelago than inside. Other countries with sizeable Cape Verdean immigrant communities are Portugal and Spain (40,000), Angola (35,000), Senegal (22–25,000), France (10–15,000), the Netherlands (8–10,000), São Tomé and Príncipe (8,000), and Italy (8–10,000). Smaller concentrations are found in the South American countries of Brazil, Uruguay, and Argentina.

Historically, and to this day, emigration has been a crucial socio-economic strategy for coping with the disastrous effects of drought, for reducing unemployment, lowering population growth rates, and providing an essential source of income through remittances to those who remain at home. For example, early in the first wave of Cape Verdean-American immigration (q.v.) during the late 19th and early 20th centuries, it became clear that not only would the newcomers themselves benefit from the opportunities they found in America, but that their savings could mean the difference between survival and starvation for their loved ones at home. The influx of American dollars into the islands not only meant a difference at the subsistence level, but its effect fueled the Cape Verdean economy as a whole. Many merchants depended on American capital to start businesses and to stock the stores, while some sharecroppers, with the help of remittances from the United States, were able to become owners of the land which they farmed. In some instances, particularly on the island of Brava (q.v.), even the continued celebration of traditional religious *festas* was only made possible by contributions from relatives living in the United States or from returned *Mericanos.*

Today in Cape Verde remittances account for almost 50 percent of the Gross Domestic Product. As of 1962 the United States still led the list of the five countries which represent 86 percent of the total remittances to Cape Verde. The other four are the Netherlands, Portugal, France, and Angola. The economic and social benefits to Cape Verde of large-scale emigration have thus far greatly outweighed the drawbacks of losing productive members of the population to other countries. Thus the government's policy has been to encourage emigration but also to attempt to ensure that the movement will serve the welfare of the Cape Verdeans at home and that remittances will continue to be channeled back into the domestic economy. *See* CAPE VERDEAN-AMERICAN IMMIGRATION; CONTRATADOS; DEMOGRAPHY.

CAPE VERDEAN-AMERICAN IMMIGRATION. The socio-economic structure of Cape Verde has long been dependent upon large scale emigration as a response to the conditions that have resulted from frequent drought (q.v.) and poor land distribution. To relieve the catastrophic consequences of diminished food supplies and famine as well as the demographic pressure on the islands, the inhabitants have had to leave their homeland to survive. Nowhere has this phenomenon been more profound than in the flow of emigration to the United States. Pioneering this transatlantic migration in the first half of the 19th century were the young men of Brava (q.v.) island who were recruited by United States' whaling (q.v.) vessels to fill out their crews during stopovers in Cape Verde. Some of these recruits eventually settled in the United States, particularly in and around the whaling port of New Bedford, Massachusetts. Thus began the settlement of a single Cape Verdean-American community that currently numbers in the tens of thousands at the very least.

By the late 19th century, with the advent of steamship travel and the decline of the whaling and sealing industries, the old sailing vessels became obsolete and, as a result, were available at a very low cost. Some of the early Cape Verdean immigrants took advantage of this opportunity to buy up these old Essex-built "Gloucester Fishermen." They pooled their resources and converted them into cargo and passenger ships, known as packet boats for regular sailings between fixed destinations. With the purchase of a 64-ton fishing schooner, the *Nellie May,* Antonio Coelho became the first Cape Verdean-American packet owner. He hired a former whaleman as captain and the ship set sail for Brava in 1892. Before long Cape Verdean-American settlers came to own a fleet of these former whalers and schooners that regularly plied between the ports of New Bedford, Massachusetts, and Providence, Rhode Island, and the islands of Cape Verde, particularly Brava. Thus, in a situation unlike that of most immigrant groups, the Cape Verdeans came to have control over their own means of passage to this country.

During the same period, cheap sources of labor were being sought for the expanding textile mills and the cranberry (q.v.) industry of southeastern Massachusetts. Large numbers of Cape Verdean immigrants were arriving to fulfill the demand, fleeing the hardships of their land.

In the first decade of the 20th century, drought conditions became even more intolerable, accelerating the economic disintegration of the islands. The people booked passage on the packet ships, with hope of surviving through emigration to America. This movement continued steadily until the enforcement of the restrictive immigration laws of 1921 and 1924 in the United States as well as obstacles imposed by the Portuguese colonial government. What followed was a long period of dormancy which contributed heavily to the demise of the packet trade itself.

Prominent among this first generation of settlers were several Cape Verdean attorneys who contributed to the definition and formation of the Cape Verdean-American community. Alfred Gomes was the first Cape Verdean to practice law in the city of New Bedford while George Leighton went on to become a United States Circuit Court judge. Lawyer Roy Teixeira provided legal counsel to a good number of the packet captains and owners concerning the intricacies of immigration law, and in this way, was instrumental in making it possible for many Cape Verdeans to gain entry into the United States.

While irregular record-keeping, clandestine departures and arrivals, and the extent of return migration make it difficult to determine the exact total of Cape Verdean-American immigrants, recent research indicates the most accurate estimate is that between 35,000–40,000 Cape Verdeans arrived in the United States during the years 1820–1976. Since the independence of Cape Verde in 1975, emigration from the archipelago to the United States has increased again, with an annual average of 914 persons arriving between 1975 and 1980. *See* CAPE VERDEAN EMIGRATION; DEMOGRAPHY; ERNESTINA.

CAPITAÇÃO.Head tax, especially as a source of revenue during the colonial era in Guinea-Bissau.

CAPITÃO. Military governor representing the Portuguese crown, especially in Cape Verde. Each *capitão* would rule a *capitania* or captaincy sometimes known as *residências* in Cape Verde. *See* DONATARIOS.

CARDOSO, PEDRO MONTEIRO (1890–1942). Cardoso was born in Fogo (q.v.) and was the author in 1933 of the significant *Folclore caboverdiano.* This work appeared earlier than the *Claridade* movement (q.v.). As a poet, Cardoso celebrated Cape Verdean cultural uniqueness as a resolution of the tension between Portuguese and African culture. Cardoso explored other African dimensions (especially music [q.v.]) in Cape Verdean literature (q.v.) but perhaps in a cautious or half humorous spirit of ''approach-avoidance.''

CARDOSO, RENATO DE SILOS (1 December 1951–29 September 1989). Cardoso served as a special advisor to Pedro Pires (q.v.) and had a Secretarial appointment in the Ministry of Labor and Public Affairs. He had been a PAICV (q.v.) member until 1980 when he was dismissed from the party for ''Trotskyism.'' He went to Brazil for additional practical training, but returned in 1985 to serve the party in these important positions. On 29 September, Cardoso was found, mortally wounded, at a beach with his rented car, near Praia. A short time later he died in the Agostinho Neto Hospital in Praia. Although an arrest took place, the lack of evidence in a poorly conducted investigation could not result in a trial. The only known witness, a woman companion, has offered conflicting testimony, and with the lack of evidence the case was not pursued by either the PAICV or the MpD (q.v.) governments.

The death of Cardoso became a political issue cited often in the 1991 elections (q.v.). Some say there was a love triangle, others claim he was trapped in a scandalous circumstance in which a struggle ensued and he was accidentally killed. Robbery does not seem to be a factor. It has also been suggested that a rapist who frequented ''lovers' lanes'' was responsible. Cardoso was considered to be very intelligent and ambitious with a potential for promotion within the PAICV. Alternatively, with his considerable knowledge about the inner workings of the PAICV, and his past of liberal and independent thought, he was considered to be an inspiration of the movement which became the MpD. Was this an accident, or an internal political struggle, or a crime of passion? The answer is not yet known about the mysterious end to Cardoso, whose death was as controversial as his life. He now lies buried in Varzea cemetery in Praia.

CASABLANCA GROUP. African organization formed in January 1961 which sought to unify the socialist oriented states such as Egypt, Guinea-Conakry, Mali, Algeria, and Ghana in opposition to the moderate Brazzaville Group which was formed in December 1960. The Casablanca Group was officially disbanded in 1963 upon the formation of the Organization of African Unity (q.v.). As a result of the emergence of the Casablanca Group the Conferência das Organizações Nationalistas das Colônias Portuguesas (q.v.) was formed in April 1961. This represented a major African effort to unify the three leading nationalist movements fighting in the Portuguese colonies.

CASA DOS ESTUDANTES DO IMPÉRIO (CEI). This semi-official African student center in Lisbon was a center for African *assimilados* (q.v.) and intellectuals including figures such as Marcelino dos Santos of Mozambique, Amilcar Cabral (q.v.) of Guinea, and Mario de Andrade of Angola. From the CEI, revolutionary thinkers formed the MAC (q.v.) in 1957. In 1965 the CEI was finally closed by the Salazar (q.v.) government which termed it subversive.

CAVAQUINHO. SEE: MUSIC.

CENTRO DE INSTRUÇÃO POLÍTICO MILITAR (CIPM). In order to develop ideological unity within the PAIGC (q.v.) cadres, Amilcar Cabral (q.v.) founded the CIPM in the earliest period of the operation of an exile base in Conakry in about 1961 when a number of the leading figures such as João Vieira, Francisco Mendes (qq.v.), Domingo Ramos, Constantino Teixeira, and others attended this seminal party school. One of the functions was to link ideological and military training in the formation of *bi-grupos,* the basic guerrilla army unit. The CIPM also trained those returning from abroad and offered basic education (q.v.). In the early 1970s, 200–300 students in groups of 25 would be trained through a series of formal, informal, and role-playing exercises during a program of several months. The curriculum included national and world history, a PAIGC code of behavior, lessons on the party program and organization, military and political tactics, decolonization, foreign relations as well as developing a strong sense of national unity and purpose. Stress was laid on the political, rather than the military, dimensions of the struggle.

CESARIA. SEE: ÉVORA, C.

CHABETA. SEE: BATUKO.

CHAMPALIMAUD. One of the major financial and industrial conglomerates of Portugal with ties to the BNU and extensive colonial interests. Champalimaud virtually controls the Portuguese steel industry although it is, in turn, dominated by West German finance capital. Champalimaud operated the cement and puzzolane company in Cape Verde. *See* BANCO DE CABO VERDE; MINERALS.

CHURCHES. SEE: RELIGION.

CID, COMMANDER PAULA. At the turn of the 19th century, Commander Cid was Governor of Cape Verde, São Tomé, and Benguella. While Governor of Benguella in 1908 he served on a commission to investigate the labor conditions in São Tomé (q.v.) which had been exposed for their harshness, but his impartiality was questioned since he had been appointed by the Portuguese government. *See* BIKER, J.; CONTRATADOS.

CIMBOA. SEE: MUSIC.

CLARIDADE MOVEMENT. The literary review *Claridade* was founded in 1936 by a group of Cape Verdean intellectuals and writers including Baltasar Lopes, Jorge Barbosa, and Manuel Lopes (qq.v.). The primary purpose of the journal was the examination of the roots of Crioulo culture (q.v.) as well as the development of an original regional Cape Verdean literature (q.v.). *Claridade* was inspired by the modern continental Portuguese literary magazine, *Presença,* as well as by a group of Brazilian writers of the same period who were also breaking away from the classical Portuguese forms in order to create a modern regionalistic fiction. With the contributions of such local social commentators as Felix Monteiro and the sociologist João Lopes, *Claridade* became more than a literary review. It encompassed a socio-economic analysis of the archipelago as well. Though published only sporadically over the years, *Claridade* has served a crucial function in establishing a distinctive Crioulo cultural and literary expression on the islands. The most heralded writers of this movement are known as *Claridosos*. *See* LITERATURE.

CLASS STRUCTURE. For a small island nation, the class structure of Cape Verde is rather complex in its diversity, but simple insofar as it is overwhelmingly based upon agricultural production, even if its main income is derived from trade (q.v.) and services. About 90 percent of the working population is in primary production. Essentially one may apply the term ''peasant'' to describe the relations of production in Cape Verde inasmuch as there is the dominance of agriculture (q.v.), a cultural heritage of feudal-like values and participation in the ''Great Tradition'' of Portugal. Feudal class structure in Cape Verde was wholly imported from Europe, as the islands were reckoned only to be part of the Kingdom of Portugal. The privileged nobility or *fidalgos* not only represented the king, but owed their positions to him. Faithful service was rewarded; violations of the feudal trust were regulated by a balance of imprisonment and pardons for those convicted of infractions and subject to the restrictions of *degredados* (q.v.). The owners of the royal charters, monopolies, and landgrants could become wealthy by using slave labor and regularly producing a share for the royal treasury. This imported Cape Verdean aristocracy could also include foreigners placed in dominant economic and administrative positions, such as those from Genoa, Venice, Brazil, and Spain.

During the long centuries of colonialism, the Cape Verdean systems of sharecropping and absentee landlords were maintained until the end of the colonial period with ownership of the land in *capelas, capitanias, donatarios, morga-*

dos, by *feitors* and *lançados* (qq.v.) who held royal trade monopolies. A small civil service of functionaries, and a commercial group of importers and shopkeepers were found through the colonial era.

The largest part of the population, until recent decades, lived in rural areas as small-scale farmers, such as the peasant-like *badius* (q.v.), and other sharecroppers known as *rendeiros.* The sharecroppers grew subsistence crops for themselves and worked on other lands as wage laborers or sharecroppers. Crops such as bananas, sugar cane, and coffee have been some of the more important, but still limited, cash crops.

The working class proper was very small and was centered around the light industry processing agricultural and animal products including the fishing (q.v.) industry. Cape Verde also has a working class sector in the transport and port workers. Service sector positions of drivers, repairmen, mechanics, street vendors, secretarial and clerical jobs, and domestic servants are to be found. Some traditional artisans such as weavers and musicians may also be seen.

Another group of wage-earners in the public sector were the "road brigades" which were very heavily made up of women and children since much of the male working class has emigrated to Europe or North America to send back remittances. Thus one may speak of an absentee working class in Cape Verde since these overseas males play a vital role in the Cape Verdean economy even though they are physically absent. Another segment of the working class is physically present yet absent in production due to staggering levels of unemployment ranging between one-third and half of the potential working force. Such peculiarities in the local economy also resulted in a sizeable minority of *lumpen* or déclassé strata of criminals and prostitutes, although during the period since independence the state has sought to curb such elements with innovative social programs.

The military of Cape Verde during colonial times was very largely derived from Portuguese conscripts. Presently the small Cape Verdean armed forces (q.v.) are made up of Cape Verdean volunteers. Those from the mercantile strata in Cape Verde usually came from the islands and the more prosperous merchants, hotel operators, and bankers form the upper strata of Cape Verdean society at present, much as they did during the late days of colonialism. High-ranking civil servants and government officials are also associated with the upper classes. The departure of the Portuguese colonial authorities meant that top positions in Cape Verdean society were vacated and the socialist orientation of the PAIGC/PAICV (qq.v.) resulted in a sharp struggle for power between the battle-hardened cadres and a relatively weak *petite bourgeoisie* which either welcomed the end of colonialism or was not able to organize an effective opposition.

After feudalism was diminished by the Pombal (q.v.) reforms of the 18th century, and after the Crown was toppled in the early 20th century, the Portuguese state turned to highly concentrated state power, indeed to fascism itself, to maintain the colonial empire and the class structure therein. Little class or social mobility was tolerated except for the case of the *assimilados* (q.v.), and Cape Verde became valued for its strategic position and as a source of cheap labor in the case of the *contratados* (q.v.), and road brigades. Institutions of repression were brutally maintained in the case of the prison camp at Tarafal (q.v.) and through ideological control in the schools and churches which functioned in support of colonialism. The modern class structure in Cape Verde can also incorporate a diasporic middle class of professionals and a working class in maritime trades. Even if located off of the islands, they play an important economic role in remittances to the islands. A small urban informal economy also exists with women (q.v.) selling foods such as fruits, vegetables, and fish, and many street merchants of both Cape Verdean and African origins are active in selling clothing and light manufactured items. *See* BADIUS; RACE AND RACISM; SLAVERY.

COLADERA (COLA, COLADEIRA, KOLADERA). In traditional usage *coladera* may denote: 1) an open-air procession dance, accompanied by drums and whistles, performed at the festivals of Saint John and Saint Peter, on the islands of São Vicente and Santo Antão (qq.v.); or, 2) one of a group of women who perform improvised topical verses in a lively call-and-response style during certain festivals, accompanied by male drummers.

At present, the term more commonly denotes a popular dance song in fast duple meter, sung with alternating verse and chorus. This modern *coladera* is of recent origin, emerging in the 1960s; it appears to have been influenced by Caribbean and Afro-American dance music (q.v.), by the *morna* (q.v.), and, perhaps, by the processional *coladera.* The genre is widely popular throughout the archipelago as well as among Cape Verdean emigrant communities. The *coladera* may be played by an ensemble using traditional instruments such as are associated with the *morna,* or by a modern dance band with drum set and amplified stringed and keyboard instruments. The appeal of the *coladera* lies in its fast, danceable rhythm; its harmonies and lyrics lack the sophistication of the *morna. Coladera* texts are generally simple, topical, light-hearted, and often satirical or humorous. It accompanies couple dancing or, more traditionally, a line dance. PETER MANUEL

COLUMBUS, CHRISTOPHER (b. ca. 1450–20 May 1506). Columbus was born the son of a Genoan wool-sorter. As a young man, he sailed into the eastern Mediterranean off the Turkish coast where there was a Genoan trade post at the island of Chios. After his marriage to Felipa Moniz di Perestrello he gained information from his father-in-law who was a seafarer and great collector of maps and navigational material available in the 14th and 15th centuries.

As a result of the voyages undertaken for Prince Henry, the Portuguese knight Diego Da Azambuja (q.v.) was assigned the tasks of constructing a slave and gold trading fortress at Al-Mina in Ghana to protect their regional trade. In December 1481 Azambuja left Portugal with building materials, craftsmen, and some 500 soldiers, in ten *caravelas* from Portugal. It is believed that Christopher Columbus and probably his brother Bartólomeu were hired, respectively, as official pilot and cartographer on the Azambuja mission in 1482, and perhaps on a second trip in 1483. It is likely that they stopped in the Cape Verde Islands on these voyages.

In 1484 King João II (q.v.) rejected an additional request

for Christopher Columbus to sail under the Portuguese flag along the Guinea coast. But in December 1488, Columbus was waiting in Lisbon to greet his brother Bartólomeu, returning from his voyage under Captain Bartólomeu Dias (q.v.), who had headed a resupply mission to Al-Mina, and was the first Portuguese navigator to round the Cape of Good Hope in 1487.

As a result of these West African voyages, Columbus was prompted to seek Portuguese financing for further voyages, but only succeeded with the Spanish Queen Isabella who backed his plans. Despite his familiarity with the Guinea coast, Queen Isabella of Spain specifically ordered him under a royal *cedula* that Columbus sail directly west so as to not challenge the Portuguese and Papal authority in Guinea or Al-Mina. The goal was also to avoid all Portuguese and Moorish lands and seas, and seek a shorter and different sea route to the East, by sailing west.

As a result of this epic voyage, Columbus is alternatively credited with, or blamed for, being the first European navigator to reach the New World. After his epic 1492 voyage across the Atlantic, Columbus visited King João II again, but it was only the Spanish Crown which was willing to finance a second voyage, which included a black crewman named Juan from the Canary Islands.

It was on his third voyage, starting on 30 May 1498, that Christopher Columbus visited Cape Verde as the fleet commander. Unlike the previous voyages, the Spanish started to test the Portuguese coastal monopoly and Columbus planned to sail down to the latitude of Sierra Leone and then travel due westward. On this voyage he left the Canary Islands on 21 June and reached the Cape Verde archipelago on 27 June 1498 when he sailed past Sal Island to Boa Vista (qq.v.) where he anchored probably at Porto Sal Rei and was received by the Portuguese captain of the island, Diogo Afonso (q.v.), who had himself discovered some of the Cape Verde Islands in 1462. Afonso was the nephew and heir of Prince Henry (q.v.) the Navigator.

Boa Vista already had a small population which existed on a trade of salt, salted meats, hides, and as a leper colony for wealthy Europeans. Three days stay at Boa Vista was enough for Columbus who sailed on to Ribeira Grande on the island of São Tiago (q.v.). Eight days of Saharan dust and tropical heat was sufficient for Columbus and he finally set off to the Indies on 4 July 1498.

As he left, he noted in his diary that the Cape Verde Islands were given "a false name," ". . . since they are so barren that I saw no green thing in them and all the people were infirm, so that I did not dare to remain in them. . . ."

King João II also asked Columbus to report on any sightings of ocean-going African canoes described in Cape Verdean waters as such tales had been circulated among 15th century navigators. Sailing southwest from an erupting Fogo (q.v.) island, Columbus sought further unknown New World lands, but there are no reports of any contacts with Africans at sea.

COMISSÃO PERMANENTE. SEE: PERMANENT SECRETARIAT.

COMPANHIA DO CACHEN E CABO VERDE. SEE: CACHEU.

COMPANHIA GERAL DO GRÃO PARÁ E MARANHÃO. This Brazilian commercial company, operating under a Royal Portuguese charter obtained by the Marquis de Pombal (q.v.), had great economic and political influence in Cape Verde. It was the main economic activity in the islands during the administration of Cape Verdean Governor Manuel António de Sousa e Menezes. With the Companhia's virtual autonomy it not only controlled the base of authority in Cape Verde, but also the coast since Guinea was itself under Cape Verdean administration. The main objective of the Companhia in Africa was to supply the slave (q.v.) labor needs of the two northern, coastal Brazilian states of Pará and Maranhão.

Following Dutch and French rivalries for control of northern coastal Brazil, the Portuguese appointed their first Governor there in 1626. Although African slaves were used as early as the 16th century, the Portuguese could rely on Amerindian labor for gold mining. Because of disease, brutality and effective genocide, the Portuguese turned toward Crown-backed trading companies to import African slaves for labor in agriculture and mining. The depression in Portugal's economy in the 1670s to 1690s caused all of these companies to fail. By sending Portuguese *degredados* (q.v.) and Açorean settlers to Brazil an effort was initiated to restart the local economy. The arrival of the Marquis de Pombal in Portuguese ruling circles was to introduce still greater change beginning with the appointment of his younger brother, Francisco Xavier de Mendonca Furtado as the governor and *capitão* of Maranhão in 1751.

In 1752, with the approval of the Overseas Council, the Portuguese residents in these Brazilian captaincies were given the authority to trade in African slaves. The plan went forward with an initial investment of 30,000 cruzados. On 15 February 1754 the nascent Companhia sent a representative of Grão Pará to the King and the Marquis to seek the needed investors in Lisbon. On 7 July 1755 the Companhia was offically established with formal provisions for its internal organization. The head of the Companhia reported directly to the King and was not required to observe local legal jurisdiction. The Companhia was also in charge of a fleet of cargo and war ships. As the Companhia began its operation it had a total investment of 1.2 million cruzados.

Economic development was greatly increased as a result of the Companhia, especially in rice and cotton, as well as potatoes, sugar, cacão, hides, wood, and gold. The growth of the Industrial Revolution and the American Revolutionary War only helped to increase the demand for these agricultural products. By 1759 the Companhia controlled some 41 ships to manage its diverse products and services.

Initially there was a 20-year lease on the slave trade in Guinea-Bissau (q.v.) but with provisions for this to continue. The large scale of operation, brutal treatment of slaves, great amounts of wealth generated, and distant supervision by the King inevitably led to abuses and corruption. The Companhia ended in 1778, a year after the fall from power of the Marquis. It was then renamed the Companhia para Comércio Exclusivo. This successor company revived the dying slave trade in Guinea, but it also came to an end by about 1786.

COMPANHIA UNIÃO FABRIL (CUF). The CUF was one of the very largest Portuguese conglomerates with huge investments in Africa and approximately 10 percent of Portugal's total corporate capital. It was a multinational concern involved in textiles, agriculture, petrochemicals, steel, and shipbuilding. It had its own merchant ships and tens of thousands of employees. The CUF was primarily owned by the powerful Mello family which, in turn, had links to the BNU and the Champalimaud (q.v.) conglomerate which shared the CUF's dominance of the Portuguese, and formerly the colonial, economies. The CUF had important ties to American and French capital as well. *See* BANCO DE CABO VERDE.

CONFERÊNCIA DE ORGANIZAÇOES NACIONALISTAS DAS COLONÍAS PORTUGUESAS (CONCP). The Conference of Nationalist Organizations in the Portuguese Colonies was founded in April 1961 in Casablanca, Morocco, where it maintained a Permanent Secretariat at Rabat under Marcelino dos Santos, who was to become a central leader of FRELIMO in Mozambique. The CONCP replaced the former umbrella organization FRAIN (q.v.). The Second CONCP Conference was held in Dar es Salaam, Tanzania, in October 1965. In addition to other liberation movements and organizations, the PAIGC (q.v.) sent a five-person delegation consisting of Amilcar Cabral, Vasco Cabral, Abílio Duarte, José Araujo (qq.v.), and Vitor Maria as well as representatives from the UNTG and UDEMU (qq.v.).

CONSELHO. In Portuguese the term *conselho* can have multiple meanings related to "council" ranging from a *conselho municipal* (city administration) to the *conselho de guerra* (q.v.) deliberating on military policy, or *conselho executivo* (q.v.), or to regions of public administration or elections (q.v.). In short, a *conselho* is an administrative part of a hierarchical political organization.

CONSELHO DE GUERRA (WAR COUNCIL). SEE: CONSELHO EXECUTIVO DA LUTA; CONSELHO SUPERIOR DA LUTA; PERMANENT SECRETARIAT.

CONSELHO EXECUTIVO DA LUTA (CEL). The PAIGC's (q.v.) Executive Council of the Struggle was elected during the annual meetings of the Conselho Superior da Luta (CSL) (q.v.) and functioned between CSL meetings. The CEL met at least every four months or more often if needed. Its main function was to act as the Political Bureau of the PAIGC. There was only one female member of the CEL. After the 1964 PAIGC Congress a 20-member (15 regular, five alternate) Political Bureau was organized and functioned until it was replaced and enlarged by the CEL in 1970. The CEL was central to the regulation of political and military affairs during the period of the nationalist war. This regulation was achieved inasmuch as the CEL contained the seven-member Conselho de Guerra (War Council) and PAIGC's powerful three-member Permanent Secretariat (Commission) (q.v.). Members of the CEL constituted about one-third of the CSL.

CONSELHO SUPERIOR DA LUTA (CSL). The High Council of the Struggle functioned within the PAIGC (q.v.) as an organ roughly equivalent to a central committee, that is, it was the highest body except for the irregular meetings of the Assembléia Nacional Popular (ANP) (q.v.). Within the CSL were the CEL (q.v.), the Conselho de Guerra, and the Permanent Commission (q.v.). The CSL met annually since its first session in August 1971 when it replaced the PAIGC Central Committee (65 members) that emerged from the Second Party Congress. In 1964 the Central Committee had seven departments but these were reduced to five by 1967. In 1970 the Central Committee was initially enlarged to 70 members and was newly named the CSL with about one-third of its members also being on the CEL. At the time of the 1973 Second Party Congress the CSL increased its membership from 81 to 85. The membership was raised to 90 at the 1977 meeting of the ANP. At the CSL meetings, members of the CEL are elected to serve between the yearly CSL meetings.

CONSTITUTION. The Constitution of the Republic of Cape Verde, the first in the country's history, was approved on 5 September 1980. It defined Cape Verde as a ''sovereign, democratic, unitary, anti-colonialist and anti-imperialist republic.'' The Head of State is the President of the Republic, who is elected by the Assembléia Nacional Popular (ANP) (q.v.) and has a mandate of five years, as do the ANP deputies elected by universal adult suffrage. The Prime Minister is nominated by the same Assembly, to which he is responsible. The President of the ANP may act as interim head of state, if necessary. He is not a member of the government.

The Constitution abolishes both the death sentence and life imprisonment. Citizens have equality of rights and duties, without sexual, social, intellectual, religious or philosophical distinction. This extends to all Cape Verde emigrants throughout the world. Citizens also have freedom of thought, expression, association, demonstration, religion, rights and duties and the right to health care, culture and education.

On 12 February 1981 all articles concerning plans for eventual union with Guinea-Bissau (q.v.) were revoked, and an amendment was inserted to provide for the creation of the Partido Africano de Independência de Cabo Verde (PAICV) to replace the Cape Verde section of the PAIGC (qq.v.), which was then defined, in the Constitution, as the leading force of society. Constitutional revisions in 1991 allowed multi-party elections which replaced the PAICV with the MpD (q.v.) as the ruling party.

CONTRADANCE. SEE: MUSIC.

CONTRATADO. A contract laborer who agrees to sell his labor for a prescribed period of time to a specific employer, used extensively in Cape Verde to reduce the population especially at times of drought (q.v.) and famine and to generate remittances to be sent back to the islands. Probably the largest single source of *contratados* was from the *badiu* population of São Tiago (qq.v.), but other islands also contributed to their numbers. Often the *contratado* system was used for agricultural production and for public works. *See* BIKER, J.

CRANBERRY INDUSTRIES. In the latter part of the 19th century, the wild cranberry, native to Cape Cod, Massachusetts, became an important agricultural crop which required a large and intensive workforce. The Italians, Poles, and Finns residing in southeastern Massachusetts all provided the necessary labor in turn, but by 1910 the Cape Verdean immigrants completely dominated the harvest. Working the cranberry bogs became one of the major sources of income for the new arrivals who could earn enough during a good season to take them through the cold winter months with extra to send back to the Cape Verde Islands, or in some cases, to make the return trip themselves. The money would also be used to bring other family members to the United States in a pattern of chain migration. Approximately one-quarter of the total arriving immigrants from Cape Verde during the period of mass migration between 1900–20 listed Plymouth county, the heart of the cranberry district, as their intended destination. Cranberry pickers came primarily from Fogo (q.v.), the island which most closely resembled the cranberry region in terms of its agricultural economy. Although the economic success of the cranberry industries became completely dependent upon the labor of all the Cape Verdean immigrants who were a fundamental part of it, very few Cape Verdeans themselves became owners of these productive bogs.

CRIOULO CULTURAL MARKERS. When Cape Verdean and Guinea nationalists began to question the legitimacy of Portuguese colonial rule, they also began to study their respective strengths and weaknesses. The 20th century nationalists also began to investigate how a foreign power so far from its own continental home could come to rule uninvited, and for so long. True enough, there was the monopoly of the force of arms, but perhaps more effective still were the ideological weapons of divide and rule, racism (q.v.), and denial of self-identity and Crioulo origins (q.v.).

In Cape Verde, the new, questioning intellectuals noted that their own society was only accepted as a residual or hybrid culture of Portuguese. It was given no self-generating legitimacy or authenticity. At best it was viewed as a "bastard society" which could be useful to the colonizers for cheap labor and as colonial middlemen. Even the unique role of the Cape Verdean language, Crioulo, was projected just as poorly spoken Portuguese. These new thinkers found that a people with no effectively expressed awareness of their history, culture, and language, would never be destined to rule themselves and hold their fate in their own hands. The first active explorations in this search for a new consciousness were found in literary movements which spoke about the Cape Verdean life experience. At first this literature (q.v.) was in Portuguese, then later in the early written forms of Crioulo language (q.v.). By the early decades of this century the movement crystalized in the *Claridade* (q.v.) literary journal. Symbolically it spoke with the clarity of a personal, then national vision. But the democratic republicanism in Portugal was not to last; the New State of Portugal's fascist leadership was quick to grind down the faintest threat to its authority. A heavy darkness fell on *Claridade* and its illuminating *Claridosos.* Not so easily deterred, the new nationalists sought self-expression in sports teams, arts, literature and music (q.v.), seeking to throw off the intellectual and cultural monopoly of the Portuguese identity which strangled their self-discovery and self-identity.

Key markers of Cape Verdean or Crioulo culture appear in women's dress, in their use of *panos* (q.v.) and headscarfs tied in distinctive ways. Markers appear in music and dance in the form of *batuko, coladera, finaçon, funana* (qq.v.), *mazurkas, mornas, tabankas* (qq.v.), and *valzas.* There were Crioulo cultural expressions on television and radio, and in the form of poems, novels, short stories, and films. Foods which are typically Cape Verdean include *cachupa* (q.v.), *conj* (soup), *djagacida* or *jag* (a chicken dish), *grogga* (q.v.), *gufong* (corn bread). Key Crioulo values are expressed in the image of *saudade* (the Crioulo soul), and the lament that it is always the *hora di bai* (time to leave), but that the Crioulo community can be kept intact through *mantenas* (supportive and informational greetings). Cape Verdean culture can also be identified by games and handicrafts such as the popular board game *ouri* (q.v.), and in ship models, coconut and shell carving, horn sculpture, pottery, weaving of *panos,* and embroidery. *See* CLASS STRUCTURE; CRIOULO CULTURAL ORIGINS; CRIOULO LANGUAGE; RACE AND RACISM.

CRIOULO CULTURAL ORIGINS AND SYNTHESIS. Many of the very first European settlers in Cape Verde died or returned to Portugal. But by the end of the 15th century and into the early 16th century more came to replace them. Of this group of Europeans, most were Portuguese. Many of these were from the Lisbon area, but a notable number came from the Algarve region of southern Portugal, not so far from the ancient Phoenician trading and supply town of Gades (Cadiz). Portuguese-speaking people were added from the Madeira and Açores islands for those who were seeking the promise of new lands and new opportunities.

Following the Inquisition substantial numbers of Portuguese Jews (q.v.), or *Novos Cristãos* (New Christians), after their forced conversion, were added to this mixture. Most of the Portuguese were functionaries of the state or church, some military officers, colonial officials, a few *fidalgos* (noblemen), and small-scale merchants. The Crown enticed settlement with promises of free trade, even for slaves, on the coast. The promise was kept but only for a very few years, when only select merchants were involved in the Royal slave (q.v.) trade monopoly. In a census of 1513, after more than a half century of settlement, Ribeira Grande officially had the grand total of 162 residents, of whom 58 were "Whites" (*Brancos*), 12 were priests, and 16 free "Blacks" (*Pretos*). The rest of these were soldiers, *degredados* (q.v.), and landlords. The *degredados,* or those convicted of criminal or political crimes, were also to play an important role in the early settlement of the islands. Some were sentenced to life; others received a pardon but may still have stayed, having little inclination to return to Portugal. It is worth recalling that some of the boats used in those early days still relied on galley slaves for rowing and this was "ideal" work for *degredados.* The population of slaves (q.v.) at this time was about 13,000, but they were recorded on lists of property and existed as "non-people."

Those of Italian extraction were also among the very first inhabitants such as the De Noli family from Genoa. António De Noli (q.v.) had been one of the discoverers and first captains of the southern *donatario* (q.v.) of São Tiago (q.v.). The Italian and Jewish components of the "White" population, a few Lebanese, and Chinese, and Moroccan Jews were also to leave their descendants down to the 20th century. The inventory of Europeans who left their traces in names and genes must also include the pirate attackers, passing sailors, and maritime merchants from Spain, France, England, Holland, Brazil, and America. Some of these came in a spirit of open aggression with the goal of looting and raping the resources, slaves, and women. Others were more friendly. But the poverty on the islands also found a few women willing to accept prostitution to help sustain their families. Cape Verdeans, especially the men, are a traveling folk and there is a long tradition of women having to rely on their own hard work just to get by.

However, it is mainly the "Guinea Rivers," from Cap Vert in Senegal to Sierra Leone, also known as the Upper Guinea coast, that was the origin of the slaves arriving in and exported from Cape Verde. The still extant slave registers document the specific ethnic origins of these mostly coastal Senegambians and some Mandingos and Fulas (qq.v.). Quickly Portuguese priests baptized the slaves to transform them to the status of *ladinos* (q.v.), who were given a Latin name and perhaps the name of his or her owner. Speaking the languages of Africa was actively discouraged so that one might not be able to find a fellow member of the same language group in the ethnic mosaic of Cape Verdean slave communities. The Crioulo language and later literature (qq.v.) evolved in this context of commerce and multi-culturalism in the very first decades of the settler and slave experience.

Despite the practice of ethnocide relative to African cultural traditions, some African-based beliefs and practices relating to animism still survive, such as the notion of spirit possession and the evil eye. Some Mandingo and Senegambian words linger on in the Crioulo language even while its dominant structure and lexicon is derived from Portuguese. Among the *badius* (q.v.) and within Crioulo cultural markers (q.v.) are such African elements as traditional weaving on a narrow band loom used in the important *panos* (q.v.) and the practice of carrying children bundled on the back and carrying head loads for human porterage. Also of African origin is the use of the heavy wooden mortar and pestle (*pilão*) for grinding corn and husking rice. Crops and foods of Africa such as rice, bananas, papayas, melons, millet, and peppers carry on as well. The very popular game of *ouri* (q.v.), played widely in Cape Verde, is of ancient origin. Indeed, it has been known for thousands of years before Christ in the ancient Nile Valley. Similarly, African musical (q.v.) traditions carry on in various forms. On the other hand, the Cape Verdean *mornas* (q.v.) are unique to the islands but have some Portuguese influence.

CRIOULO LANGUAGE. The mother tongue of the Cape Verdean people based predominantly on a Portuguese root vocabulary and simplified grammar to which elements of Mandingo and Senegambian (qq.v.) phonetic systems and some loan words are added. While derived from Portuguese it is not understood easily by native-speakers of that language. Informally it is used everywhere in the archipelago, by the young and old and especially in a variety of musical (q.v.) traditions. In education (q.v.) it is used in elementary schools but not formally in the *liceu* (q.v.). It also has a growing published literature (q.v.) as well as some small dictionaries. However the language is still not fully conventionalized nor formally taught.

Likewise for formal or official occasions it is not used, as the official language in the Cape Verde Islands is Portuguese. Crioulo is the expressive instrument of the people, the language most suitable for sharing intimacy and feelings, for expressing the "soul" of the archipelago. Although varying from one island to another, Crioulo is the vehicle of everyday communication in Cape Verde for everyone at all levels of society. It is the language for joking, singing, storytelling or affection. It is also a defining feature of the Cape Verdean cultural identity that has been transmitted to the United States and other parts of the world. The term Crioulo has come to refer not only to the creolized language of the Cape Verdeans but also to identify the distinctive and dynamic culture also including folklore, customs, and cuisine, of this people of mixed European and African heritage.

CRIOULO POLITICAL RELATIONS. The land proprietors and *fidalgos* (when they were present), ranking military officers, colonial functionaries, large-scale merchants and shippers, the bishops and priests, who all held authority over their captaincies and their inhabitants, were part of the social, political, and indeed, biological process of Crioulo synthesis. It is from this group that one may derive a *capitão* (q.v.) model of Cape Verdean power relations. All of these privileged members of Cape Verdean society were able to keep their rank and position by virtue of their relationship to the external power represented by the Kings and Presidents of Portugal. They could rest assured that any revolt or rebellion would be rare and they would only have to await reinforcements from other islands or the coast, or perhaps from Portugal, before their position might be restored. This persistent threat was sufficient to keep the colonial administrative structure in place for five centuries. The key here is that the reference point was an external power base with its own economic interests which gave the ruling classes in Cape Verde their self-confidence and security.

Another model of Cape Verdean power relations emerging in its long history can be derived from the coastal traders and their island counterparts. These so-called *lançados* (q.v.) of the 16th and 17th century, very often of Jewish (q.v.) origins, existed to benefit the Portuguese Crown, or at least so it thought. Having been subject to Portuguese pogroms and vicious anti-Semitism, the *lançados* were not so keen to be economically loyal. They were linked to the *tangamãos* (q.v.) who played a role as intermediary translators of African languages. Thus the *lançados* fit into a love-hate relationship with the Lisbon authorities. Always suspicious of their economic freedom and success, the Portuguese regularly sought new controls and measures to ensure the payment of taxes and tariffs. Yet, without a measure of freedom in their enterprise, the flow of slaves, gold, hides, ivory, honey, and wax would begin to wane and the *lançados* would look for merchant ships of other nations. If we can liberally expand the role of the *lançados* to a rival model of economic power we can see that they and their potential for economic abuse were only tolerated and seldom enjoyed.

Their power never rested with royal favor or patronage, but because they were at the economic crossroads, or the roots, of what constituted the bulk of the Cape Verdean import and export economy. Their strength was their strategic position and grassroots link, which kept their position secure on the coast without much more than a bodyguard of *grumetta* (q.v.) mercenaries to protect their warehouses and residences.

At most points in Cape Verdean history one may find a certain tension pushing and pulling between the external interests of the state represented by the *capitãos* versus the local interests of the *lançados* serving as the gatekeepers of the critical commerce between the islands and coast. Between these two models rests the Cape Verdean majority, ever more Crioulized, and ever more powerless until independence. *See* CLASS STRUCTURE; LANÇADOS.

CUMBIA. SEE: MUSIC.

-D-

DADDY GRACE. SEE: DA GRAÇA, M.M.

DA GAMA, DUARTE LOBO. Da Gama was the first Governor of Cape Verde appointed in 1587. This appointment ended the captaincy system which had prevailed in Cape Verde from 1460.

DA GAMA, VASCO, (b. ca. 1460–d. 1524). Da Gama was the first Portuguese soldier-navigator to round the Cape of Good Hope in 1488 and in 1497 on his way to India. The flagship, São Gabriel, 120 tons, was captained by Da Gama himself. The São Raphael, 100 tons, was commanded by his brother Paulo, while a 50-ton caravel, Berrio, was under the authority of Nicolau Coelho. A stores-ship, the Santa Maria, was under the control of Gonçalo Nunes. On Saturday, 8 July 1497, the four-ship fleet set sail from Restelo, Portugal, on a course to the Canaries which they reached in one week's time. The Cape Verde Islands, settled just four decades earlier, represented the next port on the trip. All captains agreed to meet there if separated by fog or bad weather at sea.

Sailing under King Manuel I Da Gama initiated the Portuguese trade monopoly of the region. His first trip was undertaken from 1497 to 1499. On 22 July 1497 they sailed in sight of Sal (q.v.) Island and met the other vessels that had, in fact, become separated. Becalmed for several summer days in the waters off Sal, they did not arrive in São Tiago (q.v.) until 27 July 1497 when they were received by its small Portuguese settler community. The ships had suffered some from the weeks at sea so for almost one week they made repairs, took on water, wood, meat, and supplies. At last, all was ready to continue. On 3 August the fleet hoisted sails and took an easterly course back along the African coast and then a huge curving course out to sea with the hopes that further discoveries of land might be made. They finally rounded the Cape on 22 November, and on 17 December they sailed their three ships beyond the furthest point reached by Bartólomeu Dias (q.v.). On Christmas day (Natal) they were on the coastal part of South Africa which still bears the name he gave it. In 1498 he encountered Muslims at Quelimáne on the east coast, then sailed to Malindi and on to Malabar and Calicut, India, which he reached on 20 May 1498, almost one year after starting out from Portugal. About a year was spent along coastal India, but by 25 April 1499 the four small ships were on the return voyage and were in the ocean waters off of modern Guinea-Bissau (q.v.), and again landed in the Cape Verde Islands, probably in May 1499 for his second visit there.

The second stop in Cape Verde was, however, not a pleasant one. Vasco Da Gama had lost 55 of his men on the voyage through sickness and accident and the remaining 63 men were simply not sufficient to crew the four vessels. Moreover, his brother Paulo was in poor health and not expected to live. Hard decisions had to be made. Da Gama placed João da Sá in charge of the São Gabriel with orders to sail directly back to Portugal. Apparently in waters off-shore from Cape Verde the ships São Maria and São

Raphael were ordered burned so as not to fall into Moorish or Spanish hands. Vasco and his dying brother Paulo sailed on to Terceira in the Açores in mid-summer 1499, where Paulo died and was buried. Probably on 29 August Vasco Da Gama at last returned to Portugal from this difficult voyage.

On his second voyage to India in 1502–04 Da Gama had relatively advanced navigational equipment, which allowed him to sail directly from the bulge in West Africa to the South African Cape. The specific details of this voyage are not as well known, but one may assume that he repeated his visits to Cape Verde in the early spring of 1502 on the out-bound voyage and in the summer of 1503 on the return leg. From these exploits generating wealth and fame, Portuguese King João III appointed him, in April 1524, the Viceroy of India, until his death on 24 December 1524.

DA GRAÇA, MARCELINE MANUEL (1881–1960) (DADDY GRACE). Born in the island of Brava (q.v.), Da Graça emigrated to the United States just after the turn of the century. Preaching an unorthodox style of baptism and faith healing to all who would listen, the flamboyant ''Sweet Daddy Grace'' rose to prominence almost overnight. He was a charismatic evangelical leader and founder of the United House of Prayer for All People in a former New Bedford synagogue. Grace established hundreds of congregations in numerous cities throughout the United States, with an estimated following of half a million by the late 1930s, when his central headquarters was based in Harlem.

Riding in Cadillacs, and dressed in suits of bright purple, chartreuse and yellow, with his famed four-inch-long manicured fingernails painted in similar colors, this cult figure was to engender more fame than any other Cape Verdean-American immigrant. If estimates of 350 ''houses of prayer'' are correct, he can also be considered one of the great evangelist money-makers at the time of his death in Los Angeles. SEE: RELIGION.

DA LUZ, SILVINO (1939–). While in Portugal studying medicine at the University of Coimbra, Da Luz was drafted as a Lieutenant in the Portuguese army and was sent to Angola to help suppress the nationalist uprisings which had begun in 1961. He gained practical military experience there but also witnessed the savagery of colonial "pacification" in which tens of thousands were killed. He deserted and escaped to Zaire and Nigeria where he narrowly missed capture. He made his way through Ghana and finally to Conakry in 1963 to make contact with the PAIGC (q.v.) headquarters there. He received additional military training in Algeria and was then sent to Dakar for more "medical" studies while working in the PAIGC underground. Later he went for military training in Cuba. He became known as a successful and clever Commander of the FARP (q.v.) during the armed struggle and he served as the Cape Verdean Minister of Defense and of Foreign Affairs as well as being a member of the Cape Verdean National Council. Just before independence he is credited with, or blamed for, organizing the takeover of Radio Barlavento on 9 December 1974. This radio station had remained in the hands of anti-PAICV/pro-colonial forces. After the electoral defeat of the PAICV (q.v.) in 1991 he began working for a commercial firm in Mindelo, São Vicente (q.v.).

DARWIN, CHARLES (1809–1882). Famed biologist and author of *The Origin of Species* (1859), which established evolutionary theory. The occasion of Darwin's visit to the Cape Verde Islands was during his almost five-year voyage (1832–36) around the world in the ship *Beagle.* His task was to collect specimens and study geological formations which would finally lead to his understanding of the great age of the planet and the transformations of plants and animals which we now accept as the process of evolution.

Charles Darwin set sail from Plymouth, England, on 27 December 1831 and first saw land in the Madeira Islands, but the *Beagle* sailed on to the next port, the Canary Islands. Sailing on to Cape Verde, Darwin noticed unusual cloud formations, the result of two clashing fronts of air riding upon the confrontation of the Canary Current (q.v.) from the north and the stream of warmer water coming from the south along the tropical coast of West Africa. By 10 January Darwin and the *Beagle* crossed the Tropic line and on the

15th they reached the vicinity of São Tiago (St. Jago, in his notebook). His first reference expressed a degree of anxiety. "St. Jago is so miserable a place that my first landing in a Tropical country will not make that lasting impression of beauty which so many have described."

The strong currents and light winds kept the *Beagle* tacking all about the northwest end of São Tiago, but on Monday morning, January 16th, they sailed down the west coast of the island and by 3 PM they anchored in the port of Praia. Darwin's diary entries (pages 24–26) for his first two days give some of his varied views; here are his words exactly:

> Jan. 16th. St. Jago viewed from the sea is even more desolate than the land about Santa Cruz. The Volcanic fire of past ages, and the scorching heat of a tropical sun, have in most places rendered the soil sterile and unfit for vegetation. The country rises in successive steps of table land, interspersed by some truncate conical hills, and the horizon is bounded by an irregular chain of more lofty and bolder hills. The scene, when viewed through the peculiar atmosphere of the tropics was one of great interest: if, indeed, a person fresh from sea, and walking for the first time in a grove of cocoa-nut trees, can be a judge of anything but his own happiness. At three o'clock I went with a party to announce our arrival to the 'Governador.' After having found out the house, which certainly is not suited to the grandeur of his title, we were ushered into a room, where the great man most courteously received us. After having made out our story in a very ludicrous mixture of Portuguese, English and French, we retreated under a shower of bows. We then called on the American Consul who likewise acts for the English. The Portuguese might with great advantage have instilled a little of his well-bred politesse into this quarter. I was surprised at the houses: the rooms are large and airy, but with uncommonly little furniture, and that little in vile taste. We then strolled about the town, and feasted upon oranges: which I believe are now selling a hundred per shilling. I likewise tasted a Banana: but did not like it, being maukish and sweet with little flavour. The town is a miserable place, consisting of a square and some broad streets, if indeed they deserve so respectable a name. In the middle of these 'Ruas' are lying together goats, pigs and black and brown children:

> some of whom boast of a shirt, but quite as many not: these latter look less like human beings than I could have fancied any degradation could have produced. There are good many black soldiers; it would be difficult, I should think, to pick out a less efficient body of men. Many of them only possess for arms, a wooden staff. Before returning to our boat, we walked across the town and came to a deep valley. Here I saw the glory of tropical vegetation: Tamarinds, Bananas and Palms were flourishing at my feet. I expected a good deal, for I had read Humboldt's descriptions, and I was afraid of disappointments; how utterly vain such fear is, none can tell but those who have experienced what I to day have. It is not only the gracefulness of their forms or the novel richness of their colours, it is the numberless and confused associations that rush together on the mind, and produce the effect. I returned to the shore, treading on Volcanic rocks, hearing the notes of unknown birds, and seeing new insects fluttering about still newer flowers. It has been for me a glorious day, like giving to a blind man eyes, he is overwhelmed with what he sees and cannot justly comprehend it. Such are my feelings, and such may they remain.

The next day Darwin and the Captain went to "Quail Island" to make a headquarters and observatory for their expedition. At first he was likewise intimidated by the barren landscape, but with the eyes of a naturalist he quickly saw the true beauty of corals, ocean life, and diverse geological samples.

On Thursday, January 19th, he was still profoundly struck by the interplay of bold Cape Verdean barrenness with a spiritual solitude and grandeur and his "unspeakable pleasure of walking under a tropical sun on a wild and desert island. It is quite glorious the way my collections are increasing." So much was he enjoying the experience that his arrival three days earlier seemed like "a period long gone by."

On page 27 of his entry two days later, for Saturday, January 21st, he began to process and analyze his geological samples noting that these stones gave him a "comparative nearness of time" as he felt drawn close to the period that the volcanos had been active so stripped they were of vegetation. By January 30th, two weeks after arriving, his collecting and recording continued with so many exciting things to see that he lamented that he was "in the position of the ass between the two bundles of hay." The same day he noted a few drops of rain.

A third week went by with his collecting of marine animals and experiments on magnetism, but the Captain was preparing to set sail and on pages 33–34 of Darwin's diary he wrote that "upon the whole, the time has been for me of proper length and has flown away very pleasantly."

Further diary entries give extremely detailed information of the nature of the geology of the port of Praia and of its varied marine animals, especially the sea-slugs and octopuses he found. In his "Red Notebooks" one may find 34 numbered papers of field observations from his stay in Cape Verde. These notes cover a variety of subjects such as shells, birds, geology, plants, marine life, and even monkeys.

On 8 February, Wednesday, the *Beagle* lifted anchor and took a course southwest toward South America having spent 23 days in the Cape Verde Islands his very first stop on this historic voyage. On the return voyage, Darwin left Bahia on 12 August 1836 and stopped again briefly at Cape Verde before finally landing in Falmouth, England, on 2 October 1836, four and three-quarter years after the voyage had begun.

DA SILVA, BALTAZAR LOPES (23 April 1907–28 May 1989). Da Silva is often known by his name Lopes. He was a celebrated writer and author of *Chiquinho,* the seminal novel of Cape Verdean emigration, first published in 1947. Lopes was born in the town of Ribeira Brava on the island of São Nicolau (q.v.) and earned degrees from the Faculties of Law and Letters at the University of Lisbon. After spending several years teaching in Portugal, Da Silva returned to Cape Verde in the 1930s to work at the Liceu Gil Eannes on the island of São Vicente (q.v.) where he was the director for many years, retiring in 1972. As one of the founding members, in 1936, of the literary review *Claridade* (q.v.), Da Silva became one of the leading figures in the development of modern Cape Verdean literature (q.v.).

He was a poet, short story writer, and essayist as well as novelist, writing his poetry under the pseudonym Osvaldo Alcantara. With the publication in 1957 of the monograph *O dialecto crioulo de Cabo Verde,* Da Silva spearheaded the movement to legitimize Crioulo (q.v.) as a viable language in its own right. In 1960 Da Silva edited the pioneering anthology of Cape Verdean stories, *Antologia de Ficção Cabo-Verdiana Contemporanea,* which included six of his own works. Although offered a prestigious faculty position at the University of Lisbon in the 1940s, Da Silva chose instead to live and write in his native Cape Verde. Following his death in 1989, he was buried in the cemetery at Mindelo. Da Silva is considered one of the literary greats of Cape Verdean culture.

DA SILVA, TOMÉ VARELA. Da Silva is a Cape Verdean scholar from the interior of São Tiago (q.v.) who has published a series of books in the 1980s and 1990s documenting some of Cape Verde's oral and musical traditions. His works include collections of folktales (e.g., *Na Boka Noti,* 1987), poetry, and biographies of *batuko* and *finaçon* (qq.v.) leaders which include the lyrics and an analysis of chosen performances (e.g., *Nha Bibinha Kabral: Bida y Obra,* 1988; *Finasons di Nha Nasia Gomes,* 1985; and others). Da Silva publishes his books in Crioulo rather than Portuguese and is an advocate of the expanded use and recognition of Crioulo (q.v.) as an official language. He lives in Praia where he is in charge of the Institutu Cabuverdiano do Livro (the Cape Verdean Institute of Books). *See* LITERATURE. SUSAN HURLEY-GLOWA.

DEGREDADOS. Exiled Portuguese criminals, often charged with political crimes, who settled on the coast or in the Cape Verde islands or were confined there for a period of punishment or exile. Some *degredados* became an important part of the permanent settler population where they were sometimes regarded as *lançados* (q.v.). In the 1550s and 1560s large numbers of *degredados* were used as rowers in the galleys sent overseas. In the 17th century female Portuguese *degredados* were sent to Cape Verde to increase the European gene pool to little lasting importance. *Degredados* were excluded from high political and administrative appointments.

DEMOGRAPHY. The historical data for Cape Verdean demography should be considered relative rather than absolute. Under the best of conditions unknown numbers of people avoided the census-takers for fear of increased taxes or military conscription. Thousands were away from home in search of work under various circumstances and the conditions of the drought (q.v.) distorted the demographic picture still further. Nonetheless the statistical image is far more accurate than many other African countries which have unconfined populations and nomadic groups. Some statistical reports go back for several centuries and all accounts illustrate tremendous variations in population as a result of sustained out-migration, famine, and volcanic activity on occasion.

By comparison with other Luso-African and neighboring countries it underscores just how small Cape Verde really is. According to the World Bank data for 1991 other related populations are:

Moçambique	15.30 million
Angola	9.70 million
Senegal	7.20 million
Guinea-Bissau	0.96 million
Cape Verde	0.34 million
São Tomé/ Príncipe	0.12 million

The health (q.v.) conditions in Cape Verde have improved substantially since independence as the rise in population might suggest. However, the level of sanitation and available drinking water are limiting factors. The still high infant death rate correlates with limitations in maternal nutrition, dehydration, and protein deficiencies. The presence of a hot dry climate has the advantage of avoiding a variety of debilitating tropical diseases. The limited areas suitable for human occupation in the islands cause a relatively high population density of 83/square kilometer or 215/square mile. The population is distributed very unequally on the various islands with São Tiago having 44.0 percent of the total population; next is Santo Antão with 17.3 percent, Fogo with 12.4 percent and Santa Luzia and São Vicente (qq.v.) at 10.3 percent. The other islands have between 1 and 5 percent of the population. The population in 1980 is about 25 percent urbanized in various villages and three main towns: Praia (39,000) on São Tiago, Mindelo (40,000) on São Vicente, and São Filipe on Fogo.

Population of Cape Verde

Year	Population	Year	Population
1550	15,708	1910	142,552
1580	9,940	1920	159,672
1650	13,980	1927	148,300
1720	23,130	1930	146,299
1730	38,000	1936	162,055
1800	56,050	1939	174,000
1810	51,480	1940	181,286
1832	60,000	1950	148,331
1861	89,310	1960	199,902
1864	97,009	1970	270,999
1867	67,357	1983	318,816
1871	76,053	1984	326,212
1878	99,317	1985	333,128
1882	103,000	1986	338,560
1890	127,390	1987	347,060
1900	147,424	1990	336,798

(Sources: Duncan 1972 pp. 255–57; Cape Verde Censuses)

While these figures clearly chart the overall population growth of the archipelago, it would be in error to conclude that each island has experienced the same pattern of continued growth. Turning to the latest data for each island, it is clear that Boa Vista and Brava (q.v.) are islands of relative demographic stagnation, while the islands of Sal, São Tiago, and São Vicente have shown remarkable growth in their populations. In these three cases the largest growth has been that of urbanization (q.v.), especially for the cities of Praia and Mindelo and for the small scale, but rapid growth of tourist and airport services in Sal. In the cases of Fogo, Maio,

Santo Antão, and São Nicolau the population has shown some increase, but also notable fluctuations. *See* CAPE VERDEAN EMIGRATION; DROUGHT; LIFE EXPECTANCY; SEX RATIOS; URBANIZATION; VITAL STATISTICS.

DE NOLI, ANTÓNIO. De Noli was a Genoese navigator and merchant in Portuguese service. In 1457, at Arguim, De Noli and Gonçalo Ferreira were reported as trading slaves for horses from Diogo Gomes (qq.v.). Perhaps on this voyage, or perhaps one in 1455, De Noli and Diogo Afonso (q.v.) may have been the first Portuguese navigators to set foot in the Cape Verde islands. Both Afonso and De Noli were awarded captaincies in the Barlavento and Sotavento islands respectively, but it was mainly De Noli in 1462 who developed the captaincies on São Tiago (q.v.) island from which trade on the Guinea coast could be regulated. De Noli, his brother Bartólomeu, his nephew, Portuguese Jews (q.v.), and other Genoans settled in Ribeira Grande with slaves imported from the Guinea coast to create a slave plantation economy much like that already established in Madeira.

DENTE D'ORO, ANTÓNIO. SEE: BATUKO.

DGS. SEE: PIDE

DIAS, BARTÓLOMEU. Bartólomeu Dias was a Portuguese navigator who rounded the Cape of Good Hope, South Africa, in his 1487–88 voyage and returned along the Guinea coast to Portugal in December of that year. Dias also saw service in supplying the Portuguese fortress at Al-Mina. Bartólomeu Columbus sailed with the Dias' fleet on the 1487–88 voyage, just as Dias sailed in escort in the first leg of the voyage of Vasco da Gama (q.v.).

DIAS, DINIZ. Portuguese navigator who "discovered" the mouth of the Senegal River and the Cap Vert of Senegal in 1444–45.

DI NHA RENALDA, ZECA. SEE: FUNANA.

DI NHA RENALDA, ZÉZÉ. SEE: FUNANA.

DONATARIOS. The system of local rule in Cape Verde and some other colonial holdings in which a *capitâo* (q.v.) (captain) was given a royal grant to administer with a high degree of local autonomy. The captain was appointed under Crown authority and was subject to inspection, review, and appeal by Lisbon. It was normal to farm the *donatario* by slave (q.v.) labor.

DOS SANTOS, JOSÉ HENRIQUES "ZECA SANTOS" (6 February 1946–4 February 1974). Dos Santos was an early militant of the PAIGC (q.v.) and a guerrilla soldier in the forests near Madina Boé, where he was killed in 1974 just before the end of the war. The PAICV Association of Combatants considers him a National Hero who fought for the freedom of his nation. His remains were returned to Praia after independence and his tomb has become a shrine of distinction to his supporters.

DRAKE, SIR FRANCIS. Drake was born some time between 1539 and 1543. His family was counted among the prosperous shipowners of Plymouth, England, in the 16th century. His family was related to the Hawkins family which was noted for its role in shipping and especially in the commerce of slaves (q.v.) from the Upper Guinea coast.

When John Hawkins sailed along the Upper Guinea coast in 1563–64 to raid for slaves among the villages of the Sapeis, Wolofs, and Sambas, one of his young officers was Francis Drake. Drake was wounded by an arrow shot by Africans resisting his assault. Three years later, in November 1567, Captain John Lovell dispensed with the dangers of raiding African villages and turned instead to seizing slaves and booty of other nations on the high seas. Sailing with Captain Lovell, as his first mate, was again Francis Drake. Cruising in the waters near São Tiago (q.v.) in the Cape Verdean archipelago, they seized Portuguese ships under sail, and took their slaves, sugar, and other goods to sell in

Spanish America, while killing the crewmen who resisted. So it happened that the irregular trade in slaves was devolving to irregular warfare on the high seas, especially between Britain, Spain, and Portugal.

From his experiences in slaving in 1563 and Crown-backed piracy in 1567, Francis Drake was emboldened to more aggressive attacks. In 1577, now captain of his own ship, Francis Drake and his younger brother Thomas, sailed down the Moroccan coast as he had done several times before. Brazenly seizing a bigger ship he sailed on and came across two Portuguese passenger ships, one well supplied with fabrics, wine and a Portuguese pilot from Oporto, Nuño da Silva, who knew the Brazilian coast. Pleased with these trophies he sailed on to Brava (q.v.) in the Cape Verde Islands to drop off the other Portuguese passengers he had seized. With his stolen pilot he sailed on and reached Brazil in April 1578.

Repeating this route in 1585, Drake sailed along the Portuguese coast in his famous ''Golden Hind'' with hopes of intercepting a Spanish treasure fleet returning from Mexico. In this he failed and thus determined to sail on to Cape Verde again, hoping to loot Spanish or Portuguese ships at sail. On 16 November 1585 he reached São Tiago in Cape Verde. In the evening he landed 1,000 soldiers under the command of Carleill. A brisk night march took the force to the outskirts of the capital town, now known as Cidade Velha. With some advance warning, all of the inhabitants had already fled into the mountains for safety. Showing the English flag from the fortress of this 15th century town, on the morning of 17 November 1585 was a signal to the fleet to move into town. It happened as well that this was an anniversary of Queen Elizabeth's coronation. The festive atmosphere was augmented when Carleill fired off the 50 loaded cannon of the town while Drake's fleet responded in kind from the adjoining sea.

The easy victory provided water and food supplies, but any hope of gold bullion was not fulfilled. Frustrated in this failed attack, Drake sent word to the Governor that every town would be burned if gold were not supplied. Drake learned that the Governor and Bishop had fled twelve miles to the interior town of Santo Domingo. He marched 600 troops again, but neither gold nor inhabitants were found and in disgust he burned the town and went on to Praia which was reported to have hidden gold. Failing again, Praia was torched and he returned to Cidade Velha, which had also produced little treasure for Drake.

Cape Verdeans lost scores of homes, buildings and supplies by fire, but casualties were nil and whatever gold they had was still theirs to possess. Drake's frustrated troops, desirous of plunder, were in a mutinous mood and he felt compelled to have them renew their oaths of obedience to the Queen before they sailed again. Further revenge of Cape Verdeans was still to come. Some 18 days' travel west at sea a ''malignant fever'' acquired in Cape Verde spread among Drake's crew, killing as many as 300.

On he sailed to plunder the Spanish in the Caribbean in 1586, although his dreams of Spanish humiliation, ransom, and treasures were far less than he had wished. On still another voyage, on 28 January 1596, this pirate-sailor passed away and was buried at sea as befits a man of his life and character.

DROUGHT. The Sahelian drought in Africa is a continuation of centuries of desiccation of the Sahara and the Cape Verde archipelago. The drought in Cape Verde is accompanied by a substantial demographic transformation of the population of the islands, either by increased mortality or by emigration (q.v.). Droughts and the resultant famines have often cut the population of Cape Verde by 10–40 percent. The two main factors for the recurrent droughts are poor water conservation and abusive patterns of land ownership, on the one hand, coupled with a poor location, on the other. The archipelago is essentially a maritime extension of the Sahara and its location is at the border of the Inter-Tropical Convergence Zone (ITCZ) which causes the two-season weather pattern of the region. If the moist hot winds of the rainy season only reach south of the Sotavento islands there is no rain at all and no restoration of the water table.

The first reported case of drought or famine was in 1580–82 followed by another in 1592. Data for the 17th century are scattered, but it is assumed that recurrent patterns of drought were known. With better record preservation for the 18th century one finds droughts and/or famines in 1719, 1746, 1748, 1750, 1754, 1764, and a very grave period from 1774 to 1776 which caused the death of 22,666 people in the archipelago. Smaller droughts were recorded in Boa Vista in 1789 and in Brava (qq.v.) in 1790. Statistics kept from 1747 to 1970 show 58 years of famine and over 250,000 related deaths in some dozen drought periods, which also caused massive loss to agriculture and livestock (qq.v.).

In the 19th century droughts were reported in 1809–10, 1813 (in Maio and São Tiago [qq.v.]), 1814 (in Boa Vista and Fogo [qq.v.]), 1825, and 1831–33, which killed about 30,000 people or about 10 percent of the population. In this drought cycle food aid from the United States (q.v.) was received. Harvests failed in 1845–46 in São Tiago and São Nicolau (q.v.) and in 1850–51 the harvests of the Barlavento islands also failed. In 1853–54 the crops of Sal (q.v.) and Boa Vista failed. The drought of 1854–56 killed an estimated 25 percent of the population, especially in Fogo, São Vicente, and Santo Antão. This was associated with a cholera epidemic in some islands. In Fogo alone 800 died. As a result, the population of the islands fell from over 120,000 to less than 100,000. From 1858 to 1860 poor harvests were reported in Maio, São Tiago, and Brava. Major drought and famine returned in the 1862–67 period which left 29,845 dead while thousands of others emigrated. In 1875–76 the crops failed in São Tiago and Santo Antão. The 1883–86 drought was termed as grave as that of the 1860s. In 1896–98 crops failed in Boa Vista and Sal while a drought in 1899–1900 caused a famine in Fogo.

For the 20th century grave famine and drought are recorded for 1902–03, and smaller droughts for 1911–13, 1921–23, and 1934–36. In the drought of 1941–42 all islands were affected and major out-migration took place. Some islands were stricken by drought in 1947–48, 1959–60, the late 1970s and mid-1980s.

Because of this, the unpredictable role of agriculture has forced emigration from the islands for workers to seek cash employment elsewhere. Thousands of Cape Verdeans, males in particular, have left as *contratados* (q.v.). This resulted in an island demographic (q.v.) pattern composed disproportionately of elderly, children, and women. A large factor in the drought and desiccated conditions has been a serious lack of proper land management and water conservation. Colonial rule and European labor markets actually benefitted from cheap Cape Verdean labor. They had no inclination to invest the necessary funds for meaningful economic or resource development of the islands. The PAICV (q.v.) leadership has already initiated plans for reforestation, deep well drilling, desalinization plants, erosion control and catchment dams to reduce the disastrous effects of the natural causes and colonial inheritance which are associated with the drought.

DRUGS. SEE: GROGGA.

DUARTE, ABÍLIO AUGUSTO MONTEIRO (1931–). Duarte had formal training in the fine arts in the Sorbonne in Paris, but became an early militant of the PAIGC (q.v.). Duarte is considered one of the PAIGC "old guard" having played a critical organizational and recruiting role in the early years. In 1958 he was the main member of the PAIGC underground in the islands. Duarte is the son of a Catholic priest and studied at the *liceu* in Mindelo, while serving as a recruiter and party organizer, especially among the strategic dock workers. His recruits included: Luís Fonseca, Silvino da Luz, Joâquim Pedro da Silva, Ignácio Soares, and Manuel dos Santos. He fled the islands in November 1960 to avoid arrest by a few days, reached Paris and went on to Algeria for military training. He served the PAIGC in many ways including numerous foreign missions.

After independence Duarte was the CEL (q.v.) member in charge of National Reconstruction and he served as the Minister of Foreign Affairs for the Republic of Cape Verde. He was a key member of the Cape Verdean National Council and as a member of the PAIGC General Secretariat. Duarte became the Chairman of the Unity Commission and was the Cape Verdean Ambassador to the United Nations (q.v.). While serving as the President of the ANP (q.v.) (1975–91) he declared Cape Verde independent on 5 July 1975 and signed the important Agrarian Reform Law in April 1982.

DUARTE, DULCE ALMADA. A sociologist by training and a liberationist by practice, Duarte was a very early member and supporter of the PAIGC (q.v.). In June 1962 she addressed the UN Committee on Decolonization, then meeting in Rabat. She is the wife of Abílio Duarte (q.v.).

DYULAS, DIULAS, JOOLAS. This economically important ethnic group is mainly from the Soninke branch of the Mandingo people with some Fula (qq.v.) admixture. Functioning as a specialized class of itinerant traders, the Dyulas integrated the Portuguese and Cape Verdean economic concerns along the coast with those of people in the interior, especially in the early 16th century until the coming of the colonial era. During the decline of Mali (q.v.), the Dyula influence appeared in a series of petty chiefdoms on the shores of the Gambia and Cacheu (q.v.) Rivers and at the Dyula commercial center of Kankan. The Dyulas stimulated local production of gold, kola nuts, and the exchange of slaves (q.v.) for imported products from Cape Verde and Portugal such as salt, textiles and firearms during precolonial times. These items were traded throughout Guinea-Bissau (q.v.) and in much of the upper Niger River. The Dyulas often worked in close association with Mali and various Mandingo (q.v.) sub-kingdoms. Most Dyulas were Muslims, but they did not carry out conversions or *jihads.* The penetration of the interior by the Portuguese and Cape Verdean traders broke into Dyula commerce, sparking the Dyula revolts from 1835 to the 1880s in the upper Niger and in Guinea-Conakry when they tried to reestablish their commerical authority.

-E-

EANNES, GONÇALO. As a representative of the Portuguese Crown, Eannes was sent to visit the Prince of Tekrur (q.v.) and the Lord of Timbuktu of Mali (q.v.) in the last quarter of the 15th century in order to establish commercial and political relations.

EANNES, GIL. Sailing for Prince Henry (q.v.) in 1434 and 1435, Eannes made two trips in a cumbersome 50-ton square-sailed *barca.* More efficient *caravelas* were operational after 1441. After returning to Lisbon in 1435 he later set sail with Afonso Gonçalves Baldaio and went south of the Tropic of Cancer. These voyages were the first recorded in that region since the time of the Phoenicians (q.v.) in 813 BC. In subsequent expeditions, Eannes made three consecutive trips in 1444, 1445, and 1446 using the more advanced caravel-type of ship.

ECONOMY AND TRADE. The history of trade in Cape Verde had been largely a history of sporadic and limited independence but generally in the context of a struggle between local commercial interests and those of the Portuguese Crown and its colonial monopolies. In the 20th century decades would pass with an unfavorable balance of trade for Cape Verde. For example, during the 1951–73 period imports increased almost 11 times in value while exports have not even increased threefold. In other words, the deficit between exports and imports in this period increased by 370 percent. Recent data suggest that the deficit may be slowing but only to a small degree. The 1981 deficit was $103 million, while in 1983 it dropped to $90 million.

A contributing source of this fundamental economic imbalance has been the prolonged drought (q.v.) which necessitated, in the 1970s, considerable imports of food (about two-thirds of the total import value). Significant imports also include manufactured items, cement, and textiles. Portugal (q.v.) is the primary trading partner of Cape Verde. In 1981, a typical year, Portugal accounted for 39.9 percent of all imports from and 62.5 percent of all exports to Cape Verde. If Portugal's former colonies are included then 75 percent of Cape Verdean imports are from this group of Lusophone nations. Other principal partners are Germany, the Netherlands, the United Kingdom and the United States (q.v.). Imports cover a wide range of products but foodstuffs and beverages are usually the most important commodities.

Like imports, the major recipient of Cape Verdean exports was Portugal and the Portuguese African colonies which received about two-thirds of the meager volume of total exports. The other major recipient of Cape Verdean exports was the United States which purchased 15–25 percent of total exports, especially fish products. Exports of goods and services increased substantially between 1979 and 1983, from 30 percent of GDP to 44 percent. The expansion is largely a consequence of increased aviation services through the international airport at Sal (q.v.) and improvement in services at the port of Mindelo, São Vicente (q.v.). Cape Verde's main export is still its emigrants. However Cape Verdeans who live overseas send remittances to the islands which count for a very substantial source of foreign exchange.

By value, exports in recent years have covered only 5–6 percent of all imports thus requiring heavy government subsidies, emigration (q.v.), burdensome poverty and remittances for Cape Verdeans overseas. The estimated per capita income for 1985 was $350, up from $329 in 1982. Economic development plans include improved port and aviation infrastructure, shipping and fishing fleets, a small textile industry, a fish processing factory, tourism, and commercial production of salt and puzzolane. Thus the foreseeable future promises more of the same; this can be worsened with drought (q.v.), or improved by the development of the manufacturing sector and maritime services. *See* AGRICULTURE; FISHING; LIVESTOCK.

EDUCATION. Since independence the government of Cape Verde has made education a top priority, in contrast to the low level of commitment to public education that the Portuguese exhibited during the colonial years. Metropolitan Portugal (q.v.) was itself notable in Europe for limited educational opportunities and low school enrollments. For example, in 1960 only 9.8 percent of the population was enrolled in primary school while the comparable statistic for Holland was 13.0 percent, the USSR 14.2 percent, and the United States 18.4 percent. In Portugal's colonial territories the situation was expectedly worse. The percentages for enrollment in primary school were 4.7 percent for Cape Verde and 3.8 percent for Guinea-Bissau (q.v.). These low rates were typical of the European colonies in Africa, but after independence the percentage in primary school tended to increase rapidly as the function of education changed from producing an effective colonial administration to one of nation-building and social reconstruction.

In Cape Verde contract labor was an essential element of the colonial economy but Cape Verdeans were also important in the entire African colonial infrastructure. In 1866 a seminary (*liceu* [q.v.]) was established in São Nicolau (q.v.). For several generations this educational institution offered excellent formal instruction to its students, many of whom were from the poorer segments of society. The seminary produced missionaries, writers, teachers, and public servants, but also included facilities such as a bindery, and carpentry and blacksmith shops for the training of skilled craftsmen. Not only was this the sole facility of its type in the Cape Verde islands, it was also unique to the Portuguese colonies as a whole. The resources of the São Nicolau seminary provided an oasis of intellectual and literary life in the overseas provinces while at the same time giving those who were forced to leave the islands a solid educational foundation upon which to make a new start.

By 1945 there were 100 primary schools operating in Cape Verde. Yet, it is clear that these few schools were grossly inadequate in meeting the social needs, since the literacy rate in 1950 was placed at about 28 percent, and about 63 percent in 1970. Of those who were literate, some 90 percent were only literate at the primary level. The educational system was designed to meet colonial needs of ideology, labor, and services and therefore it was not in the interests of colonial Portugal to have a large, well educated population.

Although the expressed goal of the Cape Verdean government to eradicate illiteracy by the year 1990 appears to be an unrealistic one, steady progress toward this objective is currently being made. Officially there is compulsory education for all children in Cape Verde between the ages of 7 and 14 years. However, due to a general lack of facilities, this cannot be enforced, although it is estimated that 80 percent of this age group attends school full-time. In 1980/81, the adult literacy rate (age 14 and over) was 37 percent.

Statistics on enrollments, facilities, and staff are:

	Schools	Teachers	Pupils		
	1982/83		1982	1988	1990
Primary	436	1,459	50,000	53,265	64,895
Preparatory	13	500	7,262	12,514	97,401
Secondary	3	103	192	6,439	18,341
Teacher Training	3	32	199	N/A	N/A
Industrial/ Commercial	1	40	724	N/A	N/A

(Source: Cape Verde Census and United Nations)

Enrollments in basic elementary education are fairly close between boys and girls, but the number of males increases in secondary school. The three secondary schools, *liceus,* provide a three-year general course or a two-year pre-university course. In recent years the number of secondary (*liceu* [q.v.]) students has expanded rapidly. The government is currently giving serious consideration to opening a second technical school in Praia since it is very difficult for students from the Sotavento islands to attend the Mindelo school. On an irregular basis, the Ministry of Health and Social Affairs conducts training courses for nurses, laboratory technicians, and social workers, as needs are identified and resources become available. Specialized training is also offered at the Maritime Training Center in Mindelo, São Vicente, and professional education is available at the Center for Administrative Training and Promotion. In 1985 the government created the Instituto Nacional para l'Investigação Agricola (INIA) (q.v.) for the development of a research program in the agricultural and social sciences.

At present there is no university in Cape Verde and there are no immediate plans to establish one. All Cape Verdeans pursuing university studies do so abroad and these students can be found in countries all over the world. In 1982/83 approximately 1,000 Cape Verdeans were out of the country studying at universities and technical schools (up from 688 abroad in 1980). Of these, some 100 were enrolled in medical schools.

The network of kindergarten facilities is estimated to be serving only 10–15 percent of the children 5 to 6 years of age with the current number of kindergarten applicants exceeding the number of available positions by a two to one margin. Preliminary studies do confirm that those who have gone through the kindergarten system are more successful at the elementary levels than those who did not receive pre-elementary instruction. In terms of adult literacy programs, as of 1982, 146 cultural centers for literacy instruction serving a population of 2,147 students were in operation.

ELECTIONS. Since the 1975 election which voted exclusively for PAIGC (q.v.) candidates (within a constitutional one-party state) there were no other major elections in Cape Verde, except for delegates to the Assembléia Nacional Popular (ANP) (q.v.). This was changed in 1991 when the PAICV (q.v.) allowed constitutional revisions permitting an opposition party, the MpD (q.v.), to run for the 79 seats in the ANP, and to have an independent candidate run for President. These elections took place on 13 January 1991 and resulted in the MpD winning 56 seats and the PAICV only 23. The validity of the elections may be judged by the fact that the ruling party was voted out of power.

Cape Verdean-Americans and emigrants tended to support the PAICV. The Comissão Eleitoral Nacional (CEN) reported 15–20 percent abstentions, and 159,988 registered voters in the islands and 6,830 among the emigrants. The MpD opposition won 69 percent of votes, PAICV had 22 percent. Three seats in the National Assembly were reserved for emigrants, i.e., 2 for the PAICV from Africa and America, and one for the MpD from Europe.

In the direct popular vote for the separate Presidential elections in February 1991, the CEN announced 72 percent of the votes for António Mascarenhas Monteiro and 26.2 percent for Aristides Pereira (qq.v.). Of the 159,667 registered voters Monteiro got 70,582 and Pereira got 25,722. There were also 372 blank votes at 0.28 percent, and 1,363 nullified votes at 1.39 percent. The President of the CEN is Onofre Lima. Elections were calm and tranquil. Former Prime Minister Pedro Pires (q.v.) said that despite the outcome, the elections represented a victory for *pluripartidarismo* (multi-partyism). Pires did claim that Bishop D. Paulino Evora encouraged voters to turn toward the MpD, but now Pires considers himself a member of the loyal opposition. The next election will be held in 1996.

1991 Election Results

Islands	*Electoral Seats*	*PAICV*	*MPD*
Boa Vista	São João Baptista/Santa Isabel	2	0
Brava	São João Baptista/N.S. Do Monte	1	1
Fogo	N.S. Ajuda	2	0
	N.S. Conceição/Santa Catarinha	2	1
	S. Lorenço	1	1
Maio	N.S. Da Luz	1	1
Sal	N.S. Das Dores	1	1
São Tiago	Praia Urbano	4	8
	Praia Rural I	0	2
	Praia Rural II	1	1
	S. Catarina	1	5
	S. Salvador do Mundo	0	2
	S. Lorenço dos Orgãos/São Tiago Maior	1	4
	S. Amaro Abade/S. Miguel	1	4
Santo Antão	N.S. do Livramento/N.S. Do Rosario	0	2
	S. Crucifixo/S. Pedro Apostolo	0	2
	S. Antonio Das Pombas	0	2
	S. Andre	0	2
	S. João Baptista	0	2
S. Nicolau	N.S. Do Rosário	1	2
	N.S. Da Lapa	0	2
S. Vicente	N.S. Da Luz	2	10
Diaspora:	Africa	1	0
	America	1	0
	Europe	0	1
TOTALS		23	56

Electoral Notes: (The abbreviation S. stands for São/Santo or Saint; the letters N.S. stand for Nossa Senhora or Our Lady.)

In the urban area of Praia the vote was 70 percent for Monteiro and in S. Catarina it was 89 percent. There was also strong support for Monteiro in São Vicente and Santo Antão. Monteiro was projected as the candidate for youth and for change. He had been briefly in the PAIGC (q.v.) but left for his studies in Belgium. He had been Judge-President of the Supreme Court of Justice for the last ten years.

After the MpD electoral victory of 13 January 1991, a new government was formed on 17 February 1991. The main cabinet appointments are listed in Appendix B.

EMIGRATION. SEE: CAPE VERDEAN EMIGRATION; CAPE VERDEAN-AMERICAN EMIGRATION; DEMOGRAPHY.

ERNESTINA. This 19th century schooner is of great practical and emotional significance to Cape Verdeans. She is the last surviving sailing ship to bring Cape Verdean immigrants across the Atlantic. Designed by George M. McClain to classic schooner proportions, she was built in Essex, Massachusetts, at the James and Tarr Shipyard from 1893 to 1894 at a cost of $16,000. She was launched on 1 February 1894 as the *Effie M. Morrissey,* to fish the Grand Banks for cod, herring, haddock, and mackerel. For 30 years she fished from Gloucester, Massachusetts, and Nova Scotia as a standard ship of its type.

In 1924 she was reequipped for a series of Arctic explorations under Capt. Bob Bartlett, who had sailed with the famed explorers Peary and Henson. For a wooden sailing ship she probably sailed closest to the North Pole. These voyages were recorded in a popular Movietone News series and in the National Geographic. The oceanography, biology, and ethnography of the Arctic were substantially advanced during these voyages of the *Morrissey*. During World War II, the *Morrissey* carried out secret sounding and supply missions in the Arctic for submarine warfare. Bartlett died in 1946.

After the war she went to Staten Island, New York, where she caught fire and was deliberately scuttled to extinguish the fire. Later she was raised, and in 1948 the vessel was sold for $7,000 to Henrique Mendes of Cape Verde who renamed it the *Ernestina* and converted it to an immigrant packet ship plying between the Cape Verde Islands and the United States, and as a "floating country store" she sailed along the Senegambian and Guinea with trade items of great variety.

She sailed into Providence as recently as 1965 with immigrants from the Cape Verde Islands. The trip across was always of uncertain length; sometimes as little as three weeks, sometimes as long as two months. Many Cape Verdean families can note ancestors who came on these packet ships. The rise of steamships in the late 19th century had brought an end to most sailing ships, but for smaller and less lucrative routes the schooners kept at work far into the 20th century. Other similar ships well known to Cape Verdeans were the *Maria Sony* and *Madelane*.

Failing in a 1976 effort to bring her to the United States, she finally came back in 1982, after receiving new masts and major repairs to the hull with strong African hardwoods. The 112-foot schooner was presented as a gift and symbol of cooperation from the government of the Cape Verde Islands to the United States. Currently, the *Ernestina* is docked in New Bedford, Massachusetts, and is used to teach sailing and seafaring skills, whale-watching, as well as maritime and cultural history. In "Tall Ships" festivities of the 1980s and 1990s, the *Ernestina* was unique in that it was the only participating sailing vessel which actually brought migrants to America. In this period the Cape Verdean communities in New England always look forward to a visit by the *Ernestina* on 5 July, Cape Verde Independence Day, to India Point or Fox Point Park in Providence.

In 1991 she was to sail back to Cape Verde but a hurricane brought a series of problems which halted this plan. Her overall sparred length is 152 feet; hull length 112 feet; length on deck is 106 feet, and at the waterline she is 94 feet. Her maximum breadth is 24 feet, 5 inches and she draws 13 feet. The sail area is 7,937 sq. ft. and her weight is 98 gross tons. She now is at the full standards by the United States Coast Guard and has all modern life-saving, safety, and pumping equipment as well as a 295 HP Cummins Diesel engine for better manuevering. *See* SAILING VESSELS.

ÉVORA, CESARIA. Born in São Vicente (q.v.) in 1941, Cesaria Évora, nicknamed Cize, has had significant international success with her recordings. A singer with a warm, dark voice, she has become the foremost interpreter of *mornas* and *coladeras* (qq.v.), particularly the songs of B. Leza (1905–1958, born Francisco Xavier da Cruz), who was a family friend and important Cape Verdean composer. Évora's recent successes are a strong contrast to the struggles she experienced in earlier life. These hardships seem almost palatable in her voice when she expresses life's pain in the *mornas* she sings. Always struggling for her basic existence, she did not take her singing seriously until she was selected by the Organization of Cape Verdean Women (q.v.) to be sent to Portugal to record several songs for a compilation in 1986. In Portugal she met the musician, Bana, who recognized her talent and arranged a U.S. tour for her. Her public grew bigger in France and she was offered recording contracts. Since 1989 she has produced several highly esteemed recordings including the C.D., "Miss Perfumada," which has sold over 100,000 copies, 70,000 just in France. Although she has performed in the most important halls in Paris and Brussels, Évora remains a down-to-earth woman who is most comfortable singing in her bare feet after a few drinks with Cape Verdean friends. SUSAN HURLEY-GLOWA

-F-

FEITOR, FEITORIA. Portuguese royal trade monopolies and private mercantile concerns were usually represented by a *feitor* or local business agent, often with very considerable powers. A *feitor* occupied a *feitoria* or sometimes fortified trading outpost such as in Cacheu (q.v.).

FERNANDES, GIL VINCENTE VAZ (10 May 1937–). Born in Bolama, Guinea-Bissau, Fernandes attended high school in Bissau (qq.v.). Because of his early affiliation with the PAIGC (q.v.) he fled to Senegal in September 1960. With plans to study in Poland, he was instead recruited to attend the University of New Hampshire from which he earned a B.A. degree in political science in 1965. Later he received an M.A. from American University in Washington, D.C. Fernandes is a pioneer of the PAIGC on the international scene. From 1970–72 he was the party representative in Cairo, and from 1973–74, in Scandinavia. At the time of independence he was a roving ambassador of the Foreign Affairs Commission. He played a significant role in representing the party at the United Nations (q.v.). He was the first ambassador of the Republic of Guinea-Bissau to the United States.

FERRO, FERRINHO. SEE: FUNANA; MUSIC.

FINAÇON. *Finaçon* is another women's musical and lyrical form common to the São Tiago *badius* (qq.v.). In this instance, one or two vocalists improvise topical verses, while other women join in by beating on cushions held between their legs, producing polyrhythmic patterns corresponding to those used in *batuko* (q.v.). The verses, covering a broad range of subjects, are rendered in an intense, highly rhythmic, but at most semi-melodic style. *Finaçon* is sometimes performed as a competitive song duel which leads to gaiety and laughter. *Finaçon* is also the name of one of the most successful *funana* bands in Cape Verde. *See* MUSIC.

PETER MANUEL

FISHING. Artisanal fishing is a mainstay of the Cape Verdean economy (q.v.). Until recently the state had supported the fishing industry, especially in the export of tuna and lobster. In the past, fishing has represented 28 to 36 percent of all export earnings. Indeed it had been a growing dimension of the Cape Verdean export economy. However, throughout the late 1980s the contribution of fishing to the GNP has steadily declined to about 2 percent. Following the privatization policy of the MpD (q.v.), the state-run fishing company, PESCAVE, is slated for liquidation. With the potential for fishing still great there is discussion about leasing Cape Verdean waters to foreign firms with large factory ships. Meanwhile, small-scale artisanal (domestic) fishing has shown significant growth in value. The export of live lobsters has been sustained during the collapse of commercial fishing in Cape Verde. This is due to their popularity in Europe and relatively high value.

Despite the mid-Atlantic location of the islands, the volcanic origins result in a very narrow coastal shelf which provides for limited trawling for many commercial fish. This industry could be expanded significantly if not for shortages of capital, port facilities, modern scientific fishing technology, and processing equipment. There is a substantial potential for the development of light industry related to canning and freezing of fish products.

FLAG OF CAPE VERDE. From 1975 to 1992 the flag of Cape Verde was that carried by the PAIGC/PAICV (qq.v.) in the liberation war and in the first 17 years of independence. The background colors of this flag are red, yellow and green. These colors are found in the flags of several other independent African nations. In the Cape Verdean case the color red stands for the blood that was shed in the long struggle for Cape Verdean independence. Yellow symbolizes the harvest in a dual sense: the harvesting of crops, and the metaphorical sense of harvesting the strengths and skills of the Cape Verdean people. Green indicates the green fields of vegetation so needed and valued in the Cape Verde islands.

On this background rests a five-pointed black star which is the symbol of Pan-African unity since the days of the Marcus Garvey Pan-Africanist movement. Two corn stalks surround the star, indicating the traditional foodstuff of the islands. The small sea shell is typical of a variety of shells found on the islands' beaches and thus symbolizes the islands themselves.

Following the electoral victory of the MpD (q.v.) in January 1991, the idea of changing this flag was first mooted. Since the unity with Guinea-Bissau (q.v.) had already been broken and the former flag could be construed as a party, rather than national flag, a competition was held for a new flag design and constitutional changes were made to adjust for a new flag and national shield. The winning entry was the design by Pedro Gregorio, an architect from São Nicolau (q.v.). In August 1992 the new flag appeared. It has an overall appearance which suggests inspiration from the flags of the European Community as it is dominated by a field of blue and a circle of gold stars. The larger upper blue field is the sky over the archipelago, while the lower and smaller blue field represents the water surrounding the islands. The two horizontal white bars symbolize both peace and the horizon on which the islands are located. Between the white bars is another horizontal bar of red symbolizing the struggle for freedom. The ten gold stars located above and below the horizon indicate the nine main islands and the tenth star is said to represent the Cape Verdean diaspora population. This change of flags did provoke some anti-MpD opposition demonstrations in 1992 in Praia.

FOGO. (14° 55′N; 24° 25′W). Fourth largest island (476 sq. km.) in the Cape Verde archipelago. Fogo also has the highest point (2,831 meters) among all of the islands. Fogo was first known as São Filipe, but today it is known as Fogo in reference to the volcanic "fire" of the island. At times the red glow of the central volcano has been a valuable and prominent navigational aid. The round, rocky cone-shaped island continues to have periodic eruptions. Some of the more notable activity of the volcano took place in 1680, 1847, and 1951. The most recent activity was in March 1962.

Fogo lies just east of Brava, but it may even be seen from São Tiago (qq.v.) on a clear day. It is one of the four members of the Sotavento group of islands. Fogo was the second island to be settled and its main town and port is still known as São Filipe. The island has about 12.5 percent of the population of the archipelago (1960, 25,457; 1970, 29,692; 1980, 31,115). São Filipe (population about 3,500) is the third largest Cape Verdean town. The other main villages are Igreja and Cova Figueira.

The earliest settlement was based on the substantial introduction of slaves (q.v.) from the mainland as early as the late 1460s. Most land holdings were initially derived as *donatarios* (q.v.) to settlers related to Prince Fernando. The settlers grew some agricultural trade items and dealt extensively in slaves. Most of the first settlers left by the end of the 15th century and only after 1510 was the island settled more widely. By 1582 the slave population of the island had reached 2,000 and the relative autonomy in coastal trade gave the island some atmosphere of prosperity.

The volcanic eruptions in various years also caused some shifts in population, usually with temporary relocation to neighboring Brava. This island has also attracted a number of settlers from Portugal and from the Madeira islands. Today Fogo is often regarded as the island of Cape Verdean "first families" since some may still control land held in their families for centuries.

Since independence the government has organized construction of some 330 water conservation dikes (73 kilometers in total) and 42 kilometers of terracing, in addition to the repair and maintenance of existing dikes and terraces for rainwater control. A reforestation scheme in Fogo is also addressing the same issue. Local development projects in Fogo have focused on road building and coffee production when there is adequate rainfall and there are plans to develop facilities for small-scale tourism.

Population of Fogo

1580	1,200
1650	2,500
1720	5,000
1800	8,000
1890	20,225
1900	17,600
1927	22,596
1930	21,563
1940	22,914
1950	17,520
1960	25,457
1970	29,692
1980	31,115
1990	33,902

(Sources: Duncan 1972; Cape Verde Censuses)

FORÇAS ARMADAS REVOLUCIONARIAS DO POVO (FARP). This was the regular armed forces of the PAIGC (q.v.) during the war. The FARP was formed in 1964 in order to wage a more aggressive war against Portuguese colonialism. The function of civilian defense was then handled by the PAIGC local militia units called Forças Armadas Locais (FAL). The armed forces of Cape Verde are derived from the FARP but became separate following the 1980 coup d'état in Guinea (q.v.). The total armed forces of Cape Verde number about 3,500 with a ratio of 1:98 in the military versus the general population. The Cape Verdean armed forces are mainly in the army, but there is also a tiny navy and air force. The annual military budget is about $15 million or about 5 percent of the total government budget.

FORCED EMIGRATION. SEE: CONTRATADOS; SÃO TOMÉ.

FOROS. SEE: TABANKA.

FORTES, FERNANDO FERREIRA (1929–1983). One of the original six founders of the PAIGC (q.v.). He is buried in the prominent party memorial tomb at the cemetery in Mindelo.

FRENTE DE LIBERTAÇÃO DA GUINÉ PORTUGUESA E CABO VERDE (FLGC). The FLGC emerged in 1960 under the leadership of Henri Labéry (q.v.) the founder of the União Popular da Guiné in 1957. Essentially the FLGC replaced the MLGCV (q.v.) of Dakar and its three constituent organizations. The FLGC included the MLG and the MLICV (qq.v.) so as to broaden the base of support to provide more effective opposition to the growing PAIGC (q.v.) founded four years earlier. While the FLGC united new groups it lasted only one additional year until it was replaced by the FUL (q.v.) following factional divisions within the FLGC. The FUL and some former FLGC members led to the formation of the FLING (q.v.) in 1962.

FRENTE DE LUTA PELA INDEPENDÊNCIA NACIONAL DA GUINÉ-BISSAU (FLING). The FLING was the only serious rival of the PAIGC (q.v.) during the period of anti-colonial nationalism. The principal differences lay in the moderate program, ethnic allegiances, and exclusion of Cape Verdean unity and independence for the FLING, versus the social reforms, anti-tribal program, and the projected unity of Guinea-Bissau (q.v.) and Cape Verde for the PAIGC. The FLING emerged in a July-August 1962 meeting in Dakar, Senegal, which formed a coalition of seven ethnically-based groups such as the MLG (q.v.), UPG, and RDAG under the leadership of Henri Labéry (q.v.).

In 1966 Jaime Pinto Bull became the President of the FLING and the main operation continued from a Dakar office. As the successes of the PAIGC mounted, the FLING undertook direct actions against the PAIGC and was implicated in the assassination of Amilcar Cabral (q.v.). The FLING undertook some military activities shortly after being founded but not after 1963. Some members of the FLING were openly hostile to Cape Verdeans given the role of Cape Verdean merchants during the period of slavery (q.v.) and the presence of some Cape Verdean administrators during colonialism. Between 1963–67 the OAU (q.v.) sought to merge the FLING and the PAIGC with active encouragement by Senegal's moderate President Senghor. After 1967 Senghor reluctantly accepted the supremacy of the PAIGC although Senegal's support for the FLING continued quietly from 1967 to 1970. It was long assumed that the Portuguese PIDE (q.v.) and the American CIA favored the FLING to divide the supporters of the PAIGC.

The most militant members of the FLING were the former MLG members, while most of the other member groups held reformist, rather than revolutionary goals. In 1970 the FLING was reorganized with Domingos Joseph Da Silva as the new Secretary General of the FLING-UNIFIÉ. In 1973 the leadership passed again to Mario Jones Fernandes. The FLING was charged with creating disturbances in Bissau, Bolama (qq.v.) and Bafatá in May 1974 and FLING members were arrested by the Guinea-Bissau government in April 1976. Since then there has been no reported activity of the FLING in either Guinea-Bissau or Senegal.

FRENTE REVOLUCIONÁRIA AFRICANA PARA A INDEPENDÊNCIA NACIONAL DAS COLONIAS PORTUGUESAS (FRAIN). This umbrella organization was formed in Tunis, Tunisia, in 1960 to link the PAIGC (q.v.) and the MPLA of Angola in their common programs against Portuguese colonialism. The first leader of the FRAIN was Mario de Andrade of the MPLA. Just as the FRAIN replaced the MAC (q.v.), it was replaced in 1961 by the CONCP (q.v.), which continued the same function but included the FRELIMO of Mozambique as well.

FRONT UNI DE LIBÉRATION (DE GUINÉE ET DU CAP VERT) (FUL). In July 1961 Amilcar Cabral (q.v.) again sought to unify the PAIGC (q.v.) with Henri Labéry's FLGC (qq.v.) and some other groups. This attempt to form a united front failed because of the hesitating support of the FLGC and the refusal of the MLG (q.v.) to participate due to its concern about the role and future of Cape Verde. The effort to create the FUL was the last attempt to form a united front for national independence. Once the FUL became moribund Cabral returned to organize the PAIGC in Conakry in 1962. The other leaders agreed to form the FLING (q.v.) which subsequently proved to be the only substantial rival to the PAIGC during the years of armed struggle.

FULA (FULBE, FULANI, PEUL, FELLANI, FUL, FOULAH, FELLATA). The Fula are known by a variety of names depending upon local usage. They are members of the West-Atlantic sub-branch of the Niger-Congo language stock but their history is quite different from the other Senegambians (q.v.). They belong to two main categories, i.e., the Islamized sedentary Fula and the less-Islamized migratory groups of Fula. It is the first category which is more representative of the Fula in Guinea-Bissau (q.v.). The Fula reached Guinea-Bissau as early as the 12th or 13th centuries and had periods of explosive spread in the 15th and 16th centuries under the leadership of Coli Tenguella. In 1867 the Fula, with some support from the Portuguese, attacked and destroyed the Mandingo kingdom of Gabu (qq.v.) which still held control of the interior of Guinea-Bissau at the time. Subsequently the Fula themselves came under Portuguese control, but the Portuguese also used the hierarchical structure of Fula society for the maintenance of local colonial authority.

Until the 19th century period of Fula dominance it was not uncommon that Cape Verdean slavers and *lançados* (q.v.) would take Fula captives in trade from Dyulas (q.v.) and Mandingos from Gabu. By the time that the Fula influence in the interior of Guinea-Bissau was established slavery (q.v.) was beginning its decline, but the Fula themselves were involved in similar arrangements with foreign slave traders.

FUNANA. *Funana* is a music (q.v.) and dance genre from the island of São Tiago (q.v.) associated with the *badius* (q.v.). In its traditional form, it is played on the *gaita* (q.v.), a two-row button melodeon, a member of the accordion family, and a homemade percussion instrument called the *ferrinho* or *ferro,* a length of end iron that is balanced on one palm and one shoulder and scraped like a rasp with a simple table knife. *Funana* can be either a strictly instrumental dance music or a music with words, depending on the inclination of the players. When performed as a song, the musician who plays the *gaita* usually sings, although the *ferrinho* player or a third person occasionally takes this role. Listeners clap along with the music using a contrasting rhythm, making *funana* polyrhythmic at times. Although *funana* songs are sometimes improvised on the spot, some musicians have worked with fixed texts and melodies. *Funana* song texts often have themes such as a nostalgic remembrance of a journey, problems due to lack of rainfall, woes with women, and difficulties with earning a living. Some songs address contemporary issues such as AIDS (q.v.) or local politics.

Historically, *funana* and other musical genres of the *badius* were discouraged by the Portuguese government because musicians expressed their dissatisfaction and frustrations with the system in their songs, although the meaning was sometimes veiled in parables and stories that could not be easily deciphered by outsiders. The church authorities objected to the dance done to *funana,* a close dance similar in style to merengue and lambada. It is done by couples and may be erotic. This music censorship came to a climax in the 1970s during the struggle for independence from Portugal. The extent to which *funana* musicians actually played a role in boosting anti-Portuguese sentiment has not been determined, but since independence *funana* and other *badiu* folkarts have become symbols of Cape Verdean defiance and pride.

About the time of independence, some young musicians from Santiago including ''Katchás'' Martins (q.v.), Zeca and Zézé di Nha Renalda, and Norberto Tavares (q.v.) began to take interest in the songs of *funana* players and started to play them with their bands, replacing the *gaita* with keyboards or guitar and the *ferrinho* with a drum set. Katchás' band, Bulimundo (q.v.), made this new style of *funana* popular not only with the lower economic classes but with Cape Verdeans from other islands and higher income classes. The music of Bulimundo borrowed heavily from the repertoires of several well-known acoustic *funana* players, namely, Kodé di Dona (b. 1940) from São Francisco, Sema Lopi (b. 1941) from Santa Cruz, and Caiteninho (now deceased) from Achada di Santo António, Praia. The *funana* dance also became popular with the general public in a modified form. The success of the new sound made by Bulimundo led to the establishment of many more *funana* bands. Bulimundo itself split into two bands in the mid-1980s when the lead singer, Zeca di Nha Renaldi, virtually ''the voice'' of modern *funana,* broke away to form the group Finaçon with his brother, Zézé, and other musicians. When Katchás died in an automobile accident in 1988, Bulimundo continued without him and still produces fine music. Finaçon, however, has had more international success, being one of the only Cape Verdean groups to be produced and distributed by a major recording company (CBS). Along with Bulimundo and Finaçon, there are several important *funana* bands in the immigrant communities, especially Tropical Power led by Norberto Tavares (q.v.) in New Bedford, Massachusetts, and Livity in Rotterdam, Holland.

Harmonically, *funana* typically consists of the alternation of just two chords played with the left hand on the *gaita* while the right hand plays a melody. *Funana* is usually in quadratic meter and has a fast tempo. The chords alternate every four beats when the *gaita* bellows are moved from one direction to the other. *Funana*'s melodic structure is related directly to the physical limitations of the *gaita;* it is a diatonic instrument whose pitches change depending on whether the bellows are pulled apart or drawn together. The structure of *funana* songs is built from the repetition of harmonic blocks with four melodic phrases. The chords that are used as a harmonic foundation for *funana* can be major or minor. Alternation between adjacent chords is prevalent (for example, A minor to G major) but many songs use standard I-V-I relationships. Although the pop version of *funana* has become standardized using minor chords (usually a minor one chord and a minor five) and very fast tempo, traditional *funana* musicians play music that they consider to be *funana* that is not fast, minor, or even quadratic. Their broader definition of the genre includes slow *funana,* fast and slow sambas (not the same as Brazilian samba), marches, and even waltzes. *See* FINAÇON. SUSAN HURLEY-GLOWA

-G-

GABU. Gabu was a tributary kingdom to the Mandingo Empire of Mali (qq.v.). It was founded in the mid-13th century by Tiramakhan Traore, a general under the notable Malian king Sundiata. It was located on the southern bank of the Casamance and throughout most of northeastern Guinea-Bissau (q.v.) until its fall in 1867. During its heyday in the 17th and 18th centuries Gabu conducted numerous military operations in the region. These wars generated many of the slaves (q.v.) traded on the coast with Portuguese and Cape Verdean *lançado* (q.v.) merchants. The Fula (q.v.) people became a largely subject population to Gabu and this led to a long pattern of Fula-Mandingo clashes, which generated thousands of captives used in the Cape Verde-based slave trade. Playing on this conflict the Portuguese supported the Fula insurgents since they also wanted to conquer Gabu and to generate more slave/war captives for their trade.

GAITA. SEE: FUNANA; MUSIC.

GOMES, DIOGO. Portuguese navigator and pilot. In 1455, along with the Venetian Cadamosta (q.v.), Gomes established commercial relations with the Wolof people at the mouth of the Senegal River and with the Mandingo (q.v.) states on the Gambia thereby strengthening these early Portuguese relations with Mali (q.v.) itself. In 1457 Gomes reportedly arrived with four horses (q.v.) at Arguim, where one horse usually brought 10–15 slaves (q.v.). Gomes found Gonçalo Ferreira and the Genoese António De Noli (q.v.) already trading at Arguim at that time. By exercising the royal Portuguese trade monopoly Gomes gave De Noli and Ferreira seven slaves per horse, but received 14–15 slaves per horse from the African traders. Gomes is credited with being one of the discoverers of the Cape Verde Islands. This occurred when he was blown off course returning from a coastal exploration in 1460. He landed at what is now São Tiago and he also visited Fogo (qq.v.). Since he landed on São Tiago on 1 May he named it in honor of that saint's day. Later he reported on Boa Vista, Maio, and Sal (qq.v.) islands as he sailed northward. In 1461 Gomes sailed to coastal Liberia and Sierra Leone.

GOMES, FERNÃO. Fernão Gomes was a Lisbon merchant. In 1468 Gomes received a lease for Guinea trade for five years from King Afonso V (1438–81) for the price of 200 milreis a year on the condition that he explore 100 leagues of West African coastline to the east of Sierra Leone. This lease excluded land opposite the Cape Verde Islands. Gomes was also required to sell ivory to King Afonso V at a fixed price. Between 1469 and 1475 Gomes carried out his explorations and he is credited with the discovery of the Gold Coast (Ghana) during this period. In 1477 Gomes reached the Bight of Biafra. In 1482 a Portuguese fort was constructed at Al-Mina as a result of Gomes' travels and reports. The Crown granted Gomes a trading monopoly along the Guinea coast, but the operation was based in the Cape Verde Islands, which had only been settled a few years earlier.

GOMES, FLORA. This filmmaker from Guinea-Bissau (q.v.) has pioneered in this field for his nation. His film *The Return of Cabral* in 1976 paid homage to Amilcar Cabral (q.v.) who was assassinated in 1973. In 1978 Gomes released his film

Anos no Ocaluta and in 1990 his film *Mortunega* won the Bronze Prize in the Carthage Film Festival. This popular film focuses on a Guinean woman in the context of the long armed struggle for national liberation. The film features Bia Gomes and Tunn Eugenio Alurada.

GOMES, IRENEU. Gomes was trained in Brazil as a physician and psychologist who pioneered in these fields in Cape Verde. She is also a women's rights activist and a long-time member of the PAIGC (q.v.). She served as the Minister of Health and Social Affairs under the PAICV (q.v.) government. *See* WOMEN.

GOMI, N. SEE: BATUKO; DA SILVA, T.V.

GONÇALVES, ADRIANO. Gonçalves, commonly known as "Bana," is one of the best known recording artists from Cape Verde. Born on 11 March 1932 in Mindelo, São Vicente (q.v.), he has been singing for 50 years and since 1959 he has been featured in 45 recordings, six C.D.'s and four films. A giant of a man at nearly two meters tall, he has a deep, resonant voice that is much admired and imitated and his interpretations of *mornas* and *coladeras* (qq.v.) have set the standard for years to come. Since 1959 "Bana" has lived and worked in France and Holland, finally moving to Portugal in the 1970s. Over the years he opened several clubs in Lisbon that became Cape Verdean meeting points with music and cuisine from the islands. His most recent restaurant is called Monte Cara. In quasi-retirement now, Bana has finally moved back to Mindelo and has opened a nightclub there where he and others regularly perform Cape Verdean music. SUSAN HURLEY-GLOWA

GONÇALVES, ANTÃO. With Nuño Tristão (q.v.), Gonçalves was the first to capture Moorish slaves at Cape Blanc and thus began the age of slavery (q.v.) in 1441. The Africans were initially seized for information and ransom. With this cargo of slaves and gold dust, Gonçalves returned to Portugal to stimulate further exploration. Gonçalves made at least five voyages in 1441, 1443, 1444, 1445, and 1447 to the Upper Guinea coast in West Africa.

GONÇALVES, ANTÓNIO AURELIO. Cape Verdean writer of novelettes (such as "O Enterro de Nha Candinha Sena," "Prodiga," "Noite de Vento," and "Virgens Loucas") and short stories (such as "Recaida" and "Historia de Tempo Antigo") which are highly regarded examples of the Claridade (q.v.) period. Although influenced by 19th century French writers, he dealt with realistic themes as far ranging as the dilemmas, struggles, and independence of Cape Verdean women and critical social commentary.

GRACE, MARCELINE MANUEL. SEE: DA GRAÇA.

GRIOT. Greatly respected poet, oral historian, itinerant musician, arbitrator, and keeper of lineages, especially in Senegambia (q.v.) and points east in the Sahel. Committing oral history and praise-singing to memory was enhanced by musical accompaniment, especially with the multi-stringed hand-held African harp or korah. *See* MUSIC.

GROGGA, GROG, GROGGO, GROGGU. An alcoholic drink made in Cape Verde out of sugar cane. *Grogga* is present at most parties and celebrations and is the preferred beverage of many people; drinking it is virtually a national pastime. The best *grogga* comes from Santo Antão (q.v.) although it is manufactured on other islands as well. All *grogga* contains a high percentage of alcohol and can sometimes contain a dangerous level of methyl alcohol.

Upper classes prefer whiskey, brandy, and vodka, while middle classes often drink domestic or imported wines. The consumption of *grogga* is especially popular among the poor, that is, the majority. In recent years there is evidence that alcoholism has reached serious levels among all classes, but especially among the poor. While the traditional *grogga* is made of Santo Antão sugar cane, there is reason to believe that large-scale sugar imports from Cuba and elsewhere are used to make an inferior, abundant, and cheaper *grogga* which adds to the problem of alcoholism, and even death. The use of other drugs in Cape Verde, such as smuggled cocaine and home-grown marijuana, is also known.

SUSAN HURLEY-GLOWA AND RICHARD LOBBAN

GRUMETTAS, GRUMETES. African sailors and ship crews, occupying low ranks of irregular armed forces. Other reports suggest that they were Christianized slaves, especially as private slave armies of the Crioulo *lançados* (q.v.) and their *tangomãos* (q.v). Occasional reports of *grumetta* revolts and mutinies suggest their informal, but strategic role in policing the economy and society, especially in the years before formal Portuguese colonialism.

GRUPO DE ACÇÃO DEMOCRATICA DE CABO VERDE E DA GUINÉ (GADCVG). The Democratic Action Group emerged in the period after the fall of the Caetano (q.v.) government in Lisbon and essentially represented the position of the PAIGC (q.v.) regarding the unity of Guinea-Bissau and Cape Verde. The GADCVG rapidly became a mass organization which blocked the organizing efforts of the UDCV and the UPICV (qq.v.) particularly in mid-November 1974 when it organized a 24-hour general strike to back the PAIGC demand that it alone would be in the negotiations with Portugal (q.v.) regarding independence in 1975.

GUERRA, SOFIA POMBA. Guerra was a Portuguese pharmacist working in Bissau in the early years of the PAIGC (q.v.). In her semi-exile from Portugal as a supporter of the Portuguese Communist Party she had access to Marxist literature which was passed on to PAIGC members, such as Osvaldo Vierra. Basil Davidson notes that in this way she became significant in the ideological understanding and analysis which helped to create the PAIGC political program and strategy.

GUINEA-BISSAU (GUINÉ PORTUGUESA [Port.], GUINÉE PORTUGAISE [Fr.]). The centuries-long relations between Cape Verde and Guinea-Bissau have been intimate and complex from the start. It was as the 15th century Portuguese explorers made their way along the West African or Upper Guinea coast in the first half of that century that they discovered the Cape Verde archipelago. As the islands were settled it was through the trade in slaves (q.v.) and other goods from the Guinea coast that early development was achieved. From these earliest times the Portuguese economic, cultural, linguistic, and religious presence on the coast was fortified and maintained in the Cape Verde islands. Deep cultural and genetic roots were thereby established.

From the 1460s until 1879 the Portuguese administered Portuguese Guinea from Praia in Cape Verde. On the eve of the Berlin Congress (q.v.) this changed and in 1879 a separate colonial administration was established in Bolama and later in Bissau (qq.v.). The overthrow of the Portuguese king and the establishment of colonial and fascist rule in Lisbon did little to change this relationship. However many of the middle-level colonial administrators in Guinea were of Cape Verdean extraction.

In 1956, at the time of the founding of the PAIGC (q.v.), the recovery of the long-standing unity between the two lands was proclaimed as one of the central objectives of this political party which had both Guinea-Bissau and Cape Verde in its name. Cape Verdeans fought and died alongside Guineans during the period of the nationalist struggle from 1963 to 1974 and at independence steps were made to consolidate the political unity of the two lands. President Luís Cabral (q.v.), of Cape Verdean extraction but Guinean birth, was the first head of state and for six years two branches of the same party ruled in the two countries.

In November 1980 Cabral was overthrown by João Vieira (q.v.) in the context of political disputes in the Guinean PAIGC and in a spirit of Guinean nationalism which opposed the persistent dominance of those of Cape Verdean extraction in many important positions. In 1981 the Cape Verdean government created the PAICV (q.v.) while the PAIGC with new leadership continued to function in Guinea-Bissau. Despite this deep fracture in political administration diplomatic relations were restored in 1982 and there continues to be a wide variety of arenas of mutual cooperation in transport, communication, and other exchanges. Both countries meet regularly on various matters and both are functioning members of the Group of Five Luso-African nations. The mutual goal to recover and intensify a greater degree of unity is shared by both administrations who know each other personally. This goal is still to be fully realized at the present time.

GUIZA. A traditional form of wailing for the deceased. The *guiza* is a mournful lament that is usually led by a woman who is closely related to the person who has died. As she chants in tribute to the departed loved one, her emotional expression of grief spills over into uncontrolled weeping and elicits from others around her a refraining chorus of sobs.

-H-

HAWKINS, SIR JOHN (1532–1595). Like his father, William Hawkins, John was a merchant adventurer from England, but the main items of commerce for John Hawkins were African slave (q.v.) captives. In 1559 John moved from London to the port town of Plymouth, where he married the daughter of Benjamin Gonson, Treasurer of the Navy, an office that John Hawkins was later to hold. Backed by English merchants Hawkins left for Africa in 1562 in three small ships named *Salomon, Swallow,* and *Jonas.* This first adventure in English slaving was sufficiently profitable that it attracted the secret financial backing of Queen Elizabeth and several of her Privy Councillors as secret stockholders. The second voyage took place in 1564 and met armed resistance by the Portuguese which was forcefully broken by Hawkins, who seized several Portuguese ships. For these successes Hawkins was knighted by the Queen and given a royal emblem showing an African slave in chains. The rapid gain in popularity of sugar as a sweetener encouraged a third voyage in 1566 under a different captain and in 1567 with Hawkins again in charge. On his last trip Hawkins was attacked and beaten by Spanish ships, thus ending this first period of English slaving.

HEALTH. The standard of health in the Cape Verde Islands is not high but has been improving substantially in recent years. The ratio of doctors to people was recently 1:14,000. However, at the time of independence the ratio was 1:25,000 people with only a dozen doctors in the whole archipelago. Several islands had no doctors and Santo Antão (q.v.), the second largest island, had only one doctor. The islands had only two hospitals: a 200-bed facility in Praia and a 120-bed hospital in Mindelo or 2.2 beds/1,000 inhabitants. Not only are the facilities very inadequate, the basic diet does not even yield the minimum daily caloric intake thus making disease and a short life expectancy (q.v.) endemic. Aside from the two main hospitals there were 21 health posts and 54 nurses in the islands at independence in 1975. Even with various additional technical and medical assistants the health delivery system was notably deficient. In the mid-1960s there were at least double the number of doctors, but many left just before independence. Since 1975 a dozen more Cuban doctors arrived to make up for this void.

A high priority in the post-independence era has been to elevate the health conditions in the islands, but the limited infrastructure described above, poor inter-island transport, inadequate personnel, and inaccessible regions have frustrated these efforts. By 1980 life expectancy had improved and infant mortality had declined. The number of doctors had increased so that by 1982 the ratio of doctors to population was put at 1:6,120. Still there are only 51 doctors in the whole archipelago of whom only half are Cape Verdean nationals. The number of hospital beds has steadily increased but it is still short of internationally recognized standards. In short, the efforts and advances in health care have been impressive and considerable, but the health conditions and services inherited from the colonial era were so starkly inadequate that there is still substantial improvement needed. The expansion of Basic Sanitary Units and Sanitary Posts at the community level and expansion of Maternal and Child Health Care Units is an encouraging sign in recent years.

The most pressing health issues relate to neonatal and post-neonatal care and the rather high incidence of infectious diseases. Poor public sanitation and the limited supply of clean water are clearly exacerbating factors. Inadequacies in health management systems, health statistics, and numbers of beds, hospital, doctors, and nurses are contributing factors. The main causes of death are those typical of developed nations such as heart disease, malignant neoplasms, and accidental deaths, but there are also patterns of mortality similar to underdeveloped nations with the elevated incidence of protein calorie malnutrition, upper respiratory infections, and gastro-intestinal diseases. Even diseases such as malaria and measles have been problems in Cape Verde.

Special note must be made of the role of famine and drought (q.v.) as factors in the health environment which have repeatedly caused massive increases in mortality throughout the history of the archipelago. *See* AIDS; DEMOGRAPHY; DROUGHT; LIFE EXPECTANCY; VITAL STATISTICS.

HENRY, PRINCE (1394–1460). Prince Henry "The Navigator" was the son of King João I (1358–1433) and Philippa, daughter of the Englishman, John the Gaunt. Henry was responsible for organizing about one-third of the early Portuguese exploration of the West African coast during the great age of Portuguese maritime innovation during the first half of the 15th century. Henry led the military expedition against Ceuta, Morocco, in 1415 for the Royal Portuguese House of Avis. Stimulated by reports of the mysterious Christian, Prester John, and lured by the knowledge of gold mines feeding trans-Saharan trade, Prince Henry sent ships along the coast of Morocco looking for an easier route to the interior of Africa. Since Moors were still ruling considerable portions of the Iberian peninsula and all of north Africa they had controlled the trade to the east and had blocked Portuguese and European penetration of Africa. In 1434 ships of Prince Henry reached Cape Bojador, the furthest point reached by Portugal until that time, due to the limitation of prevailing winds, navigational skills, and equipment. In 1436 Prince Henry led an unsuccessful military effort against Tangiers. In 1441 a ship captained by Antão Gonçalves (q.v.), sailing for Prince Henry, returned to Portugal with the first documented African slaves (Moors from an area probably along southern coastal Morocco). Prince Henry usually received 20 percent of slave cargoes.

In 1453, Gomes Eanes de Azurara (q.v.), a well-known chronicler for Prince Henry, wrote *Crônica de Guiné* which described some of the aspects of this early exploration and slave trading. In 1456 the Genoan captain Usodimore and the Venetian captain Cadamosta (q.v.) both sailed under Prince Henry's flag when they reached the Geba River in today's Guinea-Bissau (q.v.). During the period 1419–60 there were at least 35 voyages under the Portuguese flag. Of these, eight were initiated directly by Prince Henry and two were cosponsored by him, although at his death in 1460 he had never actually participated in an exploration mission as it was not considered appropriate for a man of his status.

HODGES, JR., SAMUEL (27 January 1792–22 October 1827). Hodges was born in Taunton, Massachusetts, the son of a grist mill and real estate merchant. He attended Wrentham Academy and later joined his father's business in Easton, Massachusetts. On 1 September 1813 he joined the 40th Infantry Regiment as a 1st Lieutenant to serve in the War of 1812. After leaving the military in 1814, he worked briefly as an attorney for gaining veterans' land bounties. In about 1815 he moved to work in Stoughton, Massachusetts, to be employed as a Proprietors' Clerk for the Gay Cotton Manufacturing Company, which made cotton and woolen yarns. He unsuccessfully sought several more remunerative and interesting government posts, but sailed for Cape Verde in 1817 to be officially appointed in 1818 the first American Consul. This was one of the first American diplomatic posts in all of West Africa. At first Hodges' appointment was somewhat informal and differing sources suggest that his full recognition was not granted by the Portuguese government until 1823.

His post allowed Hodges to engage in active commerce as well as file reports to the Secretary of State, John Quincy Adams, about the movement and nature of American shipping. His consular letters also reported about the slave trade, legitimate trade, cargoes, shipwrecks, and pirate attacks. His assignments often required the arrangement for the return passage of destitute American seamen and whalers left behind in the islands. Other tasks included evaluating shipwrecks and selling American vessels at auction if he deemed them unseaworthy. He also reported on the effort of Afro-Americans to resettle back on the African coast. During his service there were occasional attacks of American privateers who sometimes raided the islands for salt, booty, and slaves.

Hodges traveled extensively throughout the archipelago and probably to the coast. He appointed Vice Consuls, such as Ferdinard Gardner, a later successor, to some of the other islands. The consular powers of appointment extended to the Guinea coast as well, just as the Portuguese administration in Cape Verde regulated the affairs of Guinea until 1879. Hodges maintained his Consulate in Praia, in São Tiago (q.v.). His role as Consul strengthened the American presence in the islands following the War of 1812 between the United States (q.v.) and Britain. The British intensified their patrols against slaving (q.v.) and pirate ships in 1819 and as a "legitimate trader" Hodges was probably in support of this policy except that the British were competitors of American (especially New England) merchants.

In 1821 he took his first home leave and married Polly Wales in Stoughton. He returned with her to Cape Verde where they had four children. On his second home leave in 1823 he acquired major commercial interest in at least two American brigs, the *Oswego* and *"Old Ironsides."* Indeed, he sailed both directions on this leave in the *Oswego.* The famed *Ironsides* was registered in Boston, and its master was George Hodges, the younger brother of Samuel. It was used in trade between Cape Verde and the Guinea coast such as in visits to Bathurst and Cacheu (q.v.) in 1823 and to Cape Verde in 1824 and 1825.

In his official and private capacity, Hodges was also personally active in buying and selling ships. For example he bought the Maine schooner *First Attempt* in December 1824 and in the same month he sold the brig *Oswego* to a Portuguese who may have used this ship for the slave trade. Such commerce may have been in violation of the economic protocol which reserved such trade for Portuguese flagships, but in such cases Hodges' close personal and private relations with the businessman Manuel António Martins, with the Portuguese Governor General, and with the British Consul, could overcome such technicalities. Hodges also coordinated trading activities with British merchants all along the coast. Trade included urzella, water, provisions, and salt. He also helped to provide for cheap Cape Verdean crews on American whaling (q.v.) and sealing voyages.

Hodges formed a significant commercial alliance with Martins, a wealthy Cape Verdean merchant, and was deeply involved with a wide variety of trading ventures including salt, lime, and hides. His diary of 1823 describes the merchant community of Praia numbering 25 families including those with "a constant trade" in African slaves. It appears that Hodges' own commercial dealings may also have involved smuggling. However, it should be noted that some of the smuggling of American merchandise to Africa, in 1818 for example, was in the context of an American policy of undermining the British colonial trade monopoly in West Africa. Likewise Portuguese policy and practice were not always consistent. As a result of his business successes, Hodges built a handsome mansion in Praia. The Hodges-Martins alliance resulted in establishing the long commercial and diplomatic relations which have existed between the United States and Cape Verde. Martins subsquently became the U.S. Vice-Consul in Mindelo, São Vicente (q.v.).

Hodges is also credited with starting the earliest known Crioulo-English dictionary of some 100 words alphabetized by Crioulo; Hodges did not speak Portuguese. Hodges died on 22 October 1827, at only 35 years of age, of an attack of malaria. His immediate successor to the position of U.S. Consul was William G. Merrill who was appointed on 19 December 1828.

HORSES. Horses in West Africa and Cape Verde have a long history. Given high demand horses were popular items in the slave (q.v.) trade. They were exported from both Portugal and Spain and then raised in Cape Verde for use in the slave trade. Sixteenth and 17th century traders could fetch three to five slaves for an excellent mount. Some horse traders chose only to export stallions because of their strength and size, but also without mares, the horse population could not be regenerated while the demand stayed high. The Cape Verdean nobility often used horses for fast transport and recreation. At times of Cape Verdean drought (q.v.) horse flesh was consumed in desperation.

-I-

INDIGENA. SEE: ASSIMILADO.

INDIGO. Indigo (*Indigofera sp.*) and urzella (*Litmus roccella*) are both dyes originally from the Rio Nuño area on the Guinea coast which have been exports from Cape Verde. Indigo is a leguminous plant while urzella or orchil is a lichen collected in the mountains of Cape Verde. Both produce a blue dye. Indigo and urzella were used to dye Cape Verdean textiles, especially *panos* (q.v.), which were important in the slave trade (q.v.). At times they became significant agricultural (q.v.) exports although today this role is largely taken over by other cash crops.

Both crops were developed in the context of slavery and in the 18th century a Brazilian monopoly held the exclusive right to trade in these dyes. Later this commerce was controlled by the British to the disadvantage of Cape Verdeans. Under the strict control of foreign monopolies and in the context of the slave trade, the production of these dyes never truly developed the generally stagnant agricultural sector of Cape Verde.

INSCRIPTIONS. Mysterious inscriptions are claimed for Cape Verde in the cases of two epigraphic notations. One case is found on an exposed stone face on the north coast of São Nicolau (q.v.) near the village of Ribeira Prata. It is commonly known as the *Rotcha Scribida* (written rock). In this case, there are some fairly regular hard stone intrusions into sedimentary rock where some have thought they represented an ancient writing system. Having closely examined photographs prepared by the photographer Lawrence Sykes, who processed and enlarged negatives provided by José Maria Almeida of the National Historical Archive, I have concluded that this is not human writing at all. This view is supported by the Cape Verdean historian Daniel Pereira.

The other case is found on a large free-standing stone in a deep valley on the north coast of Santo Antão (q.v.) near the town of Janela. It does not appear to have any published literature or critical analysis. Written in a form unlike modern Portuguese, Arabic, Hebrew, Berber, or Tifnaq, it has been problematic and undeciphered.

Research on the possible origin of the Janela inscription has led in several directions including Hebrew written in a type of Aramaic, Phoenician, or an archaic Portuguese. The case for Hebrew in the Archaic Aramaic form is not likely since the modern ''box-like'' form of Hebrew seems to be the only form used by Portuguese Jews. Some have thought of the possibility that the inscriptions are Phoenician, but this rests on the assumptions that Phoenicians (q.v.) circumnavigated Africa in the 7th or 6th century BC under Pharaoh Necho II or under Hanno in the 5th century BC.

However, the most fruitful investigation rests upon a comparison with the Portuguese incription of a similar appearance, on a stone at Yellala Falls about 150 kms. above the mouth of the River Congo. This was almost certainly inscribed by Diogo Cão in 1485 on his second voyage in the region; it carries a cross in a very similar style to that of the cross which appears on the Janela stone. This inscription appears to have two types of writing systems which range from archaic Portuguese as well as letters which are in a distinctly different style which is the only form of writing in the case of Janela. The Portuguese portion of the inscription is confidently translated (cf. Axelson 1973). Another 15th century Portuguese inscription is that known on stone crosses erected by Diogo Cão at Cape Lobo in 1483. In his 1485 voyages, *padrões* (stone monuments) were raised at Cape Cross in Namibia. The authoritative Pacheco Pereira states that the original inscription was in Portuguese, and Latin, with Arabic numbers. Bartólomeu Dias (q.v.) also raised a cross in 1488 at Kwaaihoek, in South Africa. All of these crosses are quite tall and free-standing, but the crosses in the Cape Verdean and Yellala inscriptions are on vertical surfaces of natural stone surfaces. Most intriguing, is that the Janela case, and a small portion of the Yellala inscriptions contain a similar writing style.

It was also common for the 15th century Portuguese explorers to mark their landings and passages with stone inscriptions, especially with crosses. Still another instance of this would be the case of Dighton Rock in New England which has reasonably been attributed to Manuel Corte-Real in 1511. In short, the Janela inscription in Santo Antão was probably placed there by a 15th century Portuguese. It is tempting to conclude that it was written by Diogo Gomes or by Diogo Afonso in the 1460s, or by Diogo Cão (qq.v.) or his pilots in the 1480s, but the condition of the inscription, the contemporary use of Latin abbreviations and signature monograms makes this still worth additional investigation.

INSTITUTO NACIONAL PARA L'INVESTIGAÇÃO AGRICOLA (INIA). The National Institute for Agricultural Research was established by the Cape Verde Government under the Ministry of Rural Development in 1985 as a semi-autonomous research group with facilities located near Praia. The Institute has national scope and is responsible for socio-economic research throughout the country. The facilities include laboratories, a library, and a computing center. The Social and Economic Studies Division assumes the responsibility of providing Cape Verdean and foreign scholars the necessary information to facilitate their respective research efforts in agriculture and livestock (qq.v.) production.

-J-

JEWS. Jewish history plays a role in Cape Verde and Guinea (q.v.) that is far greater than expected or recognized. Despite the important role of Portuguese Jews in navigational sciences and in the cartography of Africa, they faced deep anti-Semitism, especially after the Spanish and Portuguese Inquisitions when they became termed *Marannos* (Moorish

Jews) or *Judeus Segredos* (Secret Jews). This led to forced conversions and to Jews becoming known as *Novos* Cristãos (New Christians). It was not until 1768 that Portugal officially abolished the distinction between "Old" and "New" (i.e. Jewish) Christians. In turn, these circumstances caused a diaspora of as many as half of the Jewish population which was sent to Cape Verde, Senegambia (q.v.), the Guinea coast, São Tomé, and Príncipe as galley rowers and *degredados* (convicts).

The excellent research of Jean Boulegue has brought to light many fascinating details of the Portuguese Jewish presence in Senegambia and Guinea. For example, in 1517 Portuguese King Manuel I made reference to a group of *lançados* (q.v.) on the Senegambian coast; most of these were Portuguese Jews who had been deported. The term *lançados,* derived from the Portuguese verb "to throw out," is related to their outcaste or fugitive role in Luso-African coastal commerce. Although a notable portion of the Senegambian *lançados* were Portuguese Jews, this term also applied to Christian traders as well. While seeking to convert or expel Jews from Portugal, the Crown in the 16th and 17th century allowed, or even encouraged, the Jewish *lançados* to settle along the Senegambian and Upper Guinea coast to trade for ivory, hides, slaves (q.v.), gold, gum, wax, and amber while based in Cape Verde. Within the islands Jews would receive these same items for later resale to those traders who wanted to avoid the risks of coastal trade even if it meant higher costs in the islands. Jews in Cape Verde were also active in the trade of hides, urzella (q.v.), and coffee.

Restrictions for the *lançados* prohibited them from selling iron bars, firearms, and navigational instruments, yet the *lançados* were clearly critical in the economic network which linked the Crown trade monopolies to the coast. Spanish and English smugglers using ties to the *lançados* were frequent violaters of these Portuguese prohibitions.

Thus, as early as the later 15th century and through the 16th and even 17th centuries, a Jewish coastal presence was deeply established. This brought on an important synthesis dynamic which was responsible for playing a central role in the creation of Crioulo culture (q.v.). These Jews, both in the

Cape Verde Islands and on the coast, were at the heart of the Afro-Portuguese merging which became Crioulo culture. The anti-Semitism of Spain and Portugal and the financial goals of the Portuguese Crown were constantly trying to restrict their success. The more successful, the more restrictions, but also the more deeply struck were the commercial and cultural roots of these people. The *lançados* were themselves undergoing a transformation because of their intermediary and collaborative relation with African cultures. This contradictory nature at once set them apart, while embedding them in a multi-racial and multi-cultural identity that was being concurrently synthesized. In Cape Verde this was to become the essence of Crioulo culture. This process has its close parallels in East Africa with the commercial presence of Omani and Shirazi Muslims who were trading for ivory and slaves from the African interior. A trade language and an entire cultural group, now known as KiSwahili evolved in this context. In the Senegambian case, French and British expansion finally reduced the presence of the *lançados* and their military associates, the *grumettas* (q.v.), to only Portuguese Guinea and to urban and coastal entrepôts. Until the war of national liberation (1963–1974) in Guinea-Bissau, Crioulo people, culture, and language were still mainly in urban areas. During the war the use of Crioulo spread throughout the countryside.

Jews from Cape Verde and Portugal were already known in Joal as early as 1591 and a synagogue was noted there in 1641. In 1606, in Portudal, also on the Senegalese coast there were 100 Portuguese following the "Laws of Moses." Boulegue notes that in 1614 the Governor of Cape Verde recorded that the greatest number of *lançados* were Jews. In 1622 the Cape Verdean Governor, Dom Francisco de Mourra, reported to the Portuguese King that the Guinea coastal rivers were "full of Jews who were masters of the local regions and were quite independent of the Crown." No doubt such information relating to "the Jewish danger" gave "justification" to the Portuguese to punish two wealthy members of the Jewish comunity around the synagogue in Rufisque, Senegal, for economic excesses in 1629. When a branch of the Portuguese Inquisition was established in Cape Verde in 1672, one result was the seizure of Jewish-owned merchandise. As the 17th century evolved, the Portuguese were steadily displaced from Senegambia, but they retained their bases in the Cape Verde islands and in Guinea at Cacheu, Bolama, Bissau (q.v.), Buba, Geba, Mansoa.

In the 16th and 17th centuries the term *ganagoga* was also used in the Upper Guinea/Cape Verde region to imply Jewish *lançados,* but in practice *ganagoga* also meant people who were able to speak many local African languages. Allied with them were the *tangomãos* (q.v.) who represented a still deeper connection to the African interior for the *lançados.* It seems most likely that the term *tangomão* is a corrupted form of *targuman,* which means "translator" in Arabic. Muslims and Arabic-speakers were and are widespread in this area, especially the northern and interior regions where the *tangomãos* or *lançados* traded.

The Jewish and Moorish alliance was already of very great historical depth. This relationship was based upon several factors. On the one hand, the Portuguese Crown and its *feitors* and *capitãos* (q.v.) gained tremendous wealth from the slave trade and they did little to oppose it; however, they were pleased to have a social pariah group, like the *lançados* be responsible for the front line operation of the trade. Meanwhile, the commercial skills, and higher level of literacy put the Jews in a strong position to have a critical role in an economy and society which otherwise shunned them. It should be made very clear that, by no means, were all Portuguese slavers Jewish, nor were all Portuguese involved in the slave trade; likewise the slave trade in the interior necessitated strategic African collaboration.

A reference to a *lançado* expedition to the goldfields of Bambuk in 1785–88 refered to a Jewish *ganagoga* who married a daughter of the Imam of Futa Toro. In their heyday, the *lançados* owned and operated their own ships, river craft and canoes, as well as carrying firearms, daggers, and swords. Above all they were traders in wax, gold, hides, cloths, ivory, and cotton. However, by the late 18th century, a clearly defined *lançado* community in Senegambia was gone, but not really departed. Virtually all *lançados* had African wives and consorts and their subsequent generations continued to play a central and substantial role in the culturo-linguistic melange which consitutes Cape Verdean Crioulo culture. This was formed in the context of the merging and blending of Iberian, Moorish, Jewish, and African peoples.

Following the ''Liberal Wars'' in Portugal in the 1820's, some ''Miguelista'' Jews fled to the mountains of Santo Antão (q.v.). Several became leading traders and professionals according to Meintel. In the mid-19th century the population of Cape Verdean Jews was increased by some small scale Jewish migration from Rabat, Morocco, especially for the trade in animal hides which was important in Boa Vista. Although there is no formal Jewish synagogue in Cape Verde today and there is no official rabbi, an elder named David Cohen was reported to lead other Jews in prayer in the 20th century. Historically there was a very definite Jewish presence amongst early Cape Verdeans. Jews first came to the island of São Tiago as refugees from religious persecution during the Inquisition. They were shunned by the wider society of the islands at that time and they were confined to a separate ghetto-like community in Praia. During the early nineteenth century, Jews also came to settle in Santo Antão where there are still traces of their influx in the name of the village of Sinagoga, located on the north coast between Ribeira Grande and Janela, and in the Jewish cemetery at the town of Ponta da Sol. The family names of Cohn (priest) and Wahnon are prominent in Santo Antão. Other Jewish settlers such as the Ben Oliel family migrated to Boa Vista (q.v.), trading in salt, hides, and slaves. Jewish-derived surnames can be found amongst the inhabitants of the islands. Such names can include Auday, Benros, Ben David, Cohn, DaGama, and Seruya.

The family of Salomão Ben Oliel is still active today in trading activities of the Sociedade Luso-Africana, Ltd. This hyphenated company name suggests the long historical roots between two cultural regions. Jewish cemeteries or graves are in Brava (at Cova da Judeu), Boa Vista, São Tiago (in

Praia and Cidade Velha), Santo Antão (especially at Sinagoga), São Nicolau (at Mindelo), Fogo (qq.v.), and probably in other islands as well. In the 19th and 20th century Praia cemetery, for example, there are about eight grave markers still extant with Hebrew inscriptions (q.v.). These were originally outside of the cemetery walls, but as it expanded, the walls were relocated and thereby integrated these deceased Jews with their Crioulo cousins.

Since Portugal was heavily involved in the slave trade through its Crown slave trade monopolies, it is not surprising that Cape Verdean Jews and other coastal *lançados* were also involved in the slave trade. The Atlantic slave trade has also been known as the Triangle trade as it described a vast triangular shape linking West Africa with the Caribbean and then to New England and Europe and thence back to Africa. As a result, in the Caribbean, in Curação, Surinam, and Jamaica, there were Jewish populations similar to, and linked with, those in West Africa. The case of Jamaica parallels that of the *lançados* since it was in its period of growth from the 1630s to 1670s. Eighteenth century Portuguese Jews in Jamaica include names such as Alvarez, Cardoso, Corea, DaCosta, Gomes, Gonsalis, Gutteres, Lamego, Quisano, and Torres. *See* BENROS; CRIOULO CULTURE; INSCRIPTIONS; LADINOS; LANÇADOS; RELIGION; SLAVERY.

JOÃO II (ruled 1477, 1481–1495). Portuguese king during the later period of the Age of Maritime Exploration. He was the son of King Afonso V. During his reign, settlers began arriving in the Cape Verde Islands. Under João II chartmaking expanded in Lisbon, including the work of Bartólomeu Columbus, brother of Christopher Columbus (q.v.). In 1484 João II turned down a request by Christopher Columbus to finance further voyages after he had visited the Guinea Coast between 1482–84. Columbus visited João II again in 1493 after his historic voyage to ''India'' (the New World).

JUVENTUDE AFRICANA AMILCAR CABRAL (JAAC). SEE: PIONEERS OF THE PARTY

-K-

KABRAL. SEE: CABRAL.

KATCHAS. SEE: FUNANA; MARTINS, C.

KODI. SEE: FUNANA.

KRIOULO. SEE: CRIOULO.

-L-

LABÉRY, HENRI. Founder of the UPG in 1957 which led to his direct involvement in the founding of the FLGC (q.v.) in 1960. Some elements of the FLGC appeared in 1961 as the FUL (q.v.). In 1962 Labéry emerged as the head of the FLING (q.v.). Labéry is of Cape Verdean extraction and was an early associate of Amilcar Cabral (q.v.). He went to schools in Lisbon, but lived mainly in Guinea-Bissau (q.v.). Labéry's program was less clear on ideological matters, and was essentially concerned with the independence of Guinea.

LADAINHA. SEE: TABANKA.

LADINOS. This social group constituted a portion of early migrants to the Cape Verde Islands. Some references use this term for the people and language of 16th and 17th century Sephardic Jews (q.v.) from the Iberian peninsula. In the case of such groups exiled to the Guinea coast to serve as merchants, they are also known as *lançados* (q.v.).

Other references use the term *ladinos* to refer to baptized African slaves (q.v.). In either case, the reference was often racist, and derogatory, and implied a lying, wandering, sneaky, and thieving group which was particularly untrustworthy. In certain social contexts it could be used affectionately to mean a scamp.

LANÇADOS. Literally the term *lançados* means "outcastes." They were usually fugitive Portuguese settlers including those exiled *degredados* (q.v.) following their conviction for some "crime." Often they were charged with political crimes, such as was the case for Jews (q.v.) following the Inquisition, but Christian *lançados* were also known. *Lançados* were reputed for being resourceful and courageous, and having initiative. The term also connotes the mixed-race traders living in the trading communities in the islands or on the coast where they conducted trade. They often had African wives from the local groups and, as such, their children can be said to be the nucleus of the future Crioulo (q.v.) population. They were economic intermediaries or middlemen for the Portuguese regional trade. *See* TANGOMÃOS.

LANÇAROTE (LANZRATE). This ship captain sailed under the Portuguese flag in the early to mid-15th century, but may not have been of Portuguese extraction. There is one well known passage written in 1444 which is credited to Lançarote which details the capture of 165 men, women, and children to be taken to Portugal as slaves (q.v.). It also notes that others were slain in resisting the raiders. This event probably took place on the coast of Mauretania. Similar events were also reported by Afonso Gonçalves Baldaia, Gil Eannes, Antão Gonçalves, and Nuño Tristão (qq.v.).

LANDU, LANDUM. A music and dance genre of Boa Vista (q.v.), associated with wedding celebrations. *See* MUSIC.
PETER MANUEL

LEEWARD ISLANDS. SEE: SOTAVENTO, ILHAS DE.

LEGISLATIVE ASSEMBLY (PORTUGUESE). The 130-member Legislative Assembly of Portugal (q.v.) provided for two representatives from Cape Verde and one from Guinea-Bissau (Guiné-Portuguesa)(q.v.). In the two colonies there were separate Legislative Assemblies replacing the former legislative councils. In Guinea-Bissau the Assembly consisted of 17 members: five elected, three traditional chiefs, three administrative representatives, two commercial representatives, two from workers organizations, and two representing "cultural and moral" concerns. In Cape Verde there were 21 members of the Assembly expanded from the 18-member Council. The composition included: 11 elected by vote, four administrative appointments, two commercial representatives, two workers' representatives, and two representing "moral and cultural" concerns. Both Guinea and Cape Verde were "Overseas Provinces" of Portugal after 1971 with subdivisions of *conselhos* (q.v.) (municipalities) and civil parishes (administrative posts). *See:* PORTUGAL.

LEITE, ANTÓNIO JANUÁRIO (10 June 1867–10 June 1930). Januário Leite was one of the early members of the new literary (q.v.) generation of Cape Verde which helped to launch the cultural liberation of the islands. He was born the son of João José Leite and Irene Candida in Pombas. Through his life he was considered humble and modest. He is especially famous for his works of poetry including "Sonhos," and a maternal, "Saudade."

He taught for more than two years in the *conselho* (q.v.) of Porto Novo in Santo Antão (q.v.), but it was his life in Mindelo which caused him to meet other Cape Verdean *literati* such as José Lopes (q.v.) and Guilhêrme Ernesto. His political outlook was that of a Portuguese Republican and as such he found himself involved in "the 1886 troubles" and he was arrested as a result of the 1894 revolt in Santo Antão. His poetic expression was intensified as a result of the injustices he witnessed. His works were collected and published posthumously in 1952 in the form of *Poesias* and *Versos da Juventude.* Literary researchers, Luís Romano and Tomas Benros, have collected and analyzed the works of Leite.

LEZA, B. SEE: ÉVORA, C.

LICEU. A *liceu* functions in the Portuguese or Cape Verdean system of education (q.v.) as the equivalent of an advanced secondary school. In Cape Verde this has long been the highest level of education available locally thus, in a land of widespread illiteracy, considerable social status was achieved by those who completed the *liceu.* Some discussion has begun over the question of offering university level educational centers. In addition to the *liceus* of Mindelo and Praia, there is a famed *seminário* of São Nicolau (q.v.) which offered a secondary education, while training Cape Verdeans for the Catholic priesthood. This seminary was central in the development of Cape Verdean literature (q.v.) and in the birth of the *Claridade* (q.v.) literary movement.

LIFE EXPECTANCY. With centuries of drought (q.v.) and famine, life expectancy in Cape Verde has often been short. The hardships and high mortality were frequently escaped by emigration (q.v.) to the New World, Europe, and São Tomé. One of the most severe aspects of shortened life expectancy was a rather high rate of infant mortality. However, in recent years this has been greatly improved according to data from Cape Verdean Dr. João Soares.

In research done by Robert Tidwell, Waltraud Coli, and Richard Lobban a data base was formed by coding 777 obituaries from the Cape Verdean press. This has been analyzed and published in Lobban, Coli and Tidwell (1986). This data base was recently expanded to 1,049 cases by Chris Wrenn and analyzed further by Robert Tidwell. The results of this collective work are presented below.

Comparative Life Expectancy in America

Cape-Verdeans born in:		
Cape Verde	81.15	N = 322
Other Places	62.50	N = 275
America	59.66	N = 452
All Places	67.00	N = 1,049
All Americans (1993)	75.5	
"Black" Males	64.6	
"White" Males	72.9	
"Black" Females	73.8	
"White" Females	79.6	

(Sources: Lobban and Tidwell study; National Center for Health Statistics)

It should be noted that the higher life expectancy for Cape Verdean-born Americans inherently excludes those already dead from high infant mortality or those who did not migrate to the United States for other reasons including health (q.v.). Thus, this is a population skewed toward the older age cohorts. On the other hand, the life expectancy for Cape Verdean-Americans is more representative of the entire Cape Verdean population in the United States, and is lowered by including a broader range of younger Cape Verdean-Americans. When controlling for this difference, Tidwell found little significant difference in the overall life expectancy of Cape Verdean-born or American-born Cape Verdeans.

However, when Tidwell looked at survival statistics generated for each ten-year age cohort there is a somewhat greater life expectancy for those born in the Islands, and in almost all cases, women outlived men by about two years when controlling for place of birth and age cohort. The highest life expectancy was consistently seen among those with professional occupations, while shorter lives were experienced by those in construction and maritime trades. The reasons for this difference require further investigation in epidemiology, behavior, health, diet, and nutrition conditions in the two populations.

Despite these methodological issues, it is also useful to compare Cape Verdean life expectancy with that in other West African countries. *See* HEALTH; VITAL STATISTICS.

Country	*Average Number of Years Lived*
Sierra Leone—Males	39.0
Sierra Leone—Females	43.0
Gambia—Males	41.0
Gambia—Females	45.0
Guinea-Bissau—Males	43.0
Guinea-Bissau—Females	47.0
Senegal—Males	44.0
Senegal—Females	47.0
Cape Verde—Males	57.0
Cape Verde—Females	61.0

(Source: World Health Organization, 1990)

LIMA, ARISTIDES RAIMUNDO (31 December 1955–). Lima was born in the town of Sal Rei on Boa Vista (q.v.) where he later worked as a teacher of Portuguese and French just before and after independence. In 1976 he became a journalist for the Cape Verdean newspaper *Voz di Povo* until pursuing a law degree from the University of Leipzig, from which he graduated in 1983. Lima worked in the Ministry of Justice from 1985–86 in the section concerned with the support and dynamization of district tribunals. Concurrently Lima was a member of the third legislature of the Assembléia National Popular (ANP) (q.v.) from 1985–90 while also serving, from 1986 to 1989, as an adviser to the President on constitutional and legal affairs and as a teacher of constitutional law at the Amilcar Cabral Institute. Within the PAICV (q.v.) Lima was the Director of State Institutions where he played a critical role in the transition to democracy starting with the liberalizations of 1988, and the major PAICV reforms leading to revisions of the constitution (q.v.), formation of the electoral Code of Conduct, and electoral procedures throughout 1990 which provided for the formal abolition of one-party rule to the transition to the multi-party system with the MpD and UPICV (qq.v). Lima's book, *Reforma Política em Cabo Verde (Do paternalismo a modernização do Estado)* (1992), sets out the details of this transition.

After the 1991 elections (q.v.) and the defeat of the PAICV, Lima worked from 1991–92 in the Cabinet for Studies and Legislation of the Ministry of Justice dealing with public administration and labor issues, while teaching public law in Praia. It was widely expected in 1991–92 that the party leadership of former Prime Minister Pedro Pires (q.v.) would have to change, and in the 1993 PAICV Party Congress it was determined that Pires would move into a behind-the-scenes position with Lima brought forward as the party's new Secretary General. Thus, Lima continues to be the leader of the minority opposition party (PAICV) in the ANP during its fourth legislative period from 1991–96, but he is strengthened by also being the PAICV Secretary General. In this capacity, he intends to address the issues of minority representation and oversight, as well as seeking to curb the strength of the MpD, especially in areas of economic policy.

Lima is the author of numerous legal publications in German, English and Portuguese which make him both a sophisticated observer of and active participant in the Cape Verdean legal system and a significant number of national and international conferences focusing on legal issues.

LINDBERGH, CHARLES A. and ANNE MORROW. The famed aviators, Charles A. and Anne Morrow Lindbergh played a small role in Cape Verdean history during their flight which circumnavigated the North Atlantic to prepare for an era of commercial trans-Atlantic airplane travel. The Lindbergh adventure began in Flushing Bay, Long Island, on 9 July 1933, when their specially designed Lockheed Sirius, equipped with pontoons and a 710 horsepower Wright Cyclone F engine took off to the northeast. The plane was named "The Tingmissartoq" (a big flying bird in a Greenland Annuit language). Through the summer and fall they flew in Newfoundland, Labrador, Greenland, Iceland, and the Scandinavian nations and on south to western Europe. By 15 November they reached Lisbon, Portugal, to work their way toward subsequent stops in the Açores and Canary Islands. On 26 November they finally landed on the African continent at Villa Cisneros in Rio de Oro, now incorporated within the Kingdom of Morocco.

On the next morning they took off for a long six hour flight to the Cape Verde Islands, flying over Boa Vista (q.v.) and landing in the harbor at Praia at 3 o'clock in the afternoon. The landing was especially difficult as they were pursued by a very strong tail wind following the powerful Canary Current (q.v.) along the northwest African coast. Indeed, the winds and waves typical of a Cape Verdean November were much more than they had anticipated. Even as they arrived they were both worried that they would have to adjust their plan to cross the Atlantic from Cape Verde as many ocean navigators had done before. While sailing ships often favor a strong tail wind, the wings of a heavy plane prefer the lift of a head wind.

After securing "The Tingmissartoq" for the night, Charles and Anne stopped for a courtesy call at the Portuguese Governor's Headquarters, where he provided them with assistance in supplies. The Lindberghs did carry two charts of the archipelago but they were not very familiar with its culture, people, or history and they struggled to communicate in French and expressed some anxieties about their sleeping accommodations. Anne noted that "nearly every woman had on a red bandanna, a ragged calico skirt and shirtwaist, and, wound about hips and abdomen, a wide band of material making a heavy belt. It seemed to me a strange place for a belt, until I realized that the band was exactly the right position to support the weight of a child if the woman were pregnant. And most of them were." Clearly they did not know the African roots of a Cape Verdean *pano.*

The Governor tried to explain some of the history and geography of the Islands by informing his guests about the 15th century discovery by Cadamosto of the Barlavento and Sotavento island (qq.v.) groups, as well as the harmattan season, but the Lindberghs had not done much homework in this regard and seemed more shocked than informed. Later, her diary reported that "It's boring here" in the Islands and their preoccupation to fly on was growing in intensity. In the morning of the third day, 30 November, the Lindberghs calculated that a more favorable course to Brazil would be made from Bathhurst, in The Gambia, which lay southeast of Cape Verde. Their stay in the Islands was at an end. A week in The Gambia and abandoning many pounds of heavy supplies they crossed the Atlantic westward and worked their way back to Flushing via South America and the Caribbean, finally returning to New York on 19 December 1933. In 1938 this adventure was recorded in the book of Anne Morrow Lindbergh, *Listen! the Wind.*

LITERATURE. The history of Cape Verdean literature can be roughly divided into three major periods. The first comprises the generation of writers who made up the classical school before 1936. The second period includes the writers, known as *Claridosos,* who emerged in the 1930s to form a school of regional literature. The third is the modern period since the

Claridosos. The first was based largely in Portuguese literary traditions; the second probed the uniqueness of Cape Verdean culture; the third stressed realism including African roots and revolutionary themes.

The literary generation of the classical period revolved around the *liceu* in São Nicolau (qq.v.) and included such writers as José Lopes, Januário Leite, Pedro Cardoso and Eugénio Tavares (qq.v.). The latter is best known for his renditions of the uniquely Cape Verdean art form, the *morna* (q.v.), which combines poetry, song, and dance to express the ''soul'' of the archipelago. During this period the first literary annual was published, *Almanach Luso-Africano,* in 1894 in Ribeira Grande, São Nicolau, as well as the first book of poetry, *Caboverdeanas* by Pedro Cardoso, published in Praia in 1915. Generally speaking, the classical writers followed Portuguese forms and did not directly address the Cape Verdean condition in their verse. However, Tavares and Cardoso were exceptions to this rule and even wrote in their native Crioulo (q.v.).

The modern period commenced with the publication in 1936 of the literary review, *Claridade* (q.v.), and included such figures as Baltasar Lopes, Manuel Lopes, and Jorge Barbosa (qq.v.). The *Claridade* movement gave birth to a new Cape Verdean literature that addressed the particular Crioulo experience and culture as well as the socio-economic conditions of the archipelago. Out of this period came the first Cape Verdean novel, *Chiquinho,* by Baltasar Lopes Da Silva (q.v.) published in 1947, the first anthology of Cape Verdean short stories, *Anthologia da ficção cabo-verdiana contemporânea* in 1960, and a wealth of essays concerning *Crioulo* culture and language. Of the better works in English on Cape Verdean literature see Burness, 1977, 1981; Ellen, 1988; Hamilton 1975; Parsons, 1923. *See also* AMARILIS, O.; BARBOSA, J.; CARDOSO, P.; CLARIDADE; CRIOULO CULTURAL ORIGINS AND SYNTHESIS; DA SILVA, B.L.; GONÇALVES, A.; LEITE, A.; LOPES, J. and M.; MARTINS, O.; MORAZZO, Y.; TAVARES, E.; VIRGINIO, T.

LIVESTOCK. SEE: AGRICULTURE; HORSES.

LIVITY. SEE: FUNANA.

LOPES, BALTASAR. SEE: DA SILVA, B.L.

LOPES, JOSÉ (15 January 1871–2 September 1962). Prolific poet of the first generation of Cape Verdean writers and legendary figure in São Vicente (q.v.) as the poet laureate of the classical period. Lopes was born in Ribeira Brava, São Nicolau (q.v.), one of seven children. At the age of ten he became an orphan and although he was able to attend the seminary for a time, by age 15 he was forced to leave as more family members passed away. From that time, Lopes was self-educated, mastering Latin, French, and English well enough to write verse in those languages. Under the influence of the poet Custodio Duarte, the literary talent of Lopes was cultivated. Lopes married Dona Isabel Ben Oliel of Boa Vista (q.v.) in 1891 but he left to live in Angola until 1894 when he returned to Boa Vista. From 1900 to 1928 he lived in Ponta do Sol, Santo Antão (q.v.). From 1928 until his death he resided in São Vicente, where he served as a school teacher while writing a number of weighty volumes of poetry including *Hesperitanas, Jardim Das Hesperides* (in Portuguese); *Ombres Immortelles* (in French); *Ode on England, Braits,* and *The Nurses of Hong Kong* (in English). In addition, his two-volume *Alma Arsinaria* collected his works in Portuguese, French, English, and Latin. These works earned him medals, awards, and international recognition as one of the great Cape Verdean poets. *See* LITERATURE.

LOPES, JOSE LUÍS FERNANDES LOPES (1948–). Cape Verdean Ambassador to the United States (q.v.). He was a student of history at the University of Classeca, Lisbon, and has a degree in agriculture from the University of Santarem. He also has M.A. degrees in international relations and development from Johns Hopkins University. Lopes was a member of the team which negotiated Cape Verdean independence in 1975. He was credentialed in the United States in August 1980 making him one of the most senior in the Washington diplomatic corps. He left the Foreign Ministry and he had sought to run as a PAICV (q.v.) candidate in the elections, but because of his long absence, he failed to meet a residency requirement for candidates. Now out of public office, but with his preference for economic liberalism, he presently serves as the President of PROMEX, an American export promotion company in Praia.

LOPES, MANUEL (23 December 1907–). Distinguished poet and writer of prose fiction who, with Baltasar Lopes and Jorge Barbosa (qq.v.), was one of the founders of the literary movement that produced the journal, *Claridade* (q.v.), in 1936. Lopes was born on the island of Santo Antão (q.v.) and educated at the University of Coimbra, Portugal. He returned to Cape Verde to work for Western Telegraph on the island of São Vicente (q.v.) but his job then took him to the Azores and finally back to Portugal. His writings focus on themes particular to the Cape Verdean experience and, as such, Lopes was instrumental in defining the regional literature (q.v.) of the archipelago. He has been the recipient of several distinguished literary awards and his works have been translated into a number of different languages.

His first novel *Chuva Braba* (Wild Rain) is considered a classic, as is his second novel, *Flagelados do vente leste* (Victims of the East Wind), which was the basis for the first Cape Verdean-produced feature length motion picture. The film carried the same title and was shot on Lopes' native island of Santo Antão. He also wrote a collection of short stories, which preserve some African elements of folklore such as trickster tales and the game of *ouri* (q.v.).

-M-

MAIO. (15° 10′N; 23° 10′W). Sixth largest island (269 sq. km.) in the Sotavento group of the Cape Verde archipelago. This relatively low (maximum altitude, 436 meters), sandy island lies just to the east of São Tiago (q.v.). Maio has the two main towns of Vila do Maio and Santo António, but the population is small. The island was not effectively settled until the early 16th century and its economy was based on livestock and slave (qq.v.) trading. The periodic droughts (q.v.) in Cape Verdean history have always had disastrous effects on Maio and the very limited amounts of water and grazing land have kept the livestock and human populations small. However, the population has increased slightly over recent decades.

Population of Maio

1580	50
1650	120
1720	250
1800	700
1900	1,900
1950	1,879
1960	2,680
1970	3,466
1980	4,098
1990	4,964

(Source: Duncan 1972; Cape Verde Censuses)

In the 17th century the administration of Maio was granted to João Coelho da Cunha to run profitably for the King. As early as 1643 slave ships from New England traded at Maio. American ships did not always come in peace, and coupled with weak Portuguese control, a pirate ship from Baltimore sacked the port of Maio in December 1818. Trade in salt was also an important feature of the Maio economy until about 1850. Salt was traded on the coast for slaves and to passing ships for manufactured goods. Since the working population was small, and Portuguese administration slight, some ships stopped at Maio and gathered their own salt supplies. With a 1,400 meter airstrip there was a colonial plan under consideration to develop tourism through the TURMAIO agency, but little progress had been made at the time of independence in 1975.

MALI. Following the collapse of the Empire of Ghana, the Empire of Mali entered its formative phase in the late 11th century. Mali's formal beginning occurred in 1230 when Sundiata (Sundjata) and his general Maridiata defeated the Susu leader Sumaguru. Sundiata ruled Mali from 1230 to

1255 and made Islam the state religion.

Mali's economy was based on trans-Saharan and Sahelian trade, especially in slaves (q.v.), salt, gold, and subsistence agriculture of the Sudanic crops. The most important group of Mande traders upon whom Mali was built were the Soninke-derived Dyulas (qq.v.) (sometimes known as Wangarawa) who were instrumental in the Islamization of Mali. Islamic conversion of the Malian ruling class and large numbers of the farming people took place between the 11th and 13th centuries. Mali was very hierarchical in socio-political structure including nobility, soldiers, traders, artisan castes, and slaves.

According to the Arab historian Umari, Mansa Musa related to the Governor of Cairo that sea-faring Malians had actually ventured to the New World before 1312. Under the rule of Mansa Muhammad (son of Qu) 200 ships of men and 200 of gold, water and supplies were sent. One of the ships returned to be followed by another 1,000 of men and 1,000 of supplies. These interesting reports have not been fully substantiated but were considered as a factor in the explorations initiated by Prince Henry and Columbus (qq.v.).

It was during the reign of Mansa Kankan Musa (1312–37) that Mali reached its greatest influence. In 1324–25, for example, Mansa Musa is reported to have made a flamboyant pilgrimage to Mecca via Egypt with an entourage of thousands of followers carrying gold gifts of astonishing abundance. By 1375 Mali was noted on European maps even though Europeans had still not traveled along the West African coast. At its peak, Mali included the Mandingo kingdom of Gabu (qq.v.) in an area between the upper Corubal and upper Cacheu (q.v.) Rivers, to the Gambia River, then all the way to the Atlantic coast through Wolof, Serer and Tukulor areas northward up the coast until just north of the mouth of the Senegal River.

Through the late 14th and early 15th centuries Mali thrived as it supplied as much as one-sixteenth of the entire world supply of gold. The Arab traveler and early historian Ibn Batuta visited Mali in 1352–53 and brought impressive reports about its glories to northern Africa and Europe. However, by the 15th century the fortunes of Mali began a long decline. The Portuguese were on the scene in the late 15th century and noted the state of hostility between Mali and its neighbors, but the Portuguese, who only wanted African products and slaves, could not be concerned with the outcome and gave no aid to Mali. In 1473 Jenne was lost to the Empire and this prompted Mansa Mahmoud I of Mali to send a message to King João II (q.v.) of Portugal requesting military aid against Fula (q.v.) and Songhai enemies. The Portuguese still did nothing so by the 16th century Mali's power eroded even further, although it is interesting to note that it was still producing more gold than the New World gold mines of the time. In 1534 another request for aid was directed to Portugal's King João III and ambassadors from Mali actually traveled to Portugal. Needing slaves and war captives, and not wanting to back a loser, Portugal again declined to provide any aid to Mali. This trend reached its climax in 1546 when Songhai invaders sacked Niani, the Malian capital, thereby bringing to an end this major West African empire.

MANCHUPA. SEE: CACHUPA.

MANDINGO (MANDING, MANDINKA, MALINKE, MANDE). The Mandingo and related peoples of Guinea-Bissau (q.v.) are representatives of the Nuclear Mande or Manding language family of the Niger-Congo linguistic stock. Manding is a major language of Africa and is spoken in one form or another in about nine West African countries with as many as ten million speakers. The Mandingo began to arrive in their present distribution in the mid-13th century with the expansion of the Empire of Mali (q.v.) to which they are all related to various degrees. However, even after the fall of Mali in 1546, the Mandingo kingdom of Gabu in Guinea-Bissau (qq.v.) continued on until 1867. Many Senegambians (q.v.) such as the Balantes, Banhuns, and Beafadas were either driven west toward the coast or were simply stranded in pockets within expanding Gabu.

During these times of Gabu's formation and internal migration in Guinea there were great numbers of slaves (q.v.) generated for trade to Cape Verde and other Portuguese commercial partners. Throughout the centuries of slaving, the Mandingos of Gabu had important trade centers at Farim on the Cacheu River headwaters, at Cacheu (q.v.) at the river's mouth, at Ziguinchor in the Casamance, and at Geba on the Geba River. These posts permitted contact with Europeans (e.g., Portuguese, Cape Verdeans, French, English, and *lançados* [q.v.]) and access to firearms in exchange for war captives/slaves.

By the time of the Berlin Congress (q.v.), Portuguese incursions to the interior were laying the groundwork for the colonial wars against the Mandingo in the early 20th century. The African dimension of Cape Verdean peoples has been supplied in part by the Mandingo people.

MANJACO (MANDYAKO). Ethnic group of the Senegambian (q.v.) cultural stock, Atlantic sub-family of the Niger-Congo or Nigritic language group. The Manjacos show very slight Islamization and some hierarchical organization which they may have acquired through contact with the Mandingos (q.v.). Their economy is based on shifting agriculture and rice cultivation. The Manjacos provided stiff and early resistance to Portuguese settlement between 1878–90, when they were among the first to try to halt the Portuguese penetration of the interior. They also fought vigorously in 1913–15 during the "pacification" campaigns of Teixeira Pinto.

MANSOA, RIO (MANSOA RIVER). The fourth longest river of Guinea-Bissau (q.v.), the Mansoa courses about 192 kilometers from the coast and is navigable for at least two-thirds of the way. Its route is roughly parallel to that of the Farim-Cacheu which flows on the north. The headwaters of the Mansoa are found to the east of Mansaba in the Farim *conselho* (q.v.). The Mansoa was used as a corridor through the coastal swamps for trade to the interior.

MARTINS, CARLOS "KATCHÁS" ALBERTO SILVA (8 August 1951–29 March 1988). Martins was born in the town of Pedro Badejo in São Tiago (q.v.) and lived part of his life in Europe before rediscovering his musical roots in Cape

Verde. Considered by many to be the "King (or Father) of Funana" (q.v.) Martins was a guitar player and founding member of the prominent group Bulimundo. Katchás became interested in the songs of *funana* musicians and sought them out, eventually adapting *funana* into a new style using keyboards, guitar, bass, sax, and drums. He was one of the first to form a *funana* band and is considered a musical pioneer in Cape Verde who helped to liberate and legitimate the African musical traditions which had been suppressed by Portuguese colonialism.

It is said that "he brought funana to the plateau" through the huge success of his band, Bulimundo, and his recordings since the 1970s. Although his music (q.v.) was rooted in folk traditions, previously viewed with disdain, its popularity made it acceptable to higher income Cape Verdeans of the Praia plateau and to Cape Verdeans from other islands. Many modern popular singers have been influenced by the musical tradition of Katchás, who died in a car accident in 1988. *See* FINAÇON. SUSAN HURLEY-GLOWA and RICHARD LOBBAN

MARTINS, OVIDIO. This Cape Verdean writer was born in São Vicente (q.v.) in 1928. There he finished secondary school and had further education in Portugal. He was a proponent of Crioulo-based literature (q.v.) and was a founder of *Suplemento Cultural.* He was especially active in the 1960s and 1970s and is well known for his work *Tutchinha* and *Caminhada,* which were collections of poems in Portuguese and Crioulo. This work was confiscated by the PIDE (q.v.) which was strongly opposed to independent Cape Verdean cultural expression. His poems are known in Europe, Brazil, and North America. Typical poems such as "Sing, My People," and "Rain in Cape Verde" are celebrations of Cape Verdean independence and cultural uniqueness.

MASTRO. The ceremonial raising of a *mastro* (mast) at the feast of a saint is a Crioulo cultural (q.v.) form deriving from their religious tradition. A structure is built which is supposed to resemble the mast of a sailing ship, with fruit, baked goods and candy attached. Children especially enjoy this ritual with the daring older ones attempting to climb the *mastro* in order to pluck off the goodies, while the rest wait for it to be lowered before scrambling to snatch the treats. The custom is typically carried out on the feast days of Saint John and Saint Anthony.

MAZURKA. SEE: MUSIC.

MENDES, FRANCISCO (''CHICO TE,'' 1939–1978). Prime Minister of Guinea-Bissau (q.v.), Mendes did not complete his formal education because he joined the PAIGC (q.v.) in 1960 at the age of 21. He was born in southern Guinea-Bissau in the village of Enxude. From 1960 to 1962 Mendes was the political commissioner at the PAIGC training program in Conakry. From 1962 to 1963 he was assigned to underground organizational work in the eastern town of Bafatá and from 1963 to 1964 he served as the political commissioner in the North Front. At the time of the first PAIGC Congress in 1964, Mendes became a member of the Political Bureau and in 1965 he was made a member of the Conselho de Guerra (q.v.) in the capacity of political commissioner. From 1970 to 1971 his War Council responsibility was military logistics. In 1972 Mendes was appointed to the CEL (q.v.) and, following the independence of Guinea-Bissau, he became the Prime Minister of the Permanent Secretariat of the nation. Mendes died in an automobile accident in Bafatá in July 1978.

MENDES, R. SEE: MUSIC.

MESTIÇOS (MESTIZOS). Those people of a ''mixed'' racial heritage and often incorporated into middle administrative and economic strata in the African colonies of Portugal. In a sense the majority of the population of Cape Verde may be termed *mestiço*. *See* CRIOULO CULTURAL ORIGINS; RACE AND RACISM.

MINDELO. SEE: SÃO VICENTE; URBANIZATION.

MINERALS. Cape Verdean salt has been processed for centuries as an important element in the slave trade and as an export in other foreign commerce. It is also used in the preparation of salted meats which are sometimes exported from Cape Verde. Most salt production has been located in Sal, Boa Vista, and Maio (qq.v.) islands. This export item had been irregularly developed by a Franco-Portuguese firm.

The other main mineral export of any consequence for Cape Verde has been pozzolana, a variety of porous volcanic ash used in making cement. The Champalimaud (q.v.) monopoly owned the Companhia de Cimento Pozzolana de Cabo Verde which had its main operations on Santo Antão (q.v.). Production has steadily declined and an original staff of 300 was put at less than 70 in the most recent count.

MIRANDA, LINEU (1912–24 January 1992). Miranda has been a Senior School Inspector for Santo Antão (q.v.) and was a long-time PAIGC (q.v.) activist who had been aware of the plan to land guerrillas in the islands, but was doubtful about its potential for success especially because of the drought (q.v.) conditions which prevailed in the year for which it had been planned. Because of his work in education Miranda was allowed certain mobility and managed to go to Lisbon in 1967 after the war had already begun in Guinea-Bissau (q.v.). Basil Davidson notes that he then went to see Amilcar Cabral (q.v.) in Conakry via Paris.

His travels were not sufficiently obscure and, although he just missed arrest by Spanish fascist police in the Canary islands, he was arrested in Santo Antão in October 1967. A public trial was held in which Miranda was supposed to be isolated, but his low-key manner, revolutionary optimism, and fundamental sense of humor was able to turn the trial into a celebrated discussion of colonialism itself and since he had done nothing but meet Cabral there was little substance to the charges. Nonetheless, he was found guilty and sentenced to the notorious prison of Chão Bom near Tarrafal, São Tiago (qq.v.). It was there he met other liberation fighters and Portuguese anti-fascists who were likewise incarcerated under poor conditions.

Miranda survived his imprisonment and was freed on 1 May 1974 in the wake of the Lisbon coup. After liberation he was made the first Director of the Cape Verdean Institute of Solidarity (ICS) which survives today. He was also elected a

Deputy in the first Assembléia Nacional Popular (q.v.) of Cape Verde. Miranda was especially well known in Santo Antão where he had founded the first primary cycle day school on the island. He was living in his favorite canyon abode at Ribeira Grande in Santo Antão until his death.

MONTEIRO, ANTÓNIO MANUEL MASCARENHAS GOMES (16 February 1944–). Monteiro was born in Santa Catarina, São Tiago (q.v.), as the son of Manuel Gomes Monteiro and Ernestina Varela dos Reis Mascarenhas Monteiro. He attended primary and secondary schools in Cape Verde and then studied law at the Universities of Lisbon and Coimbra in Portugal. He joined the PAIGC (q.v.) in 1969, but broke with it over policy in 1971. He continued his study of law from 1974 to 1977 as an Assistant at the Catholic University of Louvain in Belgium. He also became a researcher at the Inter-University Center for Public Law there.

In July 1977 Monteiro was appointed Secretary General of the Assembléia Nacional Popular (ANP) (q.v.). He held this position until 1980 when he was appointed President of the Cape Verde Supreme Court, where he served until 1990. In this position he participated in numerous international judicial meetings. These included meetings to adopt the OAU (q.v.) Charter for African Human Rights, the Addis Ababa Conference to Revise the OAU Charter, and other major conferences in Kenya, France, Portugal, and Holland.

In 1990 Monteiro became an independent candidate for President in the multi-party elections (q.v.) of January 1991 against the PAICV (q.v.). According to Cape Verdean electoral law the President must be unaffiliated with any political party. The President is elected by direct popular vote and not by the ANP. He, and the MpD (q.v.) candidate for Prime Minister, Carlos Veiga (q.v.), both won. Monteiro was elected President of the Republic on 17 February 1991; he was formally inaugurated in this role on 23 March 1991. As President, he continues to be active in supporting the movement for multi-party democracy in Cape Verde.

Monteiro still attends international conferences on human rights, such as the Strasburg conference in 1992. He also served on a high-level OAU mission to Angola which faced renewed civil war after the free elections there were opposed by the losing party. In 1993 his legal expertise was focused on a Colloquium in Belgium which dealt with the complex legal issues of constitutional transition in Africa. His dedicated, practical, and legal work in the national and regional movement for democracy and human rights has earned him the Portuguese distinction of the Grand Collar of the Order of Freedom. Monteiro will serve as President at least until the elections scheduled for 1995. He is married to Maria Antonina Bettencourt Pinto Monteiro and they have two daughters, Marisa and Liliana, and one son, Kwame Gamal.

MORAIS, LUIS. SEE: MUSIC.

MORAZZO, YOLANDA. This Cape Verdean poet was born in São Vicente (q.v.) in 1928 and was a founder of *Suplemento Cultural* which published literary (q.v.) and cultural works in the islands. Her early poems appeared in *Claridade* (q.v.), and she has published in *Arquipelago.* Having lived in Angola for a short while, she published a book of poetry, *Cantigo de Ferro,* in Angola just after independence there. Her poetry often explores the complex themes of Cape Verdean identity in the diaspora.

MORGADOS. Large private tracts of feudal-like land ownership for agricultural production. *Morgados* were transmitted under the principle of primogeniture. Injustices by the proprietary "lords" of the *morgados* were infamous. The *morgado* and *capela* (q.v.) systems of ownership were instituted when the royal colonization and trading companies were closed down. However, the *morgado* lands (known in general as the *latifundio* system) were officially abolished in 1863 and were further weakened after the 1876 land reforms. Likewise, extensive agricultural production by slaves had been sharply curbed when slavery (q.v.) was abolished in the Cape Verde Islands. While the *morgado* system has come to an end it resulted in a scattered pattern of land ownership which complicates the modernization of agriculture. *See* CAPELA; CAPITÃO; DONATARIO.

MORNA. *Morna* is the most popular poetic and musical genre of Cape Verde, and is regarded as one of the most characteristic and quintessential expressions of national culture and of Cape Verdean *saudade* (soul). The appeal of *mornas* extends to all classes and individual islands. *Morna* may denote an instrumental song, or an independent poem, but most typically it refers to a poem consisting of a series of quatrains set to music (q.v.). *Morna* is typically sung in medium-tempo quadratic meter by a solo vocalist, accompanied by stringed instruments such as the violin (*rabeca*) and the guitar-like *violão,* viola, and *cavaquinho.* A variety of formal structures may be used. Most typically, a melodic line is sung and repeated, and then followed by another phrase, which is also repeated resulting in an aabb pattern. This pattern may be repeated three or four times, occasionally incorporating an instrumental solo.

The origin of *morna* is obscure, although it appears to have first emerged in Boa Vista (q.v.) in the mid-19th century, possibly influenced by the Portuguese and/or Brazilian *modinha.* In its vocal style, instrumentation, and use of harmony, the *morna* is predominantly European rather than African in character. *Morna* texts, generally in Crioulo (q.v.), often reflect considerable sophistication. They are topical, frequently expressing sadness, nostalgia, longing for loved ones, and other serious or philosophical subjects. *See* BATUKO: COLADERA; FINAÇON; FUNANA; MUSIC.

PETER MANUEL

MOUVEMENT DE LIBÉRATION DES ÎLES DU CAP VERT (MLICV). The MLICV was formed in 1960 and immediately joined the FLGC (q.v.) in the same year. Its role was very minor and it represented little more than a paper organization. The MLICV was based in Dakar and was led by Mello e Castro. At times the MLICV called for the liberation of the Cape Verde Islands by armed struggle, but this tactic and goal was only enunciated, not practiced by the MLICV in the islands.

MOUVEMENT DE LIBÉRATION DE LA GUINÉE «PORTUGAISE» ET DES ÎLES DU CAP VERT (MLGCV). This united front organization was based in Dakar and was constituted primarily of the UPG of Henri Labéry (q.v.). The other two member organizations, the UDG and the UDCV, were of far less significance. The MLGCV joined with the União das Populações de Angola (UPA) in 1962 to form a front called the Frente Africana Contra O Colonialismo Português (FACCP). While little is known of the MLGCV it is established that the UPA was receiving funds from the American CIA at the time and that the FACCP was set up to rival the more militant FRAIN (q.v.) founded two years earlier. The MLGCV was a temporary affiliate of the PAIGC (q.v.) in 1960 and some reports suggest that Amilcar Cabral (q.v.) sought to establish unity with the MLGCV in 1958 but soon realized it would be impossible to find a common program.

MOVIMENTO ANTI-COLONIALISTA (MAC). The MAC was formed in Lisbon in 1957 by revolutionary intellectuals from Portuguese African colonies. The MAC was thus the precursor of the FRAIN (q.v.) which started in 1960 and the CONCP (q.v.) which began in 1961. The unity spawned in the MAC effectively persisted with common elements in the programs of the PAIGC (q.v.), FRELIMO, and MPLA until the present time.

MOVIMENTO DE LIBERTAÇõO DA GUINÉ (MLG). The MLG was headed by François Mendy Kankoila who based much of the organization on the Manjaco (q.v.) ethnic group partly residing in southern Senegal and northwestern Guinea-Bissau. In July 1961, while Amilcar Cabral (q.v.) was trying to develop the FUL (q.v.), Mendy launched attacks at Suzanna and at a Varela hotel. With these and other isolated acts, the MLG was the most militant member group of the FLING (q.v.). Mendy was anxious about any loss of autonomy within the FLING to which he gave only hesitating support just as he had to the FLGC which preceded the FLING. Neither the MLG nor the FLING had programs relating to the independence of the Cape Verde Islands. The MLG joined the RDAG in 1961, forming the FLG, which joined the FLING in 1962.

As a result of the military efforts of the MLG in 1961 the Portuguese staged a swift counterattack finally resulting in the breaking of diplomatic relations between Senegal and Portugal. Despite this result, the government of Senegal was lukewarm at best to the PAIGC (q.v.) at that time and preferred to support the MLG and, more broadly, the FLING which had some base of support with Senegalese Manjacos and was anti-PAIGC. The MLG also sought to divide Cape Verdean supporters from the PAIGC and it is alleged that it bribed PAIGC members to stimulate desertion. The MLG was dissolved in 1964.

MOVIMENTO PARA DEMOCRACIA (MpD). The Movement for Democracy can be understood with a view of its founder, Carlos Veiga (q.v.) and his contemporary political context. This includes the post-independence history of Cape Verde as well as global events. Veiga had pursued a professional legal career under colonialism, but after independence he returned to Cape Verde to work in public legal service. These rapidly evolved to his position as the Attorney General of the Republic under the PAIGC (q.v.) government by 1978. At this time, the Constitution (q.v.) only allowed for a single party state. In 1980, just before the PAIGC changed names to the PAICV (q.v.), Veiga began to have disagreements with governmental polices relating to the lack of democracy and centralized control of the party as well as limits placed on free enterprise. As a result he resigned to continue his private legal practice, but was still involved in counseling public legal projects. In particular, it was his experience with the Special Commission on Constitutional and Judicial Issues of the Assembléia Nacional Popular (q.v.) from 1985 to 1990 that kept him involved but without direct responsibility to the PAICV.

Playing upon fears of increased centralization of the PAICV in the ANP and upon some harsh measures taken against opponents and dissidents, a group within the PAICV began to formulate a political program allowing for broader discussion and participation. The PAICV leadership assumed it to be small and isolated. To increase this perceived isolation, the PAICV Prime Minister, Pedro Pires (q.v.), allowed the MpD to be formed and to compete in elections provided by a revision of the one-party Constitution.

Meanwhile, as a close observer of Cape Verdean politics, Veiga became a leading member of the MpD which he had started to organize in early 1990. In November 1990 the MpD nominated him as their party candidate for Prime Minister in the forthcoming elections promised by the PAICV democratization effort. Surprising the PAICV leaders, the national ANP elections (q.v.) in January 1991 ousted the PAICV which had ruled since independence in 1975. In the elections the MpD won 69 percent of the popular vote which earned it 56 seats in the ANP, while the PAICV won only 23 seats. Veiga has served as the Prime Minister of the Republic since February 1991. The elections also gave the Independent candidate for President, António Mascarenhas Monteiro (q.v.), an even greater popular vote, and he replaced the former PAICV President Aristides Pereira (q.v.). Thus, Cape Verde has joined a number of other African states in their drive toward political pluralism.

Various factors have been proposed to account for this victory including the strong role of the Catholic Church which felt restrained by some PAICV policies such as liberal access to abortion. The lack of armed conflict in the islands during the war of liberation meant that only the PAIGC/PAICV leadership had experienced this important front-line struggle, while other Cape Verdeans had positions opposed to the PAICV. The 1975 elections failed to include parties other than the PAIGC/PAICV so that the intervening years saw their complete control of power erode some degree of mass participation. Anti-state agitation followed by measures including the suspension of habeas corpus and brutality, were taken by the former government; these widened the gap. To its credit the PAICV demonstrated its commitment to the plural, democratic process by its willingness to step aside after the elections. This transition was accomplished without bloodshed or subsequent recriminations.

The collapse of the socialist system in eastern Europe also weakened the PAICV government. Aside from the international and regional context in which the Veiga government is situated, it has a significance much greater than one would expect for a small, insular nation. This is due to Cape Verde's chair on the Security Council at the United Nations (q.v.), and because of the large Cape Verdean constituency in southeastern New England. Newly elected Prime Minister Veiga visited Massachusetts and Rhode Island from 30 September to 6 October 1992, where he first raised the new flag (q.v.) of Cape Verde.

The Veiga government has endorsed privatization of the economy and has reversed some of the nationalization and state control of a wide range of enterprises by the PAICV. Human rights, expansion of a mixed free market political economy, and an irreversible commitment to plural democracy and human rights are also stated as guiding principles. Given the widespread diaspora population which contributes significantly to the Cape Verdean economy, the MpD also intends to have a more integrated and effective policy for these emigrants. A new constitution, flag, and national emblem have already been approved. The MpD intends to rule by consensus and local level empowerment and involvement. Future political debates will be balanced by the existence of the PAICV opposition. Veiga is the Prime Minister of Cape Verde at least until the planned elections for 1995.

MOVIMENTO PARA INDEPÊNDENCIA NACIONAL DA GUINÉ PORTUGUESA (MING). The MING was founded in 1954 but soon proved to be ineffective. However, it was the direct forerunner of the PAIGC (q.v.) which was formed in 1956. The MING was organized by Amilcar Cabral (later the founder of the PAIGC) and Henri Labéry (qq.v.) (later the founder of the UPG). The MING was formed clandestinely in Bissau (q.v.) by commercial workers and civil servants. There was no reference to the Cape Verde Islands in its initial program.

MUSIC. Dancing and music-making are an important part of daily life in Cape Verde for people of all ages. The blend of African and European traditions has resulted in a music culture like no other, and one of special pride to Cape Verdeans. It is common to see young children earnestly practicing the dance steps that elders perform. A good *festa* or celebration always has music and dancing. Although people have little spare money, there are many *festas* in Cape Verde. Typical occasions for them are Christian celebrations including saint's days, weddings, baptisms, Christmas, and Easter. In the country, music is often made by impromptu ensembles of family members and neighbors who get together for a night of singing and dancing accompanied by acoustic instruments. If the spirit moves someone to sing a favorite *morna* or *coladera* (qq.v.), he or she is welcomed to join the musicians for the song. For some important occasions, local musicians are hired to play for the event. In São Tiago (q.v.), a *batuko* (q.v.) group may assemble and sing and dance the whole night. At other times, music is played on a battery powered cassette deck or radio (prized possessions of most families). No matter how provided, music and an opportunity to dance must be present if a *festa* is to be a success.

On weekends in larger towns, dance clubs with popular bands fill up around 11 P.M. and are full of enthusiastic dancers until the wee hours of the morning, even when admission prices seem too high for many people to afford. Whether in the country or in towns, dressing up in one's finest and dancing is a favorite entertainment because it allows people to forget for awhile the difficulties that life in the islands regularly brings. When Cape Verdeans emigrate, their music remains an important symbol of ethnic identity in the new country, persisting longer than the active use of Crioulo language (q.v.). Social clubs and night clubs with Cape Verdean music open wherever there is a substantial immigrant population.

The traditional musics of Cape Verde can be viewed as existing along a continuum with European influences on one end and African influences on the other. While all of the traditional musics are unique forms that have evolved over the 500 years that Cape Verde has been inhabited, the musics from São Tiago and Fogo (qq.v.) have a stronger African influence while the musics from the Barlavento islands and Brava (qq.v.) have more resemblance to Portuguese folk musics. For example, the traditional folk music of the

Barlavento islands is played on the violin (*rabeca*), ten and six string guitars, the *cavaquinho* (a small four string instrument like a ukelele), string instruments common to Portugal (q.v.). The musicians generally emphasize melody more than rhythm and the vocal style and harmonies are similar to those found in Portugal. The primary musical genres are the *morna* and *coladera,* although forms found in European dance musics such as mazurka, waltz, march and contradance exist as well. Nearly all of these genres have been adapted by popular dance bands using electronic instruments, although the acoustic traditions continue to exist.

In São Tiago and Fogo, islands where there has historically been a large population of *badius* (q.v.), the music and dance traditions have more resemblance to some African musical forms. As in other parts of the African diaspora, the slave (q.v.) population did not originate from just one ethnic group but from many, resulting in a music culture that draws from diverse African traditions. The degree to which these traditions reflect any specific African music culture is perhaps less significant than the fact that many *badius* believe that their traditions come from Africa and tend to see themselves as Africans. The primary African-influenced genres of São Tiago today include *batuko, finaçon, funana,* and *tabanka* (qq.v.). All of these emphasize rhythm over melody, feature call-and-response structures, much repetition, simple harmonies, and an open, loud, singing style without the use of vibrato. The dances have more in common with African and Afro-Caribbean traditions than European ones, especially the *batuko* style of dancing.

Unlike the refined and highly literary *morna* texts, these genres have songs that are sometimes created on the spot through improvisation. Singers tell stories that provide social commentary and express the concerns of people living in the villages and countryside of São Tiago. There is often no sharp definition between the musicians and the public, since anyone may participate in the musical event by singing, clapping, and dancing. Rather than using instruments from the string family, *batuko* and *finaçon* performers traditionally beat surrogate drums in the form of rolled-up *panos* (q.v.) covered with plastic bags and held between the legs.

Tabanka members use conch shell horns and drums and include *batuko* ensembles at various times in their rituals. Musicians play *funana* on the *gaita,* a two-row button accordion, and on the *ferrinho,* a scraper made of iron used as a percussive accompaniment instrument. In the past, a one-stringed bowed fiddle called the *cimboa* was used as a solo instrument in São Tiago, but it has all but disappeared from popular use in the folk tradition. It had a strong resemblance to instruments found in West Africa and probably originated from there rather than from Europe.

As in São Tiago, the people from the other islands have their own special dances and festivals: Fogo has *pilão,* a musical genre somewhat similar to *batuko* that accompanies the grinding of corn with pestles in large wooden mortars in preparation for various feast days; São Vicente and Santo Antão (qq.v.) have a processional dance called *cola* or *coladera,* that is performed on their special feast days. Although there are differences in the folk traditions from the various islands, the *morna* and *coladera* are widely popular on all of the islands. The *morna* is often said to express the essence of the Cape Verdean soul. In contrast, the musics of the *badius* had limited appeal to Cape Verdeans from other islands before independence and were often considered coarse and primitive when Cape Verde was governed by Portugal. Since independence, *funana* and other musics from São Tiago have become symbols of the Cape Verdean resistence to Portuguese domination and have become widely popular, especially in the commercial form popularized by bands such as Bulimundo and Finaçon.

In the past, the limited recordings of Cape Verdean music featured the *morna* and *coladera.* The history of recorded Cape Verdean music is difficult to reconstruct since Cape Verde lacked the facilities to produce its own recordings and thus Cape Verdean artists were forced to record and produce their works in Europe or the United States. Recordings were usually made and distributed in small batches at the expense of the musicians. When the last record was sold, no more were manufactured. With no written transcripts or master recordings, historical continuity is sketchy.

While recordings exist of early acoustic string ensembles

playing *mornas,* the recordings of the singer ''Bana'' (A. Gonçalves [q.v.]), a much admired and imitated singer whose career stretches across four decades, and the group Voz di Cabo Verde, were the first to became widely popular in the 1960s, attracting a degree of interest in Europe as well as in Cape Verde. These recordings were influenced by Latin American and Brazilian rhythms and styles, particularly *cumbia.* The works of these musicians and other fine *morna* and *coladera* composers and interpreters established Mindelo as the musical center of Cape Verde. Somewhat earlier, the instrumentation in some Cape Verdean ensembles gradually changed from acoustic instruments to that similar to dance bands in Europe and America, featuring electric guitar, drum set, congas and claves, and woodwinds. The violin as the lead instrument was sometimes replaced by clarinet or saxophone, represented most clearly in the music of the band leader, composer, and arranger, Luís Morais. He has produced high quality recordings with his ensemble from Mindelo for decades.

Another group with a long history in Cape Verdean music is the band Os Tubarões. It was established in 1969 and has been one of the most popular bands in Cape Verde, producing five albums since 1976, with two C.D.'s soon to be released. The band changed personnel over the years but has been closely identified with the distinctive voice of lead singer Ildo Lobo since 1973. Although Os Tubarões is based in Praia, its members have striven for a national rather than regional sound. They try to remain close to the acoustic origins of the *mornas* and *coladeras* they play, in part by using drum set and saxophone instead of electronic instrumentation.

Since the mid-1970s, Praia was established as a second musical capital of Cape Verde. Local genres provided the inspiration for musicians who include Norberto Tavares, and the members of Bulimundo, and Finaçon (qq.v.), among others. These musicians developed the accordion-based *funana* genre into a high energy dance music that created a mini-revolution in the world of Cape Verdean popular music. Many of the artists make their homes in Europe or America; yet they remain very popular in Cape Verde. They make regular tours to the various Cape Verdean communities abroad and distribute their latest albums or C.D.'s.

The superstar of the Cape Verdean music industry is uncontestably Cesaria Évora (q.v.). She is an interpreter of *mornas* and *coladeras* from São Vicente with an unforgettable deep, rich contralto voice and a silky smooth singing style. Since 1990 she has produced a series of recordings that have received widespread popular and critical acclaim. Her C.D., "Miss Perfumado," has sold more than 100,000 copies, and is very popular in France where she sang at the legendary Olympia music hall in Paris. One of Cesaria's trademarks is to sing without shoes. The current success of her works is in part the result of her collaboration with several fine Cape Verdean composers and arrangers, namely, Paulino Vieira and Ramiro Mendes. Both of these musicians were born in the 1950s and received formal training in music and arranging. Vieira now lives and works in Lisbon. Mendes studied at the Berklee School of Music in Boston and now lives in Brockton, Massachusetts. Although they have recently become associated with Cesaria, they are both important musicians in their own right. Cesaria's recent successes have focused international attention on Cape Verde and, because of her popularity, more of the country's fine musicians may have an opportunity to reach a wider audience than in the past.

Still, the future of traditional Cape Verdean music is in jeopardy because Cape Verdeans often value diverse types of music, especially reggae, zouk, soukous, and popular music from Africa, Brazil, Portugal, and America, at the expense of their own. In a search for the new and modern, traditional Cape Verdean musical forms are pushed aside and replaced by musics from other countries. Fewer young people are learning to play acoustic instruments in the Cape Verdean style and genres like *batuko, finaçon,* and *tabanka* seem to be gradually disappearing. In a country that is struggling to meet the basic needs of its population, there is little money for programs supporting the arts, although there is a small school for music in Mindelo. Formal musical training is the exception in Cape Verde, but a few talented composer/ scholars including Vasco Martins and Eutroppio Lima da

Cruz (a former priest who is now the mayor of Boa Vista) are taking Cape Verdean music in new directions by using folk melodies for their inspiration in writing compositions in the Western artistic tradition. It remains to be seen whether the music that helps the next generations of Cape Verdeans define themselves will still be the *morna, coladera,* or *funana.* What seems certain is that music and dance will continue to be important to Cape Verdean self-identity.

SUSAN HURLEY-GLOWA

-N-

NHO LOBO. The ''(lazy) wolf'' of Cape Verdean folklore. *Nho Lobo* stories comprise a rich part of the Crioulo culture (q.v.) and oral tradition as the tales have been passed down through the generations. At informal gatherings, a storyteller would repeat the *Nho Lobo* stories, particularly for the children who would delight in their telling. Typically, the adventures of *Nho Lobo* contain a lesson about life to be learned by the young listeners.

NIGER-CONGO LANGUAGES. This large family of African languages is also known by the term Nigritic or Congo-Kordofanian languages; the classification is subject to various interpretations and organization of the various member language groups. In any case the Niger-Congo languages include the West Atlantic and Senegambian (q.v.) stocks as well as the Mandingo (q.v.) languages which are spoken in Guinea-Bissau (q.v). Even the Fula (q.v.) languages which also have Berber derivation have a basic origin in the West Atlantic group of the Niger-Congo family. In Cape Verdean Crioulo language (q.v.) and in a variety of other ways, such as through the *badius* of São Tiago and the *pano* (qq.v.) textiles, there are important cultural expressions which have their roots in the Niger-Congo language family.

NORTH ATLANTIC TREATY ORGANIZATION (NATO). At the conclusion of World War II the United States (q.v.) proposed the creation of a military alliance of the capitalist nations of the North Atlantic. The pact came into effect on 18 March 1949, the same year in which Portugal (q.v.) joined. While areas to the south of the equator were officially out of NATO's jurisdiction, Portugal's membership permitted NATO to contribute very significant military and economic aid to Portugal thus directly assisting the Portuguese with their counter-insurgency wars in its African colonies. Portugal carefully portrayed the African wars as part of a global anti-Communist campaign during an intense period of the Cold War. As such, all NATO members overlooked African aspirations for national independence seeing the African nationalists as simply pawns of the Soviet Union or China.

Before 1958 Portugal spent between 3–4 percent of GNP on the military which was similar to other Western European nations. By 1964 Portugal's "defense" requirements had reached 8 percent of GNP. In 1965 more than half of the state revenues went to the military. Portugal was supported mainly by West Germany and the United States through military loans and grants and by purchases of Portuguese colonial products.

United States aid to Portugal through NATO was measured in the hundreds of millions of dollars. Between 1949 and 1968 U.S. military aid to Portugal officially reached $349 million, but this does not include other bilateral agreements which eased Portugal's own hard-pressed economy. In 1972 alone the United States arranged financial assistance to Portugal of well over $400 million. The vast portion of Portugal's NATO committed forces were actually in Africa and NATO equipment, especially heavy artillery, armored vehicles and aircraft, not to mention U.S.-trained counter-insurgency specialists, all figured importantly in Portugal's prosecution of its wars in Africa from 1961 to 1974. *See* CAETANO; SALAZAR.

-O-

ORGANIZAÇÃO DE MULHERES DE CABO VERDE (OMCV). This political group is the women's auxiliary of the PAICV (q.v.) and was so-named in the wake of the 1980 coup d'état in Bissau which caused the PAIGC (q.v.) to be renamed as the PAICV. The former name of the OMCV was the União Democrática das Mulheres (q.v.). Essentially the objectives and policies to further the interests and needs of women (q.v) of the OMCV continue those of the former organization.

ORGANIZATION OF AFRICAN UNITY (OAU). This first modern Pan-African organization was formed on 25 May 1963 by the then independent African nations. The African Liberation Committee of the OAU sought to coordinate political and military support for the liberation movements such as the PAIGC (q.v.). From 1963 to 1967 the OAU sought to unite the FLING (q.v.) with the PAIGC to build a broader and more moderate unity. After 1967 it only gave recognition to the PAIGC as the sole legitimate political expression of the people of Guinea-Bissau (q.v.) and Cape Verde. The Republic of Guinea-Bissau became the 42nd member nation of the OAU when it joined in November 1973. The Republic of Cape Verde joined the OAU on 18 July 1975.

OS TUBARÕES. SEE: MUSIC.

OURI, OURIN, WARI. *Ouri* is one of the most ancient Middle East and African "store-and-capture" games derived from dynastic Egypt or the Levant. *Ouri* is considered to be the evolutionary forerunner of backgammon. This game is known by a wide variety of names, such as *mankala*, *ohwaree*, and *omweso* and is now played extensively throughout Cape Verde, the Middle East, Africa, the Caribbean, and among some Afro-American populations. The game is more complex than checkers but less complicated than chess and can be played with two, three, or four players. The object is to hoard defensively your own seed, pebble, or button markers, which usually number 48 or 60 to start. While in an offensive "seeding" play, the objective is to seize the markers of your opponents from their game board "territory." *Ouri* is played enthusiastically in Cape Verde and within Cape Verdean diaspora enclaves. A family's hand-carved wooden *ouri* board is considered a prized possession. *See* CRIOULO CULTURE.

-P-

PACKET TRADE. SEE: CAPE VERDEAN-AMERICAN EMIGRATION; ERNESTINA.

PANO. A unique form of untailored Cape Verdean textile which has been produced for centuries. *Panos* are woven from cotton fiber grown in the islands and are made on a narrow loom of Mandingo (q.v.) or Wolof style. Six strips (about 15–17 centimeters each) are sewn together to make a wider cloth of typically dark blue and white colors. This weaving technique is of Mande origin and reached Cape Verde through its trade with Africa. African weavers often use more than two colors, however.

The blue is from the urzella and indigo (qq.v.) dyes found in the Cape Verde Islands while the white is natural cotton. *Panos* are worn exclusively by women as a shawl or waist sash as part of the traditional costume and for folk dancing. *Panos* are wadded in a tight ball and beaten by the women to accompany the *batuko* (q.v.) dance chants. Mothers also use *panos* to carry their infants on their hips in a typically African manner.

Both the dyes and the *panos* have been important exports from the islands in the past. Higher value would be ascribed to those *panos* with more intricate designs in the weaving and better skills in sewing the strips together. The islands of Fogo (famed for the deep indigo *panos pretos*) and São Tiago (qq.v) had excellent reputations in the volume and quality of *pano* production.

Facing a relative scarcity of iron bars to exchange in the slave (q.v.) trade, the *panos* came to be a measure of value by the 16th century when they were used widely in barter exchange as elsewhere in Africa such as for the raffia cloths of the Congo. The local economy of *pano* production incorporated cotton growing, dyeing, spinning and weaving and there was a high price set for the sale of slaves who were skilled in weaving.

By 1680 two high quality *panos* were standardized in value as equal to one standard iron bar. Gradually individual Cape Verdeans were becoming successfully and independently involved in the slave trade. However, the Decree of 23 January 1687 proclaimed that the sale of locally-made *panos* to foreigners was punishable by death; indeed, selling raw cotton could face the same penalty. By 1721 the Portuguese still declared that the trade in *panos* was illegal, carrying severe penalties, in an effort to reassert the Crown monopoly in trade and to keep Cape Verdeans from dealing in this trade. *See* CRIOULO CULTURE.

PARCERIA. Colonial ''partnership'' sharecropping system, especially in Cape Verde. Some 26,000 *parceria* contracts were abolished by the PAIGC (q.v.). *See* CAPELAS; DONATARIOS; MORGADOS.

PARTIDO AFRICANO DA INDEPENDÊNCIA DE CABO VERDE (PAICV). This is the direct successor political party to the PAIGC (q.v.) which ruled in the Republic of Cape Verde until 1991. The PAICV was formed in January 1981, following the November 1980 Bissau coup which toppled Luís Cabral as President of Guinea-Bissau (qq.v.). With this breach in party policy and decision-making, the PAIGC in Cape Verde was renamed to symbolize its separate path despite the years of effort to unify the two nations, peoples, and parties under the single nationalist banner. The major policies and leading figures of the PAICV stayed the same as the former PAIGC. The PAICV pursued a program of non-alignment in international relations, with friendly ties to the socialist nations, and a large state-controlled public sector in Cape Verde.

From 1981 to 1991 the PAICV was constitutionally the ''partido unico'' (sole ruling party). Indeed, the lack of change in the PAICV ruling structure led to some notable defections such as Carlos Veiga (q.v) who went on to form the MpD (q.v.) opposition party, as well as the intrigue surrounding the death of Renato Cardoso (q.v.). The old guard also used charges of "Trotskyism" to justify party purges and repressive measures taken against the opposition especially the UCID (q.v.). To one degree or another, these policies and practices of the PAICV led to declining credibility and legitimacy. Seeking to recover from these problems the PAICV accepted revisions in the Constitution (q.v.) which paved the way for two-party elections (q.v.).

This resulted in the defeat of the PAICV which was replaced by the MpD as the new ruling party in 1991. PAICV Prime Minister and Secretary General Pedro Pires (q.v.) then became a member of the "loyal opposition" when the new Prime Minister, Carlos Viega (q.v.), was installed in this position. Aristides Pereira, the former President of Cape Verde under PAICV rule, has made some steps to distance himself from his defeated party. In addition, the PAICV Congress in September 1993 has elected Aristides Lima as the new Secretary General, but with Pedro Pires still playing an active role in party affairs. The MpD has taken a number of steps to delegitimize the PAIGC/PAICV by changing the national flag (q.v.) which had been the PAICV banner, by large-scale privatization and liquidation of public firms, by defending political pluralism, and by reducing the prominence of some national figures closely associated with the PAIGC/PAICV.

PARTIDO AFRICANA DA INDEPENDÊNCIA DE GUINÉ E CABO VERDE (PAIGC, or PAI). The PAIGC was the victorious nationalist organization based in Guinea-Bissau and Cape Verde which was founded clandestinely in Bissau (q.v.) on 19 September 1956. The PAIGC was the organizational descendant of the MING (q.v.) founded in 1954 by Henri Labéry and Amilcar Cabral (qq.v.). The main difference between the MING and the PAIGC arose over the inclusion of independence for the Cape Verde islands in the PAIGC, but not the MING. Also, there were more craftsmen and manual workers in the PAIGC than in the MING grouping. Labéry later went on to form the FLING (q.v.), a small, but persistent rival to the PAIGC, while Amilcar Cabral and his associates were the founders of the PAIGC.

As the PAIGC began to grow it attracted some port and transport workers who later helped to organize the União Nacional dos Trabalhadores da Guiné (q.v.) (UNTG) in 1961. In 1958 the PAIGC and these workers helped to organize a wave of nationalist strikes with a PAIGC membership of only about 50 people.

The independence of Guinea-Conkary in 1958 aided in stimulating an effort to hold a nationalist oriented strike of the Pijiguiti dockworkers in Bissau on 3 August 1959. To counter the nationalist demands and labor militancy the Portuguese soldiers and armed settlers reacted with 20 minutes of gunfire, killing perhaps 50 and wounding about 100 and subsequently resulting in the conviction of 21 persons for subversion. In September 1959 the PAIGC General Secretariat was moved to Conakry and in the following year the Portuguese began a more serious effort at arrests and repression of the PAIGC. The PAIGC responded in a period from December 1960 to September 1961 with an agitation program calling for a peaceful end to colonial rule by distributing some 14,000 tracts and writing two open letters to the Portuguese people as well as sending various documents to the United Nations (q.v.) with the same appeal. April 1961 saw the creation of the CONCP (q.v.) in Casablanca with the PAIGC playing a leading role in this organization which linked the struggle in Guinea and Cape Verde to those initiated in Angola and Mozambique. Toward the end of 1961 the PAIGC determined that a course of direct armed action would be the only realistic approach to bring national independence. In order to block this move the Portuguese secret police, PIDE (q.v.), arrested Rafael Barbosa (q.v.) in March 1962, the same month when the PAIGC staged an abortive attack on Praia in the Cape Verde Islands. In June and July the PAIGC responded again with acts of sabotage inside Guinea-Bissau. This escalation soon put Bissau under martial law with upwards of 2,000 suspected activists arrested and the Portuguese military strength reaching about 10,000 soldiers.

The years from 1959 to 1963 were carefully devoted to building a hierarchical structure of groups and sections united into 13 zones and six regions so that all activities could be closely coordinated. In January 1963 the movement entered a new phase of protracted armed struggle when it launched a series of attacks in the southern regions of the country. By July 1963 the PAIGC had opened a second front of military activity in northern Guinea-Bissau. By November Portugal (q.v.) made a feeble effort to conceal the colonial status of Guinea-Bissau and a special decree from Lisbon was issued saying that Guinea-Bissau had become an "overseas province," hence an integral part of metropolitan Portugal. This was a case of too little, too late, and the PAIGC continued to consolidate its gains to such a degree that, from 13–17 February 1964, the first Party Congress was held in the liberated zones in the southern front at Cassaca. Some of the notable positions taken at this Congress were: 1) an enlargement of the Central Committee from 30 to 65 members; 2) the establishment of the following seven departments: armed forces, foreign affairs, cadre control, training and information, security, economy and finance, and mass organizations; and 3) the formation of the Forças Armadas Revolutionárias do Povo (FARP) (q.v.) as well as People's Stores, and an expansion of medical and educational services.

In April 1964 the PAIGC engaged the Portuguese in an intensive military confrontation on the large southern, coastal island of Como. This 65-day offensive forced the Portuguese to withdraw 3,000 troops after losing hundreds. By 1965 approximately 50 percent of the countryside was under PAIGC control even though the Portuguese soldiers now numbered about 25,000. From 1965 to 1966 there was something of a military standoff until, in the later part of 1966, the PAIGC reintensified its efforts to gain the initiative, particularly in the newly opened eastern front which included parts of the former northern and southern regions. The December 1966 reorganization of the FARP helped to restore momentum to the struggle. The military headway accounted for political gains at the OAU (q.v.) which now gave its full support to the PAIGC in 1967, thus abandoning efforts to reconcile the FLING (q.v.) with the PAIGC. Other accomplishments of the Party in that year included the start of the Party's Radio Libertação and the restructuring of the original seven departments of the Central Committee by reducing them to the following five: control, security, foreign relations, national reconstruction, and internal organization and orientation. In 1968 the main thrust was the consolidation of the political organization and strengthening of the infrastructure in the liberated zones. On 19 February 1968 the PAIGC military forces stunned the Portuguese occupation forces by attacking the Bissalanca International Airport at Bissau. By February 1969 the Portuguese were forced out of Medina Boé in the south, thus giving the FARP units of the PAIGC a much broader area of entry. Throughout 1969 and 1970 more notable military and political reverses befell the Portuguese despite their claims of 614 PAIGC dead in 1969 and 895 killed in 1970.

In Rome, Italy, on 1 July 1970, Amilcar Cabral and leaders of the FRELIMO from Moçambique and the MPLA from Angola were given an audience with the Pope. As a strongly Catholic nation the Portuguese ruling class was enraged at this diplomatic victory for the liberation forces. In a futile and frustrated gesture, on 22 November 1970, a Portuguese raiding party from Bissau invaded the neighboring capital city of Conakry with the intention of overthrowing the government of Sekou Touré and killing the leading members of the PAIGC who then had offices based in that city. The abortive invasion failed after bloody fighting but served to underscore the frantic efforts to halt the spread of PAIGC control and influence. The Portuguese made another effort in the early 1970s to halt the PAIGC with the introduction of General Spínola's (q.v.) "Better Guinea" program which proclaimed certain minimal reforms. The PAIGC response in 1971 was even bolder attacks with rockets and light artillery against the main towns of Farim, Bafatá, and Bissau. The Portuguese claim for PAIGC dead in 1971 reached 1,257, the highest such statistic for the war and served to indicate the heightened intensity of the fighting. Revisions of the Portuguese Constitution in 1971 and the Overseas Organic Law of 1972 gave still more formal autonomy to the "overseas provinces" of Guinea and Cape Verde, but the pace set by the PAIGC was now beyond the control of the Lisbon authorities.

New anti-aircraft guns and small but effective Surface-to-Air missiles from the Soviet Union permitted the PAIGC to open competition for the airspace over Guinea-Bissau which had formerly been the exclusive domain of Portuguese helicopter gunships and deadly napalm and white phosphorus dropped by fighter-bombers. As a rule, the PAIGC was beginning to bring down two or three enemy aircraft each month by this time. In April 1972 a unique mission of the United Nations actually visited the liberated zones and the 848th sessions of the UN Decolonization Committee recognized the PAIGC as the only effective movement operating inside Guinea-Bissau. The observations and recognition of the Special Mission were endorsed by the 27th session of the United Nations General Assembly later in the same year. This was a major diplomatic triumph for the PAIGC's long effort to isolate and discredit Portuguese colonial rule. In August 1972 another first occurred with the elections in the liberated zones for 273 regional commissioners and 99 representatives to the PAIGC's Assembléia Nacional Popular (ANP) (q.v.) to be held in late 1973.

In an address in the United States, Amilcar Cabral announced that soon the PAIGC would declare that the national independence of Guinea-Bissau had been achieved, but, on 20 January 1973, this towering African nationalist and revolutionary philosopher was assassinated in Conakry in an intricate plot to take over the PAIGC and protect certain strategic interests of the Portuguese. The conspiracy had been well organized using PAIGC dissident elements, FLING partisans, and logistic and intelligence support from the Portuguese. While the loss was sharply felt, the organization that Amilcar Cabral had carefully built went on to greater achievements. In May 1973 "Operation Amilcar Cabral" resulted in the seizure of Guiledge, a large fortified base near the southern frontier. This was possible, in part, because of the introduction of the new anti-aircraft weapons, but especially because of the collective resolve of the PAIGC military organization to redress the loss of Secretary General Cabral.

From 18–22 July 1973 the PAIGC held its second Party Congress at Boé which elected Aristides Pereira (q.v.) as the new Secretary General, made certain revisions in the proposed Constitution (q.v.), enlarged the Conselho Superior de Luta (CSL) (q.v.) from 81 to 85 members, and created a Permanent Secretariat (q.v.) of the Executive Committee. This new formation was headed by Pereira with the Deputy Secretary General being Luís Cabral (q.v.); the two other members were Francisco Mendes and João Vieira (qq.v.). The July Congress put the last official touches to the preparations for the 23–24 September 1973 historic meeting of the First Assembléia Nacional Popular (ANP [q.v.]) which formally proclaimed the Declaration of State, adopted the constitution, and elected the executive organs of the state including Luís Cabral as the President of the 15-member Council of State, eight State Commissioners (Ministers), and eight Sub-Commissioners of State (Deputy Ministers). Immediately scores of nations around the world recognized the new Republic and by early October 1973 diplomatic recognition had been extended by 61 nations even though Portuguese troops still occupied the major towns.

Elsewhere in Africa, especially in Mozambique, the liberation movements were showing comparable gains and it was increasingly clear that the end was near for Portuguese colonialism. On 25 April 1974 the Portugese Armed Forces Movement (MFA) overthrew the colonial, fascist regime of Prime Minister Caetano and made General Spínola (qq.v.), recently returned from Guinea-Bissau, the new President of Portugal. The leader of the Portuguese Socialist Party, Mario Soares, met with Aristides Pereira on 15 May 1974, and negotiations for full independence were under way. By 27 July Portugal officially stated that it was prepared to grant independence and, in accords reached at meetings held in Algiers in August, the final details were determined. On 4 September the first representatives of the Comité Executivo da Luta (CEL [q.v.]) entered Bissau and on 10 September Portugal gave de jure recognition to the new Republic of Guinea-Bissau. Luís Cabral and Aristides Pereira officially entered Bissau on 19 October 1974.

Meanwhile, in Cape Verde, matters were more complicated as the PAIGC had had a different history in the islands and had not engaged in any meaningful armed struggle but had concentrated on clandestine political organizing. A number of rival Cape Verdean groups emerged and a climate of uneasiness prevailed through late September and into October until it was made clear in discussions, negotiations, demonstrations, and a general strike that the PAIGC was to be the sovereign political party in the islands. On 18 December 1974 a transitional government had been formed from members of the PAIGC and of the MFA. In early 1975 relations between Portugal and Guinea-Bissau became strained over financial matters and the PAIGC nationalized the Portuguese Banco Nacional Ultramarino. In this context of instability the moribund FLING movement was prompted to make another attempt at bringing down the PAIGC in a poorly planned coup d'état on March 21. The apparatus of the new state became more fully engaged with the 28 April-6 May Assembléia Nacional Popular held for the first time in Bissau, and the first meeting of the ANP since the Declaration of State in the southern forests a year earlier. On 30 June 1975 there was an election for representatives to the Cape Verdean ANP and, with this act, the islands became the independent Republic of Cape Verde on 5 July 1975. However, since the PAIGC program called for unity between the sister republics there were already many agreements which united the two lands in commerce, transport, education, and communication. Most importantly, the PAIGC was the ruling party in both countries although there were two separate national assemblies.

Notable events in 1976 as a result of PAIGC policy included the creation of the Guinean *peso* to replace the Portuguese *escudo* on 28 February and the Second Session of the Assembléia Nacional Popular from 22 April to 3 May as well as visits to Bissau from President Samora Machel of Mozambique and President Agostino Neto of Angola. On 15–20 November 1977 the PAIGC held its Third Party Congress. After some delays and about a year of meticulous and widespread preparation the central themes of this major event were unity between Guinea-Bissau and Cape Verde, economic development and political consolidation. The former Permanent Secretariat of four members was enlarged to eight, the CSL was increased to 90 members, and the new

CEL was expanded from 24 to 26 members. The four new members of the Permanent Secretariat were Pedro Pires (q.v.), Umaro Djalo, Constantino Teixeira, and Abílio Duarte (q.v.). The new thrust of the PAIGC was to form a vanguard political party which would organize, dynamize, and mobilize the peoples of Guinea-Bissau and Cape Verde.

Since the November 1980 coup d'état of João Vieira the two Republics have become separated and the PAIGC is no longer considered the ruling party of the Cape Verde Islands; it was replaced by the PAICV (q.v.) in 1981 and in 1991 the PAICV was voted out of office. The very high level of unity between the two lands which existed in the immediate post-independence period has been sharply reduced. *See* CABRAL, A. and L.; CEL; CSL; FLING; MENDES, F.; PAICV; PEREIRA, A.; PIRES, P.; VIEIRA, J.

PARTIDO SOCIAL DEMOCRATICA (PSD). This small splinter group of UCID (q.v.) was formed in the 1990s in Cape Verde by João Alem. It has never competed in elections or demonstrated any broad base of support.

PEREIRA, ARISTIDES MARIA (1924–). A founder of the PAIGC (q.v.), born on Boa Vista (q.v.) island where he attended the *liceu* (q.v.) before receiving specialized training as a radio-telegraph technician. Pereira was one of the organizers of the Pijiguiti strike in 1959 and he worked in Bissau (q.v.) as the Chief of Telecommunications until 1960 when he left for security reasons to join Amilcar Cabral (q.v.) in Conakry. Pereira was a member of the Political Bureau of the Central Committee who organized in Bissau and other urban areas. In 1964 Pereira was the joint Secretary General of the PAIGC and a member of the Conselho de Guerra (q.v.) after 1965. Following organizational restructuring in 1970, Pereira became a member of the Permanent Commission of the CEL with Luís and Amilcar Cabral (qq.v.). In this position his chief responsibilities were security and control, and foreign affairs.

Before the death of Amilcar Cabral, Pereira was the Deputy Secretary General of the Party, but after Cabral's passing, Pereira became the top political officer of the

PAIGC. Subsequent to the independence of Cape Verde on 5 July 1975, Pereira also became the President of the Republic of Cape Verde. In this position he maintained his commitment to social democracy and non-alignment and has often been a mediator among the non-aligned nations. After the PAICV (q.v.) electoral defeat in 1992 Pereira was replaced by President António Monteiro (q.v.). Pereira went into semi-retirement but continued to play a role as senior statesman in African affairs.

PEREIRA, CARMEN (1937–). Born in Guinea-Bissau (q.v.), the daughter of a lawyer she joined the PAIGC (q.v.) in 1962. Her husband Umaru Djallo was a party activist and when he fled to avoid arrest she stayed in Bissau (q.v.) to work as a dressmaker and care for her children. In 1964 she also left Guinea-Bissau to engage in full-time party assignments. In 1965 Pereira headed a nurses training delegation to the Soviet Union. As the liberation war progressed she became the Political Commissioner for the entire South Front. She was the only woman in the 24-member Comité Executivo da Luta (CEL) (q.v.) of the PAIGC and she was the head of the Women's Commission which operated in both Guinea and Cape Verde from 1975 to 1981. Pereira was the Second Vice-President of the Assembléia Nacional Popular (q.v.) in Guinea, and she was one of the 15 members of the Council of State. *See* UDEMU; WOMEN.

PEREIRA, DUARTE PACHECO. Pereira was a frequent 15th and 16th century visitor to Cape Verde and the African coast. He may have been at the site of Al-Mina as early as 1475 when he reported on a Flemish ship with a Spanish captain which took on a cargo of gold. A few years later this Portuguese pilot, explorer, and cosmographer accompanied Azambuja (q.v.) in the founding of Al-Mina in 1482. He was at Al-Mina when Cão (q.v.) sailed south from that fort. His glowing accounts of the great profits to be made from the sale of Portuguese goods and the return cargo of gold were an important factor in the decision of the Portuguese to build at that site.

As the commander of a supply ship in the 1480s and 1490s

he made numerous trips to Africa. Once Pereira was rescued by Barthólomeu Dias (q.v.) on his return from the Cape of Good Hope. Pereira later sailed to India. Between 1505 and 1508 he wrote *Esmeraldo de Sita Orbis*, a book of sea routes, in which he described the West African coast. He also gave details about coastal trade in gold, ivory, and slaves at Arguim at a time when Lisbon eagerly backed slavery (q.v.). For his long experience Pereira, of *fidalgo* social rank, was appointed Governor of Al-Mina from 1519 to 1521. However, when the flow of gold slowed from its former high of 240,000 cruzados per year, he was recalled to Lisbon for reassignment.

PERMANENT SECRETARIAT/COMMISSION. Within the Comité Executivo da Luta and the Conselho de Guerra (qq.v.) was found the Permanent Secretariat of the PAIGC (q.v.). Until 1973 the Permanent Secretariat was composed of Amilcar Cabral (q.v.), the PAIGC Secretary General in charge of political and military affairs, Aristides Pereira (q.v.), Vice Secretary General and ''Responsable'' for economy and security, and Luís Cabral (q.v.), ''Responsable'' for national reconstruction, health, and education. After the 1973 death of Amilcar Cabral and the Second Party Congress, the Secretariat changed its name to the Permanent Commission and was expanded to include João Bernardo Vieira and Francisco Mendes (qq.v.) as Secretaries of the Commission. The Commission handled the day-to-day decisions of the government and during the war all members were also members of the seven-man Conselho de Guerra (War Council [q.v.]). After independence the Commission was expanded again to eight members.

PETROFINA and SOCIEDADE ANONIMA DE REFINAÇÃO DE PETROLEOS (SACOR). These two oil companies have been the main suppliers of petrochemical products in Guinea-Bissau (q.v.) and Cape Verde. Both Petrofina and SACOR are affiliated with the Portuguese Banco Nacional Ultramarino (BNU) and are thus linked to the CUF (q.v.) through political alliances and interlocking directorates. *See* BANCO DE CABO VERDE; CHAMPALIMAUD.

PHOENICIANS. Phoenicians were masters of the eastern Mediterranean Sea as early as the time of Old Kingdom Egypt in the 3rd millennium BC. However, in the 1st millennium BC their voyages extended throughout the Mediterranean and by the 9th or 8th centuries BC they had knowledge of the Red Sea as well as the coastal Atlantic as far north as France and as far south as Morocco. It is reported by Herodotus that during the reign of Pharaoh Necho II (610–594 BC) a three-year exploration of the entire African coast took place with stops long enough to plant food for the next leg which kept Africa on their right for the whole voyage.

According to the book of Pomonius Melo, *De Situ Orbis*, the Phoenician captain Hanno sailed from Cadiz in 445 BC southward along the African coast until he reached the Red Sea on a five-year voyage. He passed the Fortunate (Canary) islands and then some small islands which he called Hesperias because of their westerly location a few days' sail off the coast. It is now clearly known that these were, in fact, the Cape Verde Islands since they are the first islands to reach after sailing south from the Canaries. On one voyage he reported seeing a large volcano off the west African coast, which one might consider to be the volcano at Fogo (q.v.). This smoke plume might be seen at great distance, and the fire of Fogo was noted as a useful navigational beacon by Christopher Columbus (q.v.) in Cape Verdean waters.

Also, there is speculation that the obscure stone inscriptions (q.v.) found in the Cape Verde Islands are Phoenician, but it seems more reasonable on several grounds to assume that they are 15th century Portuguese writings instead. Indisputable proof of the Phoenicians as the first to discover the Cape Verde Islands is not established, but one may consider this a strong possibility.

PILON, PILÃO. SEE: MUSIC.

PIONEIROS DE PARTIDO (PP). The Pioneers of the Party was a youth organ of the PAIGC (q.v.) during the period of armed struggle and afterward. It sought to educate children under the leadership of the Party. The PP acted as the political branch of the education (q.v.) policy in the liberated areas and at the Pilot School especially after 1972. Children from 10–15 were eligible to join and participate under the slogan of "Study, Work, Struggle." While the PP was relatively small in the begining, it was very active at PAIGC boarding schools (*semi-internatos*) and carefully cultivated youth leadership qualities within Guinea and in youth contacts at international youth forums and festivals. The organ of the PP, called *Blufo*, was published more or less quarterly and featured educational, cultural, and political articles and puzzles.

Since 12 September 1974 the main work of youth organizing was channeled through the Juventude Africana Amilcar Cabral (JAAC), which had chapters in most schools or neighborhoods. The JAAC concentrated its efforts on national reconstruction projects such as drug eradication, literacy campaigns, and general youth improvement. It was particularly targeted for work among urban youth who had not been integrated into the structures of the liberated zones during the war.

After the 1980 coup in Bissau (q.v.) the JAAC changed its name to JAAC-CV, but its form and functions continued to serve the needs and interests of the one-party state. With democratic reforms and the elections of 1991, the MpD (q.v.) has sought to create non-party youth groups and organizations to replace the JAAC-CV.

PIRES, GENERAL PEDRO VERONA RODRIGUES (1934–). Pires was born on Fogo (q.v.) island in an isolated village within the volcanic crater making up the bulk of the island. After school in Cape Verde he went on to Lisbon to study engineering where he met other nationalists from Africa. By 1959 he was already involved with the underground movement in Lisbon for the liberation of Portugal's African colonies. Being subject to military draft in the Portuguese colonial army, he deserted and fled to Ghana with the hope of meeting Amilcar Cabral (q.v.).

After joining the PAIGC forces he received additional military training in Algeria and in 1966 was sent to Cuba to be a member of a 30-man team to prepare for a two-pronged invasion of the Cape Verde Islands. This plan was never implemented. He served as the "Responsable" for Health and Education in the Southern Front and was the Commander for this region. Pires was a leading member of the Comité Executivo da Luta (CEL) and a member of the Conselho de Guerra (qq.v).

In 1974 Pires led the PAIGC (q.v.) delegation in London and Algiers which resulted in the independence of Guinea-Bissau. He was also the principal negotiator for the independence of Cape Verde on 5 July 1975. With the independence of Cape Verde, the first Assembléia Nacional Popular (q.v.) elected him the nation's first Prime Minister. His foreign policy was one of non-alignment, anti-apartheid, and regional peace and stability. Domestically he developed a program of ecological conservation, and fiscal accountability, especially to donor nations. In Cape Verde his policies of national reconstruction and development were widely regarded as effective. Pires was the Chairman of the Cape Verdean National Committee of the PAICV.

He was also able to convince American Congressmen that Cape Verde would not be used as a Soviet base thereby gaining critical U.S. aid and support. Some people give great credit to these pioneering achievements, while others, now in the MpD (q.v.), criticize his administration as too centralized and inherently undemocratic as a result of the one-party state and the military means which brought the PAIGC to power.

After the 1980 coup d'état in Bissau, Pires continued as the leader of the newly founded PAICV (q.v.). Through the 1980s Pires and the PAICV accumulated enemies who opposed him for being too close to the Soviet Union and for advancing extensive nationalization and land reform. As a result of such criticism the PAICV took steps to isolate the opponents within the party by expulsion and some of those outside the party were arrested. Due to these measures, the PAICV created more opponents, ultimately leading to pressure for pluralistic democracy rather than a one-party state.

In January 1991 Pires and the PAICV lost the first multi-party elections (q.v.) in Cape Verdean history to the new ruling party, the MpD. The peaceful transition of power was heralded around Africa and the world as a model to follow. Pires is now a member of the "loyal opposition." In

July 1992 Pires attended the Democratic Party convention in the United States. His formal leadership as Secretary General of the PAICV ended with the appointment of Aristides Lima (q.v.) to that post, but Pires is likely to play an important behind-the-scenes role.

POLICIA INTERNACIONAL E DE DEFESA DO ESTADO (PIDE). The major Portuguese fascist secret police organization. As early as 1957 the PIDE arrived in Guinea-Bissau (q.v.) to assist in intelligence, counter-insurgency operations, and especially widespread arrests of suspected nationalists. In 1961 an additional organ, the Polícia de Segurança Pública (PSP), was introduced to curb the anti-fascist and anti-colonial movements in Portugal and in the African colonies. In 1971 a contingent of 105 PIDE agents arrived in Cape Verde to infiltrate and break up underground operatives of the PAIGC (q.v.). By the early 1970s the PIDE had received such notoriety that it changed its name to the Direção Geral de Segurança (DGS).

POMBAL, MARQUIS DE. The Marquis de Pombal was the title given to Sebastião José de Carvalho e Melo who served as the Prime Minister of Portuguese King José I (1750–77). The Marquis was of lower level aristocratic birth and had served as a diplomat in the late 1730s. His administration can be characterized as relatively enlightened economic development coupled with increasing state despotism. The Pombal Laws of 1751–53 brought greater centralization of state powers, especially the repressive powers of the police. Under the Pombal administration there was also strong opposition to the liberal perspectives of the Jesuits.

His administration included expanded foreign trade, and more autonomy from English trade, but import replacement from a budding Portuguese industry. He founded a number of state-backed monopoly trading companies, most of which were failures. Of those *companhias* which were successful one traded Douro Wine, and another promoted commerce in Pernambuco-Paraiba. In 1755 he created the Companhia do Grão Pará e Maranhão (q.v.) for the development of these two states in Brazil. Relative to Cape Verde, the Companhia called for expanded slave (q.v.) trade to the Guinea coast to meet the labor needs through substantial imports of slaves. This company persisted until 1778.

An assassination attempt against King José in 1758 resulted in the 1759 expulsion of the Jesuits whom he accused of involvement and who had allegedly opposed him. In 1760 the Marquis instituted a "reform" of the kingdom's police. In 1761 he founded the Royal Treasury and formally abolished slavery in Portugal (q.v). Contributing to wider literacy and publishing, he launched the Royal Printing Press in 1768, but this was coupled with vigilant political censorship. In Cape Verde, in 1769 he arranged for the permanent transfer of power to Praia from Ribeira Grande, and he introduced his "Law of Good Reason" which, in the name of Enlightenment, gave more restrictions to the feudalists. His reforms in education, the university system and his creation of a more secular state were likewise significant. His attacks against the Jesuits were renewed in 1773 when their order was formally dissolved.

Thus, the liberal economic policies were matched with a carefully controlled enlightenment, increasingly centralized and repressive police and state structures, intensified African slavery, a decline of the feudal relations which had prevailed and the beginning of a more powerful state bureaucracy. The Marquis de Pombal represented a major turning point in Portugal's history and he set it on the path leading substantially to the present.

POPULATION. SEE: DEMOGRAPHY.

PORTUGAL. In 1143 Portugal broke away from the Spanish monarchy and established its own king under Dom Henriques. From 1384 to 1910 the House of Aviz (Knights of Calatrava) was the royal ruling lineage. Between 1420 and 1470 Portugal was absolute master of the seas and, under the influence of João II, Prince Henry's (qq.v.) significant navigational achievements and exploration of Africa took place. The coast of Guinea was reached in the 1440s and the Cape Verde Islands in the 1460s. In West Africa, Portugal's dominance declined rather quickly to the French, English, and Dutch through the following centuries, but Portugal continued to be a major supplier of slaves (q.v.) to the New World, especially to Brazil until the late 19th century. From 1580 to 1640 Portugal was ruled under the Spanish Crown. The repression known under the Spanish Inquisition resulted in some additional migration to the Cape Verde Islands by political exiles and Jews (q.v.) from Portugal.

In 1656 private Cape Verdean tax collection was eliminated and a direct officer of the Portuguese Crown was appointed to strengthen Portugal's hold on the islands and along the African coast. Throughout the 17th and 18th centuries Guinea-Bissau (q.v.) and Cape Verde continued to supply slaves to the New World through the services of Luso-African traders (*lançados* [q.v.]) on the coast. In 1836 Portugal officially ended the slave trade, but it continued for several more decades. In 1868 England yielded its claims on Bolama (q.v.) to Portugal and, following the 1884–85 Berlin Congress (q.v.), Portugal and France agreed on the southern and northern borders of Guinea-Bissau. At the close of the 19th century Portugal was virtually bankrupt and the monarchy sought dictatorial powers to make certain reforms. Following the assassination of the King and Crown Prince in 1908 and a popular revolt in 1910, the monarchy was abolished and the House of Bragança was banished. The Republican government prevailed from 1911 until 28 May 1926, when a military putsch overthrew the democratic republic and installed the fascist Estado Novo government. A case of resistance to the fascist government is recorded in Guinea-Bissau in 1931 with a month-long revolt of deported politicians.

From 1886 to the 1930s the Portuguese conducted military expeditions of ''pacification'' against most of the coastal peoples of Guinea-Bissau. The Colonial Act of 1933 brought Portugal's relations with Africa into the Portuguese Constitution and were maintained until the 1974 revolution. In 1963 the nationalist movement in Guinea, led by the PAIGC (q.v.), began a protracted armed struggle which paralleled those in Angola and Mozambique. As a result of these wars and economic and political contradictions inside Portugal, the Armed Forces Movement (MFA) overthrew the dictatorship on 25 April 1974 and thereby brought an end to Portuguese fascism. Amidst considerable political instability in Portugal itself, the question of colonialism had to be resolved. During the second half of 1974, conservatives still were hopeful that Cape Verde could be persuaded to keep a special relationship with the colonial power, but independence was to be complete.

Indeed, the change of power in Lisbon was a consequence of the wars in Africa and thus it led directly to the independence of Guinea-Bissau on 24 September 1974 and of Cape Verde on 5 July 1975. However, both countries have maintained close and vital economic ties with Portugal since independence. Portugal is Cape Verde's primary trading partner (39.9 percent of imports and 62.5 percent of exports in 1981). Cape Verde's main export, its people, have settled in large numbers in Portugal where more than 30,000 Cape Verdeans have emigrated just since the beginning of the drought (q.v.) of 1968. *See* AFONSO, D.; AZAMBUJA, D.; AZURARA, G.; CAETANO, M.; DEGREDADOS; DE NOLI, A.; GOMES, D.; HENRY; JEWS; LANÇADOS; NATO; PIDE; POMBAL; SALAZAR, A.; SLAVERY; SPÍNOLA, A.; TARRAFAL; TRADE.

PRAIA. SEE: SÃO TIAGO; URBANIZATION.

PRINCIPE. SEE: SÃO TOMÉ.

-R-

RACE AND RACISM. While anthropologists and others have long noted variations in human types, the 19th century classification—Negroid, Caucasoid, and Mongoloid—has long shown its hopeless inadequacies with even supposedly homogeneous populations. For the population of Cape Verde, where merging and blending has been the central theme, such a classification is also "in the eyes of the beholder" and has little scientific validity or usefulness. The phenotypes of skin color, hair texture, and nose shape obscure the less obvious genetic characteristics such as blood type, resistance to specific diseases, or internal anatomical structures.

The top colonial officials of Cape Verde were typically of a lighter complexion relative to the light tan, darker tan, brown, and darker brown majority. As such the rulers were termed *Brancos* (Whites) in Portuguese. The Moorish, Jewish, and Mediterranean diversity which is found deeply embedded in Portugal's racial inheritance is overlooked and *Brancos* in positions of power is the essential feature. This minority faced a majority of *Pretos* (Blacks) who at the very beginning were almost all slaves (q.v.), with some exceptions. Quickly a population of *Mestiços* (q.v.) emerged as the majority. *Mestiços* are also known as *Mulatoes*, or *Mistos*, and *Pretos* (or *Blacks*) were those of African origin such as Papeis, Balantas, Bijagos, Jalofas, Felupes, Fulas (q.v.), Mandingos (q.v.), and Manjacos (q.v.).

Percentage of "Racial" Composition of Cape Verde

Year	*"White"*	*"Mestiço"*	*"Black"*
1550	1.96	69.61	28.38
1930	3.98	59.80	36.27
1936	3.89	75.23	20.86
1940	3.19	62.47	34.34

(Sources [or calculated from data provided]: 1582 Carreira 1983:298–299; 1807, 1869 Meintel 1984:24; 1930–1940 Cape Verde Censuses; 1950, Duncan 1972:195)

In some Cape Verdean slave records one finds observations about ethnic origins and various features deemed of significance. Color was most often reported simply as *preto*(*a*) or black, but there are many who are recognized as *preto fula*, or simply *fula* colored, with reference to the somewhat lighter complexion of the interior Fula people who had figured among the slaves while the Mandingo kingdom of Gabu was in power, but Fulas were rare in the 19th century slave lists. Colors could also take the reference of *pardo*(*a*) or brown, and *mulato*(*a*), or *mulato*(*a*) *claro*(*a*) (light tan) or *mulato*(*a*) *securo*(*a*) (dark tan). If this were not sufficient, the complex system of racial taxonomy could then turn to types of noses which might be *chato* (flat) or *muito chato* (very flat), while faces (*rostos*) were *arab fula* (like a Berber or Moor), or *rosto comprido* (long), or *rosto redondo* (round). Stature (*estatura*) might be noted as *regular, medianna, robusto* (strong), *alto* (tall), or *picado* (smallish). Other notable features were also reported such as *aleijado* (crippled), *coxo* (limping), *maneta* (one handed), *bexigosa* (pockmarked), and, *pescoco* (thin-necked). Note was also made of hair types including the *cabeca seca* (dry or wiry headed), the *cabo crespo* (frizzy hair), and *cabo encrespado* (curly hair). In studies in Brazil and Lusophone African countries some have easily counted a score of terms, while others making finer distinctions have surpassed 100 subtle differences.

In Cape Verde the system of racial taxonomy was confounded by higher levels of wealth, power, educational status, and class which "lightened" one's appearance, while poverty, uncouth behavior, and illiteracy "darkened" it. Complicating Cape Verdean self-identity further was the legal status *assimilado* (q.v.), as well as negative colonial images of Africanity, and seeing that some Cape Verdeans served as strategic intermediaries in the colonial system as local administrators and functionaries in all parts of the Luso-African world. In these complex and even contradictory ways, Cape Verdeans, especially those in top positions of administration, were trapped in a system in which they might be both victims and victimizers. *See* CLASS STRUCTURE; CRIOULO CULTURAL ORIGINS.

RASO. SEE: BRANCO AND RASO ISLETS

REBELADOS. A religious movement in the early 1960s originating among peasants in remote areas of São Tiago (q.v.) in rebellion against the attempts of Portuguese Catholic missioniaries to control the religious practices of the native population. The *rebelados* rejected the authority of priests and would perform their own traditional baptisms, weddings, and other rituals. Followers worked the land communally, refused to deal with money, and forbade the killing of living creatures. When, during a government anti-malaria campaign, they would not allow their homes to be fumigated, the colonial authorities began to see their movement as a threat. The leaders were subsequently arrested, interrogated, and banished to other islands. *See* BADIUS.

REIS, CARLOS. Long-standing PAIGC (q.v.) supporter and Minister of Education in Cape Verde under the PAICV (q.v.) administration. In 1986 he served as the Ambassador to Lisbon.

RELIGION. Although the inhabitants of Cape Verde are overwhelmingly followers of the Catholic religion, a Protestant sect, the Church of the Nazarene, was introduced in Brava (q.v.) in the early 1900s by emigrants returning from the United States who were successful in converting a significant number to their faith. In collaboration with another sect, the Sabbatarians, they built two Protestant churches and began to translate the Gospels into Crioulo (q.v.). Some of the converts were drawn to these evangelical groups out of disillusionment with the corruption of the Catholic Church under colonialism. The *rebelado* movement actively resisted some teachings of the Church. All of the larger islands have several Catholic churches and these have roots going back to the earliest times in the islands and on the Guinea coast where the authority of the Church also lay. As of 1982, 297,304 people (98 percent of the total population) were considered to be of the Roman Catholic faith, while the two Protestant groups represented about 2 percent. In centuries gone by there was also a Jewish (q.v.) presence in the islands.

RESISTANCE. Most of the history of Cape Verde included the direct administration of the coastal regions in which the African inhabitants made enduring efforts to resist Portuguese penetration and slaving. While there was critical African collaboration with the slave trade (q.v.) there was also intense resistance against the Portuguese *lançados* and their *grumettas* (qq.v.). After slavery ended in the 19th century, the Berlin Congress (q.v.) stimulated further attempts at territorial conquest of Africa which were met with numerous local uprisings especially in Cacheu and Bissau (qq.v.). These were countered with intensive military activity and brutal "pacification" campaigns in the late 19th and early 20th centuries. The highest expression of African and Cape Verdean resistance was seen in the successful war of national liberation led by the PAIGC (q.v.) (1963–74) which resulted in the independence of Cape Verde. In the islands, the oppressive and confined circumstances did not allow for sustained revolt, but there are numerous examples of tax revolts, flight to the interior, protests, petitions, strikes, resistance of the *badius* and *rebelados* (qq.v.), and demonstrations and agitation led by the PAIGC.

ROMBOS (or SECOS) ISLETS (14° 58′N; 20° 40′W). The small islets of Grande, Luís Carneiro, Sapado and Cima consitute the main members of the Rombos islets in the Sotavento (q.v.) group of islands in the Cape Verde archipelago. These lie to the north of Brava (q.v.) and are uninhabited.

-S-

SACOR. SEE: PETROFINA.

SAILING VESSELS. Ocean-going craft were absolutely central to the discovery, development, piracy, slavery, economy, whaling, migration (qq.v.), and even shipwrecks of Cape Verde. The earliest ships included modest dugout canoes on the Guinea coast and perhaps the *triremes* of the Phoenicians (q.v.) as well as the *barcas* and *caravelas* of the 15th and 16th century Portuguese. These early forms often used galley rowers and lateen sails.

The historian Richard Bailyn states that the first Yankee trader had reached the Cape Verde islands as early as 1643. By the 18th and 19th centuries trans-Atlantic commerce became regularized in the form known as the Atlantic or Triangle Slave Trade.

Ocean-going craft were largely defined by the rigging patterns. According to the Kendall Whaling Museum, a ship was three-masted with square-rigged yards; brigs were two-masted and were square-rigged; barks were three-masted, square-rigged on the forward two, and boom-rigged on the mizzen mast; and schooners were two or three-masted, with all mainsails gaff-rigged. For additional trans-Atlantic speed, topsails were sometimes added to schooners. All of these craft had one to three jib sails.

In M. Halter, 1993, *Between Race and Ethnicity* (Appendix, pages 179–86) data from New Bedford Public Library are presented on ship arrivals from Cape Verde to New Bedford from 1860 to 1920. From these data the following calculations were made. Of 106 vessels arriving between 1860 and 1899, 78 were schooners, 19 were barks, 9 were brigs, and there were no steam powered vessels. For this first period the average number of passengers per vessel was 27. Meanwhile, of 230 vessels arriving between 1901 and 1920, 165 were schooners, 23 were barks, 11 were brigs, and there were 15 steam vessels arriving. For this second period the average number of passengers per vessel was 75. If the carrying capacity of steamers is singled out, the 15 reported steam ships carried an average of 206 passengers. These data clearly show the powerful role of the steam age displacing the large sailing ships. However, in small-scale Cape Verdean commerce, the smaller costs of operating a schooner kept the smaller craft quite economical in years to come. One of the most famous schooners in the Cape Verdean packet trade, was the *Ernestina* (q.v.), which sailed the Atlantic engineless to Rhode Island until the 1960s.

SAL (16° 45′ N; 22° 55′ W). The third smallest (216 sq. km.) island of the Barlavento (q.v.) group of the Cape Verde archipelago. Sal is generally a low, sandy island with its maximum altitude of only 406 meters. Its current population is about 7,500 people with the largest number at the Espargos-Preguça market town of about 5,000. The village of Palmeira lies on the west coast, and Santa Maria is found on the extreme south of this narrow island. At Santa Maria there is a fish processing factory and salt works. Sal, as well as other members of the archipelago, may have been known to salt-seeking "Moors" before Portuguese "discovery."

The first settlement was by slaves from Boa Vista (q.v.),

but this was not significant until the late 17th century when the demand for salt and livestock had been intensified by coastal slaving (q.v.) at this time and into the 18th century. The island was a common stop for ships in the area to get a cargo of salt for ballast and trade at little or no cost. In the early 1970s the airport at Sal was expanded to become the largest in the archipelago and can accommodate the 747-type of commercial aircraft. Tourism was boosted at this time by the Belgian-Portuguese firm DETOSAL which has 70 beds in beach hotels. Water supply remains a serious problem and agriculture (q.v.) in Sal is almost impossible. For health and hygiene purposes a desalinization plant supplies needed water. The main sources of wage work on the island are related to the airport, tourism, the *salinas* (salt pans), and the petroleum storage facility.

Population of Sal

1890	539
1927	672
1930	764
1940	1,142
1950	1,813
1960	2,626
1970	5,505
1980	7,500
1990	7,715

(Source: Duncan 1972; Cape Verde Censuses)

SALAZAR, ANTÓNIO DE OLIVEIRA (1889–27 July 1970). Following the overthrow of the Portuguese Crown and instability of the Republican government, Salazar came to be the Prime Minister of Portugal (q.v.) in 1932. In 1933 Salazar and Marcelo Caetano (q.v.) were the chief architects of the absolutist Portuguese constitution and of the Estado Novo policy which maintained fascist control of industry, labor, and the press in Portugal and in its African colonies. Their use of the PIDE (q.v.) and domestic police as well as Portugal's membership in NATO (q.v.) allowed them to maintain decades of repression at home and in the colonies.

In Cape Verde the prison camp of Tarafal (q.v.) was notorious during this period. Salazar served until he was incapacitated by a stroke in 1968, when Caetano replaced him as Prime Minister.

SANTA LUZIA (16° 45′ N; 24° 45′ W). The smallest (35 sq. km.) of the Barlavento (q.v.) group of the Cape Verde archipelago. Santa Luzia is rather low (maximum altitude 395 meters) and lies to the southeast of São Vicente (q.v.). The island was not inhabited until the 17th century when it was granted to Luís de Castro Pireira. The island has functioned mainly for livestock (q.v.) raising when rains have been sufficiently favorable.

SANTO ANTÃO (17° 5′ N; 25° 10′ W). The second largest (779 sq. km.) and northernmost island in the Cape Verde archipelago and largest member of the Barlavento (q.v.) group. Santo Antão is rocky and mountainous with its two principal peaks reaching 1,980 meters and 1,585 meters. There are permanent sources of water for São Vicente (q.v.) lying nearby to the southeast. The main town and port is Porto Novo; other towns include Ribeira Grande, Vila Maria Pia, Pombas, Ponta da Sol, and the villages of Ribeira da Cruz, Janela, Sinagoga, and Tarrafal. Santo Antão was first settled in the early 1500s especially by families from Madeira. Rock cut inscriptions (q.v.) found near the town of Janela have long been a puzzle to the historians of Cape Verde.

Early settlers also included exiled Portuguese Jews (q.v.), who named one town in Santo Antão, Sinagoga, which was later transformed into a leper colony, since virtually abandoned. Jewish cemeteries are reported at Ponta do Sol, the site of the island's only airstrip. In the 17th century the administration and ownership of Santo Antão was granted to the Count of Santa Cruz. More significant, settlers and slaves (q.v.) arrived in the late 17th and again in the late 18th centuries, but these were mainly from the other islands. Exports from Santo Antão have included *grogga* (q.v.) (rum), slaves, livestock, and the mineral (q.v.) pozzolana for making cement.

Population of Santo Antão

1890	24,547
1910	33,838
1927	25,936
1930	23,973
1940	35,930
1950	27,947
1960	34,598
1970	47,200
1980	43,198
1990	43,845

(Source: Duncan 1972; Cape Verde Censuses)

Approximately 17 percent of the population of the archipelago resides in Santo Antão, which has fallen by 4,000 since 1980 to 43,198 inhabitants. Since independence the PAICV (q.v.) has built new roads, irrigation canals, and other water conservation projects as well as planting 30,000 coffee plants as a cash crop and 50,000 new trees.

SÃO NICOLAU (16° 35′ N; 24° 15′ W). The fifth largest island in the Cape Verde archipelago and central member of the Barlavento (q.v.) group. São Nicolau is of average size (343 sq. km.), its terrain is rocky but not exceptionally high, with the two main peaks at 1,305 meters and 663 meters. The narrow shape of the island has caused the main villages such as Preguiça, Castilhano, and Carrical and its 1,400-meter airstrip to be located on the immediate coast, although the main town, Villa da Ribeira Brava is located in an interior valley.

Several relatively permanent streams attracted settlement in the early 16th century especially by families from Madeira and their slaves (q.v.), largely from Guinea. The European population of today is quite small. Relatively productive agriculture (q.v.) and livestock raising attracted further settlement in the 17th century, when São Nicolau and São Vicente (q.v.) were jointly under the administration granted to the Marquis de Gouveia. From 1876 to 1917 a seminary (*liceu* [q.v.]) functioned on the island to train priests and teachers. In addition it served as something of a center of scholarly life for the archipelago. Recently the PAICV (q.v.) built a new water works, constructed new rural service centers and has created some 400 new jobs.

Population of São Nicolau

1890	12,425
1927	14,519
1930	10,753
1940	14,827
1950	10,316
1960	13,894
1970	16,308
1980	13,572
1990	13,557

(Source: Duncan 1972; Cape Verde Censuses)

SÃO TIAGO. (15° 5′ N; 23° 38′ W). São Tiago is the largest island (851 sq. km.) of the Cape Verdean archipelago. It is rocky and mountainous with several permanent sources of fresh water. The present capital is Praia (25,000 population) on a beach from which it draws its name. The former capital was at Ribeira Grande now known for the ruined city and fort of Cidade Velha.

São Tiago was first noted by the Portuguese in May 1460 by the ships of António De Noli and Diogo Gomes (qq.v.). Within a few years the first permanent settlers from the Algarve went to São Tiago and founded Ribeira Grande as the first capital. A commerce in slaves (q.v.) grew to develop the island as it became central to the island's export economy. By 1466 settlers and *lançados* (q.v.) traded freely in African slaves and products, soon resulting in the Crioulo (q.v.) population characteristic of the islands. As a consequence of this long history São Tiago is considered to have the most African population of the archipelago. As an example of the scale of the trade, between 1514 and 1516 almost 3,000 slaves were landed at Ribeira Grande.

The role and context of Ribeira Grande may be summed up by the expression that it was the "Goa of the Occident." In 1533 the capital was elevated to the status of "city" when the official residence of the Cape Verdean bishop was established. The Bishop represented religious and Crown authority in the islands and on the coast from Morocco to Guinea. Today the main cathedral is in Praia and the original one is in ruins.

The relative prosperity and autonomy of the *capitãos* (q.v.) on São Tiago resulted, in 1564, in rule reverting back to the Crown for a fuller monopolization of island and coastal trade. This oscillation and competition between island autonomy and colonial monopolies remained a central theme through most of Cape Verdean history.

Ribeira Grande reached a permanent population of 1,500 by 1572, although the interior town of Santa Catarina was already larger by this time. The slave plantation system was deeply entrenched, with a few dozen *Brancos* and *Mestiços* having full authority and using a small group of "free Africans" as overseers to dominate some 90 percent of the population of African slaves.

Aside from the central role of slavery in the economy, São Tiago was also a common stopping place for fresh water for ships going to South America or down the West African coast. Local production of livestock and plant dyes (urzella and indigo [q.v.]) was sometimes important and São Tiago horses (q.v.) were much prized for riding and for the slave trade. It is ironic in this regard that Matthew Perry's anti-slavery Africa Squadron (q.v.) was based in São Tiago in the 1840s and 1850s while slavery was still extant.

Population of São Tiago

1890	63,795
1927	57,554*
1930	63,154
1940	77,192
1950	58,893
1960	88,587
1970	128,782
1980	145,957
1990	171,433

(Sources: Duncan 1972; Cape Verde Censuses. [*] includes Maio)

See BADIUS; REBELADOS; TARAFAL.

SÃO VICENTE (16° 52′ N; 24° 58′ W). This island in the Barlavento (q.v.) group in the Cape Verde archipelago ranked seventh in size (227 sq. km.). While there are rocky mountains they are not of exceptional height (774 meters) for the islands. There is virtually no regular water supply in São Vicente and its settlement was retarded for this reason. Water was brought from Santo Antão (q.v.) for cooking and washing needs until the desalinization plant in Mindelo began its operation in January 1972. The island has about 10 percent of the population of the archipelago and the town of Mindelo itself is the largest urban area of all of the northern islands with some 47,000 inhabitants. There are few natural resources in São Vicente except for its excellent harbor at Mindelo (Porto Grande) facing Santo Antão. Another village is San Pedro where the 1,200-meter airstrip is located.

Population of São Vicente

1890	6,666
1927	17,709
1930	14,639
1940	15,867
1950	19,158
1960	21,361
1970	34,500
1980	41,792
1990	51,277

(Sources: Duncan 1972; Cape Verde Censuses)

In the 17th century the administration of São Vicente and São Nicolau (q.v.) was joined under a common grant to the Marquis de Gouveia. The mid-18th century saw the period of the first settlement of São Vicente as its port economy was stimulated by intense slaving (q.v.) on the Guinea coast. In about 1790 the British established a consulate and coal depot at Porto Grande to strengthen their naval dominance. With these developments substantial numbers of settlers were attracted to Mindelo from other Cape Verde islands to work as longshoremen or to join ship crews. In the mid-19th century British steamers en route to Brazil made regular stops at Mindelo. Indeed, mail from the United States usually went to England and then to Cape Verde on the Brazilian line. During the later years of the Africa Squadron (q.v.) mail went by this route at the astronomical cost of 65 cents per half ounce. A submarine communications cable reached Mindelo in 1875. By 1880 the Portuguese firm Empresa Nacional de Navegação established regular service from Portugal to São Vicente and Guinea-Bissau (q.v.). In the early 20th century Mindelo handled about five million tons of shipping annually and had become the main port for the whole archipelago.

Aside from extensive storage and bunkering facilities there is now an oil refinery and an attractive hotel. PAIGC (q.v.) development programs have already initiated a fiber glass boat-building factory at Mindelo with a fish-processing factory soon to be expanded. Other activities since independence include new road construction, hospital expansion, new social service and health centers, and the development and promotion of horticulture. *See* URBANIZATION.

SEMA LOPI. SEE: FUNANA.

SENEGAMBIANS. This large cluster of the coastal, Atlantic stock of the Niger-Congo (or Nigritic) peoples includes virtually all of the inhabitants of Guinea-Bissau who are of neither Fula nor Manding (qq.v.) (Mande) origin. Sometimes Senegambians are known as "Semi-Bantu" peoples of the Guinea Littoral. The Senegambians include the Balantas, Banyuns, Biafadas, Bijagos, Diolas (not to be confused with the Dyula [q.v.] traders), Nalus, Papeis, Brams, Manjacos (q.v.), Serer, Wolof and Mankanyas. Senegambian peoples were found as far north as Mauretania until the 11th-century expansion of the Berbers, when they were pushed back southward. They extended eastward through most of present Guinea-Bissau until the creation of Gabu (q.v.) and the secondary Mande kingdoms pushed them westward toward the coast. The southward spread of the Senegambians was similarly checked by the consolidation of power in the Guinea highlands at Futa Jallon and with the expansion of the Susu kingdom.

At an early date the Senegambians incorporated the Sudanic food complex and added rice farming as a local specialty. The numerous small Senegambian groups represent the shattering effect from the pressure on all sides by more powerful centralized hierarchies. The Senegambians are either acephalous or only slightly centralized and are mostly animist, except for more recent Islamization among some. It is mainly from Senegambian and Mande peoples that Cape Verdeans may trace their genetic and cultural roots to Africa.

SEX RATIOS. As a result of a long-standing pattern of male migration for employment off of the islands and some differentials in overall life expectancy favoring women in the overall population of Cape Verde, the proportion of females has always exceeded that of males in recent decades.

Percent Female By Year:

Year	Percent
1936:	54.5
1950:	54.7
1960:	53.7
1970:	52.5
1980:	54.2
1990:	52.1

Percent Female By Island (1990):

All Islands	52.1
Boa Vista	49.1
Brava	52.4
Fogo	53.3
Maio	53.6
Sal	48.5
São Tiago	53.0
Santo Antão	49.0
São Nicolau	51.3
São Vicente	51.5

(Source: calculated from the 1990 census)

See DEMOGRAPHY; LIFE EXPECTANCY; VITAL STATISTICS.

SILLA, ERNESTINA (?–1973). This exemplary woman militant and member of the PAIGC (q.v.) was born in the Tombali region of Guinea-Bissau (q.v.). In 1962, while still a teenager, she contacted the Party and then left home to dedicate herself to the nationalist struggle. Her main assignment was public health work in the liberated zones of the northern region. Her active work did not prevent her from marrying and raising children. On 31 January 1973 she was killed in combat on the Farim River on the way to the funeral of Amilcar Cabral (q.v.) in neighboring Guinea-Conakry. In March 1977 the "Titina" Silla Juice Factory was opened in Bolama (q.v.) in her memory. *See* WOMEN.

SILVA, LIDO. While president of the UCID (q.v.), Silva failed to meet the deadline to submit candidates for the 1991 elections (q.v.). He did not swing his support for the other candidates. Probably as a result of this failure, Silva was replaced by the rather elderly Antero Barros as UCID President in 1992, who was in turn replaced by Celso Celestino in 1994.

SLAVERY, SLAVES. The Portuguese first captured African slaves in the early 1440s on the Moroccan coast. Until the discovery of the New World, slaves were used as domestic servants in Europe and on sugar plantations in the various Atlantic islands. Slavery in Cape Verde was at its height between 1475 and 1575, but various forms of slave plantations and slave trading existed from the very beginning to the late 19th century. Guinea-Bissau (q.v.) itself did not use the slave plantation system to a great degree, but was chiefly an exporter. During the 15th century the export of slaves from Africa did not exceed 1,000 annually, but this was a uniquely Portuguese enterprise and occurred only on the upper reaches of the West African coast, and was chiefly centered in the Cape Verde islands during the period of 1501 to 1600. The slave trade in the 16th century was still dominated by Portugal, but Spanish and English slavers began to erode the monopoly in the late 16th century.

Not only was there competition for slaves between European royal trading houses, there was an endless local effort to bypass the royal taxes and to trade independently by smuggling. Unless authorized by a Crown monopoly, most free Cape Verdeans were legally barred from trading in slaves, although certainly not from owning them. As such Cape Verdean *lançados* (q.v.) were directly involved in the trade along the coast which depended upon slave wars waged in the interior. Cape Verdean *panos*, horses (qq.v.), and salt were brought from the islands to trade along the coast. The majority of African slaves were brought from Guinea in particular and Senegambia (q.v.) in general. The pace of slaving increased through the century, reaching a regional height of some 5,000 slaves annually by the 1570s. Most of these slaves went to the New World, especially to the Caribbean and to Brazil, although a small trickle still went to the Cape Verde Islands and to Europe. The need for slaves inside Cape Verde was for replacement of elderly, sick, or dead slaves in agricultural or domestic work. However, "seasoned" slaves from Cape Verde were highly valued for being more docile and because a dangerous and unhealthy trip to the coast could be avoided.

Throughout the 17th century the Portuguese slave trade in Senegambia and Guinea-Bissau declined in both absolute and relative terms. The reason was that more European powers were involved and Portuguese slavers became more active in Angola and Mozambique. In the first half of the 17th century the share of slaves from Guinea and Senegambia fell to about 6 percent of the total number of slaves from Africa, whereas it had been as much as 75 percent in the century before. Likewise, the numbers of slaves fell from previous highs of about 5,000 per year to an average of 650 per year. The earlier figures related to the various wars of the autonomous state of Gabu (q.v.) in Guinea-Bissau, which generated large numbers of slaves for trade and export. In the 17th century Gabu became less dynamic and more stable, thus slowing the production of slave captives. The early 17th century saw renewed efforts by other European powers to engage in West African slavery; the real heyday of competitive and aggressive slaving had begun. The English Royal African Company averaged some 10,000 slaves each year in the area between Senegal and Sierra Leone in the late 17th century, but this large figure represented only 12 percent of their total slave trade from Africa at the time. At about the same period two Cape Verdean companies were established as slave trade monopolies at Cacheu (q.v.) in Guinea-Bissau.

With a marked growth in the New World plantation system the demand was high and insecurity prevailed among peoples of the coast and the interior as all of the major Sudanic states in the West African savanna had come to an end. The portion of slaving done by Portuguese vessels or with Portuguese traders continued to fall. Indeed, the coastal *lançados* and Dyula (q.v.) traders had almost free reign in the context of virtual anarchy of slave commerce at this time. Slaves were being drawn from peoples located even further in the interior as the various Fula (q.v.) wars generated a high degree of insecurity in the 18th century. In 1753 a Brazilian slave trade company was given monopoly rights at Bissau (q.v.) to acquire slaves for the Brazilian states of Maranhão and Grão Pará. This accounted for a resurgence in slaving in Guinea-Bissau, as slave exports rose to average some 700 per year in the late 18th century. Many of these slaves were generated from the incessant wars between the Mandingo (q.v.) state of Gabu and the Fula people of Labé Province of Futa Jallon.

The early 19th century saw the start of European abolition when it was realized that a cash economy (rather than slave barter) and industrial exports on a massive scale would be served better by "free labor" which could purchase European goods and enter a system of colonial taxation in which unpaid slaves could not "participate." The wage-slave system began to cut away at the older system of chattel slavery. As a poor European nation, Portugal (q.v.) was slow to make this transition and slavery lingered on into the 19th century. To a limited extent there was even some slight increase in the slave trade at this time in Guinea-Bissau, as the abolition and anti-slavery patrols had resulted in a relative scarcity of the slave supply, thus temporarily forcing an increased demand. At this point, the decentralized coastal peoples were again raided. But as the century wore on there were larger numbers of slaves from the Mandingo-related peoples when the Fulas continued to press their attacks on Gabu in eastern Guinea-Bissau. The Brazilian slave company still kept its monopoly in Bissau from which it took the vast portion of its slaves, but the annual numbers had fallen to only a few hundred per year. Despite the rather rapid spread of the abolition movement, Portugal acted more often in violation of the restrictions and agreements to limit the trade.

While in the earliest days of Cape Verdean society there was an overwhelming majority of slaves, this was only so during part of the islands' history. Specific data for the mid-19th century, provided by the late historian of Cape Verde, António Carreira, show that only a minority of the population actually held slaves, and of the group of 549 slave owners from São Tiago (q.v.), where slavery was the most significant, the average owner had only 4.4 slaves. On the neighboring island of Maio (q.v.) it was only 3.4 slaves per owner. Only 17 out of 549 slave proprietors on São Tiago had 20 slaves or more. One of these had 63 and another 50, but these are most exceptional. So, while one may speak of Cape Verde as a slave society, it must be clear that for all but the start of its half millennium of history, its slave population was a minority of the total population, and slavery was not equally important to each island. Moreover, not many slaves were held even by those who had them. It was a minority of the economically powerful, usually serving the interests of the Crown or royal commerce, who were involved.

Thus, it was rather rapidly that the relative portion of slaves in society fell from the overwhelming majority to a rather stable 5–10 percent which is where it remained in the 18th and 19th century when the institution of slavery was, at long last, curbed. Although few in number, virtually all slave masters and landlords took their sexual pleasures with their slaves which also had the effect of regenerating their slave labor force without additional expense. The still extant 19th century records continue to show some steady new arrivals from the coast, but almost all of the slaves officially registered for tax purposes in each island were from that same island. This pattern included those of the highest station in church and administration and continued to be a pattern carried on to the 20th century in which a minority of births are to those of formally married mothers. A value system of male supremacy was added to this practice and sometimes resulted in dominant persons having a dozen children or more.

Several factors and circumstances led to the end of slavery in Cape Verde. The official, but not very effective, abolition of the slave trade in the United States in 1807 and official Portuguese prohibition of slave trading in its territories north of the equator in 1815 were a start. A substantial effort at abolition was made by Britain in the 1819 Anglo-American Treaty on the slave trade. The Portuguese extended their ban to the rest of their empire in 1836. Clearly, the Portuguese slave traders could see that this era was beginning to end.

Despite these formal proclamations, orders, and efforts, slave trading persisted in the shadowy world of smuggling, especially among Cape Verdean *lançados* who had dodged Crown monopoly regulations. Even while the Africa Squadron (q.v.) of the United States was stationed in Cape Verde from 1843 to 1861 to supress the trade, the Cape Verdean hosts continued a centuries-long tradition of domestic slavery and trading in slaves for the market that still existed in Spanish-speaking America and Brazil. Some Americans from northern states (like New York and Massachusetts) throughout the 1850s and even until 1861 claimed to outfit ships for whaling (q.v.). Such was the case of the *Memphis*, leaving New Bedford in 1859, but which carried 500 slaves to Cuba instead. In 1860 at least 83 northern United States ships were still engaged in the trade. When they reached Cape Verde and the African coast their true mission as slave traders and shippers became apparent even when sailing under a Portuguese flag and with the American captain identified only as a "passenger." After the "Middle Passage" to Caribbean plantations they would return to their home ports greatly enriched with a "legitimate" cargo of sugar, molasses, cotton, and tobacco.

The long and bloody American Civil War ultimately faced the often deferred and obscured, but central, issue of American slavery. President Lincoln reluctantly made the Emancipation Proclamation in the United States in 1863 as an economic tactic against the property of southern Secessionists. In short, the changed legal context, the abolition movement moralists, the need for security and stability in Africa for the growth of legitimate trade, and the American Civil War were all powerful factors leading to the sharp decline and ultimate extinction of the trade in Guinea-Bissau by the third quarter of the 19th century.

When formal slavery had ended by the close of the 19th century, it was replaced by, and evolved into, a system of "free" contract labor in which the life of a *contratado* (q.v.) was only a slight improvement, as wages were pitifully low and the conditions of employment were most oppressive, especially in São Tomé. The contract labor system was particularly important to the economy of Cape Verde which has long had great difficulty in supporting its own population by island agriculture (q.v.) because of prolonged droughts (q.v.), gross colonial mismanagement, and backward systems of land ownership. Some Africans had short-term, personal benefits from the slave trade, but the protracted brutality associated with this commerce in human beings certainly stands as one of the most exploitative and inhuman epochs in human history. Also, most Europeans in Europe or in the New World did not benefit either. Not only was there chronic insecurity and anxiety under the slave system, but only the small European and African class of slave owners and traders were the true "beneficiaries" of this launching of the great African diaspora. *See* AZAMBUJA, D.; BADIUS; BISSAU; CACHEU; COMPANHIAS; CRIOULO CULTURAL ORIGINS; DE NOLI, A.; DONATARIOS; DRAKE, F.; DYULAS; FINAÇON; FULA; GABU; GOMES, D.; GONÇALVES, A.; HODGES, S.; JEWS; LANÇADOS; MALI; MANDINGO; POMBAL; PORTUGAL; SENEGAMBIANS; SONINKE; TANGOMÃOS; TRISTÃO, N.

SONINKE. The Soninke are members of the Nuclear Mande stock of the Niger-Congo language family, but they speak a distinct Manding language. The most notable achievement of the Soninke people is their founding of the Sudanic empire of Ghana. The Dyula (q.v.) branch of the Soninke was central in the trade and Islamization of the Upper and Middle Niger, which led to the formation of the state of Mali (q.v.). When they were at the center of power they generated large numbers of slaves for export to the coast for barter to the Cape Verdean *lançados* (q.v.), the Portuguese and other Europeans.

SOTAVENTO, ILHAS DE. Southern, leeward islands of Cape Verde including Maio, São Tiago, Fogo, Brava, (qq.v.) and the islets of Grande, Luís Carneiro, and Sapado. *See* Individual entries on the major islands.

SPÍNOLA, GENERAL ANTÓNIO SEBASTIÃO RIBEIRO DE. (11 April 1910–). Born in Estrémoz, Portugal (q.v.), Spínola received a strict military education and was a noted horseman. With his family close to the ruling circles of the Portuguese government and the powerful Champalimaud (q.v.) banking group he was long a prominent military officer. In the Second World War, Spínola was invited by Hitler to inspect conquered areas of the Soviet Union and is reported to have visited the German Sixth Army during its unsuccessful attempt to seize Stalingrad. Spínola was the Commander of the Portuguese army in Guinea-Bissau during the nationalist war of the PAIGC led by Amilcar Cabral (qq.v.).

-T-

TABANKA, TABANCA. In Cape Verde, the term *tabanka* refers to organizations from the island of São Tiago (q.v.) which are associated with *badiu* (q.v.) folklife. There are *tabanka* organizations in various quarters of the city of Praia (Achada Grande, Várzea, and Achada di Santo António), as well as in Assomada (Chão de Tanque) and the village of São Jorge. *Tabanka* organizations have existed at least since the early 1800s and perhaps even earlier. *Tabanka* is generally considered a type of mutual aid association, whereby membership ensured individuals help from the group from time to time. For example, members provided agricultural assistance at planting and harvest time, food in times of famine, or occasional financial help in emergency situations. Nowadays, the mutual aid aspect of *tabanka* is no longer stressed. Rather, the group continues mostly for religious and social reasons, although members still make small monthly contributions to a fund that helps with funeral expenses when someone dies.

The *tabanka* association's primary activities are centered around a patron saint's day, usually Saint John (June 24) or Saint Anthony (June 13). Each year a complex Afro-Christian religious reenactment and celebration takes place to honor the patron saint. The story that is reenacted involves the theft and recovery of a symbolic representation of the saint, which takes the form of crossed branches from a tree that have been blessed along with a banner with the saint's name written on it. The saint is kept in the chapel that bears its name and serves as the center of *tabanka* activities.

As part of the reenactment, members of the *tabanka* association take on roles similar to a colonial court and army. These various personages include a king and queen of the court, a king and queen of the countryside, governors, commanders, judges, daughters of the saint (young girls between eight and 15), ladies-in-waiting, doctors, nurses, army troops, brides, marines, female dancers, several comic characters, a thief and his/her son, the falcon.

Although the initiation of the *tabanka* festivities is announced at the beginning of May by signals on the conch shell horns and drums, the intense period of *tabanka* activities begins when the thief steals one branch of the saint during the Catholic mass on the saint's day. The king of the court, *tabanka*'s most important spiritual leader and a position that is assigned for life, calls a session of his council to plan how to get it back. In the meantime, the thief sells the saint to a buyer. By purchasing the saint for a symbolic sum of money, the buyer (who can be male or female but must belong to a *tabanka* group) obliges himself to buy the saint again for the next seven years, with the understanding that each year he will play host to the entire *tabanka* group for a day and a night at his house.

Some eight days after the saint has been stolen, the thief and son are captured and imprisoned in a cell near the chapel and forced to tell what they have done with the saint. After they tell where it is, they are tied up and the entire *tabanka* association parades through the streets of Praia and eventually ends up at the buyer's house. During the procession, *tabanka* members wear costumes appropriate to the roles they are playing. For example, the troops have hats and wooden guns and the commanders are all in white with large hats. Members carry an assortment of flags and small banners, as well as large models of wooden boats. The group is accompanied by big military style drums (made from metal drums with skin heads) and conch shell horns. They play a rhythmic music (q.v.) based on the alternation of just two pitches. The name of the musical procession is referred to as *tabanka*, although the word can mean the entire association as well. Women called *foros* do a *batuko*-like (q.v.) dance as they march and other women wear pastel dresses and colorful hats decorated with crepe paper. The doctor and nurses give out medicine in the form of *grogga* (q.v.) to all who seem in need. When the procession arrives at the house of the buyer, the participants stay there for the rest of the day and night, praying, dancing, eating, and drinking. During the evening, the king of the court negotiates with the buyer for the saint and eventually gets it back. In other versions, the son of the thief, the falcon, steals the saint back from the buyer. The saint must be returned to the chapel within a prescribed time or it is believed that it will bring bad luck.

Although *tabanka* may appear to be primarily a social organization, members stress its religious significance. On the saint's day there is a religious ceremony in the chapel in the evening to honor the saint. The chapel is decorated with colorful banners and the altar contains a statue of the patron saint, candelabra, the conch shell horns, and the symbolic saint, which is missing one of its crossed sticks because the thief has stolen it. The king of the court leads an elaborate, lengthy ceremony during which members pay their respects to the saint. The ceremony is punctuated by the use of two large drums that beat special patterns at various points in the service. Members also perform *ladainha* (liturgy), a unique type of sung group prayer which serves as a form of purification and worship. *Ladainha* sometimes continues intermittently until dawn, interrupted with *batuko* and refreshments.

Historically, *tabanka* processions were not allowed in the center plateau of Praia. The processions and group activities made the Portuguese authorities nervous and the organizations were made illegal in the early decades of this century. The laws were later repealed when the Portuguese authorities saw it was useless to try to stop *tabanka*. Instead, they tried to control some aspects of the activities. Like *funana* (q.v.) and *batuko*, *tabanka* has become a symbol of the struggle for independence against colonial rule. The future of *tabanka* is uncertain since there seems to be a declining number of young people joining the groups. *Tabanka* processions are sometimes invited to appear at official state functions as examples of Cape Verdean folklore and some people are in favor of preserving *tabanka* by turning it into a show for tourists. If this happens, *tabanka*'s context as a religious manifestation will, of course, be altered and its original significance will be lost. SUSAN HURLEY-GLOWA

During the nationalist struggle on the mainland, *tabanka* committees were formed by the PAIGC (q.v.) in villages throughout the liberated zones of Guinea-Bissau. This linked the party with the rural peasantry.

TABARI, TCHIN. SEE: BATUKO.

TANGOMÃOS (TARGAMAN, TANGOMAUS). Tangomão is most likely derived from a corruption of the Arabic "targama" meaning "translator." They were African slavers who were middlemen for the Portuguese and Cape Verdean *lançado* (q.v.) lifestyle. As multi-lingual African traders they played a central role as enforcers and negotiators in the slave (q.v.) trade. Some reports indicate that they were fond of having body tattoos. This 17th or 18th century term became archaic as the slave trade declined on the Upper Guinea coast by the 19th century.

TARRAFAL. A notorious political prison located on the northern end of São Tiago (q.v.). Tarrafal might be confused with other places of the same name elsewhere in the Cape Verde archipelago. This prison camp began during the Portuguese fascist era in 1936 to house Communist Party members and their sympathizers who were opposed to the rule of Salazar (q.v.). As the nationalist wars began, the camp was filled with Africans as well. Tarrafal had a particularly nasty reputation for torture, brutality, and death. Its extremely isolated location made escape virtually impossible. In 1971 more than 100 PIDE (q.v.) agents arrived in Cape Verde to infiltrate and arrest members of the PAIGC, such as L. Miranda (q.v.). Nationalists were confined at the Tarrafal *conselho* (q.v.) (district council) prison also known as the work camp of Chão Bom (Good Earth). Although politically important, the overall prison staff consisted of a few dozen guards and administrators.

TAVARES, EUGÉNIO DE PAULA (5 November 1867–1930). Tavares was a popular poet best known for composing and compiling the uniquely Cape Verdean *mornas* (q.v.), poems set to music (q.v.) and typically expressing a nostalgic tone. His impact on subsequent generations of *morna* players is very great. A native of Nova Sintra in Brava (q.v.) and self-educated, Tavares worked for most of his life as a civil servant. Writing almost exclusively in Crioulo (q.v.), he played a critical role in maintaining the viability of Crioulo as the language of the people. In his verse Tavares often drew upon folkloric sources. He has become a legendary figure in the archipelago, particularly in Brava, where stories of his life and loves have become part of the popular culture. To this day in Brava, Tavares classic ''Hora di Bai'' (The Hour to Leave) is the *morna* that is traditionally the last sung, signifying the close of the evening's music. Tavares is also known for his contributions to such publications as *Luso-Africano* and *Cartas Cabo-Verdianas*, which added substantially to the patrimony and consciousness of Cape Verdean culture and the difficulties faced by its people.

TAVARES, NORBERTO (1956–). Norberto Tavares is one of the most popular and influential songwriter/performers in Cape Verdean music (q.v.) today. He is particularly famous for his unmistakable voice and unique style of *funana* (q.v.) that he composes on the synthesizer. Born on 6 June 1956 in Santa Caterina, São Tiago (q.v.), Norberto was the son of a well-known local musician, Aristides Tavares, who played the violin and other string instruments. After his father's untimely death when Norberto was nine, he taught himself how to play the guitar, keyboards, and accordion. Norberto left Cape Verde for Portugal in 1973 and formed a band there. He began experimenting with playing the *funana* that he heard as a young boy in Santa Caterina on the guitar and keyboards and put out his first album of "electric *funana*" in 1978, slightly before "Katchás" (C. Martins [q.v.]) made his version of *funana* with his band Bulimundo which became widely popular. Norberto produced several more recordings in Portugal and toured with his band before immigrating to the United States in 1979. Since then, he has continued to produce high quality recordings with songs that reflect the concerns and interests of the people of São Tiago, often using his music to express his dissatisfaction with social and political conditions in Cape Verde. He regularly performs in Cape Verdean communities in America and Europe with his band, Tropical Power, returning with them to Cape Verde in 1990 for the first time in 17 years to perform for enthusiastic crowds. His two latest albums are *Jornada di un Badiu* (1989) and *Hino di Unifição* (1992). Norberto currently lives in New Bedford, Massachusetts.

TEKRUR. One of the earliest Islamized states of the western Sudan from which the Fulas (q.v.) of Guinea-Bissau originated. Tekrur appeared at, or about, the time of ancient Ghana as early as the 3rd century AD and certainly no later than the 6th century. Tekrur was based on a trading and bureaucratic superstructure built from traditional settled village political systems and subsistence agriculture. During its height, Tekrur was linked to Marrakesh by an overland trade route about 300 kilometers inland from the Atlantic Coast.

East-west trade through Tekrur became especially important in the 12th and 13th centuries when the Empire of Mali (q.v.) (1230–1546) experienced its greatest growth. It was just after this time that the first contacts with the Portuguese were taking place on the Guinea coast and it was with riverine access to the interior that the early Portuguese acquired their slaves (q.v.) for export to the New World and for settlement in the Cape Verde Islands.

TRISTÃO, NUÑO. Portuguese navigator and captain of an armed caravel who, along with Antão Gonçalves (q.v.), captured a dozen Africans (probably Moors) at Cape Blanc (north coast of Mauretania) in 1441 and returned to Portugal with them and a cargo of gold dust. Tristão directly and personally engaged in capturing slaves (q.v.) and killing those who resisted. One of the 12 captives was of noble birth. In 1443–44 Tristão reached Arguim, seizing 29 men and women. Merchants soon grasped the idea of big and easy profits. In 1444 Tristão decided to outfit a major raiding expedition of six ships under Lançarote and Gil Eannes (qq.v.), thus initiating one of the earliest European-inspired slave raids on the African coast. In the same year Tristão became the first European to venture beyond the Mauretanian desert, as he reached the mouths of the Senegal, Gambia, and Salum Rivers, thinking they were branches of the Nile. In 1446 Tristão reached the area of Bissau and Bolama (qq.v.) but in the following year his aggressive exploits came to an end when he was killed along the Upper Guinea coast while trying to trade or slave for Portugal.

-U-

UNIÃO CABOVERDEANO INDEPÊNDENTE E DEMOCRÁTICA (UCID). One may trace UCID's roots back to as early as 23 February 1975, when the Juridical Congress of Cape Verde made its "declaration of independence" for the islands at the Boston Sheraton Hotel. This political group was also known as the UDCV (q.v.) and its supporters later emerged as the UCID.

When the PAIGC (q.v.) attained independence for the islands on 5 July 1975 parties such as the UPICV (q.v.), and others which later appeared in the UCID, were excluded from the negotiations with the Portuguese government. At this time, the left-leaning Portuguese MFA (Armed Forces Movement) and the PAIGC in Cape Verde dominated the political scene and evolutionary, rightist or pro-colonial groupings were outlawed as part of the negative forces of opposition they had finally vanquished.

In 1977 and 1978, when the PAIGC arrested some opposition members, the resolve to organize an effective opposition crystalized. The UCID claims that at least 44 people were arrested and some held as long as one year. The PAIGC claims there was a plot to blow up a power plant and take over a radio station. On the night of 31 August 1981 the PAIGC military and the POP (Public Order Police) staged some raids and arrests in Santo Antão (q.v.) which resulted in the detention, interrogation, and probably harsh treatment of about two dozen people by the internal security officers at the Morro Branco military headquarters in São Vicente (q.v.).

It was these circumstances of political isolation and frustration in 1975 and thereafter, and especially the events of Santo Antão and São Vicente, that shaped the evolution of the UCID as a genuine political party formed in Lisbon in 1981 by center-right Cape Verdean exiles. A UCID newsletter was published in 1982 which called for political pluralism, free elections, and religious freedom. The UCID took special offense at PAICV (q.v.) policies which were considered pro-Soviet and anti-American; it was also opposed to nationalization and restrictions on the Catholic Church in Cape Verde. A series of articles, largely written by John C. Wahnon, were published by the UCID in 1986 and dealt with grievances about political prisoners in Cape Verde, the PAICV association with "international terrorism," the "illegitimacy" of the PAICV government, the possibility that the Cape Verde Islands were to be used as a Soviet submarine base, cultural and political ties with Libya and the Palestinians, and expropriation of land. PAICV plans to introduce major agrarian reform were especially unpopular with the UCID as some of its members were notable land owners. Nonetheless, this became law in 1982 and was put into effect in 1 January 1983. This measure only separated the two sides even more fully. Whatever truth or merits these grievances, government actions, and policies may have had, it is clear in retrospect that the electoral defeat of the PAICV in 1991 was, in good measure, the result of an increasingly narrow base of popular support for its methods, if not its policies. In the small-scale highly personal society of Cape Verde, even many people who were not at all aligned with the policies of the UCID found that the PAICV had made excessive use of power.

In the 1991 Cape Verdean elections (q.v.) the UCID was not able to file the proper papers on time with the Electoral Commission so it did not compete. While it has never been tested in the ballot box there is some expectation that it will continue to have a political presence, and it is supposed, on the basis of the landslide victory of the MpD (q.v.), that the UCID may gain some representation in the Assembléia Nacional Popular (q.v.) should it run candidates in the elections planned for 1995. In the UCID Congress of 5–8 August 1993 party elections were held which brought new leadership. Celso Celestino, a 56-year-old, high ranking income tax administrator who had long resided in Portugal (q.v.) was proposed as the UCID candidate for Prime Minister and it agreed to support the independent President Monteiro (q.v.). Its program will feature more limited privatization and concern with social issues such as drugs, AIDS, education, and health (qq.v.). The UCID has representatives abroad in Portugal, Germany, Holland and the United States. In the United States, the UCID's First Secretary was John C. Wahnon who had been a long-time opponent of the policies and practices of the PAICV. Other UCID leaders are John Leite and Francisco Silva.

UNIÃO DAS POPULAÇÕES DAS ILHAS DO CABO VERDE (UPICV). The UPICV was led by José Leitão da Graça and his wife Maria Querido, who was named its Secretary General. The UPICV sought to preserve the Cape Verdean "personality" in its program of limited social transformation. Apparently the UPICV was first formed in 1959 in the United States as a rival to the PAIGC (q.v.). These were the heady days of African independence and many parties sought to move into influential positions to claim state power for themselves. This was also the time of the Cold War and the Sino-Soviet split. The UPICV aligned itself more closely with the People's Republic of China as the PAIGC tended to seek its primary support from the Soviet Union and Eastern Europe. The UPICV sought only independence for Cape Verde, while the PAIGC sought freedom--and unity--for both Cape Verde and Guinea-Bissau where it waged an armed struggle.

Following the MFA coup in 1974 and the 5 July 1975 independence of Cape Verde, the UPICV and the UCID (q.v.) were essentially excluded from the political arena in Cape Verde and were exiled to Lisbon and other European and North American locations. The UPICV supported the UDCV (q.v.) position of a referendum on unity with Guinea-Bissau, charging that the PAIGC would make Cape Verde "a Soviet military base." In the mid-1970s the UPICV spouted certain Maoist terminology and, on 23 May 1975, renamed itself the People's Liberation Front of Cape Verde. The UPICV claimed responsibility for a small anti-PAIGC disturbance in São Vicente (q.v.) in August 1975.

The date of 12 November 1977, when they met on the border between Holland and Belgium to determine their situation and draft a program of their party, is significant to supporters of the UPICV. Their 8-point program included provisions for the political and judicial structure, armed forces and finance, human rights, private property, freedom of religion and conscience, freedom to learn and teach, freedom of work, health, and emigration, and a design for a three-color flag (q.v.) with ten stars for the islands of the archipelago. Portuguese was to be the official language, but with provisions to advance the development of Crioulo culture and language (qq.v.).

The most persistent leader of the UPICV continues to be José Leitão da Graça. Although the UPICV still claims to exist in the 1990s, its political presence seems to be mainly a measure of the political pluralism in Cape Verde at this time. A "reconstituted" form of the UPICV symbolizes this fresh start.

UNIÃO DEMOCRÁTICA DA GUINÉ (UDG). This small group emerged in the late 1950s and merged with the UDCV (q.v.) and the UPG to form the MLGCV of Dakar in 1959. It was from such groups as the UDG that the FLING (q.v.) emerged in 1962.

UNIÃO DEMOCRÁTICA DAS MULHERES (DA GUINÉ E CABO VERDE) (UDEMU). UDEMU was a sororal organization of the PAIGC (q.v.) in mid-1960 to officially represent women's (q.v.) issues within the anti-colonial united front framework of the PAIGC. In Cape Verde after 1981 it became known as the Organização das Mulheres de Cabo Verde (OMCV) (q.v.).

UNIÃO DEMOCRÁTICA DE CABO VERDE (UDCV or UDC). The UDCV emerged in the late 1950s to join with the UDG (q.v.) and the UPG in 1959 to form the MLGCV which ultimately led to the formation of the FLING (q.v.) in 1962. Through most of the 1960s the UDCV essentially did not exist. In 1974, following the Lisbon coup, some former UDCV members supported the idea of General Spínola (q.v.) for a referendum on the question of unity with Guinea-Bissau (q.v.) regarding the possibility of separate independence for Cape Verde and a possible federation with Portugal, in order to prevent PAIGC (q.v.) control of the islands.

The most prominent leaders of the UDCV were João Baptista Monteiro, a leading Cape Verdean lawyer and rich merchant, and Jorge Fonseca, who also had extensive financial interests in the islands. Monteiro and Fonseca helped to organize some anti-PAIGC activities, mainly in São Vicente (q.v.). Both were exiled after 5 July 1975. There were also American supporters of the UDCV under the banner of the Juridical Congress whose leaders were Aguinaldo Veiga (q.v.), a Cape Verdean lawyer who served colonialism in Angola, and Roy Teixeira and his son. Some American Cape Verdeans, on behalf of the UDCV, declared the independence of Cape Verde and called for the overthrow of the PAIGC at a Boston hotel during a February 1975 rally. Some of these same people reemerged in the party now known as the UCID (q.v.), which may be considered the political descendant of the UDCV which no longer exists.

UNIÃO DOS NATURAIS DA GUINÉ PORTUGUESA (UNGP). The UNGP sought independence without revolution. UNGP leader Benjamin Pinto Bull went to Lisbon in July 1963 for negotiations which failed and prompted UNGP unity with the FLING (q.v.) a year after its formation. Benjamin Pinto Bull's brother, Jaime, was made Vice-President of the UNGP and became FLING President after 1966.

UNIÃO GERAL DOS ESTUDIANTES DA AFRICA NEGRA (UGEAN). The UGEAN was formed in Europe for militant nationalist students by the PAIGC (q.v.) and the MPLA in Angola.

UNIÃO GERAL DOS TRABALHADORES DA GUINÉ-BISSAU (UGTGB). The UGTGB emerged in 1963 in association with the FLING, and was a rival of the PAIGC's workers' affiliate, the UNTG (q.v.), which had been formed in 1959.

UNIÃO NACIONAL DOS TRABALHADORES DA GUINÉ (UNTG). The UNTG was founded in 1959 and affiliated with the PAIGC (q.v.) as a party organization. In 1961 its first statutes were drafted with Luís Cabral (q.v.) acting as the Secretary General. The UNTG's purpose was to organize the working class of Guinea and during the war it also sought to organize the working class of Cape Verde. On 1 May 1976 (International Workers' Day), the Comissão Organizadora dos Sindicatos Caboverdeanos (COSC) was formed as the complement and parallel body of the UNTG in the Cape Verde Islands.

UNIÃO POPULAR PARA LIBERTAÇÃO DA GUINÉ (UPLG). The UPLG was formed in 1961 and then merged with the FLING (q.v.) in 1962.

UNION DES RESSORTISSANTS DE LA GUINÉE «PORTUGAISE» (URGP). The URGP was formed in 1963 and became aligned with the FLING (q.v.) in 1964.

UNITED NATIONS (UN, ONU). International organization formed in 1945 for humanitarian and peace-keeping purposes. On 14 December 1960 the 1514th meeting of the General Assembly passed a resolution on global decolonization which gave strong support to the anti-colonial and nationalist movements in Africa. In 1961 the PAIGC (q.v.) submitted considerable documentation to the United Nations regarding the effects of Portuguese colonialism. On 2–8 April 1972 a special United Nations team entered Guinea-Bissau (q.v.) as the guest of the PAIGC. As a consequence of this trip, the Special Committee on Decolonization announced on 13 April 1972 that the PAIGC "is the only and authentic representative" of the people of Guinea. Subsequent resolutions in the UN General Assembly and the UN Security Council reaffirmed the "right of self-determination and independence" in November 1972, thus weakening Portugal's (q.v.) position and substantially strengthening the PAIGC. After the PAIGC declared the independence of Guinea in September 1973 the UN General Assembly adopted a resolution on 22 October 1973 condemning Portugal's continued occupation and recognized the new Republic of Guinea-Bissau on 2 November 1973. The Republic was admitted to the United Nations as a full member on 17 September 1974 following the April coup in Lisbon. These events preceded the negotiated independence of Cape Verde. Just prior to its full freedom, the UN Special Committee on Decolonization undertook a fact-finding mission in the islands to determine the health, financial, educational and developmental needs. The Republic of Cape Verde officially joined the UN on 17 September 1975.

UNITED STATES RELATIONS WITH CAPE VERDE. The United States has a relationship with Cape Verde spanning over 300 years. Even before the United States was independent from England, merchant sailors, especially from the New England states, would often stop in Cape Verde or at its coastal *baracoons* (q.v.) in the 17th and 18th centuries to trade for slaves (q.v.). In the 19th century such American stops in Cape Verde were often for acquiring crews for sealing and whaling (q.v.) expeditions. In the 20th century these ties were maintained with *contratado* (q.v.) labor supplied for the cranberry (q.v.) and manufacturing industries of Cape Cod.

Subsequent Cape Verdean emigration (q.v.) has only deepened these links. At present, the United States' economy and trade (q.v.) interests in Cape Verde are centered around the supply of American corn, and modest purchases of Cape Verdean fish products. These long historical ties to the Cape Verdean economy account for the presence of the first American consulate in West Africa being started in Cape Verde in 1818 under Samuel Hodges (q.v.). Basing the American Africa Squadron (q.v.) in Cape Verde in the 1840s and 1850s only underscored the regional strategic value of Cape Verde to the United States. Many American sailors of the Squadron were buried in the Cape Verde islands.

Since the United States was allied to 20th century Portugal (q.v.) by the NATO (q.v.) military alliance, the United States gave military, economic, and intelligence support to Lisbon's counter-insurgency effort to resist the anti-colonial war led by the PAIGC in Guinea-Bissau (qq.v.) and Cape Verde. After independence and the overthrow of the Caetano (q.v.) regime, relations between the United States and Cape Verde have generally been warm even under PAIGC/PAICV governments. The United States has continuously maintained an Ambassador in Cape Verde, which receives American AID assistance, technical aid, and a modest Peace Corps training program for Lusophone Africa. With the large diaspora community of Cape Verdean Americans there is a notable number of American social security checks sent to Cape Verde and one may speak of Cape Verde as one of the few African nations with a formal American political constituency. Since the victorious elections (q.v.) of the MpD (q.v.) in 1991, the United States has actively promoted plural democracy in Cape Verde as well as encouraging the privatization movement through the office of PROMEX.

URBANIZATION. While there are numerous villages and towns throughout the archipelago, it is only in the cities of Mindelo in São Vicente and Praia in São Tiago (qq.v.) that one may speak of urbanization in a substantial fashion. Both of these cities have become fairly large in the past decade, but Mindelo has slipped a bit recently due to a weak shipping economy and the resultant loss in employment.

Population Changes in the Two Largest Cities

	1983	*1987*	*1990*
Praia	44,718	55,258	61,644
Mindelo	42,171	48,381	47,109

Another perspective on Cape Verdean urbanization is derived from the 1990 population statistics for the archipelago which show that 32.33 percent of the population resides in primary urban places, which include Praia and Mindelo, and their suburbs. Meanwhile 12.46 percent of the population lives in secondary urban places (usually *conselho* [q.v.] capitals) and a minor 1.83 percent lives in semi-urban settlements (the small towns and villages). On the other hand, despite the rapid process of Cape Verdean urbanization, 53.39 percent of the people still live in rural areas, which are poorly served by utilities, transport, and communication.

URZELLA. SEE: AGRICULTURE; INDIGO; PANOS.

-V-

VALTZA. SEE: MUSIC.

VEIGA, AGUINALDO (14 August 1916–). Veiga was born in São Tiago (q.v.) where he attended the *liceu* (q.v.). He later studied with distinction in Lisbon earning degrees in law and political and social sciences with high honors in 1945. He immediately began a law practice in Bissau (q.v.) where he also served as the President of the Municipal Council and Substitute Delegate Attorney General of the colony as well as Director of Statistical Services. In 1950 Veiga was transferred to Angola to serve again as Delegate of the Attorney General and Judge of the Law Courts until 1956. At that time he turned to private practice in both Luanda and Lisbon. In this capacity he worked as Senior Attorney for the Central Bank of Angola, the Diamond Company of Angola, the Beer Enterprise EKA, and RIMAGA (the coffee exporting firm) as well as the large construction companies PRECOL and SOMAGUE.

During his decades in Angola before independence Veiga was also a member of the Government Council, the Legislative Chamber, and many other bodies while at the same time being a voting delegate of the colonial Overseas Council in Lisbon. At the start of the armed struggle for national liberation Veiga represented Portugal at the United Nations (q.v.). He was an active opponent of the PAIGC (q.v.) and he belatedly accepted the independence of Cape Verde, but certainly opposed unity with Guinea-Bissau (q.v.). Veiga was active in the Juridical Congress of the UDCV (q.v.).

VEIGA, CARLOS ALBERTO WAHNON DE CARVALHO (21 October 1949–). Veiga is the current Prime Minister of Cape Verde. He was born in Mindelo, São Vicente (q.v.) where he attended school. He went to Portugal to get a degree in law from the Classical University in Lisbon in 1971. He then went to Angola to work as a Registrar in the Civil Registry in Bié. He returned to Cape Verde after independence to work briefly as a public lawyer in Praia until he took a position as the Director General of Internal Administration from 1975 to 1978. Veiga then began his appointment as the Attorney General of the Republic under the PAIGC (q.v.) government.

Following the change in the PAIGC to the PAICV (q.v.) after the coup in Bissau in 1980, Veiga began to have disagreements with PAICV polices relating to centralized state control, democracy, and the role of private sector investment, which convinced him to leave the government in 1980. He then began a private legal practice representing the Banco de Cabo Verde (q.v.) and a variety of public and private businesses and projects in the islands. He gained important experience in serving as counselor to the Special Commission on Constitutional and Judicial Issues of the Assembléia Nacional Popular (q.v.) from 1985 to 1990. Veiga was a member of the Deliberative Council of the Praia Municipality from 1988 to 1989.

He worked for ten more years in private legal practice and

as the President of the Cape Verdean Lawyers Association from 1982 to 1986. As a very close observer of Cape Verdean politics, Veiga became a leading member of the Movimento para Democracia (MpD) (q.v.) which was formed in early 1990. In November 1990 the MpD nominated him as its candidate for Party President in the forthcoming elections promised by the PAICV democratization effort. The national and assembly elections in January and February 1991 ousted the PAICV and its one-party state which had ruled since independence in 1975. Veiga served as the Prime Minister of the Republic since February 1991. Cape Verde thus joined a number of other African states in their drive toward political pluralism. Veiga is the Prime Minister of Cape Verde at least until the planned elections for 1995. He is married with two daughters and three sons. He is a cousin of John Wahnon, a leader of the UCID (q.v.).

VIEIRA, JOÃO BERNARDO "NINO" (1939–). President of Guinea-Bissau's (q.v.) highest political organs since the 1980 coup d'état, including the Council of State (formerly the Revolutionary Council) and the PAIGC (q.v.) Politburo, as well as Commander in Chief of the Armed Forces and Secretary General of the PAIGC. Vieira was born in Bissau (q.v.) and was an electrician by trade. He joined the PAIGC in 1960 and in the following year attended the Party school in Conakry led by Amilcar Cabral (q.v.). From 1961 to 1964 Vieira was the political commissioner in the Catio region in southern Guinea-Bissau. Having received advanced military training in Nanking, China, Vieira was made military head of the entire Southern Front in 1964 when he was also made a member of the PAIGC Political Bureau as a result of the First Party Congress in that year. In 1965 he became the Vice-President of the Conselho de Guerra (q.v.) and continued his work as military head of the Southern Front. From 1967 to 1970 he was the ranking member of the Political Bureau assigned to the Southern Front and after 1970 he held the full national responsibility for military operations of the War Council. In 1971 he became a member of the CEL (q.v.) and subsequently was the Secretary of the PAIGC Permanent Secretariat.

Following independence Viera became the Commander-in-Chief of the Armed Forces as well as presiding over the Guinean Assembléia Nacional Popular (q.v.). In August 1978 he was appointed Prime Minister of Guinea-Bissau following the death of Francisco Mendes (q.v.) in July of that year. In November 1980 Vieira overthrew President Luís Cabral (q.v.) in a coup to become the President of the Republic and Chairman of the Revolutionary Council. Following the 1984 elections and the adoption of a new Constitution (q.v.), he became the Chairman of the Council of State. Vieira increasingly consolidated his rule between 1981 and 1986 and was promoted to the rank of Brigadier General in 1983.

VIEIRA, PAULINO. SEE: MUSIC.

VILLAGE COMMITTEES. SEE: TABANKA.

VIRGINIO, TEOBALDO. Virginio was born in Santo Antão (q.v.) and was a well known writer before his emigration (q.v.) to the United States. Probably the most prolific of modern Cape Verdean writers, he wrote seven novels from 1963 to 1986, including his almost mythical *Vida Crioula* in 1967. A common theme is a nostalgic longing for the islands. As a writer, Virginio published a collection of his poems in 1960, and short stories in 1963. His modern poetry is sentimental, but with a crisp and concise style such as seen in his *Island* and *Prisoner.* Virginio now resides in the United States (q.v.) where in 1985 he launched the cultural and literary quarterly, *Arquipelago,* which presents works in Portuguese and sometimes English. Virginio's brother Luís Romano is also a well known Cape Verdean writer, but he spent a large part of his life in Morocco and Brazil. *See* LITERATURE.

VITAL STATISTICS. At independence in 1975 the Cape Verdean life expectancy (q.v.) for males was 48.3 years and for females, 51.7 years. By 1989 this had improved substantially and the mean number of years lived was up to 57 for males and 61 for females. While this is not as high as in the United

States, it is more appropriate to compare these statistics with those of neighboring West African countries such as Guinea-Bissau where in 1989 the life expectancy for males was 43 years and for females, 47 years.

The length of life may also be expressed in the Crude Death Rate of 8.20/1,000 (for 1988); however, the rather high Infant Death Death of 65.90/1,000 is certainly a major feature of Cape Verdean demography (q.v.). In addition, it must be stressed that the population of Cape Verde is quite young, with 31 percent between the ages of four and 14 years, and within the population of young women there is a Birth Rate of 36.40/1,000 (1988). In short, this young and dynamic population can be expected to show substantial sustained growth which will only be significantly reduced by out-migration.

VOZ DI POVO. SEE: MUSIC.

-W-

WHALING. Small-scale whaling in Cape Verdean waters probably took place as early as the 15th or 16th century, but it was in the 18th century that major long-distance whalers began to visit the same waters for whales, and then for cheap Cape Verdean crewmen eager to escape the poverty and droughts (q.v.) in the islands. By the 19th century it was common to find a quarter to half of all American whaling crews made up of Cape Verdeans from harpooners to cabin boys, cooks, and later, even masters. It is clear that the connection to whaling was central in the initial emigration of Cape Verdeans to New England, especially Nantucket and New Bedford. When the cost of whaling voyages began to rival the profits, the number of Cape Verdeans increased as Yankee sailors declined. Cape Verdeans continued as whalers well into the 20th century when the industry finally collapsed.

The last notable sailing vessel (q.v.) for whaling, the *Morgan,* now part of the Mystic, Connecticut exhibit, was largely crewed by Cape Verdeans. Additional research materials on this association are also collected by the Kendall

Whaling Museum in Sharon, Massachusetts, and in the Whaling Museum in New Bedford.

WINDWARD ISLANDS. SEE: BARLVAVENTO, ILHAS DE.

WOMEN. The PAIGC and PAICV (qq.v.) had, from their inception through to the present time, put forth the full liberation of women as one of their central goals. A number of women were incorporated into leadership positions within the PAIGC's fighting forces during the nationalist armed struggle, and the Party insisted that at least two of the members of *tabanka* (q.v.) committees be women. Also, the União Democrática das Mulheres (UDEMU) (q.v.) was formed by the PAIGC in the mid-1960s and remains active today in promoting women's issues. However, the Party has not yet succeeded in placing more than a handful of women in leadership posts in the Party and government. Moreover, while educational (q.v.) opportunities for women have been expanded since independence, the male-dominated nature of the social and familial structure has not been seriously challenged, and very few women are able to pursue economic independence.

There were no formal restrictions for women being in the PAIGC, except that neither a woman nor a man in a polygynous union was permitted by the PAIGC. During the growth of the PAIGC's liberated zones, divorce was made easier for women, especially those of Muslim unions who had rather limited rights to divorce. Marriages were only permitted by joint consent and forced marriage or child marriage was opposed. The institution of bridewealth was also curbed. In general the position of women has improved given the predominant traditions which were widely based on male supremacy. Now the rights of women are legally protected. For example, children born out of wedlock must legally be supported by their fathers and the status of "illegitimacy" has been abolished. The numbers of women in industry are increasing even though the overall numbers of industrial jobs are few. Since independence, March 8, International Women's Day, has been observed.

Within the PAIGC about 12 percent of the regular members were women and there was one woman member in the Politburo and many women members in the Central Committee and in the Assembléia Nacional Popular (q.v.). Women are commonly found in the health and educational services where such possibilities were limited during colonial rule. During the armed struggle UDEMU was created to assist in the mobilization of women for the war effort. UDEMU was replaced by the Comissão Feminina (Women's Commission) toward the close of the war, but the preoccupation with military affairs and resistance to change by male chauvinists ultimately resulted in the failure of the Comissão Feminina under the leadership of Carmen Pereira (q.v.).

Since independence, the Comissão da Organizaçãos das Mulheres (COM) has made efforts to address special needs of women and to incorporate them more fully into national reconstruction. A number of women made distinguished contributions during the nationalist war; among them are Dr. Maria Boal, Director of the Pilot School and Friendship Institute, Carmen Pereira, the highest ranking woman in the PAIGC, and Ernestina Silla (q.v.), as an exemplary heroine. Articles 13, 16, and 25 of the Constitution (q.v.) of the Republic of Guinea-Bissau provide for the legal, social, and electoral equality of men and women.

After the 1981 coup in Bissau, the PAIGC changed its name to the PAICV (q.v.). Similarly, the UDEMU which had represented women in both nations was changed to the Organização de Mulheres de Cabo Verde (OMCV) (q.v.). The OMCV is organized by sectors which contain all "base groups" in a district as well as an administrative body. The OMCV continued much of the work of the former organization, and it functioned as a women's auxiliary of the single party. The position of women in Cape Verde remains hard with relatively high levels of illiteracy, hard physical work, a high level of machismo, and a relatively low level of participation. Issues such as family planning, birth control, abortion, and AIDS (q.v.) have also entered the picture. OMCV sectors sometimes help to organize *jardins* and pre-school teachers to provide day care and pre-school training for children. There are a number of Cape Verdean women writers, perhaps best known are Orlanda Amarilis and Yolanda Morazzo (qq.v.). The litarary works of A. A. Gonçalves (q.v.) reveal many of the complexities of the lives of Cape Verdean women. *See* DEMOGRAPHY; LIFE EXPECTANCY; VITAL STATISTICS.

BIBLIOGRAPHY

Introduction

Building upon the foundation of its predecessors, this edition of the bibliography attempts to present a core collection of references on the Cape Verde Islands as well as a comprehensive listing of relevant materials that have been written in English. It is an enlarged version that updates the second edition with materials published since 1988 and incorporates within it older items that round out its representation of the Cape Verdean world.

Although the general outline of the bibliography remains the same, certain changes have been made that reflect the expanded coverage. A new section, "Discovery and Travel," presents pictures of the land and people as seen by visitors or other "outsiders," ranging from early explorers and government officials to post-independence Americans rediscovering their roots. With the addition of both new works and classic pieces of scholarship, the number of entries on language, literature, music, and culture has increased considerably. Rather than focusing on the achievements of individuals, an attempt was made to select anthologies and general criticisms that bring to light the strong cultural traditions of the country. "Cape Verdean Americans," a section new to the second edition, has more than doubled in size to present comprehensive documentation on the Cape Verdean American connection, the immigrant experience, and the role of Cape Verdeans in the whaling industry. Still strong is the detailed coverage of Amílcar Cabral and the struggle for national liberation.

Particular attention has been paid in this edition to the issue of accessibility. In terms of language, orientation throughout has been to incorporate the bulk of what has been written in English because these would be most likely to be acquired and read by English-speaking researchers. However, due in part to Cape

Verde's relatively small size and Portugal's colonial monopoly on trade and information, important aspects of the islands have been addressed or recorded only in Portuguese (or occasionally another language). These have been included here. Recent years have brought new attention to this country, and there is now a steadily growing body of English-language publications.

Far more information on the Cape Verde Islands exists than might at first be assumed. Often, however, it must be extracted and pieced together from a larger canvas, such as the age of exploration, the Atlantic trade, the history of Portugal and Africa, scientific investigation, or the American whaling industry, where the focus may not be on this tiny island nation. Since independence the number of publications about Cape Verde has increased rapidly. Many have been generated by the Instituto Caboverdiano do Livro; others reflect a growing interest in the islands and its people as an area for research, study, special projects, and travel. Its current events are reported in the world press.

The topical arrangement of this bibliography will guide the researcher. Each item is listed once under the most appropriate heading. Separate parts of a whole, such as chapters in a book, are analyzed individually when warranted by their content. This tool will introduce the reader to the study of Cape Verde and its American connection. For the scholar who wishes to go further, a knowledge of Portuguese is essential since that is the language of many primary materials and classic texts.

Bibliographies, both standard reference works such as *Africa Bibliography* and the specialized titles listed below, will identify additional resources on Cape Verde, as will the source notes in many of the publications. Of particular merit for their depth of coverage are the bibliographies by Joseph M. McCarthy (1977) and Caroline S. Shaw (1991). General statistical and historical references examine Cape Verde in the context of Portugal, Africa, and the Atlantic trade. Beginning with 1587, Stewart (1989) provides a complete list of governors. Rodney (1970) describes the role of Cape Verdeans in Portugal's 16th century trade with mainland Africa; Duncan (1972) studies 17th century economics; and Brooks (1970) explores the role of Cape Verde in 19th-century trade between America and West Africa.

Though sometimes distorted because of the limited time spent, the places visited, or the agenda of the traveler, descriptive accounts from visitors provide an interesting view of the people, physical features, and daily life on the islands. They can also document the effects of drought, famine, economic conditions, and government rule. For some of the earliest chronicles see Hakluyt's *Voyages and Discoveries.* A Portuguese official, Travasso Valdez (1861), reports in detail on agriculture, commerce, and social conditions. *Black and White Make Brown* records the extensive observations of a British writer and linguist, Lyall (1938), and includes a chapter on Cape Verdean poets. Photographers Renaudeau (1978) and Bossu-Picat (1985?) present their modern day impressions with a minimum of text. Hudgens and Trillo (1990), on the other hand, include in their travel guide detailed history and background information.

Few books have been published in English on the history of Cape Verde. Of the many outstanding works by Cape Verdean historian António Carreira only one, *The People of the Cape Verde Islands: Exploitation and Emigration* (1982), is available in translation. Almeida and Nyhan (1976), Andrade (1974), and Monteiro (1979) provide capsule histories from various points of view. A 1920 handbook prepared by the British Foreign Office is unexpectedly detailed. Patterson (1988) analyzes the effects that cyclical famines have had on the population. Davidson (1989) traces the historical background of the struggle for independence and examines the first ten years of the new republic. Foy (1988) provides comprehensive coverage of its politics, economics, and society.

Works on Cape Verde's geography include studies of its volcanic origins, water problems, marine life, and winds, and descriptions of its birds, seashells, and plant life. Taken together, these selections illustrate the breadth of interests that have drawn individuals to these islands. An outstanding and frequently cited anthropological study is Meintel's *Race, Culture, and Portuguese Colonialism in Cabo Verde* (1984). Reinecke (1975) has compiled a comprehensive annotated bibliography to the language of Cape Verde. Morais-Barbosa (1967) and Silva (1984) reprint classic linguistic works. The rich literary tradition is introduced by Hamilton (1975) and studied by Araujo (1966). Moser (1992) concentrates on the post-independence literary generation. Burness (1989) and Ellen (1988) offer works in translation.

Cape Verdean music receives a good overview in Lima da Cruz

(1981) and several in-depth treatments, including one by its most famous composer, Eugénio Tavares (1932). Folklore, as told by American immigrants, is recorded by Parsons (1923). Works by Ferreira (1967) and Romano (1970) take a close look at Cape Verdean culture and society, as do the essays reprinted in *Colóquios Cabo-Verdianos* (1959). Entries on health, education, social welfare, economics, and development in Cape Verde cover a variety of specific issues. While a few are historical in their approach, most represent modern concerns and recent projects.

In addition to the brief article by Rogers (1980), good introductions to Cape Verdean Americans can be found in the Houston (1978) essay and the richly illustrated Almeida (1978) compilation. Each also contains useful bibliographical references. Many more can be found in the excellent bibliography provided by Halter (1993) in her book-length look at the first one hundred years of this community in New England. Works by Pap (1976, 1981) and the supplement by Viera (1989) include Cape Verdeans in their research on the Portuguese in America. Early studies and reports by Dillingham (1911), Bannick (1916), Weiss (1921), Taft (1923), and Tyack (1952) document the immigration experience even as they reflect the racial climate of the times in which they were written. The experiences of Cape Verdean whalers, sealers, and other men of the sea are detailed by Cohn and Platzer (1978) and Busch (1985); Malloy (1990) presents an all-inclusive guide to resources and archives on the subject. Nunes (1982) provides the first book-length biography of a Cape Verdean American.

Much has been written about Amílcar Cabral and the fight for national liberation. Two good collections of writings by Cabral are *Revolution in Guinea* (1971) and *Return to the Source* (1973). Books that study Cabral include works by Chabal (1983) and McCulloch (1983), as well as a comprehensive critical guide to his theory and practice, Chilcote (1991). Lopes (1987) writes of his mobilizing power, and Chilcote (1984) edits a set of essays created in his honor. Documents and speeches connected with the liberation movement are included in the reader edited by Wallerstein and Bragança (1982). One of the most frequently cited analyses is that by Davidson (1981). Forrest (1992) examines the struggle and discusses its aftermath.

Many of the items listed in this bibliography can be found in the libraries and archives described by Zubatsky (1977) in his research guide. Boston Public Library owns many hard to find early works and is strong in accounts by 19th century travelers; Boston University has an extensive collection on colonialism and an African Studies Library that includes documents, periodicals, and monographs from the islands. Sizable holdings on the age of exploration, literature, language, and Portuguese history and culture can be found at Brown University. Rhode Island College has a Cape Verdean Collection comprised of books, manuscripts, periodicals, papers, and other materials relevant to the islands and their American connection. New Bedford Public Library offers an extensive whaling collection and comprehensive documentation on immigration, packet ships, and other aspects of the Cape Verdean presence in New England.

In revising this bibliography I have had the good fortune to be situated in an area rich in resources on Cape Verde and the Cape Verdean American community. Using these materials as well as the interlibrary loan system of Rhode Island College made it possible to examine each item added to this new edition. Richard and I are grateful to all who contributed their ideas, support, references, and suggestions.

Marlene Lopes

CONTENTS

BIBLIOGRAPHY

A. Bibliographies

Bell, Aubrey F. G. *Portuguese Bibliography.* Oxford: Oxford University Press, 1922.

Berman, Sanford. ''African Liberation Movements: A Preliminary Bibliography.'' *Ufahamu* 3, no. 1 (March 1972): n.p.

Bibliografia Científica da Junta de Investigações do Ultramar. Lisbon: 1960.

Boletim de Bibliografia Portuguesa. Lisbon: Biblioteca National, 1935. Superseded by: *Boletim de Bibliografia Portuguesa. Documentos não Textuais; Boletim de Bibliografia Portuguesa. Monografias; and Boletim de Bibliografia Portuguesa. Publicações em Série* .

Brooks, George E. ''Notes on Research Facilities in Lisbon and the Cape Verde Islands.'' *International Journal of African Historical Studies* 6 (1973): 304–14.

Chilcote, Ronald H. ''Amilcar Cabral: a Biobibliography of His Life and Thought. 1925–1973.'' *Africana Journal* 4 (1974): 289–307.

Chilcote, Ronald H., comp. *Emerging Nationalism in Portuguese Africa,* Stanford, Cal.: Hoover Institution Press, Stanford University, 1972.

Conover, Helen F. *A List of References on the Portuguese Colonies in Africa (Angola, Cape Verde Islands, Mozam-*

bique, Portuguese Guinea, São Tomé and Príncipe. Washington, D.C.: Library of Congress, 1942.

Duignan, Peter, ed. and comp., and Helen F. Conover, comp. *Guide to Research and Reference Works on Sub-Saharan Africa,* Stanford, Cal.: Hoover Institution Press, Stanford University, 1972.

Duignan, Peter, and L. H. Gann. ''A Bibliographical Guide to Colonialism in Sub-Saharan Africa.'' *Colonialism in Africa:1870–1960,* vol. 5. London: Cambridge University Press, 1973.

Figueiredo, Jaime de. ''Bibliografia Caboverdeana: Subsídios para uma Ordenação Sistemática.'' *Cabo Verde: Boletim de Propaganda e Informação* 5, no. 49 (1953): 31.
Continued in: no. 50, p. 31; no. 54, p. 31; no. 56, p. 37.

Flors, Michel. ''A Bibliographic Contribution to the Study of Portuguese Africa (1965–1972).'' *Current Bibliography on African Affairs* 7, no. 2 (1974): 116–37.

Gibson, Mary Jane. *Portuguese Africa: a Guide to Official Publications.* Washington, D.C.: Library of Congress, 1967.

Goncalves, José Júlio. ''Bibliografia Antropológica do Ultramar Português.'' *Boletim Geral das Colónias* (1961): 281–90, 335–41, 431–71, 483–501.

Gowan, Susan Jean. *Portuguese-Speaking Africa 1900–1979: A Select Bibliography.* Braamfontein: South African Institute of International Affairs, 1982.

Instituto Português de Arquivos. *Guia de Fontes Portuguesas para a História de Africa, Vol. 1,* Conselho Internacional de Archivos/International Council on Archives. ''Guia de Fontes para a História das Nações''/''Guide to the Sources for the History of Nations''. Lisbon: Imprensa Nacional-Casa Moeda, 1991.

Kettenring, N. Ernest, comp. *A Bibliography of Theses and Dissertations on Portuguese Topics Completed in the United States and Canada 1861–1983,* Durham, N.H.: International Conference Group on Modern Portugal, 1984.

Kornegay, Francis A. Jr. ''A Bibliographic Memorial to Amilcar Cabral: Selected Survey of Resources on the Struggle in Guinea-Bissau.'' *Ufahamu* 3, no. 3 (December 1973): n.p.

Malloy, Mary. *African Americans in the Maritime Trades: a Guide to Resources in New England,* Kendall Whaling Museum Monograph, 6. Sharon, Mass: Kendall Whaling Museum, 1990.

McCarthy, Joseph M. *Guinea-Bissau and Cape Verde Islands: A Comprehensive Bibliography.* New York: Garland Pub., 1977.

Moser, Gerald M. *Bibliografia das Literaturas Africanas de Expressão Portuguesa.* Lisbon: Imprensa Nacional-Casa da Moeda, 1983.

Moser, Gerald M. *A Tentative Portuguese-African Bibliography: Portuguese Literature in Africa and African Literature in the Portuguese Language.* University Park: Pennsylvania State University, 1970.

Pap, Leo. *The Portuguese in the United States: A Bibliography,* Bibliographies and Documents Series. Staten Island, N.Y.: Center for Migration Studies, 1976.

Reinecke, John E., comp. *A Bibliography of Pidgin and Creole Languages,* Oceanic Linguistics Special Publication, 14. Honolulu: University Press of Hawaii, 1975.

Rogers, Francis M., and David T. Haberly. *Brazil, Portugal and other Portuguese- Speaking Lands: A List of Books Primarily in English.* Cambridge, Mass.: Harvard University Press, 1968.

Ryder, A. F. C. *Materials for West African History in Portuguese Archives.* London: Athlone Press, 1965.

Rydings, H. A. *The Bibliographies of West Africa.* Ibadan: Ibadan University Press, 1961.

Shaw, Caroline S., comp. *Cape Verde,* World Bibliographical Series. Santa Barbara, Cal.: Clio Press, 1991.

Viera, David J., Geoffrey L. Gomes, and Adalino Cabral, comp. *The Portuguese in the United States: A Bibliography,* Durham, N.H.: International Conference Group on Portugal, Dept. of History, University of New Hampshire, 1989. First supplement to Pap's 1976 edition.

Zubatsky, David S., comp. *A Guide to Resources in United States Libraries and Archives for the Study of Cape Verdes, Guinea (Bissau), São Tomé-Príncipe, Angola and Mozambique,* Essays in Portuguese Studies, Essay no. 1. Durham, N.H.: International Conference Group on Portugal, 1977.

B. Periodicals

Africa News 1973+.
Information on liberation struggles and reform.

Africa Report
Publication of the African-American Institute; emphasis on policy and development.

Afrique-Asie 1948+.
Reports on liberation movements. Now called: Afrique et Asie Modernes.

Arquipélago (U.S.) 1986+.
''Revista de opinião e cultura''.

Boletim Oficial da República de Cabo Verde 1842+.

Cabo Verde: Boletim de Propaganda e Informação 1949–64.

The Cape Verdean 1969+.
Cape Verdean American newspaper.

Claridade March 1936–Dec.19, 1960.
Literary and cultural journal, featuring writings of Jorge Barbosa, Baltasar Lopes da Silva, and Manuel Lopes. Modernist outlook. Sporadic: no.1,2 (1936); no.3 (1937); no.4 (1946); no.5 (1947); no.6 (1948); no.7 (1949); no.8 (1958); and no.9 (1960).

The CVN 1979+.
Cape Verdean American newspaper.

Emigrason 1985+.

Libertação
Internal PAIGC publication.

Mujêr 1982+.
Published by the Organização das Mulheres de Cabo Verde (OMCV). Covers culture, politics, child care, home economics, and other issues of particular interest to women.

Nô Pintcha 1974+.
Official PAIGC newspaper in Guinea-Bissau.

O Voz Caboverdeana (U.S.) 1933–35.

Objective: Justice 1971+.
"A United Nations review dedicated to the promotion of justice through self-determination of peoples, the elimination of apartheid and racial discrimination, and the advancement of human rights."

PAIGC Actualités 1969–74.
Information bulletin edited by the Commission on Information and Propaganda of the Central Committee of the

PAIGC. English edition published by LSM Information Center, Richmond, B.C., Canada.

Ponto & Virgula 1983+.

Raízes 1981+.
Concerned with literature, social life and customs.

Seiva 1986+.
Journal of Juventude Africana Amílcar Cabral-Cabo Verde (JAAC-CV).

Tchuba Newsletter 1975–78.
Organ of the American Committee for Cape Verde (Boston, Mass.).

Terra Nova 1974+.
Christian newspaper.

Tricontinental Magazine 1967+.
Published in Spanish, English, and French by the Executive Secretariat of the Organization of Solidarity of the Peoples of Asia, Africa, and Latin America .

Unidade e Luta 1976+.
Central organ of the PAICV.

A Voz de Cabo Verde 1911–19.
Political journal with literary contributions .

Voz do Povo 1962+.
Newspaper; superseded Arquipélago.

C. General Statistical References

Anuário Estatístico/Annuaire Statistique. Lisbon: Tipografia Portuguesa, 1947+.

Cape Verde Islands. *Secção de Estatística Geral.* Lisbon: Trimestral.

Curtin, Philip D. *The Atlantic Slave Trade: A Census.* Madison, Wis.: University of Wisconsin Press, 1969.

Lima, José Joaquim Lopes de. *Ensaios sobre a Statística das Possessões Portuguesas no Ultramar.* Lisbon: Imprensa Nacional, 1844.

Lima, José Joaquim Lopes de. *Prospecto Estatístico-Econômico da Provincia de Cabo Verde.* Lisbon: [Imprensa Nacional?], 1875.

Mendes Correa, António Augusto. ''Aspectos Demográficos do Arquipélago do Cabo Verde.'' *Garcia de Orta* 1, no. 1: 3–15

Portugal. Agência Geral do Ultramar. *Portugal Overseas Provinces: Facts and Figures.* Lisbon: [s.n.], 1965.

Serviços Aduaneiros. *Sétimo Recenseamento Geral da População da Colônia de Cabo Verde em 1940,* 3 vol. Praia: Imprensa Nacional, 1945.

Wilcox, Walter F. *International Migrations: Statistics, Vol.1.* New York: National Bureau of Economic Research, 1929.

D. General Historical and Political References

Abshire, David M., and Michael A. Samuels, ed. *Portuguese Africa: A Handbook,* New York: Praeger, 1969.

Andrade, António Alberto de. *Many Races - One Nation: Racial Non-Discrimination Always the Cornerstone of Portugal's Overseas Policy.* Lisbon: [s.n.], 1961.

Asiwaju, A. I., and Michael Crowder, ed. ''Portugal in Africa.'' *Tarikh,* with consultant ed. Basil Davidson. Entire issue. Vol. 6; no. 4. Atlantic Highlands: Humanities Press, 1980. Collection of essays. Published by Longman in London for the Historical Society of Nigeria.

Axelson, Eric. *Congo to Cape: Early Portuguese Explorers.* New York: Barnes and Noble, 1973.

Barreto, João. *História da Guiné, 1418–1918.* Lisbon: [s.n.], 1938.

Beazley, Charles Raymond. *Prince Henry the Navigator (1354–1460).* New York: G.P. Putnam, 1895.

Bénézet, Anthony. *Relation de la Côte de la Guinée,* 4th ed. London: [s.n.], 1788.

Bénézet, Anthony. *Some Historical Account Of Guinea: Its Situation, Produce, and the General Disposition of Its Inhabitants . . . ,* London: Cass, 1968.
Facsimile reprint of 2nd ed.: London, J. Phillips, 1788.

Bennett, Norman R., and George E. Brooks, ed. *New England Merchants in Africa: A History through Documents, 1802 to 1865,* Boston: Boston University Press, 1965.

Blake, John William, ed. and trans. *Europeans in West Africa 1450–1560,* 2 vol. London: Printed for the Hakluyt Society, 1942.

Boxer, C. R. *The Dutch Seaborne Empire: 1600–1800.* London: Hutchinson & Co., 1965.

Boxer, C. R. *Four Centuries of Portuguese Expansion, 1415–1825.* Berkeley: University of California Press, 1969.

Boxer, C. R. *Portuguese Society in the Tropics.* Madison: University of Wisconsin Press, 1965.

Boxer, C. R. *Race Relations in the Portuguese Colonial Empire 1415–1825.* Oxford: Clarendon Press, 1963.

Brooks, George E. *Landlords and Other Strangers: Ecology, Society, and Trade in Western Africa, 1000–1630.* San Francisco: Westview Press, 1993.

Brooks, George E. *Yankee Traders, Old Coasters & African Middlemen: A History of American Legitimate Trade with West Africa in the Nineteenth Century.* Boston: Boston University Press, 1970.

Cadbury, William A. *Labour in Portuguese West Africa,* Reprint of 1910 ed. New York: Negro University Press, 1969.

Caetano, Marcello. *Colonizing Traditions, Principles and Methods of the Portuguese.* Lisbon: Agência Geral do Ultramar, 1951.

Caetano, Marcello. *Portugal's Reasons for Remaining in the Overseas Provinces: Excerpts from Speeches Made by the Prime Minister Marcello Caetano.* Lisbon: [s.n.], 1970.

Carreira, António. *Os Portuguêses nos Rios de Guiné, 1500–1900.* Lisbon: [s.n.], 1984.

Castanheira, José Pedro, and Henrique Monteiro. " 'Perestroika' in Africa." *World Press Review* 37, no. 7 (July 1990): 55.

Chilcote, Ronald H. *Portuguese Africa.* Englewood Cliffs, N.J.: Prentice-Hall, 1967.

Clarence-Smith, Gervase. *The Third Portuguese Empire 1825–1975: A Study in Economic Imperialism.* Manchester: Manchester University Press, 1985.

Diffie, Bailey W., and George D. Winius. *Foundations of the Portuguese Empire, 1415–1580,* Europe and the World in the Age of Expansion, vol. 1. Minneapolis: University of Minnesota Press, 1977.

Duffy, James. *Portugal in Africa.* Cambridge, Mass.: Harvard University Press, 1962.

Duffy, James. *Portuguese Africa.* Cambridge, Mass.: Harvard University Press, 1968.

Duncan, T. Bentley. *Atlantic Islands: Madeira, the Azores, and the Cape Verdes in Seventeenth-Century Commerce and Navigation.* Chicago: University of Chicago Press, 1972.

Fage, J. D. ''Slavery and the Slave Trade in the Context of West African History.'' *Journal of African History* 10, no. 3 (1969): 393–404.

Ferreira, Eduardo de Sousa. *Portuguese Colonialism from South Africa to Europe.* Germany: Druckerei Horst Ahlbrecht, 1972.

Ferreira, Eduardo de Sousa. *Portuguese Colonialism in Africa: The End of an Era.* Paris: UNESCO Press, 1974.

First, Ruth. *Portugal's Wars in Africa.* London: Christian Action Publications, 1972.

Gomes, Diogo. ''As Relações do Descobrimento da Guiné e das Ilhas dos Açores, Madeira e Cabo Verde.'' *Boletim da Sociedade de Geográfia de Lisboa* 14, no. 5 (September 1898): 267–93.

Greenfield, Sidney M. ''Plantations, Sugar Cane and Slavery.'' *Historical Reflections - Reflexions Historiques* 6, no. 1 (June 1979): 85–119.

Hammond, Richard J. *Portugal and Africa, 1815–1910: A Study in Uneconomic Imperialism.* Stanford, Cal.: Stanford University Press, 1966.

Haywood, Carl Norman. ''American Whalers and Africa.'' Ph.D. diss., Boston University, 1967.

Humbaraci, Arslan, and Nicole Muchnik. *Portugal's African Wars.* New York: Third World Press, 1973.

Kaké, Ibrahima Baba. ''Coastal and Island Civilizations of Africa.'' *UNESCO Courier* 36 (December 1983): 14–18.

Lavradio, Marquês do. *Portugal em Africa Depois de 1851.* Lisbon: Agência Geral das Colônias, 1936.

Livermore, Harold. *A New History of Portugal.* Cambridge: Cambridge University Press, 1936.

Lobato, Alexandre. ''A Expansão Ultramarina Portuguesa nos Séculos XVI e XVII.'' *Ultramar,* no. 29 (1967).

Lobato, Alexandre. ''A Política Ultramarina Portuguesa no Século XVIII.'' *Ultramar,* no. 30 (1967).

Lobato, Alexandre. ''As Fontes e as Formas da Reorganização Ultramarina Portuguesa no Seculo XIX.'' *Ultramar,* no. 30 (1967).

Lobban, Richard, and Joshua Forrest. *Historical Dictionary of the Republic of Guinea-Bissau,* 2nd ed. Metuchen, N.J.: Scarecrow, 1988.

Lopes, Edmundo Correira. *A Escravatura: Subsídios para a Sur História.* Lisbon: [s.n.], 1944.

Luttrel, A. ''Slavery and Slaving in the Portuguese Atlantic to about 1500.'' *The Trans-Atlantic Slave Trade from West Africa,* [Edinburgh?]: Centre of African Studies, University of Edinburgh, 1965.

Marques, A. H. de Oliveira. *The History of Portugal from Lusitania to Empire,* 2 vol. New York: Columbia University Press, 1972.

Mauro, Frederic. *Le Portugal et l'Atlantique au XVIIe Siècle, 1570–1670: Etude Économique.* Paris: Ecole Pratique des Hautes Etudes, 1960.

Minter, William. *Portuguese Africa and the West.* Baltimore: Penguin Books, 1972.

Moreira, Adriano. *Portugal's Stand in Africa.* New York: University Publishers, 1962.

Newitt, Malyn. *Portugal in Africa: the Last Hundred Years.* Harlow, Essex, Great Britain: Longman, 1981.

Nogueira, Franco. *The United Nations and Portugal: A Study of Anti-Colonialism.* London: Tandem, 1964.

Oliveira, José Marques de. "Honório Barreto e os Interesses Portugueses em Africa." *Cabo Verde: Boletim de Propaganda e Informação* 11, no. 123 (1959): 13.

Pacheco Pereira, Duarte. *Esmeraldo de Situ Orbis,* 3rd ed. Lisbon: Academia Portuguesa da História, 1988.

Prestage, E. *The Portuguese Pioneers.* New York: Barnes and Noble, 1967.

Reade, Winwood. *The African Sketch Book,* 2 vol. London: Smith, 1873.

Rodney, Walter. *A History of the Upper Guinea Coast, 1545–1800.* New York: Oxford University Press, 1970.

Salazar, António de Oliveira. *H.E. Professor Oliveira Salazar, Prime Minister of Portugal, Broadcast on 12 August 1963: Declaration on Overseas Policy.* Lisbon: Secreteriado Nacional da Informação, 1960.

Salazar, António de Oliveira. "Policy in Africa." *Vital Speeches* 34 (15 March 1968): 325–28.

Scammell, G. V. "The English in the Atlantic Islands c.1450–1650." *Mariner's Mirror* 72, no. 3 (August 1986): 295–317.

Serrão, Joaquim V. *História Breve da Historiográfia Portuguesa.* Lisbon: [s.n.], 1962.

Serrão, Joel, ed. *Dicionário de História de Portugal,* 4 vol. Lisbon: Iniciativas, 1963.

Snelgrave, William. *Nouvelle Relation de Quelques Endroits de Guinée et du Commerce d'Esclaves Qu'on y Fait.* Amsterdam: [s.n.], 1735.

Stewart, John. *African States and Rulers: an Encyclopedia of Native, Colonial and Independent States and Rulers Past and Present.* Jefferson, N.C.: McFarland, 1989.

Teixeira, Cândido da Silva. "Companhia de Cacheu, Rios e Comércio da Guiné (Documentos para a Sua História)." *Boletim do Arquivo Histórico Colonial* 1 (1950): 85–521.

Vasconcelos, Ernesto Júlio de Carvalho e. *As Colónias,* Portuguesas, 2nd ed. Lisbon: [s.n.], 1904.

Walter, Jaime, ed. *Honório Pereira Barreto: Biografia, Documentes,* Publication, No.5. Bissau: Centro de Estudos da Guiné Portuguesa, 1947.

Wheeler, Douglas L. *Historical Dictionary of Portugal.* Metuchen, N.J.: Scarecrow Press, 1993.

Whitaker, Paul M. "The Revolutions of 'Portuguese' Africa." *Journal of Modern African Studies* 8, no. 1 (1 April 1970): 15–35.

Zurara, Gomes Eanes de. *The Chronicle of the Discovery and Conquest of Guinea,* Reprint of 1452 ed. 2 vol. London: Hakluyt Society, 1896.

E. Description and Travel

Barboza, Ronald. "Cape Verde: Portrait of an Archipelago." *Spinner: People and Culture in Southeastern Massachusetts, Vol. II,* 27–31. Edited by Donna Huse. New Bedford, Mass.: Spinner, 1982.

Barboza, Steven. "The American Connection." *Essence* (February 1988): 24.

Barboza, Steven. "Cape Verde: Islands in Limbo." *Islands* 3, no. 1 (March 1983): 66–75.

Borah, Leo A., and Chamberlin Wellman. "New Map of the Atlantic Ocean." *National Geographic* 80, no. 407–18 (1941): n.p.

Bossu-Picat, Christian, photographer. *Cabo Verde: Dez Anos de Desenvolvimento,* Boulogne, France: Editions Delroisse, 1985.

Breirly, T. G. "The Cape Verde Islands." *Geographical Magazine* 36, no. 2 (June 1963): 84–91.

Bridge, Horatio. *Journal of an African Cruiser: Comprising Sketches of the Canaries, the Cape de Verds, Liberia, Madeira, Sierra Leone, and Other Places of Interest on the West Coast of Africa,* Edited by Nathaniel Hawthorne. London: Dawsons of Pall Mall, 1968.
Reprint of 1st ed.: London, Wiley and Putnam, 1845.

Callixto, Vasco. *Viagem a Cabo Verde (1798 Quilómetros Através de 9 Ilhas): Sal, S. Nicolau, S. Vicente, Santo Antão, Santiago, Brava, Fogo, Maio, Boavista: 25 Dias.* Lisbon: Callixto, 1974.

"The Cape Verde Islands." *Littell's Living Age* 2 (1844): 673–76.

Casimiro, Augusto. *Portugal Crioulo.* Lisbon: Edicoes Cosmos, 1940.

Corry, Joseph. *Observations on the Windward Coast of Africa,* Reprint of 1807 ed. London: Frank Carr, 1968.

Costa, A. Fontoura da. *Cartas das Ilhas de Cabo Verde de Valentim Fernandes (1506–1508).* Lisbon: Agencia Geral das Colonias, 1939.

Crone, G. R., ed. and transl. *The Voyages of Cadamosto and Other Documents on Western Africa in the Second Half of the*

Fifteenth Century. Works Issued by the Hakluyt Society, 2nd series, No.80. London: Hakluyt Society, 1937.

Ellis, Alfred B. *West African Islands.* London: Chapman and Hall, 1885.

Fernandes, Valentim. *Description de la Côte Occidentale d'Afrique par Valentim Fernandes (1506–1510).* Edited by Théodore Monod, A. Teixeira da Mota, and R. Mauny. Bissau: [s.n.], 1951.

Fink, Michael. "Inside the Cape Verdean World: the Jewish Connection." *The Rhode Island Jewish Herald* (28 December 1989): 1 ff.

Freyre, Gilberto. *Aventura e Rotina: Sugestões de uma Viagem à Procura das Costantes Portuguesas de Caráter e Ação,* 2nd. rev. ed. Rio de Janeiro: J. Olympio, 1980.

Hakluyt, Richard. *Voyages and Discoveries.* Reprint of 1589 ed. Baltimore: Penguin Books, 1972.

Hudgens, Jim, and Richard Trillo. "The Cape Verde Islands." *West Africa: the Rough Guide,* pp. 475–528. London: Harrap-Columbus, 1990.

Jane, Cecil, ed. and transl. *Select Documents Illustrating the Four Voyages of Columbus,* Vol.II, The Third and Fourth Voyages. Works Issued by the Hakluyt Society, 2nd series, No. 70. London: Hakluyt Society, 1933.

Jefferson, Mark. "Cape Verd Islands: A Visit to San Vincente in 1890." *The Journal of Geography* 13 (March 1915): 224–26.

Keeler, Mary Frear, ed. *Sir Francis Drake's West Indian Voyage 1585–86.* Works Issued by the Hakluyt Society, 2nd series, no.148 . London: Hakluyt Society, 1981.

Keynes, Richard Darwin, ed. *The Beagle Record: Selections from the Original Pictorial Records and Written Accounts of the*

Voyage of H.M.S. Beagle, pp.24–32. Cambridge: Cambridge University Press, 1979.

Lindbergh, Anne Morrow. *Listen! the Wind.* New York: Harcourt, Brace, 1938.

Ludtke, Jean. *Atlantic Peeks: an Ethnographic Guide to the Portuguese-Speaking Atlantic Islands.* Hanover, Mass.: The Christopher Publishing House, 1989.

Lyall, Archibald. *Black and White Make Brown: an Account of a Journey to the Cape Verde Islands and Portuguese Guinea.* London: William Heinemann, 1938.

Meuli, Kaspar. "Cape Verde: Forgotten Islands in the Atlantic." *Swiss Review of World Affairs* 39, no. 11 (February 1990): 13–19.

Morison, Samuel Eliot. "The United States Africa Squadron at the Cape Verde Islands." *Portugal and Brazil in Transition,* pp.145–48. Edited by Raymond S. Sayers. Minneapolis: University of Minnesota Press, 1968.

Newton, Alex. "Cape Verde." *West Africa: A Travel Survival Kit,* pp.131–146. Berkeley, Cal.: Lonely Planet Publications, 1988.

Oliveira, José Osório de. *As Ilhas Portuguesas de Cabo Verde,* Colecção Educativa, 38: Série E; no. 3. Porto: Campanha Nacional de Educação de Adultos, 1955.

Oporto, Portugal. Exposição Colonial Portuguesa, 1934. "Cabo Verde." *O Império Português na Primeira Exposição Colonial Portuguesa,* pp. 265–72. Pôrto: Leitao e Coimbra, 1934.

Renaudeau, Michel, photographer. *Cabo Verde = Cape Verde Islands = Cap Vert,* Paris: Delroisse, 1978.

Roberts, George. *The Four Voyages of Captain George Roberts: Being a Series of Uncommon Events, Which Befell Him in a*

Voyage to the Islands of the Canaries, Cape de Verde, and Barbados, from Which He Was Bound to the Coast of Guiney, London: A. Bettenworth, 1726.
Attributed to Daniel Defoe.

Rodrigues-Taylor, Kathy. ''Cabo Verde: A Personal Travel Memoir.'' *Black Elegance* (September 1987): 16–20.

Saint-Lô, Alexis de. *Relation du Voyage du Cap Verd,* Microfiche reprint of 1637 ed. 3 sheets of fiche. Archives Africaines, series 5. Paris: L'Institut National des Langues et Civilisations Orientales, 1974.

Salinger, Susanne, and Harro Strehlow. ''The Travels of Carl Bolle to the Cape Verde and the Canary Islands.'' *Archives of Natural History* 18, no. pt. 2 (June 1991): 251–54.

Sousa Monteiro, José Maria de. *Dicionário Geographico das Províncias e Possessões Portuguezas no Ultramar,* Os Potuguezes em Africa, Asia, America, e Oceania, vol. 8. Lisbon: Typographia Lisbonense de J.C. de Agiuar Vianna, 1850.

Street, Don. ''An Atlantic Outpost.'' *Cruising World* 14, no. 2 (February 1988): 59–66.

''A Summer Cruise among the Atlantic Islands: Pt. IV, The Cape Verds.'' *Harper's New Monthly Magazine* 54, no. 323 (April 1877): 674–76.

Thomas, Charles W. *Adventures and Observations on the West Coast of Africa and Its Islands: Historical and Descriptive Sketches of Madeira, Canary, Biafra and Cape Verde Islands,* Reprint of 1860 ed. New York: Negro Universities Press, 1969.

Travasso Valdez, Francisco. *Six Years of a Traveller's Life in Western Africa,* Vol.1. London: Hurst and Blackett, 1861.

''Whaling at the Cape de Verdes.'' *Once a Week* 11 (6 August 1864): 194–96.

Wren, Walter. *The Voyage of Mr. George Fenner to Guinie and the Islands of Cape Verde in the Yeere of 1566.* London: J.M. Dent, 1927.

F. History of Cape Verde

Albuquerque, Luís de, and Maria Emília Medeira Santos, project directors. *História Geral de Cabo Verde,* Vol. 1-. Lisbon; Praia: Instituto de Investigação Científica Tropical; Direcção-Geral do Patrimonio Cultural de Cabo Verde, 1988+. To date, Vol. 1 (1988) and Vol. 2 (1990) have been published.

Almeida, Raymond A., and Patricia Nyhan. *Cape Verde and Its People: A Short History.* Boston: TCHUBA, American Committee for Cape Verde, 1976. Adapted from an unpublished manuscript by Deirdre Meintel Machado.

Amaral, Ilídio do. *Santiago de Cabo Verde, a Terra e os Homens,* Memorias da Junta de Investigações do Ultramar, 2nd series, no. 48. Lisbon: [s.n.], 1964.

Andrade, Elisa. *The Cape Verde Islands: from Slavery to Modern Times.* Eugene, Oregon: Third World Students Coalition Press, 1974. Published for P.A.I.G.C.-U.S.A. Committee.

Andrade, Elisa. "The Islands of Cape Verde." *UNESCO Courier* 36 (December 1983): 18–19.

Baleno, Ilídio. "Subsídios para a História de Cabo Verde: a Necessidade das Fontes Locais Através dos Vestígios Materiais." *Actas. Vol. 1: D. João II e a Política Quatrocentista,* pp. 553–57. Congresso Internacional Bartolomeu Dias e a Sua Época. Porto: Universidade do Porto: Commissão Nacional para as Comemorações dos Descobrimentos Portugueses, 1989.

Barros, António de. *Africa, Cabo Verde: o Que Se Viu, o Que Se Disse, o Que Se Cismou, de 1952 para ca.* Lisbon: Gomes & Rodrigues, 1961.

Barros, Simão. *Origens da Colónia de Cabo Verde,* Cadernos Coloniais, no. 56. Lisbon: Edições Cosmos, 1937.

Barrows, Paul Wayne. ''The Historical Roots of Cape Verdean Dependency, 1460–1990.'' Ph.D. diss., University of Minnesota, 1990.

Brookshaw, D. ''Islands Apart - Tradition and Transition.'' *Index on Censorship* 21, no. 6 (June 1992): 13–14.

Cabral, Nelson E. *Le Moulin et le Pilon: les Îles du Cap-Vert.* Paris: L'Harmattan: Agence de Coopération Culturelle et Technique, 1980.

''Cape Verde: a Mudança—Change [Country Report].'' *The Courier,* no. No.127 (May 1991): 10–26.

Cardoso, Renato. *Cabo Verde, Opção por uma Política de Paz,* Colecção Estudos e Ensaios, 1. Praia: Instituto Cabo-Verdiano do Livro, 1986. Presented at the ''Seminario sobre a Africa de Lingua Oficial Portuguesa, Portugal e os Estados Unidos da America,'' Lisbon, 14–16 May, 1985.

Carreira, António. ''Alguns Aspectos da Administração Publica em Cabo Verde no Seculo XVIII.'' *Boletim Cultural da Guiné Portuguesa* 27, no. 105 (January 1972): 123–204.

Carreira, António. *Cabo Verde: Classes Sociais, Estrutura Familiar, Migrações,* Lisbon: Ulmeiro, 1977.

Carreira, António. *Cabo Verde: Formação e Extinção de uma Sociedade Escravocrata (1460–1878),* 2nd ed. Lisbon?: Instituto Caboverdeano do Livro, 1983.

Carreira, António. *Cabo Verde: Aspectos Sociais, e Fomes do Século XX,* 2nd rev. ed. Biblioteca Ulmeiro, no. 9. Lisbon: Ulmeiro, 1984.

Carreira, António, comp. *Descrições Oitocentistas das Ilhas de Cabo Verde,* Praia: Instituto Caboverdiano do Livro, 1987.

Carreira, António. *Documentos para a História das Ilhas de Cabo Verde e "Rios de Guiné": Séculos XVII e XVIII.* Lisbon: [s.n.], 1983.

Carreira, António. *Migrações nas Ilhas de Cabo Verde,* 2nd ed. Lisbon?: Instituto Caboverdeano do Livro, 1983.

Carreira, António. *The People of the Cape Verde Islands: Exploitation and Emigration,* transl. and ed. Christopher Fyfe. Hamden, Conn.: Archon Books, 1982.

Castiel, Carol S. "Cape Verde: Searching for a Larger Goal; the Second Liberation Struggle." *West Africa* No. 3847 (27 May 1991): 866–67.

Conselho de Governo das Ilhas de Cabo Verde. *Acta.* Praia: Imprensa Nacional, 1917+.

Cordeyro, António. *História Insulana das Ilhas a Portugal Sugeytas no Oceano Occidental.* Lisbon: Na Officina de António Pedroza Galram, 1717.

Cortesão, Armando Zuzarte. "Subsídios para a História do Descobrimento da Guiné e Cabo Verde." *Boletim Geral das Colónias* 76, no. 1 (1931): 2–39.

Curti, Merle. *American Philanthropy Abroad: a History.* New Brunswick, N.J.: Rutgers University Press, 1963.

Davidson, Basil. "The Africa of Olof Palme." *New Perspectives in North-South Dialogue: Essays in Honour of Olof Palme,* 247–255. Edited by Kofi Buenor Hadjor. London: I.B. Tauris in assoc. with Third World Communications, 1988.

Davidson, Basil. *The Fortunate Isles: A Study in African Transformation.* Trenton, N.J.: Africa World Press, 1989.

Do PAIGC ao PAICV: Documentos. Mem Martins, Portugal: Gráfica Europam, 1981.

Duarte, Fausto Castilho. "A Influência de Cabo Verde na Colonização da Guiné." *Boletim da Sociedade de Geográfia de Lisboa* (1943): 57–64.

Duarte, Fausto Castilho. "Os Caboverdeanos na Colonização da Guiné." *Cabo Verde: Boletim de Propaganda e Informação* 1, no. 2 (1949): 13.

Estatuto Político-Administrativa de Cabo Verde. Lisbon: Agência Geral do Ultramar, 1964.

Ferro, Mário, A. Almeida, and M. Saldanha. *Programa da Colônia de Cabo Verde.* Lisbon: Ministério das Colônias, 1936.

Foy, Colm. *Cape Verde: Politics, Economics, & Society.* London; New York: Pinter, 1988.

Fyfe, Christopher. "The Cape Verde Islands." *History Today* 31 (May 1981): 5–9.

Gatlin, Darryle John. "A Socioeconomic History of São Vicente de Cabo Verde, 1830–1970." Ph.D. diss., University of California at Los Angeles, 1990.

Gollut, Mauricett. "Cape Verde: Back Home to the Islands." *Refugees* (February 1985): 11–12.

Great Britain. Foreign Office. Historical Section. "Cape Verde Islands." *Portuguese Possessions,* Reprint of 1920 ed. Peace Handbooks, Vol. 19, no. 117. Wilmington, Del.: Scholarly Resources, 1973.
First published by H.M. Stationery Office, London.

Greenfield, Sidney M. "The Cape Verde Islands: Their Settlement, the Emergence of Their Creole Culture, and the Subsequent Migrations of Their People." *Portuguese Migration in Global Perspective,* pp. 158–81. Edited by David Higgs. Toronto: Multicultural History of Ontario, 1990.

Haladay, Joan, and N'Koumba Karamoko. *Cape Verde: a Case Study in African Migration.* New York?: Afro-Portuguese Research Center, 1979.

Kasper, Josef E. *Ilha da Boa Vista, Cabo Verde: Aspectos Históricos, Sociais, Ecológicos e Económicos,* Estudos e Ensaios. Praia: Instituto Caboverdiano do Livro, 1987. Translated from the German by Luís Filipe da Silva Madeira.

Lacerda, João Cesário de. *Relatório do Governo Geral da Província de Cabo Verde.* Lisbon: [s.n.], 1901.

Leite, Carlos Alberto Monteiro. ''Subsídios para a História de Cabo Verde.'' *Cabo Verde: Boletim de Propaganda e Informação* 8, no. 89 (1956): 25.

Leite, John. ''Brava: da Névoa da História.'' *Arquipélago* 1, no. 4 (June 1986): 4–10.

Leite, John. *The Legacy in Cape Verde: Quoting Scientific Socialism.* [s.l.]: The Author, 1985.

Leite, John. ''Sal.'' *Arquipélago* 1, no. 1 (May 1985): 13–15.

Lereno, Alvaro de Paiva de Almeida. *Subsídios para a História da Moeda em Cabo Verde, 1460–1940.* Lisbon: Agência Geral das Colônias, 1942.

Lewis, James. *The Economic and Social Effects of Natural Disasters on the Least Developed and Developing Island Countries, with Special Reference to Antigua and Barbuda, Republic of Cape Verde, Comoros Federal Islamic Republic (and Mayotte), Republic of the Maldives, Western Samoa.* Wiltshire, England: Datum International, 1982. A report for UNCTAD VI, Belgrade 1983.

Madeira Santos, Maria Emília, and Maria Manuel Torrão. ''Subsídios para a História Geral de Cabo Verde: a Legitimidade da Utilização de Fontes Escritas Portuguesas Através da Análise de um Documento do Início do Século XVI (Cabo

Verde, Ponto de Intercepção de Dois Circuitos Comerciais).'' *Actas: Vol.1, D. João II e a Política Quatrocentista,* 527–51. Congresso Internacional Bartolomeu Dias e a Sua Época. Porto: Universidade do Porto, Comissão Nacional para as Comemorações dos Descobrimentos Portugueses, 1989.

Marinho, Joaquim Pereira. *Primera Parte do Relatório de Alguns Accontecimentos Notaveis em Cabo Verde, Reposta a Differentes Accusações Feitas contra o Brigadeiro.* Lisbon: [s.n.], 1838.

Martins, Ovídio. *Independência.* Praia: Instituto Cabo-Verdiano do Livro, 1983.

Mello, Guedes Brandao de. *Relatório do Governo Geral da Província de Cabo Verde,* 1890. Lisbon: Imprensa Nacional, 1891.

Mendes Correa, António Augusto. ''Ilhas de Cabo Verde.'' *Ultramar Português,* Vol. 2. Lisbon: Agência Geral das Colônias, 1954.
Detailed survey on a variety of topics including physical and human geography, language, culture, and politics. Portuguese with English abstracts.

Monteiro, Félix. ''The Cape Verde Story: A Long Road to Liberation.'' *Ceres* (May 1979): 28–32.

Monteiro, Júlio Jr. ''Achegas para a História de Cabo Verde.'' *Cabo Verde: Boletim de Propaganda e Informação* 1, no. 12 (1949): 23.

Monteiro, Júlio Jr. *Os Rebelados da Ilha de Santiago, de Cabo Verde.* Lisbon?: Centro de Estudos de Cabo Verde, 1974.

Mota, Avelino Teixeira da, comp. *Jesuit Documents on the Guinea of Cape Verde and the Cape Verde Islands, 1585–1617: in English Translation,* transl. by P. E. H. Hair. Liverpool: Dept. of History, University of Liverpool, 1989.

Murphy, Craig N. "Learning the National Interest in Africa: Focus on Cape Verde." *TransAfrica Forum* 4, no. 2 (December 1987): 49–63.

Partido Africano de Independência da Guiné e Cabo Verde (PAIGC). *História da Guiné e as Ilhas de Cabo Verde.* Porto: Afrontamento, 1974.

Patterson, K. David. "Epidemics, Famines, and Population in the Cape Verde Islands, 1580–1900." *International Journal of African Historical Studies* 21, no. 2 (1988): 291–313.

Pereira, Aristides. *Mensagem de Fim do Ano: Colectânea dos Discursos Proferidos por Ocasião de Apresentação de Cumprimentos do Ano Novo, 1985.* Praia: República de Cabo Verde?, 1985.

Pereira, Daniel A. *Estudos da História de Cabo Verde,* Estudos e Ensais, 3. Praia: Instituto Caboverdiano do Livro, 1986.

Pereira, Daniel A. *Marcos Cronológicos da Cidade Velha.* Praia: Instituto Caboverdiano do Livro, 1988.

Pereira, Daniel A. *A Situação da Ilha de Santiago no Promeiro Quartel do Século XVIII.* Praia: Instituto Caboverdiano do Livro, 1984.

Political and Administrative Statute of the Province of Cabo Verde. Lisbon: Agência Geral do Ultramar, 1963.

Portugal. Agência Geral do Ultramar. *Cabo Verde: Pequena Monografia.* Lisbon: [s.n.], 1961.

Portugal. Agência Geral do Ultramar. *Les Îles de Cap Vert.* Lisbon: [s.n.], 1927.

Querido, Jorge. *Cabo Verde: Subsídios para a História da Nossa Luta de Libertação, Estórias da Histórias.* Lisbon: Vega, 1989.

Rocha, Agostinho. *Subsídios para a História da Ilha de Santo Antão (1462/1983)*. Praia?: Imprensa Nacional de Cabo Verde, 1990.

Senna, Manuel Roiz Lucas de. *Dissertação sobre as Ilhas de Cabo Verde, 1818*. Praia: Instituto Caboverdiano do Livro, 1987.

Senna Barcellos, Christiano José de. *Subsídios para a História de Cabo Verde e Guiné,* 7 vol. Lisbon: Tipografia da Academia Real das Ciências, 1899.

Silva, António Barbosa da, and Domingos Barbosa da Silva, ed. *A Odisseia Crioula: as Tristezas, Alegrias e Esperanças do Emigrante Caboverdiano,* Uppsala: Alpha Beta Sigma, 1990.

Sociedade de Geografia de Lisboa. *Monografia-Catálogo da Exposição de Cabo Verde, Semana das Colónias de 1938.* Lisbon: Sociedade de Geografia de Lisboa, 1938.

Synge, Richard. ''Cape Verde: Silent Revolution, Cabral's Colleagues Bow to Change.'' *West Africa,* no. 3817 (22 October 1990): 2702.

G. Geography

Abranches, M. C., K. M. Storetvedt, A. Serralheiro, and R. Lovlie. ''The Palaeomagnetic Record of the Santiago Volcaniçs (Republic of Cape Verde); Multiphase Magnetism and Age Consideration.'' *Physics of the Earth and Planetary Interiors* 64 (1990): 290–302.

Alexander, Boyd. *Birds of the Cape Verde Islands.* London: [s.n.], 1898.

Alexander, Boyd. ''Further Notes on the Ornithology of the Cape Verde Islands.'' *Ibis* 4, Seventh Series, no. 14 (April 1898): 277–85.

Alexander, Boyd. ''An Ornithological Expedition to the Cape Verde Islands.'' *Ibis* 4, Seventh Series, no. 13 (January 1898): 74–118.

Assunção, C. Torre de. ''Geologia da Província de Cabo Verde.'' *Curso de Geologia do Ultramar, Vol.1,* 1–52. Lisbon: Junta de Investigações do Ultramar, 1968.

Azevedo, Rodolfo. ''O Problema das Chuvas em Cabo Verde.'' *Cabo Verde: Boletim de Propaganda e Informação* 1, no. 10 (1949): 15.

Bebiano, José Bacelar, ed. *A Geologia do Arquipélago de Cabo Verde,* Lisbon: Oficina Gráfica, 1932.

Benrós, Júlio Firmino. ''Estrada em Santo Antão.'' *Cabo Verde: Boletim de Propaganda e Informação* 5, no. 59 (1953): 38.

Bourne, W. R. P. ''The Birds of the Cape Verde Islands.'' *Ibis* 97, no. 3 (1955): 508–56.

Burnay, Luís Pisani, and António Antunes Monteiro. *Seashells from Cape Verde Islands.* Rotterdam, The Netherlands: W. Backhuys, 1977.
Translated by the authors. Photographs by Joaquim da Silva Correira.

Cadenat, J. ''Lista Provisória dos Peixes Observados nas Ilhas de Cabo Verde, de Primeiro de Maio a Vinte-Quarto de Junho de 1950.'' *Cabo Verde: Boletim de Propaganda e Informação* 2, no. 19 (1950): 25.

Cardoso, A. Pereira. ''Cabo Verde e o Seu Problema de Comunicações.'' *Cabo Verde: Boletim de Propaganda e Informação* 4, no. 40 (1952): 33.

Chevalier, Auguste. *Flore de l'Archipel du Cap Vert.* Paris: [s.n.], 1935.

Chevalier, Auguste. *Les Microclimats des Îles de Cap Vert et les Adaptations de la Végétation.* Paris: [s.n.], 1935.

Ferreira, Denise de Brum. *Etude sur la Secheresse dans l'Ile de Santiago (Cap Vert),* Linha de Acção de Geografia Fisica, Relatória no. 23. Lisbon: Centro de Estudos Geográficos, 1986.

Fonseca, Humberto Duarte. "Algumas Notas sobre as Chuvas em Cabo Verde e a Possibilidade de uma Interventação Artificial." *Cabo Verde: Boletim de Propaganda e Informação* 1, no. 5 (1949): 5.

Furnes, H., and C. J. Stillman. "The Geochemistry and Petrology of an Alkaline Lamprophyre Sheet Intrusion Complex on Maio, Cape Verde Republic." *Journal of the Geological Society, London* 144 (1987): 227–41.

Gils, H. van. "Mid-Altitudinal Vegetation of the Macaronesian Island Santo Antão." *Vegetatio* 74, no. 1 (1988): 33–38.

Guerra, Manuel dos Santos. *Terras da Guiné e Cabo Verde.* Lisbon: [s.n.], 1956.

Gunn, Bernard M., and Norman D. Watkins. "Geochemistry of the Cape Verde Islands and Fernando de Noronha." *Geological Society of America Bulletin* 87, no. 8 (August 1976): 1089–1100.

Henriques, Fernando Pinto de Almeida. " 'Secas' e 'Crises' no Arquipélago de Cabo Verde." *Cabo Verde: Boletim de Propaganda e Informação* 12, no. 143 (1960): 35.

Kerhallet, Charles Marie Philippe de, and Pierre Alexandre Le Gras. *The Cape Verde Islands,* Publication, No. 53. Washington, D.C.: U.S. Hydrographic Office, 1873.
Translated, with additions, by William H. Parker.

Lenhart, James H. "Modeling of Point Rainfall Processes in the Republic of Cape Verde."
Thesis (M.S.), Oregon State University, 1990.

Lopes, Vicente L., and John Meyer. "Watershed Management Program on Santiago Island, Cape Verde." *Environmental Management* 17, no. 1 (January 1993): 51–57.

Martins, Verónica Carvalho. "Preliminary Geothermal Investigations in Cape Verde." *Geothermics* 17, no. 2/3 (1988): 521–30.

Mota, Avelino Teixeira da. *Cinco Séculos de Cartográfia das Ilhas de Cabo Verde.* Lisbon: Junta de Investigações do Ultramar, 1961.

Murphy, Robert Cushman. "The Marine Ornithology of the Cape Verde Islands, with a List of All the Birds of the Archipelago." *Bulletin of the American Museum of Natural History* 50 (1924): 211–78.

Naurois, René de. "Les Oiseaux de l'Archipel du Cap Vert: Peuplements, Adaptations, Endémisme/Birds of the Cape Verde Archipelago: Communities, Adaptation, Endemism." *Bulletin de la Société Zoologique de France* 112, no. 3/4 (1987): 307–27.
In French, with English abstracts.

Ribeiro, Orlanda. *A Ilha do Fogo e as Suas Erupções.* Lisbon: [s.n.], 1960.

Rocha, A. Tavares, and G. Mateu. *Contribução para o Conhecimento dos Foraminíferos Actuais da Ilha de Maio (Arquipélago de Cabo Verde).* Luanda: Instituto de Investigação Ciêntífica de Angola, 1971.
Summary in Portuguese, French, and English.

Röckel, Dieter, Emilio Rolán, and António Antunes Monteiro. *Cone Shells from Cape Verde Islands: a Difficult Puzzle; a Look at the Workshop of Evolution.* Spain: [s.n.], 1980.

Saraiva, Alberto Coutinha. *Conspectus da Entomofauna Cabo-Verdiana,* Estudos, Ensaios e Documentos, 83-. Lisbon: Junta de Investigações do Ultramar, 1961.
Summary in French and English.

Secção de Estatística Geral. *Meteorologia e Climatologia: Resuma das Observações Efectuadas nos Postos Oficial da Colónia.* Praia: Imprensa Nacional, 1936.

Spall, Michael A. "Rossby Wave Radiation in the Cape Verde Frontal Zone." *Journal of Physical Oceanography* 22, no. 7 (July 1992): 796–807.

Stillman, C. J., H. Furnes, M. J. Le Bas, A. H. F. Robertson, and J. Zielonka. "The Geological History of Maio, Cape Verde Islands." *Journal of the Geological Society of London* 139 (May 1982): 347–61.

Stock, Jan H., and Ronald Vonk. "The First Freshwater Amphipod (Crustacea) from the Cape Verde Islands: Melita Cognata n.sp., with Notes on Its Evolutionary Scenario." *Journal of African Zoology/Revue de Zoologie Africaine* 106, no. 3 (1992): 273–80.

Vasconcelos, Ernesto Júlio de Carvalho e. *Archipélago de Cabo Verde: Estudo Elementar de Geográfia Phisica, Econômica e Política,* 2nd ed. Lisbon: Tipografia da Cooperativa Militar, 1920.

Webb, Philip Barker. "Spicilegia Gorgonea: or a Catalogue of All the Plants as Yet Discovered in the Cape de Verd Islands. From the Collections of J.D. Hooker, T. Vogel and Other Travellers." *Niger Flora,* 89–197. Edited by Sir W. J. Hooker. London: Hippolyte, Bailliere, 1849.

H. Anthropology

Almeida, António de. "Antropologia de Cabo Verde." *Boletim Geral das Colônias* 54 (1938):

Almeida, João de. *População de Cabo Verde: Trabalhos do Premeiro Congresso de Antropologia Colonial, Vol.2,* Porto: [s.n.], 1934.

Brito, Eduíno. *A População de Cabo Verde no Século Vigésimo.* Lisbon: Agência Geral do Ultramar, 1963.

Coli, Waltraud. "Cape Verdean Ethnicity." Thesis (A.M.), Rhode Island College, 1987.

Conferência Nacional das Mulheres de Cabo Verde, 1st. *Documentos,* Praia: Grafedito, 1981.

Depraetere, Marguerite. "Un Exemple d'Evolution du Statut de la Sage Femme aux Îles du Cap-Vert." *Civilisations* 36, no. 1–2 (1986): 251–57.

Finan, Timothy J., and Helen K. Henderson. "The Logic of Cape Verdean Female-Headed Households: Social Response to Economic Scarcity." *Urban Anthropology* 17, no. 1 (March 1988): 87–103.

Gonçalves, José Júlio. "A Cultura dos Bijagós." *Cabo Verde: Boletim de Propaganda e Informação* 10, no. 117 (1958): 13.

Lessa, Amerindo, and Jacques Ruffie. *Seroantropologia das Ilhas de Cabo Verde.* Lisbon: Junta de Investigações do Ultramar, [n.d.].

Lobban, Richard, Waltraud Coli, and Robert J. Tidwell. "Cape Verdean Life Expectancy." *Rhode Island Medical Journal* 69, no. 1 (January 1986): 23–26.

Lopes, Francisco. *A Importância dos Valores Expirituais no Panorama Cabo-Verdiano.* Lisbon: Centro de Estudos Políticos e Sociais, 1959.

Lopes Filho, João. *Cabo Verde: Apontamentos Etnográficos.* Lisbon: Sociedade Astória, 1976.

Meintel, Deirdre. "Emigração em Cabo Verde: Solução ou Problema?/Cape Verdean Emigration: Solution or Problem?" *Revista International de Estudos Africanos* No. 2 (June 1984): 93–120.
In Portuguese with English summary.

Meintel, Deirdre. *Race, Culture, and Portuguese Colonialism in Cabo Verde,* Foreign and Comparative Studies, African Series, No. 41. Syracuse, N.Y.: Syracuse University, 1984.

Mello, Lopo Vaz Sampayo e. "Esquisso Etnográfico da População de Cabo Verde." *Anuário do Escola Superior Nacional, Anos XII–XIII,* [s.l.]: [s.n.], 1931.

Mendes Correa, António Augusto. "Les Métis des Îles du Cap-Vert." *Zeitschrift für Rassenkunde, Vol.1,* [s.l.]: [s.n.], 1937.

Mendes Correa, António Augusto. *Raças do Império.* Porto: Portucalense Editora, 1943.

Murdock, George Peter. *Africa: Its People and Their Culture History.* New York: McGraw-Hill, 1959.

Ribeiro, Maria Luisa Ferro. "Appontamento Etnográfico sobre a Ilha de Santiago." *Cabo Verde: Boletim de Propaganda e Informação* 13, no. 148 (1961): 7.

Solomon, Marla Jill. " 'We can even feel that we are poor, but we have a strong and rich spirit': Learning from the Lives and Organization of the Women of Tira Chapeu, Cape Verde." Ph.D. diss., University of Massachusetts, 1992.

I. Language

Almada, Maria Dulce de Oliveira. *Cabo Verde: Contribuições para o Estudo Dilecto Falado no Seu Arquipélago,* Estudos de Ciências Políticas e Sociais, No. 55. Lisbon: Junta de Investigação do Ultramar, 1961.
Presented as a thesis, Universidade Coimbra, 1958.

Braga, Maria Luiza. ''Left-Dislocation and Topicalization in Capeverdean Creole.'' Ph.D. diss., University of Pennsylvania, 1982.

Brito, António de Paula. ''Dialectas Crioulos-Portugueses: Apartamentos para a Grammática do Crioulo que se Fala na Ilha de Santiago de Cabo Verde.'' *Boletim da Sociedade de Geografia de Lisboa* 7 (1887): 611–69.
Reprinted in Morais-Barbosa (1967), pp.329–404.

Cabral, Nelson E. ''Portuguese Creole Dialects in West Africa.'' *International Social Science Journal* 36, no. 1 (1984): 77–85.

Carreira, António. *O Crioulo de Cabo Verde: Surto e Expansão,* 2nd ed. Mem Martins, Portugal: Gráfica Europam, 1983.

Coelho, F. Adolpho. ''Os Dialectos Românicos ou Neo-Latinos na África, Ásia e América.'' *Boletim da Sociedade de Geografia de Lisboa* 2, no. 3 (1880): 129–96.
Continued in vol. 3, no. 8 (1882), pp. 451–78 and vol. 6, no. 12 (1886), pp. 705–55. Series reprinted in Morais-Barbosa (1967), pp. 1–234.

Costa, Joaquim Viera Botelho da, and Custódio José Duarte. ''O Criolo de Cabo Verde: Breves Estudos sobre o Crioulo das Ilhas de Cabo Verde Oferecidos ao Dr. Hugo Schuchardt.'' *Boletim da Sociedade de Geografia de Lisboa* 6, no. 6 (1886): 325–88.
Reprinted in Morais-Barbosa (1967), pp. 235–328.

Ferraz, Luiz, and Marius F. Valkhoff. ''A Comparative Study of São-Tomense and Cabo-Verdiano Creole.'' *Miscelânea Luso-Africana: Colectânea de Estudos Coligidos,* 15–39. Edited by Marius F. Valkhoff. Lisbon: Junta de Investigações Científicas do Ultramar, 1975.

Ferreira, Manuel. ''Comentários em Torno do Bilinguismo Cabo-Verdiano.'' *Colóquios Cabo-Verdianos,* 51–80. Estudos de Ciências Políticas e Sociaias, 22. Lisbon: Junta de Investigações do Ultramar, 1959.

Fontes, Ligia M. ''O Crioulo de Cabo Verde: Isolamento e Abandono como Factores de Diversificação Linguística.'' *Arquipélago* 1, no. 2 (October 1985): 16–18.

French, Robert. ''A Perspective on Cape Verdean Crioulo.'' *Spinner: People and Culture in Southeastern Massachusetts, Vol. 3,* 84–9. Edited by Donna Huse. New Bedford, Mass.: Spinner Publications, 1984.

Hamilton, Russell G. ''Lusofonia, Africa, and Matters of Languages and Letters.'' *Hispania* 74, no. 3 (September 1991): 610–17.

Hutchison, John P. ''Wh-movement and Relativization in Two Creole Languages: Cape Verdean (CV) and Haitian (H).'' *Studies in African Linguistics. Supplement 9* (December 1985): 146–50.
''Precis from the Fifteenth Conference on African Linguistics, UCLA, March 29–31, 1984''

Lopes, Edmundo Correira. ''Dialectos Crioulos e Etnografia Crioula.'' *Boletim da Sociedade de Geografia de Lisboa* 59 (1941): 415–35.
Reprinted in Morais-Barbosa (1967), pp. 405–30.

Macedo, Donaldo P. ''Aspects of Cape Verdean Phonology.'' Ph.D. diss., Boston University, 1989.

Macedo, Donaldo P. ''A Linguistic Approach to the Capeverdean Language.'' Ph.D. diss., Boston University, 1979.

Macedo, Donaldo P. ''The Role of Core Grammar in Pidgin Development.'' *Language Learning* 31, no. 1 (March 1986): 65–75.

Macedo, Donaldo P. ''Stereotyped Attitudes toward Various Portuguese Accents.'' *Focus,* no. 4 (January 1981): 1–8.
Also available as ERIC document ED 214 388.

Machado, Deirdre Meintel. ''Language and Interethnic Relationships in a Portuguese Colony.'' *Ethnic Encounters: Identities and Contexts,* Edited by George L. Hicks, and Philip E. Leis. North Scituate, Mass.: Duxbury Press, 1977.

Meintel, Deirdre. ''The Creole Dialect of the Island of Brava.'' *Miscelânea Luso-Africana: Colectânea de Estudos Coligidos,* 205–56. Edited by Marius F. Valkhoff. Lisbon: Junta de Investigações Científicas do Ultramar, 1975.

Morais-Barbosa, Jorge. ''Cape Verde, Guinea-Bissau and São Tomé and Príncipe: the Linguistic Situation.'' *Miscelânea Luso-Africana Colectâanea de Estudos Coligidos,* 133–51. Edited by Marius F. Valkhoff. Lisbon: Junta de Investigações Científicas do Ultramar, 1975.

Morais-Barbosa, Jorge, ed. *Estudos Linguísticos: Crioulos,* Estudos Linguísticos. Lisbon: Academia Internacional de Cultura Portuguesa, 1967.
Reprints of articles originally published in *Boletim da Sociedade de Geographia de Lisboa.* Cited here as Morais-Barbosa (1967).

Naro, Anthony J. ''Review of Carvalho, Estudos Linguísticos (1964, 1969), Including Carvalho (1961, 1962).'' *Foundations of Language* 7 (1971): 148–55.

Nunes, Maria Luisa. *The Phonologies of Cape Verdean Dialects of Portuguese.* Lisbon: Centro de Estudos Filógicos, 1963. Offprint from *Boletim de Filologia,* vol. 21.

Pires, João, and John P. Hutchison. *Disionariu Preliminariu Kriolu/Preliminary Creole Dictionary: Cape Verdean/English.* Boston, Mass: Funkul ño Lobu, 1983.

Schuchardt, Hugo. ''On Creole Portuguese.'' *The Ethnography of Variation: Selected Writings on Pidgins and Creoles,* Hugo Schuchardt. Edited and translated by T. L. Markey. Ann Arbor: Karoma, 1979.

Silva, Baltasar Lopes da. *O Dialecto Crioulo de Cabo Verde,* Prologue by Rodrigo de Sá Nogueira. Facsimile reprint of classic 1957 1st ed. Escritores dos Paises de Lingua Portuguesa, 1. Lisbon: Imprensa Nacional-Casa da Moeda, 1984.

Silva, Izione S. "Tense and Aspect in Cape Verdean Crioulo." *Pidgin and Creole Tense-Mood-Aspect Systems,* 143–68. Edited by John Victor Singler. Amsterdam: John Benjamins, 1990.

Silva, Izione S. "Variation and Change in the Verbal System of Capeverdean Crioulo." Ph.D. diss., Georgetown University, 1985.

Valkhoff, Marius F. "A Socio-Linguistic Enquiry into Cabo-Verdiano Creole." *Miscelânea Luso-Africana: Colectânea de Estudos Coligidos,* 41–58. Edited by Marius F. Valkhoff. Lisbon: Junta de Investigações Científicas do Ultramar, 1975.

Veiga, Manuel. *Diskrison Strutural di Lingua Kabuverdianu.* [Praia]: Institutu Kabuverdianu di Livru, 1982.

Washabaugh, William, and Sidney M. Greenfield. "The Development of Atlantic Creole Languages." *The Social Context of Creolization,* 106–19. Edited by Ellen Woolford, and William Washabaugh. Ann Arbor: Karoma, 1983.

J. Literature

Almada, Maria Dulce de Oliveira, ed. *Poètes des Îles du Cap-Vert: (1) Osvald Alcântara; (2) Jorge Barbosa; (3) Gabriel Mariano,* Conakry: Partido Africano da Independência da Guiné e Cabo Verde (PAIGC), 1962.

Almado, José Luis Hopffer Cordeiro, ed. *Mirabilis de Veias ao Sol: Antologia dos Novissimos Poetas Cabo-Verdianos,* Praia: Caminho; Instituto Portugues do Livro e da Leitura, 1991.

Andrade, Mário de. *Antologia de Poesia Negra de Expressão Portuguesa.* Lisbon: [s.n.], 1958.

Andrade, Mário de. *Literatura Africana de Expressão Portuguesa.* Lisbon: [s.n.], 1967.

Andrade, Mário de, ed. *Na Noite Gravida de Punhais,* 3rd ed. Antologia Tematica de Poesia Africana, 1. Praia: Instituto Caboverdeano do Livro, 1980.

Andrade, Mário de, ed. *O Canto Armado,* 2nd ed. Antologia Tematica de Poesia Africana, 2. Praia: Instituto Caboverdeano do Livro, 1980.

Araujo, Norman. ''Flight and Fidelity in Cape Verdean Poetry before Independence: the Revolutionary Phase.'' *Research in African Literatures* 13, no. 3 (September 1982): 383–99.

Araujo, Norman. *A Study of Cape Verdean Literature.* Chestnut Hill, Mass: Boston College, 1966.
Ph.D. diss., Harvard University, 1962.

Barbosa, Jorge Vera Cruz. ''O Ambiente Literário Caboverdiano e a Influência Brasileira.'' *Cabo Verde: Boletim de Propaganda e Informação* 6, no. 61 (1956): 9.

Burness, Donald, ed. *Critical Perspectives on Lusophone Literature from Africa,* Washington, D.C.: Three Continents Press, 1981. Reprints of previously published essays by several writers.

Burness, Donald, ed. *FIRE: Six Writers from Angola, Mozambique and Cape Verde,* Washington, D.C.: Three Continents Press, 1977.

Burness, Donald, ed. and trans. *A Horse of White Clouds: Poems from Lusophone Africa,* Monographs in International Studies. Africa Series, no. 55. Athens, Ohio: Center for International Studies, Ohio University, 1989.

Burness, Donald, ed. *Wanasema Conversations with African Writers,* Monographs in International Studies. Africa Series, no.46. Athens, Ohio: Center for International Studies, Ohio University, 1985.

César, Amândio. *Contos Portugueses do Ultramar: Vol. 1, Cabo Verde, Guiné e S. Tomé e Príncipe.* Porto: Portucalense Editora, 1969.

César, Amândio. *Parágrafos de Literatura Ultramarina.* Lisbon: Sociedade de Expansão Cultural, 1967.

Ellen, Maria M., ed. *Across the Atlantic: an Anthology of Cape Verdean Literature,* North Dartmouth, Mass: Center for the Portuguese Speaking World, Southeastern Massachusetts University, 1988.

Ferreira, Manuel, ed. *Claridade: Revista de Arte e Letras,* Prefaces by Baltasar Lopes, Manuel Lopes, and Manuel Ferreira. Linda-a-Velha, Portugal: Africa, Literatura, Arte e Cultura, 1986.
Includes facsimile reprint of *Claridade,* vol. 1–9 (March 1936–December 1960).

Ferreira, Manuel. "Introdução a Ficção Cabo-Verdiana Contemporânea." *Cabo Verde: Boletim de Propaganda e Informação 11, no. 129 (1959): 27.*

Ferreira, Manuel. *Literaturas Africanas de Expressão Portuguesa, Vol. 1,* Biblioteca Breve (Instituto de Cultura e Língua Portuguesa). Série Literatura, vol. 6. Lisbon: Instituto de Cultura Portuguesa, 1977.

Ferreira, Manuel. *Morabeza, Contos de Cabo Verde.* Lisbon: Agência Geral do Ultramar, 1958.

Ferreira, Manuel, ed. *No Reino de Caliban: Antologia Panorâmica de Poesia Africana de Expressão Portuguesa. Vol. 1, Cabo Verde e Guiné Bissau,* Lisbon: Seara Nova, 1975.

Figueiredo, Jaime de, ed. *Modernos Poetas Caboverdianos: Antologia,* Praia: Edições Henriquinas, 1961.

Frusoni, Sérgio. ''Textos Crioulos Cabo-Verdianos.'' *Miscelânea Luso-Africana Colectânea de Estudos Coligidos,* pp. 165–203. Edited by Marius F. Valkhoff. Lisbon: Junta de Investigações Científicas do Ultramar, 1975.
Reedited and translated by Marius F. Valkhoff.

Gerard, Albert S. ''The Literature of Cape Verde.'' *African Arts/Arts d'Afrique* 1, no. 2 (December 1968): 62–4.

Hamilton, Russell G. ''Cape Verdean Poetry and the P.A.I.G.C.'' *Artist and Audience: African Literature as a Shared Experience; Selected Proceedings from the 1977 African Literature Association Meeting,* 103–25. Edited by Richard K. Priebe, and Thomas A. Hale. Washington, D.C.: Three Continents, 1979.

Hamilton, Russell G. ''Language and Cape Verdean Poetry.'' *Roads to Today's Portugal: Essays on Contemporary Portuguese Literature, Art and Culture,* Edited by Nelson H. Vieira. Providence, R.I.: Gavea-Brown, 1983.

Hamilton, Russell G. ''Lusophone Literature in Africa: Lusofonia, Africa, and Matters of Languages and Letters.'' *Callaloo* 14, no. 2 (March 1991): 324–35.

Hamilton, Russell G. *Voices from an Empire: A History of Afro-Portuguese Literature.* Minneapolis: University of Minnesota Press, 1975.

Lopes, Baltasar. *Chiquinha.* S. Vicente, Cape Verde: Claridade, 1947.

Lopes, Baltasar, Manuel Ferreira, and A. A. Goncalves. *Antologia da Ficção Caboverdiana Contemporânea.* Praia: [s.n.], 1960.

Lopes, Manuel. ''A Literatura Cabo-Verdeana.'' *Cabo Verde: Boletim de Propaganda e Informação* 11 (1 October 1959): 8.

Lopes, Manuel. "Reflexões sobre a Literatura Cabo-Verdiana ou a Literatura nos Meios Pequenos." *Colóquios Cabo-Verdianos,* 1–22. Lisbon: Junta de Investigações do Ultramar, 1959.

Macedo, Donaldo P., ed. *Vozes Submersas: Poemas em Português,* Taunton, Mass.: Atlantis Publishers, 1990.

Margarido, Alfredo. *Estudos sobre Literaturas das Nações Africanas de Lingua Portuguesa.* Lisbon: Regra do Jogo, 1980.

Margarido, Alfredo. "The Social and Economic Background of Portuguese Negro Poetry." *Diogenes,* no. 37 (March 1962): 50–74.

Mariano, José Lopes da Silva. *Poetas de Cabo Verde.* Lisbon: Casa dos Estudiantes do Império, 1960.

Martinho, Fernando J. B. "America in Cape Verdean Poetry before Independence." *Research in African Literatures* 13, no. 3 (September 1982): 400–12.

McNab, Gregory. "Sexual Difference: the Subjection of Women in Two Stories by Orlanda Amarilis." *Luso-Brazilian Review* 24, no. 1 (June 1987): 59–68.

Miranda, Nuno. "Literatura e Insularidade." *Cabo Verde: Boletim de Propaganda e Informação* 13, no. 145 (1961): 1.

Miranda, Nuno. "Presença de Cabo Verde na Literatura Portuguesa e Estrangeira." *Garcia de Orta* 9, no. 1 (1961): 139–53.

Moser, Gerald M. "African Literature in Portuguese: the First Written, the Last Discovered." *African Forum* 2, no. 4 (March 1967): 78–96.

Moser, Gerald M. "Changing Africa: the First Literary Generation of Independent Cape Verde." *Transactions of the American Philosophical Society* 82, pt. 4 (1992): entire issue.

Moser, Gerald M. *Essays in Portuguese-African Literature.* University Park: Pennsylvania State University, 1969.

Moser, Gerald M. "More than Mornas: Eugenio Tavares' Other Writings." *Luso-Brazilian Review* 23, no. 1 (June 1986): 17–35.

Moser, Gerald M. "Those 'Lands to the South': Africa Seen as Exile in Cape Verdean Literature." *Literature of Africa and the African Continuum,* 61–73. Edited by Jonathan A. Peters, Mildred P. Mortimer, and Russell V. Linnemann. Washington, D.C.: Three Continents Press and the African Literature Assn., 1989.

Moser, Gerald M. "Two Cape Verdean Notes." *World Literature Today: A Literary Quarterly of the University of Oklahoma* 53, no. 4 (1979): 620–23.

Neves, João Alves das. "Poesia em Cabo Verde." *Cabo Verde: Boletim de Propaganda e Informação* 13, no. 156 (1961): 39.

Neves, João Alves das, ed. *Poetas e Contistas Africanos de Expressão Portuguesa: Cabo Verde, Guiné, São Tomé e Príncipe, Angola, Moçambique,* São Paulo: Editôra Brasiliense, 1963.

Nunes, Maria Luisa. *Becoming True to Ourselves: Cultural Decolonization and National Identity in the Literature of the Portuguese-Speaking World,* Contributions to the Study of World Literature, no. 22. New York: Greenwood Press, 1987.

Oliveira, José Osório de. *Poesia de Cabo Verde.* Lisbon: Agência Geral das Colônias, 1944.

Preto-Rodas, Richard A. "Cabo Verde and São Tomé-Príncipe: A Search for Ethnic Identity." *Negritude as a Theme in the Poetry of the Portuguese-Speaking World,* 32–54. Edited by Richard A. Preto-Rodas. University of Florida Humanities

Monograph, no. 31. Gainesville: University of Florida Press, 1970.
Reprinted in Burness, Donald, ed. *Critical Perspectives on Lusophone Literature from Africa.*

Preto-Rodas, Richard A., ed. *Negritude as a Theme in the Poetry of the Portuguese-Speaking World,* Gainesville: University of Florida Press, 1970.

Rodrigues dos Santos, E. *As Máscaros Poéticas de Jorge Barbosa e a Mundividência Cabo-verdiana.* Lisbon: Caminho, 1989.

Romano, Luís, ed. *Contravento: Antologia Bilingue de Poesia Caboverdiana,* Taunton, Mass.: Atlantis Publishers, 1982.

Santilli, Maria Aparecida. *Africanidade: Contornos Literários.* São Paulo: Editora Ática, 1985.

Saraiva, Arnaldo. "Modernos Poetas Caboverdianos." *Cabo Verde: Boletim de Propaganda e Informação* 13, no. 100 (1961): 20.

Silva, Baltasar Lopes da, ed. *Antologia da Ficção Cabo-Verdiana Contemporânea,* Praia: Imprensa Nacional, 1960.

Silveira, Onésimo. *Consciencialização na Literatura Caboverdiana.* Lisbon: Casa dos Estudantes do Império, 1963.

Silveira, Onésimo. *Hora Grande: Poesia Caboverdiana.* Nova Lisboa: Publicações Bailundo, 1962.

Simoes, João Gaspar. "A Antologia da Ficção Cabo-Verdiana." *Diário de Noticias* (1 January 1961): 13–15.

Simoes, João Gaspar. "Modernos Poetas Caboverdianos." *Cabo Verde: Boletim de Propaganda e Informação* 13, no. 143 (1961): 11.

Veiga, Manuel. "Testemunhos sobre a Literatura Africana Hoje [Cabo Verde]." *ICALP Revista* No. 16–17 (1989): 241–42.

Virgínio, Teobaldo. ''Claridade, Revista de Arte e Letras, Mindelo, 1936: Notas de uma Leitura.'' *Arquipélago* 1, no. 2 (October 1985): 5–10.

Virgínio, Teobaldo. *Poemas Cabo-Verdiano.* Praia: [s.n.], 1960.

K. Music

Hurley-Glowa, Susan. ''Cape Verdean 'Funana': Voice of the Badius.'' Thesis (A.M.), Brown University, 1991.

Leitão, Benvindo, ed. *Mornas: Cantigas que Povo ta Cantâ,* Taunton, Mass: Atlantis, 1982.

Lima da Cruz, Eutrópio. ''Cape Verde and Its Music.'' *The Courier* No. 69 (September 1981): 77ff.

Martins, Vasco. *A Musica Tradicional Cabo-Verdiana, I: a Morna,* Colecção ''Estudos e Ensais''. Praia: Instituto Cabo-Verdiano do Livro e do Disco, 1989.

Monteiro, Felix. ''Cantigas de Ana Procopio.'' *Garcia de Orta* 9, no. 1 (1961): 155–59.
Reprinted from *Claridade,* no. 9 (December 1960): 15–23.

Osório, Oswaldo, ed. and trans. *Cantigas de Trabalho,* Tradições Orais de Cabo Verde. Praia: Comissão Nacional para as Comemorações do 5°. Aniversário da Independência de Cabo Verde, Sub-Comissão para a Cultura, 1980.

Rehm, Barbara Ann Masters. ''A Study of the Cape Verdean Morna in New Bedford, Massachusetts.''
Thesis (A.M.), Brown University, 1975.

Sousa, José Maria de. *Hora di Bai: Mornas e Coladeiras de Cabo Verde,* 2 vol. East Providence, R.I.: Capeverdean American Federation, 1973.

Tavares, Eugénio. *Mornas: Cantigas Crioulas.* Lisbon: J. Rodrigues, 1932.

Virgínio, Teobaldo. ''A Morna: um Testemunho Secular.'' *Arquipélago* 1, no. 1 (May 1985): 7–8.

L. Culture

Almada Duarte, Dulce, and José C. Curto, trans. ''The Cultural Dimension in the Strategy for National Liberation: the Cultural Bases of the Unification between Cape Verde and Guinea-Bissau.'' *Latin American Perspectives* 11, no. 2, no. 41 (March 1984): 55–66.

Almeida, Manuel Ribeiro de. ''Aspectos Sociais do Povo Caboverdiano.'' *Cabo Verde: Boletim de Propaganda e Informação* 9, no. 108 (1957): 30.

Araujo, Norman. ''Civilação em Cabo Verde.'' *Cabo Verde: Boletim de Propaganda e Informação* 12, no. 141 (1960): 31.

Barros, Antero. *Subsídios para a História do Golf em Caboverde.* S. Vicente: Clube de Golfe de S. Vicente, 1981.

Cabral, Stephen L., and Sam Beck. *Nha Distino: Cape Verdean Folk Arts,* Publication no. 5. Providence, R.I.: Roger Williams Park Museum, 1982.

Cardoso, Pedro Monteiro. *Folclore Caboverdiano,* Introduction by Luíz Silva. preface by Alfredo Margarido. Paris: Solidariedade Caboverdiana, 1983.

Carreira, António. *Panaria Cabo-Verdiana-Guineense (Aspectos Históricos e Socio-Economicos).* Lisbon: Junta de Investigações do Ultramar, 1968.

Cerrone, Frederico. *História da Igreja de Cabo Verde: Subsídios.* S. Vicente: Gráfica do Mindelo, 1983.

Colóquios Cabo-Verdianos, Estudos de Ciências Políticas e Sociaias, 22. Lisbon: Junta de Investigações do Ultramar, 1959.
Collection of essays by prominent authors on a variety of topics.

Ferreira, Manuel. *A Aventura Crioula ou Cabo Verde: uma Síntese Étnica e Cultural,* Preface by Baltasar Lopes. Lisbon: Editora Ulisseia, 1967.

Levy, Bento. "Ao Povo de Cabo Verde." *Cabo Verde: Boletim de Propaganda e Informação* 13, no. 146 (1961): 1.

Lopes, Baltasar. *Cabo Verde: Visto por Gilberto Freyre: Apontamentos Lidos ao Microfone de Radio Barlavento.* Praia: Imprensa Nacional, 1956.

Lopes Filho, João. *Cabo Verde: Subsídios para um Levantamento Cultural.* Lisbon: Plátano, 1981.

Lopes Filho, João. *Contribução para o Estudo da Cultura Cabo-verdiana.* Lisbon: Ulmeiro, 1983.

Lopes Filho, João. *Defesa do Património Sócio-Cultural de Cabo Verde.* Lisbon: Ulmeiro, 1985.

Mariano, Gabriel. *Cultura Caboverdeana: Ensaios.* Lisbon: Vega, 1991.

Miranda, Nuno. *Compreensão de Cabo Verde.* Lisbon: Junta de Investigações do Ultramar, 1963.

Mota, Avelino Teixeira da. "Contactos Culturais Luso-Africanos na 'Guiné do Cabo Verde'." *Boletim da Sociedade de Geografia de Lisboa* 69, no. 11–12 (November 1951): 659.

Moura, Jacinto José do Nascimento, ed. *Crioulo e Folclore de Cabo-Verde,* Porto: Ed. da la Exposição Colonial Portuguesa, 1934.

Extracted from *Actas do I Congresso Nacional de Antropologia Colonial.*

Nyhan, Patricia, and Raymond A. Almeida. *Nho Lobo: Folk Tales of the Cape Verdean People,* Translated by Cape Verdean Educators Collaborative. Boston: The American Committee for Cape Verde (TCHUBA), 1976.
Also available as an ERIC document: ED 183 469.

Parsons, Elsie Clews. "Accumulative Tales Told by Cape Verde Islanders in New England." *Journal of American Folk-Lore* 33, no. 127 (January 1920): 34–42.
In Crioulo, with translations.

Parsons, Elsie Clews. *Folk-Lore from the Cape Verde Islands,* 2 vol. Cambridge, Mass.: American Folk-Lore Society, 1923.

Parsons, Elsie Clews. "Folk-Lore of the Cape Verde Islanders." *Journal of American Folk-Lore* 34, no. 131 (January 1921): 89–110.

Parsons, Elsie Clews. "Ten Folk-Tales from the Cape Verde Islands." *Journal of American Folk-Lore* 30 (April 1917): 230–38.

Parsons, Elsie Clews. "Three Games of the Cape Verde Islands." *Journal of American Folk-Lore* 33 (1920): 80–81.

Romano, Luís. *Cabo Verde: Renascenca de uma Civilização no Atlântico Médio,* 2nd ed. Lisbon: Edição da Revista Ocidente, 1970.

Romano, Luís. "Tradições Orais do Folclore Infantil." *Arquipélago* 2, no. 8 (December 1987): 30–36.
From: *Etnoverdianografia,* unpublished chapter, Luis Romano, Cape Verde 1983, Brasil 1985.

Schaedler, Karl Ferdinand. *Weaving in Africa South of the Sahara.*

Translated by Leonid Prince Leiven, and Judy Howell. Munich, Germany: Panterra-Verlag, 1987: 104–13.

Silva, Tomé Varela da, ed. *Na Bóka Noti: un Libru di Stórias Tradisional, Tradições Orais.* Praia: Institutu Kauberdianu di Libru, 1987.

Sousa, Henrique Teixeira da. "Cabo Verde e a Su Gente." *Cabo Verde: Boletim de Propaganda e Informação* 6, no. 63 (1954): 21.
Also: vol. 9, no. 108 (1957–58), p. 2; vol. 10, no. 109 (1958–59), p. 7.

Tenreiro, Francisco. "Acerca de Archipélagos Crioulos." *Cabo Verde: Boletim de Propaganda e Informação* 12, no. 137 (1960): 31.

Valkhoff, Marius F. "Le Monde Creole et les Îsles du Cap Vert." *Miscelânea Luso-Africana: Colectânea de Estudos Coligidos,* 59–72. Edited by Marius F. Valkhoff. Lisbon: Junta de Investigações Científicas do Ultramar, 1975.

Vaschetto, Bernardo P. *Ilhas de Cabo Verde: Origem do Povo Caboverdiano e da Diocese de Santiago de Cabo Verde.* Boston, Mass.: [s.n.], 1987.

M. Health, Education, Welfare

Albuquerque, Luís de. *A "Aula de Esfera" do Colégio de Santo Antão no Século XVII.* Coimbra: Junta de Investigações do Ultramar, 1972.

Buchrieser, C., W. Sixl, R. Brosch, V. Buchrieser, and T. Miorini. "Resistance to Antibiotics in Humans and Animals on the Cape Verde Islands." *Journal of Hygiene, Epidemiology, Microbiology and Immunology* 31, no. 3 (1987): 269–76.

Buchrieser, V., R. Brosch, C. Buchrieser, T. Miorini, and W. Sixl. "On the Drinking Water Situation on the Cape Verde

Islands, Island of Santiago.'' *Journal of Hygiene, Epidemiology, Microbiology and Immunology* 33, no. 1 (1989): 35–43.

Cabral, Tomaz António. ''Servicos de Saúde e Assistência de Cabo Verde.'' *Ultramar* 8, no. 2 (1967): 165–72.

Castro e Almeida, M. E., M. A. Gama-Antunes, and Vitor M. R. Marques. ''Some Notes about Nutrition at Praia, Cape Verde.'' *International Journal of Anthroplogy* 6, no. 3 (1 September 1991): 197–205.

Cuadrado, Raul R., Charles du V. Florey, Kenneth W. Walls, and Irving G. Kagan. ''A Comparative Serologic Study of New England and Native Cape Verdeans.'' *American Journal of Epidemiology* 86, no. 3 (November 1987): 673–682.

Dantas dos Reis, Dario L. ''Development of National Societies and Co-operation: the Viewpoint of the Red Cross of Cape Verde.'' *International Review of the Red Cross,* no. 264 (May 1988): 213–18.

del Quiaro, Robert. ''The Toll of Drought and Machismo.'' *People* 9, no. 2 (1982): 26–7.

Figueiredo, Jaime de. ''O Ensino nas Ilhas de Cabo Verde.'' *Cabo Verde: Boletim de Propaganda e Informação* 5, no. 57 (1953): 27.

Florey, Charles du V., and Raul R. Cuadrado. ''Blood Pressure in Native Cape Verdeans and in the Cape Verdean Immigrants and Their Descendents Living in New England.'' *Human Biology* 40, no. 2 (May 1968): 189–211.

Freire, Paulo, and Donaldo P. Macedo. *Literacy: Reading the Word & the World.* South Hadley, Mass.: Bergin & Garvey, 1987.

Gonsalves, Georgette Elaine. *On Teaching Cape Verdean Children: a Handbook for Administrators and Teachers.* Ross-

lyn, Va.: National Clearinghouse for Bilingual Education, 1979.
Prepared as Master's Project, Boston University, 1979.

Like, Robert, and James Ellison. "Sleeping Blood, Tremor and Paralysis: a Trans-cultural Approach to an Unusual Conversion Reaction." *Culture, Medicine and Psychiatry* 5, no. 1 (March 1981): 49–63.

Lima, Léonildo José Alfama. "Contribution à l'Etude des Alcooliques en Milieu Hospitalier en Republique du Cap-Vert/About a Group of Alcohol Addicts in a Praia Psychiatric Hospital (Cape Verde Islands)." *Psychopathologie Africaine* 17, no. 1/3 (1981): 426–30.

Lopes, José. "Instrução Publica." *Cabo Verde: Boletim de Propaganda e Informação* 4, no. 41 (1952): 29.

Loretti, A., and D. Garbellini. "Leprosy in the Cape Verde Islands." *Leprosy Review* 52, no. 4 (December 1981): 337–48.

Macedo, Donaldo P. "The Politics of an Emancipatory Literacy in Cape Verde." *Journal of Education* 165, no. 1 (December 1983): 99–112.

Miranda, Nuno. "O Cabo-Verdiano, um Portador de Cultura. Sugestões de Correcção de Educação e Ensino em Cabo Verde." *Colóquios Cabo-Verdianos,* 81–95.
Estudos de Ciências Políticas e Sociais, 22. Lisbon: Junta de Investigações do Ultramar, 1959.

Miranda, Nuno. "Sobre Educação e Desenvolvimento em Cabo Verde." *Cabo Verde: Boletim de Propaganda e Informação* 11, no. 127 (1959): 9.

Monteiro, Manuel da Costa. "Os Serviços de Saúde em Cabo Verde." *Cabo Verde: Boletim de Propaganda e Informação* 8, no. 91 (1956): 27.

Programa do Ensino para as Escolas das Regiões Libértadas. Conakry: Partido Africano da Independência da Guiné e Cabo Verde (PAIGC), [s.d.].

Regulamento das Escolas do Partido. Conakry: Partido Africano da Independência da Guiné e Cabo Verde (PAIGC). 19 September 1966.

Reitmaier, P. "The Death of Amílcar: a Case Study from Santo Antão, Cabo Verde." *Annales de la Société Belge de Medicine Tropicale* 67, Suppl. 1 (1987): 111–15.

Reitmaier, P., A. Dupret, and W. A. M. Cutting. "Better Health Data with a Portable Microcomputer at the Periphery: an Anthropometric Survey in Cape Verde." *Bulletin of the World Health Organization* 65, no. 5 (1987): 651–657.

Schweinichen, Christina von. "Cape Verde." *Housing Policies in the Socialist Third World,* 121–128. Edited by Kosta Mathéy. London: New York: Mansell, 1990.

Spencer, Maria Helena. "Ensinemos o Povo." *Cabo Verde: Boletim de Propaganda e Informação* 5, no. 49 (1953): 25.

Wennberg, A. "Anthropometric Assessment of the Nutritional Status of Preschool Age Children in Cape Verde." *Bulletin of the World Health Organization* 66, no. 3 (1988): 375–86.

N. Economics and Development

Aguiar, Armando de. "Cabo Verde: a Ilha de Santiago, Celeiro da Província Cabo-Verdiana Vive um Fase de Grande Desenvolvimento." *Cabo Verde: Boletim de Propaganda e Informação* 13, no. 155 (1961):

Almeida, Alexandre d'. *A Colônia de Cabo Verde: nas Suas Relações Comerciais com a Metropole, as Colônias Portu-*

guesas e o Estrangeiro, antes e depois da Guerra. Lisbon: Agência Geral das Colônias, 1929.
"Separata do no. 45 do *Boletim da Agência Geral das Colônias.*" Summaries in English and French.

Almeida, Raymond A., ed. *Challenge and Progress: the Role of Non-Governmental Aid in Cape Verde,* Praia: Institute of Solidarity, 1983.
Text in English and Portuguese.

Barros, A. F. Figueiredo de. *Inquerito Acerca das Indústrias de Cabo Verde.* Praia: [s.n.], 1917.

Bebiano, José Bacelar. "Alguns Aspectos Economicos de Arquipélago de Cabo Verde." *Boletim Geral das Colônias* 62 (1932):

Campos, Ezequiel de. *O Desenvolvimento da Riqueza do Arquipélago de Cabo Verde.* Lisbon: Agência Geral das Colônias, 1945.

"Cape Verde: Land Reform Spells Trouble." *Africa Now* (October 1981): 30.

Carreira, António. *Estudos de Economia Caboverdiana,* Estudos de História de Portugal e dos Portugueses. Lisbon: Imprensa Nacional-Casa da Moeda, 1982.

Castilho, Carlos, and Carlos P. Santos. "Beyond Viability." *Third World,* no. 9 (July 1987): 8–12.

Davidson, Basil. "Mass Mobilization for National Reconstruction in the Cape Verde Islands." *Economic Geography* 53, no. 4 (October 1977): 393–96.

Dreze, Jean, and Amartya Sen. *Hunger and Public Policy,* 133–38. New York: Oxford University Press, 1989.

Embassy of the Republic of Cape Verde. *Investment and Trade Opportunities in Cape Verde: an Emerging Economy and the*

U.S. Connection: Background Materials, Arlington, Va.: International Trade and Development Education Foundation, 1989.

Finan, Timothy J. "The Farm System under Duress: Agricultural Adaptations on the Cape Verde Islands." *Human Organization* 47, no. 2 (June 1988): 109–18.

"Fish Could Play a Bigger Role in Cape Verde." *Maritimes* (February 1983): 1–3.

Foy, Colm. "Cape Verde: Land and Labour." *People's Power* No. 20 (June 1982): 28–32.
Based on "A Reforma das Estruturas Agrarias de Cabo Verde" and subsequent issues of *Voz do Povo*.

Galli, Rosemary E. "The Food Crisis and the Socialist State in Lusophone Africa." *African Studies Review* 30, no. 1 (March 1987): 19–44.

Galvão, Henrique. *Informação Económica sobre o Império: Cabo Verde*. Lisbon: [s.n.], 1934.

Gomes, Adelino. "Making Its Own Rain Fall." *Africa Report* (January 1986): 21–23.

Hargreaves, George H. *Water and Conservation Programs for Cape Verde*. Washington, D.C.: Agency for International Development, 1980.

Harrison, Robert. "Famine and Poverty: The Cape Verde Islands." *Africa Today* 10 (March 1963): 8–9.

Lima, João B. Ferreira. "Estradas, Levadas, Barragems e Arborização." *Cabo Verde: Boletim de Propaganda e Informação* 8, no. 88 (1956): 40.

Loreno, Alvaro de Paiva de Almeida. "Moeda Metálica em Cabo Verde." *Cabo Verde: Boletim de Propaganda e Informação* 1, no. 12 (1949): 2.

Mayer, Jean. "Development Problems and Prospects in Portuguese-Speaking Africa." *International Labour Review* 129, no. 4 (1990): 459–78.

Meintel, Deirdre. "Cape Verde: Survival without Self-Sufficiency." *African Islands and Enclaves*, 145–64. Edited by Robin Cohen. Beverly Hills: Sage Publications, 1983.

Ministério do Ultramar. "Missão de Inquérito Agrícolas de Cabo Verde, Guiné, São Tomé e Príncipe." *Recenseamento Agrícola da Guiné, 1960–61*, Lisbon: Imprensa Nacional, 1963.

Moran, Emilio. "The Evolution of Cape Verde's Agriculture." *African Economic History*, no. 11 (1982): 63–86.

Noronha, A. R. "Banana Diseases in the Cape Verde Archipelago." *Garcia de Orta* 17, no. 2 (1969): 187–94.

Norton, L. Darrell. "Soil Erosion and Conservation on Steep Volcanic Soils of Santiago, Cape Verde." *Conservation Farming on Steep Lands*, 271–72. Edited by W. C. Moldenhauer, and N. W. Hudson. Ankeny, Iowa: Soil and Water Conservation Society, 1988.

Novicki, Margaret A. "Aristides Pereira, President of Cape Verde." *Africa Report* 28, no. 6 (November 1983): 43–46.

Pálsson, Gísli. "Cultural Models in Cape Verdean Fishing." *From Water to World-Making: African Models and Arid Lands*, 93–107. Edited by Gísli Pálsson.
Uppsala: Scandinavian Institute of African Studies, 1990.

Pires, Pedro. "A Reliable Partner." *Third World*, no. 9 (July 1987): 12–14.
Interview by Carlos Pinto Santos.

Projecto do IV Plano de Fomento: Vol. 2, Ultramar. Lisbon: Imprensa Nacional- Casa de Moeda, 1973.

Província de Cabo Verde: Comércio Externo, 1949–1955. Lisbon: Tipografia Portuguesa, 1960.

Reflexões sobre a Pesca em Cabo Verde. Praia: Secretária de Estado das Pescas, 1985.
Papers presented at the first national conference on fishing, Praia, 1985.

República de Cabo Verde: 5 Anos de Independência, 1975–1980. Lisbon: Comissão do V Anniversário da Independência Nacional, 1980.

Ribeiro, Maria Luisa Ferro. "Ilha de Santiago: Príncipais Culturas e Seu Valor Económico." *Cabo Verde: Boletim de Propaganda e Informação* 13, no. 153 (1961): 30.

Santos, António Lopes dos. *Problemas de Cabo Verde: a Situação Mantém-se Controlada.* Lisbon: Agência-Geral do Ultramar, 1971.

Seca, Mário. *A Pesca em Cabo Verde.* Praia: Serviço de Estatística, Divisão de Propaganda, 1945.

Teixeira, António José da Silva, and Luís Augusto Grandvaux. *A Agricultura do Arquipélago de Cabo Verde.* Lisbon: Agência Geral do Ultramar, 1958.
Summary in English and French.

Terry, Luís. "O Problema da Emigração Cabo-Verdiana." *Colóquios Cabo-Verdianos,* 97–112. Estudos de Ciências Políticas e Sociaias, 22. Lisbon: Junta de Investigações do Ultramar, 1959.

Topouzis, Daphne. "Determined to Develop." *Africa Report* 34, no. 5 (1989): 52–54.

"The Tuna Fisheries of Cape Verde and Senegal." *Marine Fisheries Review* 43, no. 10 (October 1981): 26–29.

Valdez, Henrique Lapa Travassos. ''O Desenvolvimento das Obras Portuárias de Cabo Verde.'' *Cabo Verde: Boletim de Propaganda e Informação* 9, no. 98 (1957): 21.

Van Cotthem, W., C. Beel, J. Danneels, J. De Keyser, and Q. Gent Vyvey. ''Restoring the Natural Vegetation on Strong Eroded Volcanic Soils of Cape Verde.'' *Soil Technology* 4, no. 2 (June 1992): 183.

Wahnon, John C. *The Legacy in Cape Verde: Expropriation of Private Rural Properties (Text of Cape Verde's Agrarian Reform Law).* [s.l.]: The Union of Capeverdeans for an Independent Democracy (UCID), 1986.

O. Documents on Cape Verdean Americans

United States. Customs Service. ''Inward Passenger Lists, 1823–99.'' *Records of the New Bedford Collector of Customs,* Record Group 36. National Archives Microfilm. 3 reels.

United States. Department of Justice. Immigration and Naturalization Service. *Crew Lists of Vessels Arriving at New Bedford, Mass., 1917–1943,* Microcopy no. T-942. 2 reels.

United States. Department of Justice. Immigration and Naturalization Service. *Index to Passengers Arriving at New Bedford, Mass., July 1, 1902-November 18, 1954,* Microcopy no. T-522. 2 reels.

United States. Department of Justice. Immigration and Naturalization Service. *Passenger Lists of Vessels Arriving at New Bedford, Mass., 1902–1942,* Microcopy no.T-944. 8 reels.

United States. Department of Justice. Immigration and Naturalization Service. *Passenger Lists of Vessels Arriving at Providence, R.I., 1911–1943,* Microcopy no. T-1188. 49 reels.

United States. Department of State. *Despatches from United States Consuls in Santiago, Cape Verde, 1818–1898,* Microcopy no. T-434. 7 reels. Washington, D.C: The National Archives and Records Service, 1960.

P. Cape Verdean Americans

Almeida, Carlos. *Portuguese Immigrants: the Centennial Story of the Portuguese Union of the State of California.* San Leandro, Cal.: Supreme Council of the U.P.E.C, 1978.

Almeida, Raymond A., ed. *Cape Verdeans in America: Our Story,* with the editorial assistance of Patricia Nyhan. Boston, Mass.: The American Committee for Cape Verde (TCHUBA), 1978.
Based on original unpublished manuscripts by Michael K. H. Platzer and Deidre Meintel Machado. Also available as an ERIC document: ED 161–773.

Antone, Joe. "Captain Joe Antone, Cape Verdean Seaman." *Spinner: People and Culture in Southeastern Massachusetts, Vol. 4,* 125–31. Interviews by Nellie Coombs. Edited by Joseph D. Thomas. New Bedford, Mass.: Spinner, 1988.
From: "We Work on the WPA," personal profiles of WPA workers.

Bannick, Christian John. *Portuguese Immigration to the United States: Its Distribution and Status.* San Francisco : R&E Research Associates, 1971.
Reprint of Thesis (A.B.), Stanford University, 1916.

Barboza, Ronald. "People of Color." *A Picture History of Fairhaven,* 206. New Bedford, Mass.: Spinner, 1986.

Barboza, Ronald. *A Salute to Cape Verdean Musicians and Their Music.* New Bedford, Mass.: Documentation and Computerization of the Cape Verdeans, 1989.

Beck, Sam. *From Cape Verde to Providence: the International Longshoremen's Association Local 1329.* Providence, R.I.: Local 1329 Publications, 1983.

Beck, Sam. ''Longshoremen's Union, Local 1329.'' *A History of Rhode Island Working People,* 76–77. Edited by Paul Buhle, Scott Malloy, and Gail Sansbury. Providence, R.I.: Institute for Labor Studies and Research, 1983.

Beck, Sam. *Manny Almeida's Ringside Lounge: the Cape Verdeans' Struggle for Their Neighborhood.* Providence, R.I: Gavea-Brown, 1992.

Berger, Joséf. *Cape Cod Pilot.* Provincetown, Mass.: Modern Pilgrim Press, 1937.

Berger, Josef. *In Great Waters.* New York: Macmillan, 1941.

Brown, Don R. ''Black Whalers: They Were Great While It Lasted; Free American Blacks and Cape Verde Islanders Crewed and Sometimes Captained the Yankee Whaling Ships.'' *American Visions* 2, no. 5 (October 1987): 26–30.

Busch, Briton Cooper. ''Cape Verdeans in the American Whaling and Sealing Industry, 1850–1900.'' *American Neptune* 45, no. 2 (March 1985): 104–16.

Calabretta, Fred. ''The Picture of Antoine DeSant: Focusing on New London's Black Maritime History.'' *The Log of Mystic Seaport* 44, no. 4 (March 1993): 93–95.

Cardozo, Manoel da Silveira, comp. and ed. *The Portuguese in America 590 B.C.–1974: A Chronology & Fact Book,* Ethnic Chronology Series, 22. Dobbs Ferry, N.Y.: Oceana Publications, 1976.

Chippendale, Harry Allen. *Sails and Whales.* Boston: Houghton Mifflin, 1951.

Cohn, Michael, and Michael K. H. Platzer. *Black Men of the Sea.* New York: Dodd, Mead, 1978.

Coli, Waltraud, and Richard Lobban. *The Cape Verdeans in Rhode Island.* Providence, R.I.: The Rhode Island Heritage

Commission and the Rhode Island Publication Society, 1990.

Conley, Beverly. ''Cape Verde: Promised Land? Mass Emigration to US and Europe.'' *West Africa,* no. 3832 (11 February 1991): 182–83.

Conley, Shirley P. ''Cross-Cultural Education: Breaking through Cultural Barriers.'' Ph.D. diss., University of Massachusetts, 1989.

Corbett, Scott. *We Chose Cape Cod.* New York: Thomas Y. Crowell, 1953.

Cozinha de Cabo Verde: a Cape Verdean-American Cookbook, New Bedford, Mass.: CVN, 1990. Looseleaf.
In English and Portuguese.

''Cranberries: Cape Verdian Negroes Pick Half of the World's Supply.'' *Ebony* 4, no. 1 (November 1948): 31–33.
For related letters to the editor, see *Ebony* vol. 4, no. 5 (March 1949): 8.

Daniels, Jonathan. *A Southerner Discovers New England.* New York: Macmillan, 1940.

Davis, Lenwood G., comp. *Daddy Grace: an Annotated Bibliography,* Westport, Conn.: Greenwood Press, 1992.

Dicker, June. ''Kinship and Ritual Kinship among Cape Verdeans in Providence.''
Thesis (A.M.), Brown University, 1968.

Dillingham, William P. ''Immigrants in Industries: Cotton Goods Manufacturing in the North Atlantic States.'' *Reports of the Immigration Commission, Vol.10,* Reprint of the 1911 Government Printing Office ed. New York: Arno Press, 1970.

Dillingham, William P. ''Immigrants in Industries: Recent Immigrants in Agriculture.'' *Reports of the Immigration Commis-*

sion, Vol.22, Reprint of the 1911 Government Printing Office ed. New York: Arno Press, 1970.

Fauset, Arthur Huff. "United House of Prayer for All People." *Black Gods of the Metropolis: Negro Religious Cults of the Urban North,* 22–30. Publications of the Philadelphia Anthropological Society, 3. New York: Octagon Books, 1974.

Ferst, Susan Terry. "The Immigration and the Settlement of the Portuguese in Providence: 1890 to 1924." Thesis (A.M.), Brown University, 1972.

Fogg, Ann. "Cape Verdean Connection." *New Bedford Magazine* 1, no. 1 (March 1981): 12–15.

"Fox Point and Its People." Written by Participants in the CETA Summer Youth Employment Program at the Fox Point Community Organization. Providence, R.I.: Fox Point Community Organization, 1979.

Fuchs, Lawrence H. *The American Kaleidoscope: Race, Ethnicity, and the Civic Culture.* Middletown, Conn: Wesleyan University Press, 1990. Brief examination of "identity" of Cape Verdean Americans, pp. 331–34.

Glassner, Barry. "Cape Verdeans: A People without a Race." *Sepia* (November 1975): 65–71.

Gomes, Peter J. "Plymouth and Some Portuguese." *They Knew They Were Pilgrims,* 179–86. Edited by L. D. Geller. New York: Poseidon Books, 1971.

Goncalves, José da Silva. "A Communidade Cabo-Verdiana nos Estados Unidos: um Caso de Ambiguidade Cultura." *Portugueses na América do Norte,* 109–17. Edited by Eduardo Mayone Dias. Lisbon: Peregrinação, 1986.

Goncalves, José da Silva. "A Presença Caboverdiana na California." *Report: First Symposium on Portuguese Presence in*

California, 18–19. San Francisco; San Leandro: UPEC Cultural Center; Luso-American Education Foundation, 1974.

Greenfield, Sidney M. ''Barbadians in the Amazon and Cape Verdeans in New England: Contrasts in Adaptations and Relations with Homelands.'' *Ethnic and Racial Studies* 8, no. 2 (April 1985): 209–32.

Greenfield, Sidney M. ''In Search of Social Identity: Strategies of Ethnic Identity Management amongst Capeverdeans in Southeastern Massachusetts.'' *Luso-Brazilian Review* 13, no. 1 (June 1976): 3–17.

Hall, Elton. *Sperm Whaling from New Bedford.* New Bedford: Old Dartmouth Historical Society, 1982.

Halter, Marilyn. *Between Race and Ethnicity: Cape Verdean American Immigrants, 1860–1965,* Statue of Liberty-Ellis Island Centennial Series. Urbana: University of Illinois Press, 1993.

Halter, Marilyn. ''Cape Verdean-American Immigration and Patterns of Settlement, 1860–1940.'' Ph.D. diss., Boston University, 1986.

Halter, Marilyn. ''Working the Cranberry Bogs: Cape Verdeans in Southeastern Massachusetts.'' *Spinner: People and Culture in Southeastern Massachusetts, Vol. III,* 70–83. Edited by Donna Huse. New Bedford, Mass.: Spinner, 1984.

Harney, Robert F. '' 'Portygees and Other Caucasians': Portuguese Migrants and the Racialism of the English-Speaking World.'' *Portuguese Migration in Global Perspective,* 113–35. Edited by David Higgs. Toronto: The Multicultural History of Ontario, 1990.

Hayden, Robert C. *African-Americans & Cape Verdean-Americans in New Bedford: A History of Community and Achievement.* Boston: Select Publications, 1993.

Holmes, Urban Tigner Jr. ''Portuguese Americans.'' *Our Racial and National Minorities: Their History, Contributions, and Present Problems,* 394–405. Edited by Francis J. Brown, and Joseph Slabey Roucek. New York: Prentice-Hall, 1937.

Houston, Laura Pires. *Cape Verdeans in the United States: Continuing a Story of Struggle, Creativity and Persistence,* Bethesda, Md.: ERIC Document Reproduction Service, ED 189 236, 1978. Microfiche.

Houston, Laura Pires, and Michael K. H. Platzer. *Ernestina—Effie M. Morrissey.* New York: Friends of the Ernestina/Morrissey Committee, 1982.

Howard, Lawrence C. ''A Note on New England Whaling and Africa before 1860.'' *Negro History Bulletin* 22, no. 1 (1958): 13–16.

Howith, Arnold M., and Rita Moniz. *Ethnicity and Political Organization: Cape Verdeans in New Bedford,* Bethesda, Md.: ERIC Document Reproduction Service, ED 166 295, 1979. Microfiche.

Inlder, John, Madge Headley, and Udetta D. Brown. *The Houses of Providence: a Study of Present Conditions and Tendencies, with Notes on the Surrounding Communities and Some Mill Villages.* Providence, R.I.: Snow & Farnham, 1916.

Jenks, Albert Ernest. ''Cranberry Bogs of Cape Cod - Their Workers.'' *The Dearborn Independent* 3 (3 January 1925): 9,14.

Jenks, Albert Ernest. ''New Englanders Who Came from the Afric Isles.'' *The Dearborn Independent* (27 December 1924): 5,15.

Jenks, Jeremiah W., and W. Jett Lauck. ''Recent Immigrant Farms and Seasonal Agricultural Laborers.'' *The Immigration Problem: A Study of American Immigration Conditions and Needs,* 94–99. Revised and enlarged by Rufus D. Smith. 5th ed. New York: Funk & Wagnalls, 1922.

Kirk, William, ed. *A Modern City: Providence, Rhode Island, and Its Activities,* Chicago: University of Chicago Press, 1909.

Lima, Lucillia. ''Lembranca: Crioulo Memories.'' *Spinner: People and Culture in Southeastern Massachusetts, Vol. I,* 92–95. Edited by Donna Huse. New Bedford, Mass.: Spinner, 1981.

Lobban, R., W. Coli, C. Connor, C. Guglielmo, C. Steffanci, and R. J. Tidwell. ''Patterns of Cape Verdean Migration and Social Association through Obituary Analysis.'' *New England Journal of Black Studies* No. 5 (November 1985): 31–45.

Lomba, Arthur. ''The Role of Cape Verdean Culture in Education.'' *Issues in Portuguese Bilingual Education,* 165–74. Edited by Donaldo P. Macedo. Cambridge, Mass.: National Assessment and Dissemination Center for Bilingual/Bicultural Education, 1980.
Also available as an ERIC document: ED 206 193.

Macedo, Donaldo P. ''A Lingua Caboverdiana na Educação Bilingue.'' *Issues in Portuguese Bilingual Education,* 183–99. Edited by Donaldo P. Macedo. Cambridge, Mass.: National Assessment and Dissemination Center for Bilingual/Bicultural Education, 1980.

Machado, Deirdre Meintel. ''Cape Verdean Americans.'' *Hidden Minorities: the Persistence of Ethnicity in American Life,* 233–56. Edited by Joan H. Rollins. Washington, D.C.: University Press of America, 1981.

Machado, Deirdre Meintel. ''Cape Verdean-Americans: Their Cultural and Historical Background.'' Ph.D. diss., Brown University, 1978.

Mazzatenta, O. Louis. "New England's Little Portugal." *National Geographic* 147, no. 1 (January 1975): 90–109.

Melville, Herman. "The 'Gees'." *Harper's* 12, no. 70 (March 1856): 507–9.
Controversial account, possibly a satire.

Millner, Darrell. "The Death of Markus Lopius: Fact or Fantasy? First Documented Presence of a Black Man in Oregon, August 16, 1788." *Trotter Institute Review* 5, no. 2 (June 1991): 19–22.

Murphy, Robert Cushman. *A Dead Whale or a Stove Boat: Cruise of the Daisy in the Atlantic Ocean June 1912 - May 1913.* Boston: Houghton Mifflin, 1967.

Nunes, Maria Luisa. "A Different Vision of a New England Childhood: the Cape Verdean Experience on Cape Cod." *Women in Portuguese Society: Proceedings of the Second Annual Symposium on the Portuguese Experience in the United States,* 32–55. Compiled by Neil Miller. Cambridge, Mass.: National Assessment and Dissemination Center for Bilingual Education, 1976. Microfiche.
Available as an ERIC document: ED 177 865.

Nunes, Maria Luisa. *A Portuguese Colonial in America, Belmira Nunes Lopes: the Autobiography of a Cape Verdean American,* Pittsburgh, Pa.: Latin American Literary Review Press, 1982.

Pap, Leo. *The Portuguese-Americans,* The Immigrant Heritage in America. Boston: Twayne Publishers, 1981.

Ramos, Lucille. "Black, White or Portuguese? A Cape Verdean Dilemma." *Spinner: People and Culture in Southeastern Massachusetts, Vol. I,* 34–37. Edited by Donna Huse. Interview by John C. Reardon. New Bedford, Mass.: Spinner, 1981.

Reid, Ira DeAugustine. *The Negro Immigrant: His Background, Characteristics and Social Adjustments, 1899–1937,* Reprint of 1939 ed. Columbia University Studies in the Social Sciences, no. 449. New York: AMS Press, 1970.
Originally presented as author's thesis, Columbia University.

Roderiques, Marlene Rae. ''Suicidal Behavior in a Population of Cape Verdean Immigrant Adolescents: A Qualitative Case Study.'' Ph.D. diss., University of Massachusetts, 1992.

Rogers, Francis M. *Americans of Portuguese Descent: a Lesson in Differentiation.* Beverly Hills, Cal.: Sage Publications, 1974.

Rogers, Francis M. ''Cape Verdeans.'' *Harvard Encyclopedia of American Ethnic Groups,* 197–200. Edited by Stephen Thernstrom. Cambridge, Mass.: Harvard University Press, 1980.

Romo, Carlos D. ''The Element of 'Sodade' in the Cape Verdean Immigrant as Seen through Individuals and Literature.'' *Report: First Symposium on Portuguese Presence in California,* 29–32. San Francisco; San Leandro: UPEC Cultural Center; Luso-American Education Foundation, 1974.

Sawyer, Kathy. ''Cape Verdean Migrants.'' *Immigrants, Refugees, and U.S. Policy,* 80–87. Edited by Grant S. McClellan. The Reference Shelf, 52, no. 6. New York: H.W. Wilson, 1981.
Originally published as ''Cape Verdeans Face Identity Problems in U.S.'' in the *Washington Post* (6 July 1980): A1.

Sharf, Susan. ''The Cape Verdeans of Providence.''
Honors Thesis (A.B.), Brown University, 1965.

Smith, M. Estellie. ''A Tale of Two Cities: the Reality of Historical Differences.'' *Urban Anthropology* 4, no. 1 (1975): 61–72.

Spirit of O.L.O.A.: Our Lady of the Assumption Church, 1905–1980. New Bedford, Mass.: O.L.O.A, 1980.

Starbuck, Alexander. *History of the American Whale Fishery from Its Earliest Inception to the Year 1876,* with a new preface by Stuart C. Sherman. Reprint in 2 vol. ed. New York: Argosy-Antiquarian, 1964.

Taft, Donald R. *Two Portuguese Communities in New England,* Reprint of 1923 ed. New York: Arno Press, 1969.
Based on thesis, Columbia University, 1923.

"Twentieth-Century Whaling Tales." *Spinner: People and Culture in Southeastern Massachusetts, Vol. II,* Edited by Donna Huse. New Bedford, Mass.: Spinner, 1982.
Interview with Quinton Degrasses by Jill Anderson, pp. 98–102. Interview with Joseph Ramos by Michael DeCicco, pp. 107–10.

Tyack, David B. "Cape Verdean Immigration to the United States."
Honors Thesis (A.B.), Harvard University, 1952.

Warner, Robert Austin. *New Haven Negroes: A Social History.* New Haven: Yale University Press, 1940.

Weiss, Feri Felix. "The Bravas." *The Sieve: Revelations of the Man Mill, Being the Truth about American Immigration,* 286–94. Boston, Mass.: Page, 1921.

Wolforth, Sandra K. *The Portuguese in America.* San Francisco: R&E Research Associates, 1978.

Q. Works by Amílcar Cabral

"Acerca da Contribuição dos 'Povos' Guinéenses para a Produção Agrícola da Guiné." *Boletim Cultural da Guiné Portuguesa* 9, no. 36 (October 1954): 771–78.

"Acerca da Utilização da Terra na Africa Negra." *Boletim Cultural da Guiné Portuguesa* 9, no. 34 (April 1954): 401–16.

"Algumas Considerações Acerca das Chuvas." *Cabo Verde: Boletim de Propaganda e Informação* 1, no. 1 (1949+): 15.

Alguns Princípios do Partido. Lisbon: Sears Nova, 1974.

Analise de Alguns Tipos de Resistência, 2d ed. Colecção de Leste a Oeste, no. 11. Lisbon: Seara Nova, 1975.

"Apontamentos sobre Poesia Caboverdeana." *Cabo Verde: Boletim de Propaganda e Informação* (1952): 28.

"Breve Análisis de la Estructura Social de la Guinea 'Portuguesa'." *Pensamiento Crítico,* no. 2–3 (March 1967): 24–48.

"Breves Notas Acerca da Razão de Ser, Objetivos e Processo de Execução do Recenseamento Agricola da Guiné." *Boletim Cultural da Guiné Portuguesa* 9, no. 33 (January 1954): 195–204.
With Maria H. Cabral.

"A Brief Report on the Situation of the Struggle (January-August 1971)." *Ufahamu* 2, no. 3 (December 1972): 5–28.

Cabral on Nkrumah. Newark, N.J.: PAIGC, 1973.

"Cinquante Ans de Lutte pour la Libération Nationale." *Questions Actuelles du Socialisme/Socialist Thought and Practice* (March 1973): 98–110.

A Consciencia Nova que a Luta Forjou Nos Homens e Mulheres da Nossa Terra e a Arma Nais Poderosa do Nosso Povo contra os Criminosos Colonialistas Portuguesas. Conakry: PAIGC, September 1971.

''Contra a Guerre Colonial: Mensagem de Amílcar Cabral ao Povo da Guiné e da Cabo Verde.'' *FPLN Boletim* (August 1965): 14–15.

''The Contribution of the Guinean Peoples to the Agricultural Production of Guinea, I: Cultivated Area.'' *Ufahamu* 3, no. 3 (December 1973): 35–41.

''The Death Pangs of Imperialism.'' *Rapport General sur la Lutte de Libération Nationale,* Conakry: [s.n.], July 1961.

Déclaration à l'Occasion de l'Anniversaire des Grèves de Bissau et du Massacre de Pigiuiti. Conakry: PAIGC, 1962.

Déclaration du PAIGC sur l'Evacuation par les Autorités Portugaises des Civils Européens du Sud. Paris: Comité de Soutien à l'Angola et aux Peuples des Colonies Portugaises, February 1963.

Déclaration Faite par M. Amílcar Cabral du Parti Africain de l'Indépendance de la Guinée et du Cap-Vert (PAIGC) Lors de la 1420ème Séance de la Quatrième Commission le 12 Décembre 1962. N.Y.: PAIGC, 1962.

Déclaration sur la Situation Actuelle de la Lutte de Libération en Guinée ''Portugaise'' et aux Îles du Cap Vert. Conakry: PAIGC, 20 January 1962.

''Determined to Resist.'' *Tricontinental,* no. 8 (September 1968): 114–26.

Discours Prononcé par le Chef de la Délégation de la Guinée ''Portugaise'' et des Îles du Cap-Vert. Conakry: PAIGC, 1962.

Discurso Proferido pelo Delegado da Guiné ''Portuguesa'' e das Ilhas de Cabo Verde. Cairo: PAIGC, 25 March 1961.

The Eighth Year of Our Armed Struggle for National Liberation. Conakry: PAIGC, 1971.

"Em Defasa da Terra." *Cabo Verde: Boletim de Propaganda e Informação* 1, no. 2 (1949): 2.
Continued in: vol. 1, no. 6: 15; vol. 2 (1950–51), no. 14:19, no. 15: 6; vol. 3 (1951–52), no. 29: 24.

The Facts about Portugal's African Colonies, Introduction by Basil Davidson. London: Union of Democratic Control, 1961.
Under pseudonym: Abel Djassi.

"Feux de Brousse et Jachères dans le Cycle Cultural Arachide-Mils." *Boletim Cultural da Guiné Portuguesa* 13, no. 51 (July 1958): 257–68.

Fondements et Objectifs de la Libération Nationale: Sur la Domination Impérialiste. Conakry: PAIGC, 1966.

"Frutos de una Lucha." *Tricontinental* No. 31 (July 1972): 61–77.

"A Guerra na Guiné." *Portugal Democrático* 8 (October 1963): 3.

"Guinea (Bissau): Polítical and Military Situation." *Tricontinental* (April 1969): 25–34.

"Guinéa: the Power of Arms." *Tricontinental Magazine* No. 12 (May 1969): 5–16.

"Guinée, Cap-Vert. Face au Colonialisme Portugais." *Partisans* 2, no. 7 (November 1962): 80–91.

Guinée "Portugaise": le Pouvoir des Armes. Paris: Maspero, 1970.

"Identity and Dignity in Struggle." *Southern Africa* 5, no. 9 (November 1972): 4–8.

"Identity and Dignity in the National Liberation Struggle." *Africa Today* (September 1972): 39–47.

''In Defense of the Land.'' *Cabo Verde: Boletim de Propaganda e Informação* 1 (November 1949): 2–5.

''An Informal Talk.'' *Southern Africa* 6, no. 2 (February 1973): 6–9.

Intervention Faite à la Première Conférence de la Solidarité des Peuples d'Afrique, d'Asie et d'Amérique Latine. Havana: [s.n.], January 1966.

''Interview.'' *NLF: National Liberation Fronts, 1960–1970,* edited by Donald C. Hughes, and Robert E. A. Shanab. New York: Morrow, 1972.

''La Guinée Portugaise et les Îles du Cap-Vert.'' *Voice of Africa* 2 (May 1962): 37, 39.

La Lutte de Libération Nationale en Guinée Portugaise et aux Îles du Cap-Vert. Conakry: PAIGC, 1962.

''La Lutte du PAIGC.'' *Remarques Africaines* 7 (26 May 1965): 19–22.

''L'Arme de la Théorie.'' *Partisans* No. 26–27 (1966):

Le Développement de la Lutte Nationale en Guinée ''Portugaise'' et aux Îles du Cap Vert en 1964. Conakry: [s.n.], 1965.

Le Peuple de la Guinée ''Portugais'' devant l'Organisation des Nations Unies. Conakry: PAIGC, June 1962. ''Présentée au Comité Special de l'ONU pour les Territoires Administrés par le Portugal.''

''Liberating Portuguese Guinea from Within.'' *The New African* 4 (June 1965): 85.

''Liberation Movement in Portuguese Guinéa.'' *Voice of Africa* 2 (March 1962): 32.

Libération Nationale et Culture. Conakry: PAIGC, 1970.

''Mankind's Path to Progress.'' *World Marxist Review* 10 (November 1967): 88–89.

Memorandum à Assembleia Geral da Organização das Nações Unidas. Conakry: PAIGC, 16 September 1961.

Memorandum Enviado ao Govérno Português pelo Partido Africano da Independência. Conakry: PAIGC, 1 December 1960.

Mensagem do Ano Novo. Conakry: PAIGC, January 1973.

Message to the People on the Occasion of the Fourteenth Anniversary of the Foundation of the PAIGC. Conakry: PAIGC, 1970.

''National Liberation and Culture.'' *Transition* 9, no. 45 (1974): 12–17.

Note Ouverte au Gouvernement Portugais. Conakry: PAIGC, 1961.

Nous Avons Lutté par des Moyens Pacifiques; Nous n'avons pas Eu que les Massacres et le Génocide. Addis Ababa: PAIGC, May 1963.

''O PAIGC Pede à ONU Auxilio Concreto.'' *Portugal Democrático* 8 (December 1963): 4.

''On the Utilization of Land in Africa.'' *Ufahamu* 3, no. 3 (December 1973): 32–35.

''Original Writings.'' *Ufahamu* 3, no. 3 (December 1973): 31–42.

''Our Army Is Our Whole People.'' *Newsweek* 75 (9 March 1970): 38–39.

Our People Are Our Mountains: Amilcar Cabral on the Guinean Revolution. London: Committee for Freedom in Mozambique, Angola & Guiné, 1971.

"PAIGC Attacks." *Tricontinental* No. 68 (November 1971): 38–39.

"PAIGC: Optimistic and a Fighter." *Tricontinental* No. 19–20 (July 1970): 167–74.

"PAIGC's Denunciation." *Tricontinental* No. 71 (February 1972): 44.

"Para o Conhecimento do Problema da Erosão do Solo na Guiné, I: Sobre o Conceito de Erosão." *Boletim Cultural da Guiné Portuguesa* 9, no. 33 (January 1954): 163–94.

"The People of Guinea and the Cape Verde Islands." (October 1972):
Speech delivered at the 27th session of the United Nations General Assembly.

"Portuguese Colonial Policy." *Africa Quarterly* 4 (1966): 287–99.

Pourquoi Nous Avons Pris les Armes pour Libérer Notre Pays. Addis Ababa: PAIGC, May 1963.

"A Propos du Cycle Cultural Arachide-mils en Guinée Portugaise." *Boletim Cultural da Guiné Portuguesa* 13, no. 50 (April 1958): 146–56.

"A Propósito de Mecanização da Agricultura na Guiné Portuguesa." *Boletim Cultural da Guiné Portuguesa* 9, no. 34 (April 1954): 389–400.

"Queimados e Pousios na Circunscrição de Fulacunda em 1953." *Boletim Cultural da Guiné Portuguesa* 9, no. 35 (July 1954): 627–46.

Rapport aux Etats-Unis. Conakry: PAIGC, 1962.

Rapport Bref sur la Lutte en 1971. Conakry: PAIGC, 1972.

Rapport Général sur la Lutte de Libération Nationale. Conakry: PAIGC, 1961.

''Realidades.'' *Tricontinental* No. 33 (1973): 97–109. Interview.

''Recenseamento Agrícola da Guiné: Estimativa em 1953.'' *Boletim Cultural da Guiné Portuguesa* 11, no. 43 (July 1956): 7–243.

''Report on Portuguese Guinea and the Liberation Movement.'' U.S. Congress (91st, 2d session). House Committee on Foreign Affairs. Hearing before the Subcommittee on Africa, 26 February 1970. Washington, D.C.: Government Printing Office, 1970.

''Report on Portuguese Guinea and the Liberation Movement.'' *Ufahamu* 1, no. 2 (September 1970): 69–103.

Return to the Source: Selected Speeches, Edited by Africa Information Service. New York: Monthly Review Press, 1973.

Revolution in Guinea: an African People's Struggle; Selected Texts, Rev. ed. London: Stage 1, 1971.

Sobre a Situação da Luta; sobre Alguns Problemas Práticos da Nossa Vida e da Nossa Luta. Conakry: PAIGC, 9 August 1971.

''The Social Structure of Portuguese Guinea and Its Meaning for the Struggle for National Liberation.'' *Translations on Africa* No. 420 (24 August 1966): 37–48.

''Solução Pacifica para Guiné e Cabo Verde.'' *Portugal Democrático* 7 (February 1963): 6.

''The Struggle Has Taken Root.'' *Tricontinental* No. 84 (1973): 41–49.

''The Struggle in Guinea.'' *International Socialist Journal* 1 (August 1964): 428–46.

The Struggle in Guinea, Reprint ed. Cambridge, Mass.: Africa Research Group, 1969.

''The Struggle of Portuguese Guinea.'' *Translations on Africa* No. 77 (1964): 29–40.

''Support for the People's Legitimate Aspirations to Freedom, Independence, and Progress.'' *Objective: Justice* 5 (January 1973): 4–7.

Sur la Situation de Notre Lutte Armée de Libération Nationale, Janvier-Septembre 1970. Conakry: PAIGC, 1970.

Sur les Lois Portugaises de Domination Coloniale. Conakry: PAIGC, 1970.

Un Crime de Colonialisme (Fondements Juridiques de Notre Lutte Armée de Libération Nationale). Conakry: PAIGC, 1961.

''Une Crise de Connaissance.'' *Third Conference of African People,* Cairo, 1961.

Unite e Lutte. Paris: Maspero, 1975.
Includes: I, ''L'Arme de la Theorie''; II, ''La Pratique Revolutionnaire''.

''The War in Portuguese Guinea.'' *African Revolution* 1 (June 1963): 103–8.

R. Works about Amílcar Cabral

''Amílcar Cabral: Profil d'un Révolutionnaire Africain.'' *Présence Africaine* No. 2 (1973): 3–19.

Andelman, David A. "Profile: Amílcar Cabral, Pragmatic Revolutionary Shows How an African Guerilla War Can Be Successful." *Africa Report* 15, no. 5 (May 1970): 18–19.

Benot, Yves. "Amílcar Cabral and the International Working Class Movement." *Latin American Perspectives* 11, no. 2, issue 41 (1984): 81–96.

Bienen, Henry. "State and Revolution: the Work of Amílcar Cabral." *Journal of Modern African Studies* 15, no. 4 (December 1977): 555–68.

Blackey, Robert. "Fanon and Cabral: A Contrast in Theories of Revolution for Africa." *Journal of Modern African Studies* 12 (June 1974): 191–210.

Bragança, Aquino de. "L'Assassinat de Cabral." *Afrique-Asie* 24 (4 March 1973): 8–15.

Bragança, Aquino de. "The Plot against Cabral." *Southern Africa* (May 1973): 4–8.

"Cabral Is Assassinated by Portuguese Agents." *African World* (3 February 1973): 1–16.

Chabal, Patrick. *Amílcar Cabral: Revolutionary Leadership and People's War.* New York: Cambridge University Press, 1983.

Chaliand, Gérard. "The Legacy of Amílcar Cabral." *Ramparts* (April 1973): 17–20.

Chaliand, Gérard. "The PAIGC without Cabral: an Assessment." *Ufahamu* 3, no. 3 (December 1973): 87–95.

Chilcote, Ronald H. "African Ephemeral Material: Portuguese African Nationalist Movements." *Africana Newsletter* 1 (December 1963): 9–17.

Chilcote, Ronald H. *Amílcar Cabral's Revolutionary Theory and Practice: A Critical Guide.* Boulder: Lynne Rienner, 1991.

Chilcote, Ronald H. "The Political Thought of Amílcar Cabral." *Journal of Modern African Studies* 6, no. 3 (October 1968): 373–88.

Chilcote, Ronald H. "The Theory and Practice of Amílcar Cabral: Revolutionary Implications for the Third World." *Latin American Perspectives* 11, no. 2, issue 41 (March 1984): 3–14.

Chilcote, Ronald H. "Unity and Struggle: Reassessing the Thought of Amílcar Cabral." *Latin American Perspectives* 11, no. 2, issue 41 (March 1984): entire issue.

Crimi, Bruno. "Les Assassins de Cabral." *Jeune Afrique* (3 February 1973): 8–12.

Cruse, Harold W. "The Amílcar Cabral Politico-Cultural Model." *Black World* 24, no. 12 (October 1975): 20–27.

Davidson, Basil. "Amílcar Cabral: Death of an African Educationist." *Times Educational Supplement* No. 3009 (26 January 1973): 6.

Davidson, Basil. "On Revolutionary Nationalism: the Legacy of Cabral." *Latin American Perspectives* 11, no. 2, issue 41 (March 1984): 15–42.

Davidson, Basil. "Portuguese Guinea Rebel [Amílcar Cabral]." *West Africa,* no. 2446 (18 April 1964): 427.

Davidson, Basil. "Sayings from Guinea-Bissau." *Journal of Peasant Studies* 1, no. 1 (October 1973): 112.

Dessalegn, Rahmato. *Cabral and the Problem of the African Revolution,* IDR Working Paper, No. 16. Addis Ababa, Ethiopia: Institute of Development Research, Addis Ababa University, 1982.

Ferreira, Eduardo de Sousa. ''Amílcar Cabral: Theory of Revolution and Background to His Assassination.'' *Ufahamu* 3, no. 3 (December 1973): 49–68.

Figueiredo, A. de. ''Amílcar Cabral.'' *Race Today* (February 1973): 40.

Hamilton, Russell G. ''Lusophone African Literature: Amílcar Cabral and Cape Verdean Poetry.'' *World Literature Today: A Literary Quarterly of the University of Oklahoma* 53, no. 1 (December 1979): 49–53.

Hill, Sylvia. ''International Solidarity: Cabral's Legacy to the African-American Community.'' *Latin American Perspectives* 11, no. 2, issue 41 (1984): 67–80.

Houser, George M. *No One Can Stop the Rain: Glimpses of Africa's Liberation Struggle.* New York: The Pilgrim Press, 1989.

Hunt, Geoffrey. ''Two African Aesthetics: Soyinka vs. Cabral.'' *Marxism and African Literature,* 64–93. Edited by Georg M. Gugelberger. Trenton, N.J.: Africa World Press, 1986.

Intelligence Report: Amílcar Cabral, A Commentary. Lisbon: Overseas Companies of Portugal, 1973.

''L'Assassinat d'Amílcar Cabral.'' *Afrique-Asie* (5 February 1975): 8–19.

Lopes, Carlos. *Guinea-Bissau: from Liberation Struggle to Independent Statehood.* Boulder: Westview Press, 1987.

Magubane, Bernard. ''Amílcar Cabral: Evolution of Revolutionary Thought.'' *Ufahamu* 2, no. 2 (September 1971): 71–87.

Magubane, Bernard. ''Toward a Sociology of National Liberation from Colonialism: Cabral's Legacy.'' *Contemporary Marxism* No. 7 (September 1983): 5–27.

Marcum, John A. ''Guinea Bissau: Amílcar Cabral, the Meaning of an Assassination.'' *Africa Report* No. 18 (March 1973): 21–23.

McCulloch, Jock. *In the Twilight of Revolution: the Political Theory of Amílcar Cabral.* London; Boston: Routledge & Kegan Paul, 1983.

Morgado, Michael S. ''Amílcar Cabral's Theory of Cultural Revolution.'' *Black Images* 3, no. 2 (1974): 3–16.

Moser, Gerald M. ''The Poet Amílcar Cabral.'' *Research in African Literatures* 9, no. 2 (September 1978): 176–97.

Nikanorov, Anatolii Vladimirovich. *Amílcar Cabral,* Translated by Filomena Maria Santos. Combatentes do Povo, 1. Lisbon: Edições Sociais, 1975.
Translated from the English edition published by Novosti Press Agency, Moscow.

Nzongola-Ntalaja. ''Amílcar Cabral and the Theory of the National Liberation Struggle.'' *Latin American Perspectives* 11, no. 2, issue 41 (March 1984): 43–54.

Partido Africano da Independência da Guiné e Cabo Verde. *Amílcar Cabral: O Homen e a Sua Obra.* Conakry: PAIGC, 1973.

Partido Africano da Independência da Guiné e Cabo Verde. *Palavras de Ordem Gerais do Camarada Amílcar Cabral aos Responsaveis do Partido, November de 1965.* Conakry: PAIGC, 1969.

Reed, Rick. ''A Song of World Revolution: In Tribute to Amílcar Cabral.'' *Institute of the Black World Monthly Report* (February 1973):

Robinson, Cedric J. ''Amílcar Cabral and the Dialectic of Portuguese Colonialism.'' *Radical America* 15, no. 3 (May 1981): 39–57.

''Tributes to Amílcar Cabral.'' *Ufahamu* 3, no. 3 (December 1973): 11–29.

Welsh-Asante, Kariamu. ''Philosophy and Dance in Africa: the Views of Cabral and Fanon.'' *Journal of Black Studies* 21, no. 2 (December 1990): 224–32.

''Without Cabral.'' *The Economist* 146 (January 1973): 29+.

S. National Liberation Documents

PAIGC. *Biographies Sommaires des Membres du Secrétariat Permanent du Comité Exécutif de la Lutte, 24 Juillet.* Conakry: 1973.

PAIGC. *Communiqués: Développement de la Lutte de Libération Nationale; l'Action du PAIGC.* Algiers: 1963.

PAIGC. *Communiqués: Extraits de Quelques Articles de l'Organe du Partido Africano da Independência de la Guinée ''Portugaise'' et des Îles du Cap-Vert.* Conakry: April, 1963.

PAIGC. *Communiqués: Le PAIGC à la Conférence des Chefs d'État et de Gouvernement des Pays Non-Alignés le Caire, Octobre 1964.* Conakry: 1965.

PAIGC. *Communiqués: Le Peuple de la Guinée ''Portugaise'' devant l'ONU.* New York: 1962.

PAIGC. *Estatutos dos Pioneiros.* Conakry: [s.d.].

PAIGC. *Le Développement de la Lutte de Libération Nationale en Guinée ''Portugaise'' et aux Îles du Cap Vert en 1964.* Conakry: [s.n.].

PAIGC. *Lei da Justiça Militar de 19 de Setembro de 1966, com as Modificações Introduzidas pelo Bureau Político do Partido, na Reunião de 20 a 23 de Dezembro de 1966.* Conakry: 1966.

PAIGC. *Manual Político,* Vol.1. Conakry: 1972.

PAIGC. *Message du Comité Exécutif de la Lutte du PAIGC.* Conakry: January, 1973.

PAIGC. *Proclamação do Estado da Guiné-Bissau.* Boé, Guiné-Bissau: 1973.
Adopted by the People's National Assembly, 24 September 1973.

PAIGC. *Programa do Partido.* Conakry: [s.d.].

PAIGC. *Projecto da Revisão de Lei da Justiça Militar.* Conakry: 1972.

PAIGC. *Regulamento de Disciplina Interna.* Quembra: 1970.

PAIGC. *Regulamento Interno dos Internatos das Regiões Libertades.* Conakry: September, 1971.

PAIGC. *Sobre a Situação em Cabo Verde.* Lisbon: 1974.

PAIGC. *Statut et Programme.* Conakry: 1962.

PAIGC. *Statuts de l'Institut Amitié.* Conakry: 1969.

PAIGC, and United Nations. *Resolution Adoptée par le Comité Spécial à sa 854ème Seance, le 13 Avril 1972 à Conakry (Guinée).* AF/109/63: 1972.

União Democrática das Mulheres da Guiné e Cabo Verde. *Status.* Conakry: [s.n.], [s.d.].

União Nacional dos Trabalhadores da Guiné. *Estatutos.* Conakry: [s.n.], August 1962.

United Nations. ''Adoption of General Assembly Resolution on Territories under Portuguese Administration.'' *U.N. Monthly Chronicle* 6 (December 1969): 23–33.

United Nations. "Developments in Angola, Cape Verde, and Sao Tome and Principe." *Decolonization* 2, no. 4 (March 1975):

United Nations. "Questions Relating to Africa: Communications Concerning Portuguese Guinea." *Yearbook of the United Nations,* 120–21. 1964.

United Nations. "Report of the U.N. Special Mission to Guinea (Bissau)." *Objective: Justice* (September 1972): 4–15.

United Nations. *Report of Visiting Mission to Cape Verde,* General Assembly, 17 April 1975.

United Nations. "Security Council Condemns Portugal and Demands Compensation." *U.N. Monthly Chronicle* 8 (January 1971): 3–19.

United Nations. "Security Council's Attention Drawn to Situation in Portuguese Territories, with Resolution." *United Nations Review* 10 (April 1963): 9–11.

United Nations. Special Committee on the Situation with Regard to the Implementation of the Declaration on the Granting of Independence to Colonial Countries and Peoples. *Working Paper on Cape Verde,* General Assembly, 23 May 1975.

United Nations. Special Committee on the Situation with Regard to the Implementation of the Declaration on the Granting of Independence to Colonial Countries and Peoples. *Working Paper on Guinea (Bissau) and Cape Verde,* General Assembly, 24 May 1973.

United Nations. *Statement of the President of the U.N. General Assembly on the Implementation of the Declaration on the Granting of Independence to Colonial Countries and Peoples,* General Assembly, 29th Session, 3 October 1974.

United Nations. "Statement on Territories under Portuguese Administration." *U.N. Monthly Chronicle* 5 (July 1968): 32–42.

T. National Liberation

''Allies in Empire: the U.S. and Portugal in Africa.'' *Africa Today* 17, no. 4 (July 1970): entire issue.

Anderson, Perry. ''Portugal and the End of Ultra-Colonialism.'' *New Left Review* No. 15 (1972): 83–102.
Continued in: no. 16, pp. 88–123; no. 17, pp. 85–114.

Andrade, F. J. H. Rebelo de. ''Armed Forces Activities in Portuguese Guinea.'' *Ultramar* 7, no. 4 (April 1968): 176–200.

Andrade, Mario de. *A Guerra do Povo na Guiné-Bissau.* Lisbon: Livraria sa da Costa, 1975.

Beetz, Dietmar. *Visite in Guiné-Bissau.* Berlin: Podium, 1975.

Bender, Gerald J. ''Portugal and Her Colonies Join the Twentieth Century.'' *Ufahamu* 4, no. 3 (1974): 121–62.

Bergersol, J. ''Guinea-Bissau Begins to Reconstruct.'' *African Development* (October 1974): 18–19.

Biggs-Davison, John. *Portuguese Guinea: Nailing a Lie.* London: Congo Africa Publications, 1970.

Bosgra, S. J., and C. Van Krimpen. *Portugal and NATO.* Amsterdam: Angola Comité, 1970.

Bragança, Aquino de. ''La Longue Marche d'un Revolutionnaire Africain.'' *Afrique-Asie* 23, no. 5 (18 February 1973): 12–20.

Bragança, Aquino de, and Immanuel Wallerstein, ed. *The African Liberation Reader: Documents of the National Liberation Movements,* 3 vol. London: Zed Press, 1982.

Cabral, Vasco. ''Foreign Capitalist Interests in the So-Called Portuguese Guinea and the Islands of the Green Cape.''

Peace and Socialism - Al Tali'a Seminar: Africa, National and Social Revolution, Ref. #36. Vol. 2. Cairo: [s.n.], 24 October 1966.

Cabral, Vasco. ''Guinea-Bissau.'' *World Problems of Marxist Peace and Socialism Review* (February 1974): 113–16.

Cabral, Vasco. *Intervention du Camarade Vasco Cabral, Membre du Comité Exécutif de la Lutte de PAIGC, au Symposium en Memoire d'Amílcar Cabral.* Conakry: Partido Africano da Independência da Guiné e Cabo Verde, January 1973.

Cabral, Vasco. ''Speech of the Delegation of 'Portuguese' Guinéa.'' *Peace and Socialism - Al Tali'a Seminar: Africa, National and Social Revolution,* Ref. #42. Vol. 1. Cairo: [s.n.], 24 October 1966.

''Cape Verde.'' *Objective: Justice* (February 1973): 1.

''Cape Verde: Agreement between Portugal and PAIGC.'' *Objective: Justice* (April 1975): 14–15.

Chaliand, Gérard. *Armed Struggle in Africa: with the Guerillas in ''Portuguese Guinea''.* New York: Monthly Review Press, 1969.

Chaliand, Gérard. *Guinea ''Portugaise'' et Cap Vert en Lutte pour Leur Indépendence.* Paris: Maspero, 1964.

Chilcote, Ronald H. ''Development and Nationalism in Brazil and Portuguese Africa.'' *Comparative Political Studies* (January 1969): 501–26.

Chilcote, Ronald H. ''Nationalist Documents on Portuguese Guinea and Cape Verde Islands and Mozambique.'' *African Studies Bulletin* 10, no. 1 (April 1967): 22–42.

Chilcote, Ronald H. ''Struggle in Guinea-Bissau.'' *Africa Today,* no. 21 (December 1974): 57–62.

Comité de Soutien à l'Angola et aux Peuples des Colonies Portugaises. *Guinée "Portugaise" et Îles du Cap-Vert, l'an Deux de la Guerre de Guinée,* Janvier–Décembre, 1964. Paria: [s.n.], 1965.

Comité de Soutien à l'Angola et aux Peuples des Colonies Portugaises. *La Lutte Continue, Janvier-Avril, 1964.* Paris: [s.n.], 1964.

Cornwall, Barbara. *The Bush Rebels: a Personal Account of Black Revolt in Africa.* New York: Holt, Rinehart and Winston, 1972.

Cruz, Luis Fernando Diaz Correia da. "Alguns Aspectos da Subverção na Província Portuguesa da Guiné." *Ultramar* 8, no. 4 (April 1968): 125–47.

Davidson, Basil. *Growing from Grass Roots: the State of Guinea Bissau.* London: Committee for Freedom in Mozambique, Angola and Guiné, [s.d.].

Davidson, Basil. "Guinea-Bissau and the Cape Verde Islands: the Transition from War to Independence." *Africa Today* (September 1974): 5–20.

Davidson, Basil. "An Independent Guinea-Bissau: Political Foundations." *West Africa* (29 January 1973): 131–33.

Davidson, Basil. "Liberation Struggle in Angola and 'Portuguese' Guinea." *Africa Quarterly* 10, no. 1 (April 1970): 25–31.

Davidson, Basil. *No Fist Is Big Enough to Hide the Sky: the Liberation of Guine and Cape Verde; Aspects of an African Revolution,* foreword by Amílcar Cabral, and preface by Aristides Perreira. New ed. London: Zed Press, 1981.
First published by Penguin Books in 1969 under the title *The Liberation of Guine.*

Davidson, Basil. "Notes on a Liberation Struggle." *Transition* 9, no. 45 (1974): 10–21.

Davidson, Basil. "Practice and Theory: Guinea-Bissau and Cape Verde." *Africa: Problems in the Transition to Socialism,* 95–113. Edited by Barry Munslow. Atlantic Highlands, N.J.: Zed Books, 1986.

Davidson, Basil. "The Prospect for Guinea-Bissau." *Third World* (April 1973): 3–6.

Davidson, Basil. "Revolt of 'Portuguese' Guinea." *Tricontinental Magazine* No. 8 (September 1968): 88–91.

Davidson, Basil. "Victory and Reconciliation in Guinea-Bissau." *Africa Today* 21 (September 1974): 5–22.

Davis, Jennifer. *The Republic of Guinea-Bissau: Triumph over Colonialism.* New York: The Africa Fund, [s.d.].

Decisão. Conakry: Partido Africano da Independência da Guiné e Cabo Verde (PAIGC), 30 August 1970.

Dias, H. " 'Portuguese' Guinea." *Portuguese and Colonial Bulletin* 5, no. 6 (December 1965): 300.

Duarte, Abílio Monteiro. "Aiding the Struggle in 'Portuguese' Guinea." *Revolution* 1 (August 1963): 44–47.

Duarte, Abílio Monteiro. *On the Question of Territories under Portuguese Domination,* United Nations. General Assembly. 29 March 1974. Document A/ AC.109/PV.966.

Duarte, Abílio Monteiro. " 'Portuguese' Guinea." *Information Bulletin (World Marxist Review)* No. 42 (13 May 1965): 53–54.

Duffy, James. "Portugal in Africa." *Foreign Affairs* 39 (April 1961): 481–93.

Ehhmark, Anders, and Per Wastberg. *Angola and Mozambique: the Case against Portugal.* New York: Roy Publishers, 1963.

Felgas, Helio. *Os Movimentos Terroristas de Angola, Guiné, Moçambique (Influência Externa). Lisbon: [s.n.], 1966.*

Fernandez, Gil. "Talk with a Guinean Revolutionary." *Ufahamu* 1, no. 1 (March 1970): 6–21.

Fernandez, Gil. "We Are Anonymous Soldiers of U.N." *Objective: Justice* 4, no. 1 (January 1972): 48.

Forrest, Joshua. *Guinea-Bissau: Power, Conflict, and Renewal in a West African Nation.* Boulder, Colorado: Westview Press, 1992.

Frente de Libertação da Guiné e Cabo Verde, Partido Africano da Independência. *Message to the Portuguese Colonists in Guiné and Cape Verde.* Conakry: [s.n.], October 1960.

Frente de Lute pela Independência Nacional da Guiné Bissau. *Charte Préambule.* Dakar: [s.n.], 1962.

Galtung, Ingegerd. *Reports from So-Called Liberated Portuguese Guinea Bissau.* Oslo: Morgenbladet, [s.d.].

Gibson, Richard. "Guiné and the Cape Verde Islands." *African Liberation Movements: Contemporary Struggles against White Minority Rule,* 243–63. New York: Published for the Institute of Race Relations by Oxford University Press, 1972.

"Guerre et Paix en Guiné-Bissau: Naissance d'une Nation." *Afrique-Asie* (23 September 1974): 66.

"Guinea-Bissau: along the People's Paths." *Tricontinental Bulletin* No. 70 (January 1972): 43–47.

"Guinea-Bissau's Liberation Struggle." *Race Today* 3, no. 11 (November 1971): 377–78.

Guiné-Bissau: 3 Anos de Independência, Africa in Struggle Series. Lisbon: CIDA-C (Anti-Colonial Center for Information and Documentation), 1976.

Guinée et Cap-Vert: Libération des Colonies Portugaises, Algiers: Information CONCP (Conférence des Organisations Nationales des Colonies Portugaises), 1970.

Guinée, Peter. *Portugal and the EEC.* Amsterdam; Geneva: Angola Comité in cooperation with the Programme to Combat Racism of the World Council of Churches, 1973.

Gupta, Anirudha. ''African Liberation Movements: A Bibliographical Survey.'' *Africa Quarterly* 10, no. 1 (April 1970): 52–60.

Hadjor, Kofi B. ''The Revolution in Guinea-Bissau.'' *Africa* (April 1974): 12–14.

Hoti, Ukson. ''The Liberation Struggle in the Portuguese Colonies.'' *Review of International Affairs* (5 November 1972): 30–31.

Hubbard, Maryinez L. ''Culture and History in a Revolutionary Context: Approaches to Amílcar Cabral.'' *Ufahamu* 3, no. 3 (December 1973): 69–86.

Ignatyev, Oleg Konstantinovich. *Along the Paths of War: War Diaries from Three Fronts of Guinea.* Moscow: Political Literature Publications, 1972.

International Union of Students. *Report of a Visit to the Liberated Areas of Guinea-Bissau.* Helsinki: National Union of Finnish Students, 1971.

Kelani, Haissam. ''Conditions in the Cape Verde Islands on the Eve of Independence.'' *Objective: Justice* (April 1975): 3–10.

''La Politique Etrangère de Guinée-Bissau.'' *La Révolution Africaine* (October 1974).

Labéry, Henri. "Le Cabo Verde Aussi Est Africain." *Afrique Nouvelle,* no. 695 (30 November 1960): 7.

Lefort, René. "Avec les Nationalistes de Guinée Portugaise." *Le Monde* No. 6–7 (November 1970):

Liberation Movement in Portuguese Guinea: (PAIGC) Totes Up 1964 Achievements, pp. 5–10. Translations on Africa, No. 220, 1964.

Liberation Support Movement, ed. *Guinea-Bissau, toward Final Victory!: Selected Speeches and Documents from PAIGC (Partido Africano da Independência da Guiné e Cabo Verde,* Richmond, B.C.: LSM Information Center, 1974.

Liberation Support Movement. *Sowing the First Harvest: National Reconstruction in Guinea-Bissau.* Oakland, Cal.: [s.n.], 1978.

"L'Indépendance du Cap-Vert: un Nouveau Pas Vers Unité avec la Guinée-Bissau." *Afrique-Asie,* no. 86 (1975):

Lobban, Richard. "The Cape Verde Islands: Colonialism on the Wane." *Southern Africa* 8 (January 1975): 4–7.

Lobban, Richard. "Cape Verde Islands: Portugal's Atlantic Colony." *Africa* (May 1973): 36–39.

Lobban, Richard. "Guinea-Bissau: A New Era." *New World Review* 43, no. 1 (January 1975): 12–14.

Lobban, Richard. "Guinea-Bissau: 24 September and Beyond." *Africa Today* 21, no. 1 (1974): 15–24.

Lobban, Richard. "Interview with President Luís Cabral." *Southern Africa* 8, no. 9 (1975): 12–14.

Marcum, John A. "A New Departure in Luso-America Relations." *Africa Today* 16, no. 1 (February 1969): 6–7.

Marcum, John A. *The Politics of Indifference: Portugal and Africa, a Case Study in American Foreign Policy.* Syracuse, N.Y.: Program of Eastern African Studies, Syracuse University, 1972.

Marcum, John A. ''Three Revolutions.'' *Africa Report* 12, no. 8 (November 1967): 8–22.

Margarido, Alfredo. ''Guinée et Guinée-Bissau: Bilan Provisoire de la Tentative d'Invasion de Novembre.'' *Revue Française d'Etudes Politiques Africaines,* no. 63 (March 1971): 18–20.

Margarido, Alfredo. ''Les Partis Politiques de Guinée Portugaise, en Angola, et aux Îles du Cap Vert.'' *Mois en Afrique,* no. 9 (July 1966):

Margarido, Alfredo. ''Partis Politiques Africains Sous Domination Portugaise.'' *Revue Française d'Etudes Politiques Africaines* (July 1968): 44–68.

Maria, Victor. ''La Guinée 'Portugaise'.'' *Voices of Africa* 2 (March 1962): 34–35.

Martelli, George. ''Progress in Portuguese Guinéa.'' *Geographical Magazine* (June 1967): 128–37.

Matteos, Salahudin Omawale. ''The Cape Verdeans and the PAIGC Struggle for National Liberation.'' *Ufahamu* 3, no. 3 (December 1973): 43–48.

McCollester, Charles. ''The Political Thought of Amílcar Cabral.'' *Monthly Review* 24, no. 10 (March 1973): 10–21.

Mendy, Justin. ''The Struggle Goes On.'' *Africa Report* (March 1973): 24.

Miranda, Nuno. ''Defesa de Portugal.'' *Cabo Verde: Boletim de Propaganda e Informação* 13, no. 147 (1961): 6.

Moolman, J. H. "Portuguese Guinea: the Untenable War." *Africa Institute Bulletin* 12, no. 6 (1974): 243–60.

Movimento de Libertação da Guiné e Cabo Verde. *Proclamação.* Conakry: [s.n.], November 1960.

"Naissance d'un Nouvel État Africain: la République de Guinée-Bissau." *Présence Africaine* 4 (1973): 248–301.

Neto, João Baptista Nunes Pereira. "Movimentos Subversivos da Guiné, Cabo Verde, e São Tomé e Príncipe." *Cabo Verde, Guiné, São Tomé e Príncipe,* Lisbon: [s.n.], 1966.

Ngwube, Douglas. "Guinea-Bissau: Decisive Phase." *Africa* (June 1974): 23–24.

"Numéro Spécial à l'Occasion de l'Indépendance du Cap Vert." *Afrique-Asie,* no. 86 (23 June 1975): entire issue.

Obichere, Boniface I. "Reconstruction in Guinea-Bissau: from Revolutionaries and Guerillas to Bureaucrats and Politicians." *Current Bibliography of African Affairs,* 13. Washington, D.C., 1975.

Ogawa, Tadahiro. *Nô Pintcha.* Tokyo: Taimatsu-Sha, 1972.

Pereira, Aristides. *Communiqué.* Conakry: Partido Africano da Independência da Guiné e Cabo Verde, 2 October 1973.

Pinto, Cruz. "Guinea-Bissau's Liberation Struggle against Portuguese Colonialism." *Freedomways* 12, no. 3 (1972): 189–95.

Portuguese Colonies: Victory or Death. Havana, Cuba: Tricontinental, 1971.

Profile of PAIGC. Geneva: World Council of Churches, Programme to Combat Racism, 1970.

Rodrigues, Manuel M. Sarmento. *No Governo da Guiné: Discursos e Afirmações.* Lisbon: Agência Geral do Ultramar, 1949.

Rudebeck, Lars. *Guinea-Bissau: A Study of Political Mobilization.* Uppsala; New York: Scandinavian Institute of African Studies; Africana, 1974.

Rudebeck, Lars. ''Political Mobilization for Development in Guinea-Bissau.'' *Journal of Modern African Studies* 10, no. 1 (1972): 1–18.

Sampaio, Mario. ''The New Guinea-Bissau: How Will It Survive?'' *African Development* (March 1974): 11–13.

Sevilla-Borja, H. et al. ''U.N. General Mission to Guinea (Bissau).'' *Objective: Justice* No. 4 (July 1972): 4–15.

Simão, José Veiga. ''Cape Verde Islands: Decolonization and Economic Assistance.'' *Objective: Justice* (April 1972): 11–13.

Simpósio Internacional Amílcar Cabral. *Continuar Cabral,* Praia?: Edição Grafedito/Prelo-Estampa, 1984.

Spinola, António de. *O Problema da Guiné.* Lisbon: Agência Geral do Ultramar, 1970.

Spinola, António de. *Por uma Guiné Melhor.* Lisbon: Agência Geral do Ultramar, 1970.

Spinola, António de. *Portugal e o Futuro.* Lisbon: Arcadia, 1974.

Sun of Our Freedom: the Independence of Guinea Bissau. Chicago: Chicago Committee for the Liberation of Angola, Mozambique and Guinéa, 1974.

''Sur les Traces d'Amílcar Cabral.'' *Afrique-Asie* No. 286 (3 January 1983): 37–68.

Tavares, Estevão. *Déposition des Ex-Détenus par la Police Politique Portugaise (PIDE) à Bissau, en Guinée "Portugaise"*. Conakry: Partido Africano da Independência da Guiné e Cabo Verde (PAIGC), 1962.

United States. Congress. House Committee on Foreign Affairs, Subcommittee on Africa. *Report on Portuguese Guinea and the Liberation Movement.* Washington, D.C.: Government Printing Office, 1970.

Urdang, Stephanie. "Towards a Successful Revolution: the Struggle in Guinéa- Bissau." *Objective: Justice* (January 1975): 11–17.

APPENDICES

A. The PAIGC Program

I. IMMEDIATE AND TOTAL INDEPENDENCE

1. Immediate winning, by all necessary means, of the total and unconditional national independence of the people of Guinea and the Cape Verde Islands.
2. Taking over of power, in Guinea by the Guinean people, and in the Cape Verde Islands by the people of Cape Verde.
3. Elimination of all relationships of a colonialist and imperialist nature; ending all Portuguese and foreign prerogatives over the popular masses; revision or revocation of all agreements, treaties, alliances, concessions made by the Portuguese colonialists affecting Guinea and the Cape Verde Islands.
4. National and international sovereignty of Guinea and the Cape Verde Islands. Economic, political, diplomatic, military, and cultural independence.
5. Permanent vigilance, based on the will of the people, to avoid or destroy all attempts of imperialism and colonialism to reestablish themselves in new forms in Guinea and the Cape Verde Islands.

II. UNITY OF THE NATION IN GUINEA AND THE CAPE VERDE ISLANDS

1. Equal rights and duties, firm unity and fraternal collaboration between citizens, whether considered as individuals, social groups or as ethnic groups. Prohibition and elimination of all attempts to divide the people.
2. Economic, political, social and cultural unity. In Guinea this unity will take into consideration the characteristics of the various ethnic groups at the social and cultural levels, regardless of the population in these groups. In the Cape Verde Islands, each island or group of identical and close islands will be able to have certain autonomy at the administrative level, while remaining within the framework of national unity and solidarity.

3. The return to Guinea of all emigrés who wish to return to their country. The return to the Cape Verde Islands of all emigrés or transported workers who wish to return to their country. Free circulation for citizens throughout the national territory.

III. UNITY OF THE PEOPLES OF GUINEA AND THE CAPE VERDE ISLANDS

1. After the winning of national independence in Guinea and the Cape Verde Islands, unity of the peoples of these countries for the construction of a strong and progressive African nation, on the basis of suitably consulted popular will.
2. The form of unity between these two peoples to be established by their legitimate and freely elected representatives.
3. Equal rights and duties, solid unity and fraternal collaboration between Guineans and Cape Verdeans. Prohibition of all attempts to divide these two peoples.

IV. AFRICAN UNITY

1. After the winning of national independence and on the basis of freely manifested popular will, to struggle for the unity of the African peoples, as a whole or by regions of the continent, always respecting the freedom, dignity and right to political, economic, social and cultural progress of these peoples.
2. To struggle against any attempts at annexation or pressure on the peoples of Guinea and the Cape Verde Islands, on the part of any country.
3. Defense of the political, economic, social and cultural rights and gains of the popular masses of Guinea and the Cape Verde Islands is the fundamental condition for the realization of unity with other African peoples.

V. DEMOCRATIC, ANTI-COLONIALIST AND ANTI-IMPERIALIST GOVERNMENT

1. Republican, democratic, lay, anti-colonialist and anti-imperialist government.
2. Establishment of fundamental freedoms, respects for the rights of man and guarantees for the exercise of these freedoms and rights.
3. Equality of citizens before the law, without distinction of nationality or ethnic group, sex, social origin, cultural level, profession, position, wealth, religious belief or philosophical conviction. Men and womem will have the same status with regard to family, work and public activities.
4. All individuals or groups of individuals who by their action or behavior favor imperialism, colonialism or the destruction of the unity of the people will be deprived by every available means of fundamental freedoms.
5. General and free elections of the organizations in power, based on direct, secret and universal voting.
6. Total elimination of the colonial administrative structure and establishment of a national and democratic structure for the internal administration of the country.
7. Personal protection of all foreigners living and working in Guinea and the Cape Verde Islands who respect the prevailing laws.

VI. ECONOMIC INDEPENDENCE, STRUCTURING THE ECONOMY AND DEVELOPING PRODUCTION

1. Elimination of all relationships of a colonialist and imperialist nature. Winning of economic independence in Guinea and the Cape Verde Islands.
2. Planning and harmonious development of the economy. Economic activity will be governed by the principles of democratic socialism.
3. Four types of property: state, cooperative, private and

personal. Natural resources, the principal means of production, of communication and social security, radio and other means of dissemination of information and culture will be considered national property in Guinea and the Cape Verde Islands, and will be exploited according to the needs of rapid economic development. Cooperative exploitation on the basis of free consent will cover the land and agricultural production, the production of consumer goods and artisan articles. Private exploitation will be allowed to develop according to the needs of progress, on the condition that it is useful in the rapid development of the economy of Guinea and the Cape Verde Islands. Personal property—in particular individual consumption goods, family houses and savings resulting from work done—will be inviolable.

4. Development and modernization of agriculture. Transformation of the system of cultivating the soil to put an end to monocultivation and the obligatory nature of the cultivation of groundnuts in Guinea, and of maize in the Cape Verde Islands. Struggle against agricultural crises, drought, glut and famine.
5. Agrarian reform in the Cape Verde Islands. Limitation of the extension of private rural property in order that all peasants may have enough land to cultivate. In Guinea, taking advantage of the traditional agrarian structures and creating new structures so that the exploitation of the land may benefit the maximum number of people.
6. Both in Guinea and in the Cape Verde Islands, confiscation of the land and other goods belonging to proven enemies of the freedom of the people and of national independence.
7. Development of industry and commerce along modern lines. Progressive establishment of state commercial and industrial enterprises. Development of African crafts. State control of foreign commerce and coordination of internal trade. Adjustment and stabilization of prices. Elimination of speculation and unfair profits. Harmony between the economic activities of town and countryside.
8. Budgetary balance. Creation of a new fiscal system. Creation of a national currency, stabilized and free from inflation.

VII. JUSTICE AND PROGRESS FOR ALL

a. On the Social Level

1. Progressive elimination of exploitation of man by man, of all forms of subordination of the human individual to degrading interests, to the profit of individuals, groups or classes. Elimination of poverty, ignorance, fear, prostitution and alcoholism.
2. Protection of the rights of workers and guaranteed employment for all those capable of work. Abolition of forced labor in Guinea and of the exporting of forced or "contract" labor from the Cape Verde Islands.
3. Fair salaries and appointments on the basis of equal pay for equal work. Positive emulation in work. Limitation of daily working hours according to the needs of progress and the interests of the workers. Progressive elimination of the differences existing between workers in the towns and those in the countryside.
4. Trade union freedoms and guarantees for their effective exercise. Effective participation and creative initiative of the popular masses at every level of the nation's leadership. Encouragement and support for mass organizations in the countryside and in the towns, mainly those for women, young people and students.
5. Social assistance for all citizens who need it for reasons beyond their control, because of unemployment, disability or sickness. All public health and hygiene organizations will be run or controlled by the state.
6. Creation of welfare organizations connected with productive activity. Protection of pregnant women and children. Protection of old people. Rest, recreation and culture for all workers, manual, intellectual and agricultural.
7. Assistance for victims of the national liberation struggle and their families.

b. On the Level of Education and Culture

1. Teaching centers and technical institutes will be considered national property and as such run or controlled by the state. Reform of teaching, development of secondary and techni-

cal education, creation of university education and scientific and technical institutes.

2. Rapid elimination of illiteracy. Obligatory and free primary education. Urgent training and perfection of technical and professional cadres.
3. Total elimination of the complexes created by colonialism, and of the consequences of colonialist culture and exploitation.
4. In Guinea development of autochthonous languages and of the Creole dialect, creation of a written form for these languages. In Cape Verde development of a written form for the Creole dialect. Development of the cultures of the various ethnic groups and of the Cabo Verde people. Protection and development of national literature and arts.
5. Utilization of all the values and advances of human and universal culture in the service of the progress of the peoples of Guinea and Cape Verde. Contribution by the culture of these peoples to the progress of humanity in general.
6. Support and development of physical education and sport for all citizens of Guinea and the Cape Verde Islands. Creation of institutions for physical education and sport.
7. Religious freedom: freedom to have or not to have a religion. Protection of churches and mosques, of holy places and objects, of legal religious institutions. National independence for religious professionals.

VIII. EFFECTIVE NATIONAL DEFENSE LINKED TO THE PEOPLE

1. Creation of the necessary means of effective national defense: army, navy and air force, linked to the people and directed by national citizens. Those fighting for independence will form the nucleus of national defense.
2. Democratic government within the armed forces. Discipline. Close collaboration between the armed forces and the political leadership.
3. The whole people will have to participate in vigilance and defense against colonialism, imperialism and the enemies of its unity and progress.

4. Complete ban on foreign military bases on the national territory.

IX. PROPER INTERNATIONAL POLICY IN THE INTERESTS OF THE NATION, OF AFRICA AND OF THE PEACE AND PROGRESS OF HUMANITY

1. Peaceful collaboration with all the peoples of the world, on the basis of the principles of mutual respect, national sovereignty, territorial integrity, non-aggression and non-interference in internal affairs, equality and reciprocity of advantages, and peaceful coexistence. Development of economic and cultural relations with all peoples whose governments accept and respect these principles.
2. Respect for the principles of the United Nations Charter
3. Non-adhesion to military blocs.
4. Protection for Guinean and Cape Verdean nationals resident abroad.

B. Current Government Officials: MpD Government of early 1993

President: António Mascarenhas Monteiro (non-partisan)
Prime Minister and Minister of Defense: Carlos Veiga

Minister of:

Foreign Affairs: Jorge Carlos Almeida Fonseca (Member of MpD Executive Committee)
Finance and Planning: Osvaldo Miguel Segueira
Rural Development and Fishing: Gualberto do Rosário
Transport and Communication: Miguel Casimiro de Jesus Chantre
Commerce and Tourism: 1992, Manuel Chantre (and Industry)
Justice and Public Administration: Eurico Correia Monteiro
Health: Luís de Sousa Nobre Leite
Education: Manuel da Paixo Faustino
Public Works: Teofilo Figueiredo Almeida Silva

State Secretaries:

Internal Administration: Maria da Silva
Youth: Rui Alberto de Figueirdo Soares
Adjunct to Prime Minister: Arnaldo Pina Pereira da Silva
Public Administration: Alfredo Teixeira
Social Promotion: Ondina Maria Fonseca Ferreira
Emigrant Communities: not known
Commerce: Jorge Spencer Lima

Officials of the Assembléia Nacional Popular (ANP):

President: Amilcar Spencer Lopes (MpD)
Majority Leader: José António dos Reis (MpD)
Minority Leader: Aristides Lima (PAICV)

C. United States Consuls in Cape Verde

1818–1827	Samuel Hodges, Jr.
1827–1836	William G. Merrill
1837–1847	Ferdinard E. Gardner
1847–1848	William Peixoto
1848–	Montgomery D. Parker
1853	John G. Forney (only from Feb. to Aug.)
1855	N. A. Haven
1857–1866	William H. Morse
1864	E. F. Wallace
1867–1869	Benjamin Tripp, Jr.
1869–	Clarimundo Martins
1871–	A. L. Onderdonk
1873–1876	Hanibal J. Silva
1873–	Joseph Hester
1876–	Thomas M. Terry
1889–1892	Henry Pease (service dates are greater)
–1898	Bartleman
1898–	Ernest Beaumont
–1916–	Will L. Lowrie

D. United States Ambassadors to Cape Verde

Melissa Wells	October 1976–September 1977
Edward Marks	September 1977–July 1980
Peter de Vos	September 1980–April 1983
John M. Yates	April 1983–July 1986
Vernon DuBois Penner	July 1986–December 1989
Francis Terry McNamara	December 1989–December 1992
Joseph Segars	January 1993–

E. Location, Size, and Elevation of Each Island

BARLAVENTO Islands (windward, northern):

Island	*Location*	*Size*	*Max. Elev.*
Santo Antão	17° 5′ N; 25° 10′ W	779 sq.km.	1,980 meters
São Vicente	16° 52′ N; 24° 58′ W	227	774
Santa Luzia	16° 45′ N; 24° 45′ W	35	395
São Nicolau	16° 35′ N; 24° 15′ W	343	1,305
Sal	16° 45′ N; 22° 55′ W	216	406
Boa Vista	16° 10′ N; 23° 50′ W	620	390
SOTOVENTO Islands (leeward, southern)			
Rombos/Secos	14° 58′ N; 20° 40′ W	6 sq.km.	96 meters
Brava	14° 50′ N; 24° 43′ W	64	997
Fogo	14° 55′ N; 24° 25′ W	476	2,831
São Tiago	15° 5′ N; 23° 38′ W	851	1,393
Maio	15° 10′ N; 23° 10′ W	267	436

F. Governors of Cape Verde (and the Guinea coast)

At first the Governors resided in Ribeira Grande, São Tiago, later at Praia; the amount of the coast under their control declined over the centuries. These data are adapted from the works of António Carreira, and expanded with additional data.

1592·	Duarte Lobo da Gama
1595	Bras Soares de Melo
1597	Francisco Lobo da Gama
1603	Fernando da Mesquita e Brito
1606	Francisco Correa da Silva
1611–1612	Francisco Martins de Sequeira
1614	Nicolau de Castilho
1618	Francisco de Moura
1622	Francisco Rolim
1622–1628	Francisco de Vasconcelos da Cunha
1628	João Pereira Corte-Real
1632	Francisco Cristovão Cabral
1636–1638	Jorge de Castilho
1639–1640	Jeronimo Cavalcanti de Albuquerque
1640–1642	Joao Serrão da Cunha
1642	Jorge de Araujo
1642–1648	Roque de Barros Rego
1650	Gonçalo de Gamboa Ayala
1650	Pedro Semedo Cardoso
1651	Jorge de Mesquita Castelo-Branco
1651–1658	Pedro Ferreira Barreto
1658–1663	Francisco de Figueira
1663–1667	Antonio Galvão
1667–1671	Manuel da Costa Pessoa
1671–	Manuel Pacheco de Melo
–1676	João Cardoso Pissaro
1676–1682	Manuel da Costa Pessoa
1685	Ignacio de Franca Barbosa
1687	Verissimo de Carvalho da Costa
1690–1691	Diogo Ramires
1692	Manuel Antonio Pinheiro da Camara
–1696	António Gomes Mena
1698	António Salgado

1702	Gonçalo de Lemos Mascarenhas
–1707	Rodrigo de Oliveira da Fonseca
1711	João Pinheiro da Camara
1715	Manuel Pereira Calheiros
1715–1718	Serafim Teixeira Sarmento de Sa
1720	António Vieira
1726	Francisco Miguel da Nobrega
1728	Francisco de Oliveira Grans
1733	Bento Gomes Coelho
1737–1738	José da Fonseca Barbosa
1738–1748	João Zuzarte de Santa Maria
1751	António José d'Eca e Faria
1751–1762	Luis António da Cunha d'Eca
1757	Manuel António de Sousa e Menezes
1761	Marcelino Pereira d'Avila
1764	Bartolomeu de Sousa e Brito Tigre
–1767	João Jacome de Brito Baena

Governors of Guinea and Cape Verde residing in Praia, São Tiago

1769–1776	Joaquim Salema Saldanha Lobo
1777	António do Vale de Sousa e Menezes
1781	Duarte de Melo da Silva e Castro
1782	Bishop D. Frei Francisco de S. Simao
1782–1784	António Machado de Faria e Maia
1789	Francisco José Teixeira Carneiro
1793	Francisco da Silva Maldonado d'Eca
1796	Marcelino António Basto
1803	António Coutinho de Lencastre
1818	António Pusich
1821	Luis Ignacio Xavier Palmeirim
1822	João da Mata Chapuzet
1826	Caetano Procopio Godinho Vasconcelos
1830	Duarte de Mesquitela da Costa Sousa de Macedo
1833	José Coutinho de Lencastre (never served in the islands)
1834	Manuel António Martins
1835–1838	Joaquim Pereira Marinho
1836	Domingos Correia Arouça
1837	Joaquim Pereira Marinho

1839	João de Fontes Pereira de Melo
1842	Francisco de Paula Bastos
1845–1848	José Miguel de Noronha
1848–1851	João de Fontes Pereira de Melo
1851–1854	Fortunato José Barreiros
1854–1858	António Maria Barreiros Arrobas
1858–1860	Sebastião José Calheiros Menezes
1860–1861	Januário Correia de Almeida (temporary)
1861–1864	Carlos Augusto Franco
1864–1869	José Guedes Carvalho e Menezes
1869–1870	Caetano Alexandre de Almeida e Albuquerque
1870	José Maria Pinto Mota (for a few months)
1870–1876	Caetano Alexandre de Almeida e Albuquerque
1876	Guilherme Quintino Lopes Macedo (for a few months)
1876–1878	Vasco Guedes de Carvalho e Menezes
1878–1881	António de Nascimento Pereira de Sampaio

In 1879 the administration of Portuguese Guinea is separated from the authority of the Governor of Cape Verde

1881–1886	João Pais de Vasconcelos
1886–1889	João Cesário de Lacerda
1889	Augusto Frutuoso Figueirdo de Barros (a few months)
1889–1890	Augusto Cesar Cardoso Carvalho (a few months)
1890	José Guedes Brandão de Melo
1894–1897	Alexandre Alberto da Rocha Serpa Pinto
1898	João Cesário de Lacerda
1922	Felipe de Carvalho

G. Slave Registries, 1856

The study of slavery in Cape Verde is fragmentary, however the 1856 slave registries in the National Archive give details of slave origins, prices, occupations, age, body characteristics, and gender, all broken down by owner and island. Some summary observations are drawn from these records, noting that there is significant variation in these categories and number at earlier historical periods.

Number of slave owners in Islands:	1,358
Total number of slaves:	5,180
Sex (when indicated): female slaves:	2,442
male slaves:	2,300
Number in Praia *conselho* only,	1,519 (M = 771; F = 748)

Average number of slaves per owner:	
All Islands	3.81
São Tiago	4.41
Fogo	4.37
Sal	4.28
Boa Vista	3.35
São Nicolau	2.54
São Antão	2.46
São Vicente	2.28
Brava	1.95

Slave Prices by Occupations:	
Herders	35–160 escudos
Weavers	25–140 escudos
Cooks (M)	75–120 escudos
Cooks (F)	25–130 escudos
Carpenters	35–160 escudos
Stoneworkers(M)	35–160 escudos
Stoneworkers(F)	25–130 escudos
Seamstresses	25–130 escudos
Washers	25–115 escudos

Slave Prices by Age:

10–15 years	65–100 escudos
15–20 years	100–140 escudos
20–40 years	115–200 escudos
40–50 years	90–140 escudos
50–60 years	70–90 escudos
60–70 years	40–70 escudos
70 plus	20–35 escudos

Group of Cape Verdean Slaves with Known Origins (n=2,871):

Same Island as Owner	74.5%
Other Cape Verde Island	9.0%
Africa	16.4%

African Ethnic Origins:

Mandingo, Bissagos, Balantas, Guinea?, Fula, Felupe, Quissi, Banhun, Bambara, Talibanca, Manjaco, Beafada.

H. American Shipping to Cape Verde, 1860–1965

Dates	Type of Vessels				Places of Origin		
	Barks	*Schooners*	*Brigs*	*Steamers*	*Other*	*N.Bedford*	*Prov.*	*Other*
1860–69	10	4	2	0	0	14	1	1
1870–79	4	22	11	0	0	37	0	0
1880–89	1	21	11	0	0	33	0	0
1890–99	16	89	3	0	0	95	8	4
1900–09	3	140	9	3	1	118	34	4
1910–19	22	118	7	3	2	132	13	7
1920–29	12	112	0	7	17	114	31	3
1930–39	0	27	0	1	1	23	6	0
1940–49	1	7	4	0	0	4	8	0
1950–59	0	7	3	0	0	0	10	0
1960–65	0	2	0	0	0	0	2	0

Source: Data Assembled by Waltraud Berger Coli from Custom House Records in the Cape Verdean Arquivo Histórico Nacional (AHN), Praia; and the National Archives, Washington, D.C.

I. Facts and Figures of Cape Verde

(Source: Public Data Base, Central Intelligence Agency)

Total Land Area	4,030 km^2
Coastline	965 km
Arable Land	9%
Population(July 1990)	374,984
Population Growth	3%/year
Birth Rate	49/1,000
Death Rate	11/1,000
Migration Rate	8/1,000
Infant Mortality	65/1,000
Life expectancy(M)	59 years
Life expectancy(F)	63 years
Fertility Rate	6.7 children/woman
Ethnic Groups	71% Crioulo
	28% African
	1% European
Primary Literacy	48%
Labor Force (1985)	102,000
in Agriculture	57%
GDP in Agriculture	16%
Rural Population	70%
Fish Catch (1985)	10,000 tons
GDP/capita (1987)	$494
Inflation Rate (1987)	3.8%
Unemployment	25%
Exports (1987)	$8.9 million
Imports (1987)	$124.0 million
External Debt (1988)	$140.0 million
Electricty	50 KWh/capita
Airports	6
Merchant ships	5
Major Airplanes	2
Telephones	1,740
Military fit to serve	40,731
Defense expenditures	11.8%/GDP
Food Imports	90%

ABOUT THE AUTHORS

Dr. Richard Lobban (PhD, Anthropology, Northwestern) is a Professor of Anthropology and the Director of the Program of African and Afro-American Studies at Rhode Island College. Since Rhode Island has a large Cape Verdean population he is also very active with local Cape Verdean groups as well as teaching courses on Cape Verde and West Africa.

Lobban has worked with Moçambican refugees in 1964; written on Portuguese Africa since 1965; walked across the nation of Guinea-Bissau during wartime with the nationalist guerrillas in 1973. After independence in 1975 he returned to Guinea-Bissau and he went to Cape Verde to witness the very last days of colonialism and the start of independence. With these long standing contacts he revisited the Cape Verde islands in 1992 while writing another book on contemporary Cape Verde which focuses on the rise of plural democracy in the islands. In 1993 he participated in the celebrations of the 20th anniversary of independence in Guinea-Bissau.

Lobban's African research also focuses extensively on Egypt, the Sudan, and Tunisia. He was a founder of the Sudan Studies Association and published numerous articles, chapters, and books on those lands including the Historical Dictionary of the Sudan with his wife Carolyn Fluehr-Lobban and John Voll (Scarecrow Press, 1992).

Marlene Lopes (M.L.S., Syracuse University) is Assistant Professor and Special Collections Librarian at Adams Library at Rhode Island College. She is the curator of the Cape Verdean Collection, a unique assemblage of books, pamphlets, papers, artifacts, sound recordings, and other materials relevant to Cape Verde and the Cape Verdean American connection. For this edition she has compiled and edited the bibliography, updating its predecessor and expanding its coverage in terms of both subject matter and the number of citations.

Lopes has been a long time bibliographer of Cape Verdean studies and is an active participant in the community. She is also a fourth generation Cape Verdean American whose family, descended from a whaler from Santo Antão, has been in the United States for more than 120 years. Lobban and Lopes work together in the Cape Verdean research collection at Rhode Island College.

Susan Hurley-Glowa (M.M., University of Louisville; M.A., Brown University) is Doctoral Candidate at Brown in ethnomusicology, and is writing on the musical traditions of São Tiago, Cape Verde. She has studied and played with Crioulo musicians in New England, and has recorded with Norberto Tavares. From 1992–93 she conducted doctoral field research in Cape Verde under a Fulbright grant. Hurley-Glowa lives in Providence and is also a professional French horn player.